# The MAILBOX®

## The Idea Magazine For Teachers™

## PRIMARY

# 1995–1996

## YEARBOOK

**Diane Badden, Editor**

The Education Center, Inc.
Greensboro, North Carolina

*The Mailbox*® 1995–1996 Primary Yearbook

Editor In Chief: Margaret Michel
Primary Grades Editorial Director: Kathy Nider Wolf
Senior Editor: Diane Badden
Editorial Manager: Julie Peck
Contributing Editors: Becky S. Andrews, Theresa Ives Audet, Irving P. Crump, Stacie Stone Davis, Jayne M. Gammons, Karen P. Shelton
Copy Editors: Lynn Bemer Coble, Jennifer Rudisill, Gina Sutphin
Staff Artists: Jennifer T. Bennett, Cathy Spangler Bruce, Pam Crane, Teresa Davidson, Susan Hodnett, Sheila Krill, Rebecca Saunders, Barry Slate, Donna Teal
Editorial Assistants: Elizabeth A. Findley, Wendy Svartz

ISBN 1-56234-137-5
ISSN 1088-5544

Printed in the United States of America.

The Education Center, Inc.
P.O. Box 9753
Greensboro, NC 27429-0753

# Contents

# BULLETIN BOARDS

# Bulletin Boards......

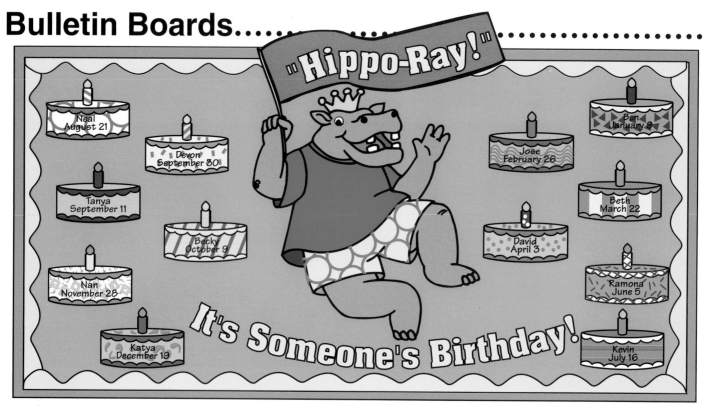

Recognize your youngsters' birthdays in a big way with this year-round display! Mount the title and a large birthday character like the one shown. Write each child's name and birthday on a white, construction-paper copy of the cake pattern on page 20. Then have each child decorate and cut out his birthday cake. Mount the completed cutouts onto the display. Plan to recognize every student's birthday during the school year—even those that occur during the summer months.

Diane Fortunato—Gr. 2, Carteret School, Bloomfield, NJ

Start the year off right with a bushel of good behavior tips. Mount the title and basket as shown. Using the apple patterns on page 20, duplicate and cut out a supply of yellow, green, and red apple shapes. Ask students to brainstorm tips for good behavior; then write the youngsters' ideas on the chalkboard. Later select and copy several of their ideas on the apple cutouts. Mount the programmed apples along with a couple of adorable worm cutouts as shown.

Sandra Daugherty—Grs. 1 & 2, Stinking Creek School, LaFollette, TN

If you want your youngsters to go bananas over school, here's the perfect display! On a paper-covered bulletin board, mount a large, three-dimensional tree, a banana-packing monkey, and the title as shown. Then, using colorful markers, have the students write their names on the display. When the project is finished, serve each child one-half of a banana. Then invite your youngsters to talk about their expectations for the new school year.

Susie Petges—Gr. 2, St. Dennis School, Lockport, IL

Reap a crop of student goals at this ever-growing display! Mount the backdrop, the title, and a tractor-driving character. You will also need one seed packet and one wooden craft stick per child. On the first day of school, ask each student to write her goals for the school year and to explain how she plans to achieve them. Then mount each student's writing onto the display as shown.

Diane Afferton—Gr. 3, Chapin School, Princeton, NJ

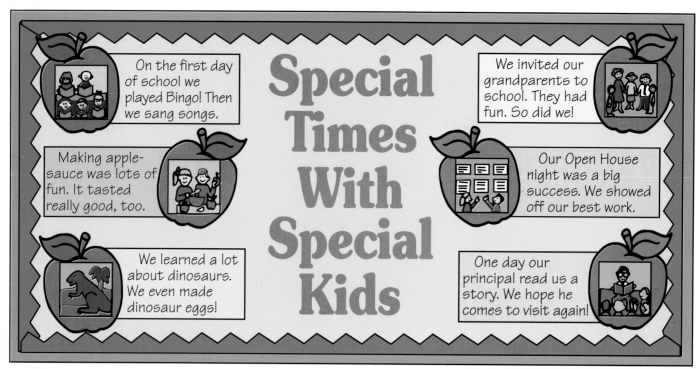

Picture this—a year-round display that's easy to maintain and loved by students! Display the title and a desired number of seasonal shapes. (See the apple patterns on page 20.) Periodically shoot and develop a roll of film. Let your students decide as a group which snapshots to display atop the seasonal cutouts. Arrange for each of several small groups to write a caption for a different picture. Mount the captions near the photos. Each month change the cutouts, photos, and captions. It's picture-perfect!

adapted from an idea by Ann Boucher—Gr. 1, Ellicott Elementary School, Ellicott, CO

Students work as a team to piece together this display. On bulletin-board paper cut to the desired size and shape, draw one interlocking puzzle piece per student. Mark the lower edge of each piece with a dot; then cut apart and distribute the pieces. Each child personalizes his puzzle piece to reflect his special interests. After students have shared their puzzle pieces with their classmates, they work together to reassemble the puzzle. Display the completed project for all to see. Now that's a perfect fit!

Diana Vrooman—Gr. 3, College Station, TX

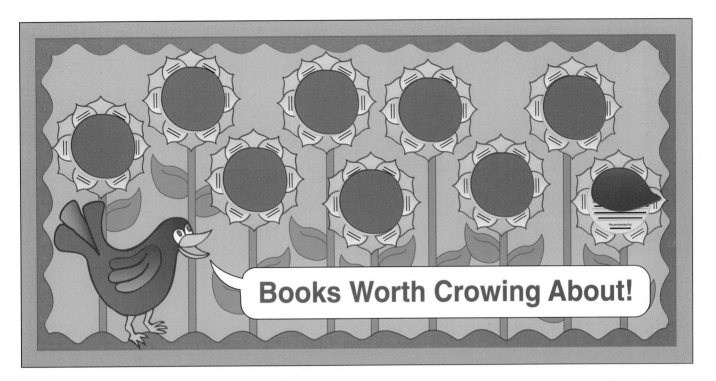

**Books Worth Crowing About!**

Take reading interest to new heights with a garden of student-made reading recommendations. To recommend a book, a student completes and cuts out a yellow copy of page 21. He puts a drop of glue at each • and attaches a programmed petal. At the ▲, he glues a 4 1/2-inch brown circle. He then glues a long, green stem bearing leaf cutouts to the back of the flower. Display the projects as shown. When a child is intrigued by a classmate's recommendation, he carefully plucks a programmed petal from the sunflower and stores it until his next trip to the library.

Tonya Byrd—Gr. 2, William H. Owen Elementary, Hope Mills, NC

You won't ruffle any feathers with this adorable door display! Once your owl decoration is in place, have each child create a smaller version of this fine-feathered fowl. Then, on a piece of light brown paper that has been trimmed as shown, have each youngster write her name and one reason why she likes school. After the students have glued their writings in place, mount the completed projects around the door decoration.

Kristy Bowling—Gr. 3
Sky View Elementary
Mableton, GA

Head down to the barn for a little foot-stompin' fun! To make a three-dimensional scarecrow, stuff a pair of child-size bib overalls and a shirt with crumpled newspaper. Add yarn hands and feet. To make the head, stitch and stuff a piece of burlap; then add hair, facial features, and a hat. Assemble and display the scarecrow holding a paper violin. Then using only construction paper and glue, each child creates a dancing scarecrow.

Cheryl Hinschberger, Challenger Elementary School, Thief River Falls, MN

When November arrives, have students brush up on nouns as they harvest a bounty of thankfulness. As students brainstorm people, places, and things for which they are thankful, write the corresponding nouns on the chalkboard. Ask each child to choose one noun, then copy and illustrate the noun. After a child shares his completed project with the class, he mounts his work in the appropriate noun category on the display.

Margaret Leyen—Gr. 2, Pineview Elementary, Iowa Falls, IA

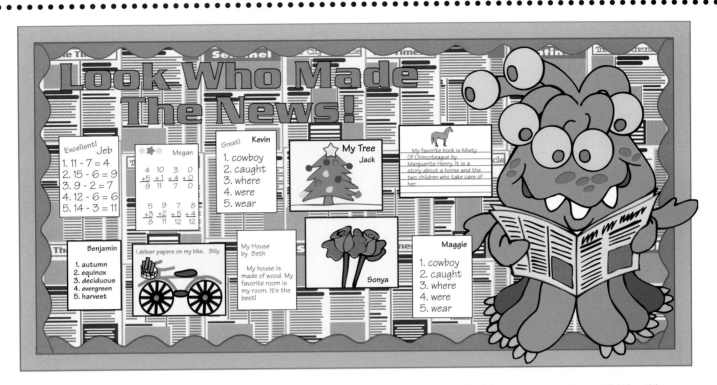

Spread classroom news at this easy-to-make display! Cover a bulletin board with newspaper; then add the title, a border, and a desired character. Showcase a perpetual assortment of outstanding student papers, classroom awards, and other noteworthy news for all to see!

Jeanine Fanto-Healy—Gr. 2, Manor Heights Elementary, Casper, WY

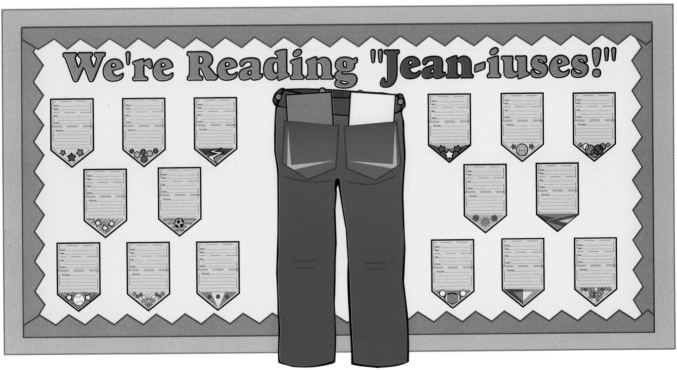

Make a fashion statement and motivate your young readers with this book-and-blue-jeans display! Poke a paperback in each back pocket of a pair of jeans; then secure the jeans to the display. Using the patterns on page 23, duplicate a supply of book-report forms on light blue construction paper. To make a book report, a child writes his name, the date, the book's title and author, and a description of the book. Then he cuts out and decorates the resulting pocket as desired.

Janet O'Bleness—Grs. 1–4, Wells–Carey Elementary, Keokuk, IA

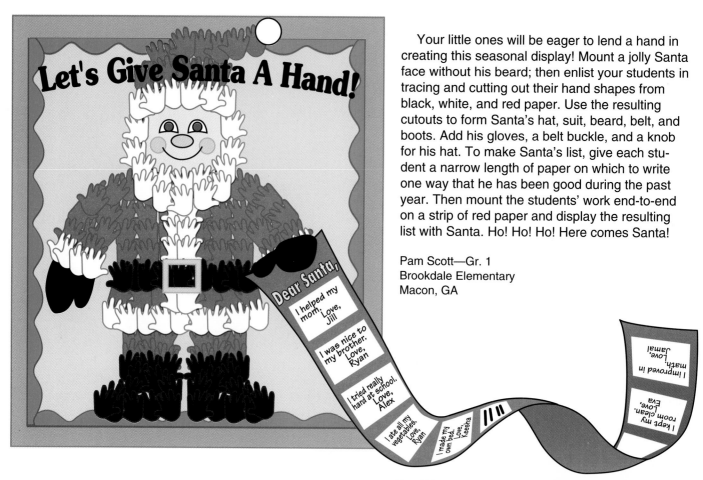

# Let's Give Santa A Hand!

Dear Santa,

I helped my mom. Love, Jill

I was nice to my brother. Love, Ryan

I tried really hard at school. Love, Alex

I ate all my vegetables. Love, Ryan

I made my own bed. Love, Keesha

I kept my room clean. Love, Eva

I improved in math. Love, Jamal

Your little ones will be eager to lend a hand in creating this seasonal display! Mount a jolly Santa face without his beard; then enlist your students in tracing and cutting out their hand shapes from black, white, and red paper. Use the resulting cutouts to form Santa's hat, suit, beard, belt, and boots. Add his gloves, a belt buckle, and a knob for his hat. To make Santa's list, give each student a narrow length of paper on which to write one way that he has been good during the past year. Then mount the students' work end-to-end on a strip of red paper and display the resulting list with Santa. Ho! Ho! Ho! Here comes Santa!

Pam Scott—Gr. 1
Brookdale Elementary
Macon, GA

Create a spectacular sight this season with star-studded greenery! Each student traces a star-shaped template on green paper and cuts out the resulting shape. Then she centers and glues a snapshot of herself on her cutout, making sure that one point of the star is directly above her picture. Each student then decorates her star as desired. Provide glitter pens, sequins, rickrack, pom-poms, and other arts-and-crafts supplies for this purpose. Be sure to fashion a star yourself! Then mount the completed projects as shown. Happy holidays!

Renee Fehr—Grs. 1 & 2
Westmoreland Elementary
Westmoreland, KS

# Happy Holidays!

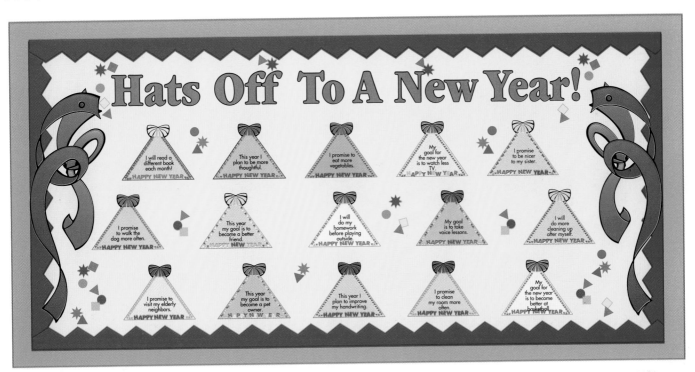

Welcome the new year with a festive display of party hats and confetti! On a white construction-paper copy of the hat pattern on page 22, have each child write a personal goal for the new year. Then have each child cut out and decorate his party hat as desired. Mount the party hats; then enlist your students' help in adding colorful confetti and streamers to the display. Happy New Year!

Ursula O'Donnell—Gr. 2, Meadow Brook School, East Longmeadow, MA

Display each student's wish for the new year with a lucky penny, and these wishes won't soon be forgotten! Give each child an index card to which you have taped a shiny new penny. Ask the youngsters to write their wishes for the new year on the cards; then mount the cards as shown. Encourage students to make wishes that would have a positive effect on several people.

Maureen Martin, Northport, NY

Reel in some valentine fun! To make a construction-paper fish, a student cuts a heart shape from each of the following: an eight-inch square (body), a four-inch square (tail), a three-inch square (fin), and a two-inch square (eye). Then he assembles his project and adds desired details with a marker or crayon. Also have each student cut out several heart-shaped air bubbles from his paper scraps. Mount the completed projects as shown.

Kathy Quinlan—Gr. 2, Charles E. Bennett Elementary, Green Cove Springs, FL

For this neighborly display, students work independently to create paper lunch-bag dwellings, then pool their projects to create a neighborhood. To make a dwelling, partially fill a lunch bag with crumpled newspaper; then fold down and staple the top of the bag closed before decorating the dwelling as desired. Use the same technique to create a schoolhouse from a large-size paper bag that has been spray-painted red. Name the neighborhood for your school principal and use teachers' names for streets. For added fun, cut the border from a discarded road map.

Emily Navidad—Art Educator, Morganton Road Elementary School, Fayetteville, NC

This year-round bulletin board is sure to steal the scene! Near the end of each week, select one student to illustrate his favorite event from that week. To make a clapboard, the student glues one end of a 1 1/2" x 12" white construction-paper strip to the corner of a 9" x 12" sheet of white construction paper as shown. Then he illustrates his scene, writes a related caption below his artwork, and designs a border for his clapboard.

adapted from an idea by Diane Fortunato—Gr. 2, Carteret School, Bloomfield, NJ

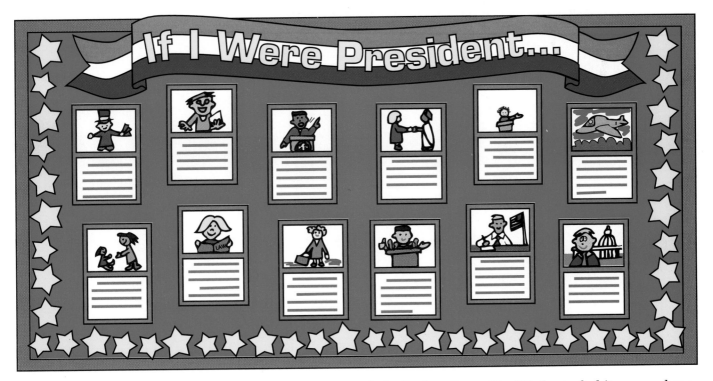

Salute your youngsters' presidential dreams at this patriotic display. On an 8" x 10" sheet of white paper, have each child illustrate herself as president of the United States. Then, on a sheet of 8" x 10" writing paper, have each youngster write a story that begins "If I were president...." Mount each student's completed projects on a large sheet of colorful construction paper and display the student work as shown. Now that's impressive!

Linda Hilliard—Grs. 1–3, Arlington, VA

Invite students to lend a hand in preserving the earth! Each student colors and cuts out a copy of the earth pattern on page 24. The student also traces one hand atop a sheet of colorful construction paper; then he cuts out and programs the resulting shape with an earth-friendly tip. Mount the hand cutouts around a large globe cutout. Display a snapshot of each child atop his earth cutout. The title says it all—"Earth: It's In Our Hands!"

Mary Jo Kampschnieder—Gr. 2, Howells Community Catholic, Howells, NE

There's no need to ponder how to decorate this display. Just mount the title and a large pond shape—then leave the rest to your students. Using a variety of arts-and-crafts supplies, students can apply their knowledge of pond life to create a pond habitat. Provide several pond-related books for reference. The outcome is a positive learning experience that results in an eye-catching display!

Desiree Palm—Gr. 1, Arrow Springs Elementary, Broken Arrow, OK

Just look what's blooming outside (or is that inside?) your window! Cover a paper-covered bulletin board with clear plastic wrap; then attach windowpanes and a series of shoeboxes—end to end—along the lower edge of the display. Cover the boxes with a student-decorated strip of bulletin-board paper. Fill the resulting window boxes with crumpled brown grocery bags (soil) and student-made flowers attached to green pipe cleaners. Display your students' "sunniest" work in the windows!

Diane Ehrhardt—Gr. 2, Taylor Mills School, Avon, NJ

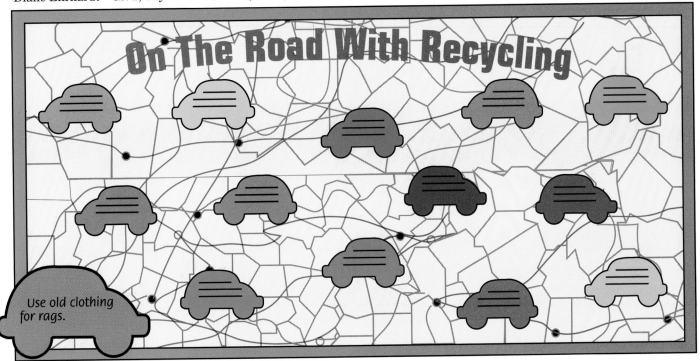

Take a recycling road trip! Cover a display area with discarded road maps and mount the title. Using the pattern on page 24, duplicate a supply of colorful construction-paper cars. Each student cuts out a pattern and writes a recycling suggestion on the resulting car shape. Ask each child to share his recycling tip before you mount his cutout on the display. Vrooooom!

Gina Parisi—Gr. 2, Demarest School, Bloomfield, NJ

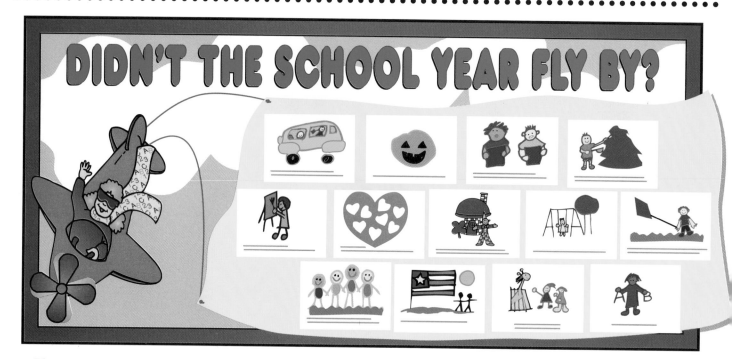

The sky's the limit! Ask each child to illustrate and write a brief description about a different event from the past school year. As a class activity, sequence the student-illustrated events; then mount their artwork on a high-flying banner like the one shown. Wow! The school year really did fly by!

Mary Mahaffey—Gr. 3, The Harrisburg Academy, Wormleysburg, PA

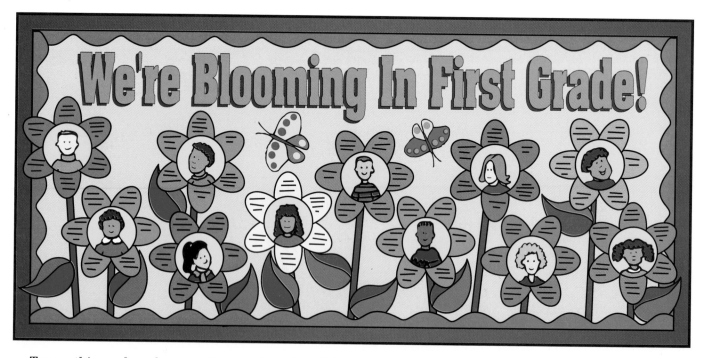

To sow this garden of success, have each student label the petals of a paper flower with things he has learned during the school year and then illustrate himself in the flower's center. As the school year draws to a close, ask one student per day to pick his flower and share it with his classmates. On the last day of school you'll have very proud youngsters and a nearly empty display!

Lynn White—Gr. 1, Ellisville Elementary, Ellisville, MO

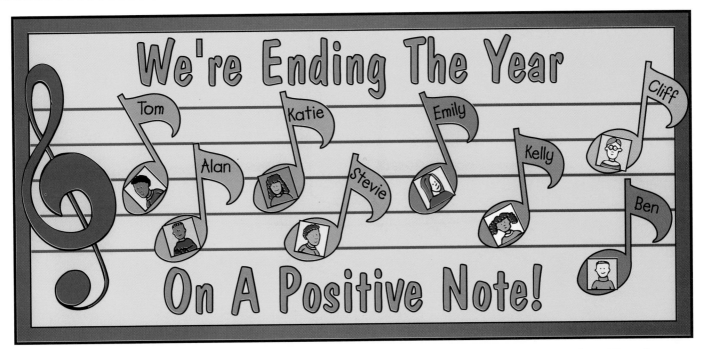

Make musical memories with this end-of-the-year display. Mount a note cutout for each student. If student photos are not available, ask each child to illustrate herself on precut paper; then attach the students' artwork to their personalized music notes. Each day spotlight a different student and write a note from the class for the student that includes fond memories about her from throughout the school year.

Lynn White—Gr. 1, Ellisville Elementary, Ellisville, MO

Summer dreams turn into summertime snapshots with a little help from your students. Follow up a discussion of your students' summer plans by having each child illustrate himself engaged in an activity he hopes to enjoy this summer. Before mounting the resulting snapshots, have each student glue a small, black triangle in each corner of his artwork. Smile for the camera!

adapted from an idea by Theodora Gallagher—Gr. 1, Carteret School, Bloomfield, NJ

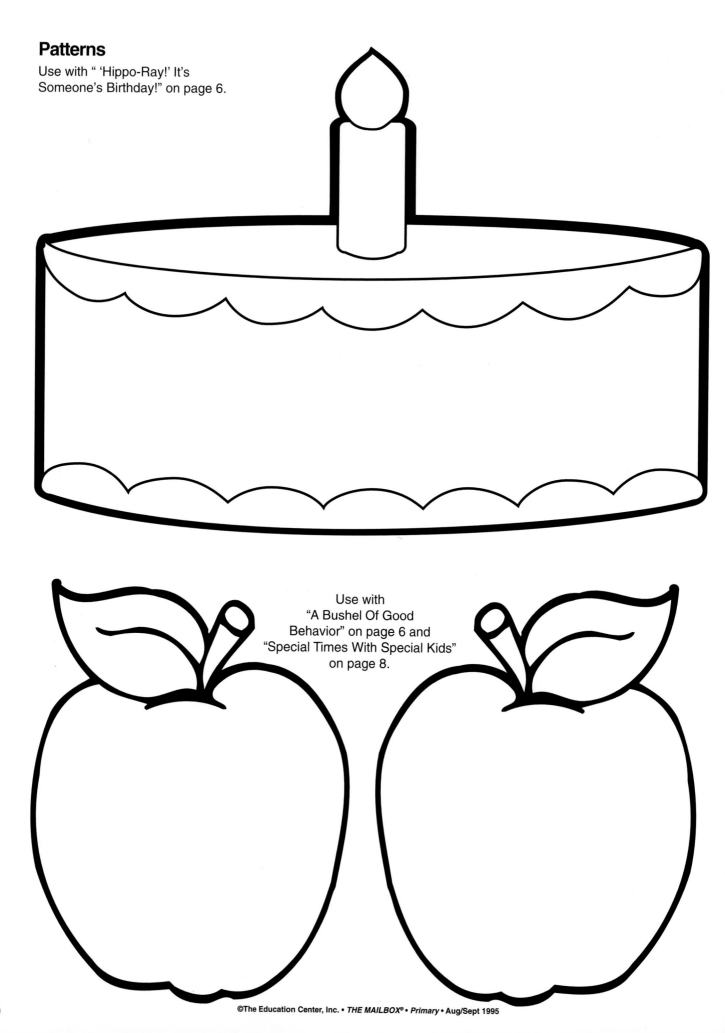

**Patterns**
Use with " 'Hippo-Ray!' It's Someone's Birthday!" on page 6.

Use with "A Bushel Of Good Behavior" on page 6 and "Special Times With Special Kids" on page 8.

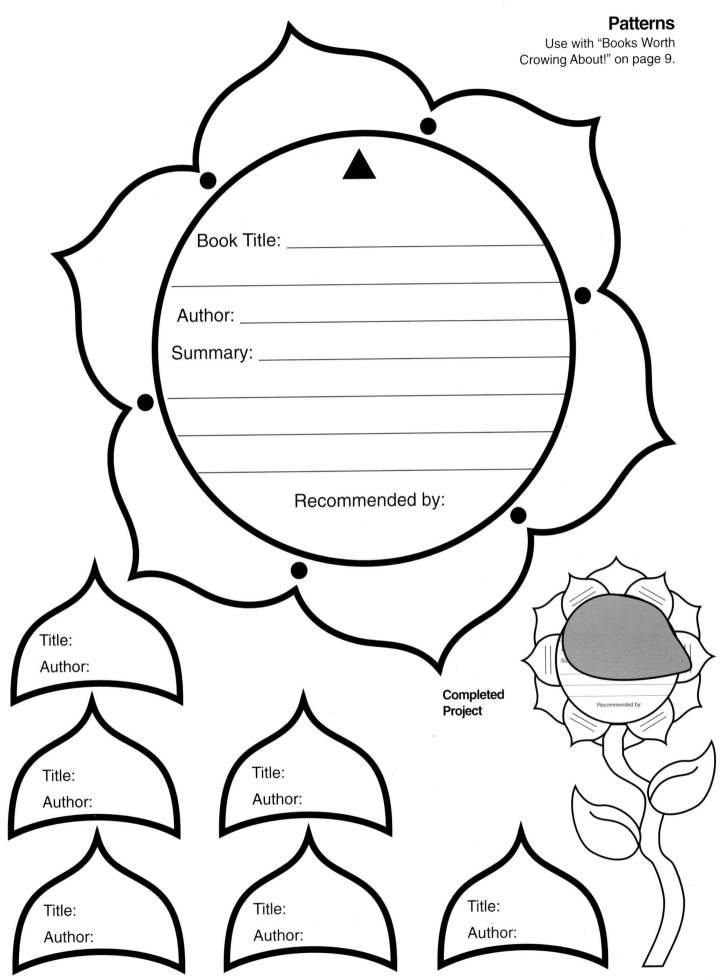

Book Title: _____

_____

Author: _____

Summary: _____

_____

_____

_____

Recommended by:

Title:
Author:

Title:
Author:

Title:
Author:

Title:
Author:

Title:
Author:

Title:
Author:

**Completed
Project**

# Pattern

Use with "Hats Off..." on page 13.

HAPPY NEW YEAR

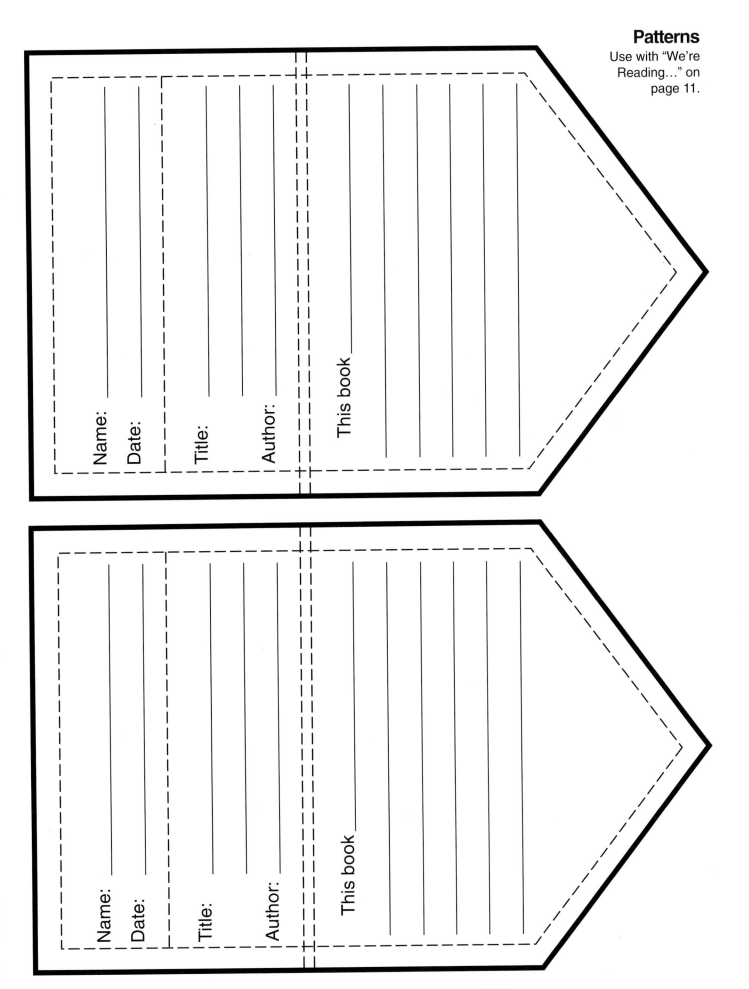

Name:
Date:
Title:
Author:
This book

Name:
Date:
Title:
Author:
This book

# Patterns

Use with "On The Road With Recycling" on page 17.

Use with "Earth: It's In Our Hands!" on page 16.

# LEARNING CENTERS

# Spotlight on Centers

### Very "Apple-tizing"!

Students get to the core of complete and incomplete sentences at this center. Create two large, tree-shaped poster-board cutouts. Label one tree trunk "Complete Sentences" and the other "Incomplete Sentences." Using the patterns on pages 20 or 38, duplicate a colorful supply of apples. Program the apples with complete and incomplete sentences; then laminate them and cut them out. Use a permanent marker to label the backs of the apples for self-checking. Place the apple cutouts in a basket; then store the basket and the two trees at a center. A student sorts the apples onto the appropriate trees by reading the words written on each apple. When he is finished, he checks his work by turning over the apples.

Tonya Byrd—Gr. 2
William H. Owen Elementary
Hope Mills, NC

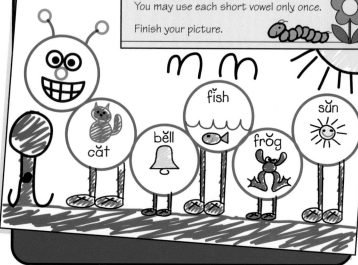

### Nifty Puzzle Packs

Perfect for the beginning of the school year, this appealing center can be ready in a jiffy. The next time you're at your favorite discount store, purchase an assortment of inexpensive, illustrated vinyl placemats. You will need two placemats of each design. Cut one placemat from one pair into several puzzle pieces. Use a permanent marker to program the backs of the pieces with a symbol. Draw the same symbol on a resealable plastic bag and on the back of the second placemat. Store the pieces inside the bag; then clip the bag to the placemat. Repeat the procedure for the remaining placemats, using a different symbol for each pair. Store the resulting puzzle packs at a center. No doubt about it! Students will visit this center time and time again!

Donna Mellor—Gr. 1
St. Theresa's Shrine
Scarboro, Ontario
Canada

> **Vowel Task Card**
>
> Draw a caterpillar.
> It needs a head and five body sections.
>
> Color a face for the caterpillar.
>
> In each body section, draw a picture of a short vowel word. Write the word, too.
> You may use each short vowel only once.
>
> Finish your picture.

### Munch A Bunch Of Vowels

Not one youngster will try to wiggle away from this vowel center! Place drawing paper, several circle tracers, pencils, and crayons or markers at a center. Add one or more task cards programmed with a vowel-related activity. A student chooses and reads an activity card. Then, using the supplies at the center, he draws a caterpillar on his paper. After decorating the caterpillar's head, the student programs the remaining body sections as described on the task card. He completes his project by adding desired details to his critter and coloring a scene around it.

Michelle Blaylock
Oviedo, FL

**Find These Five Numbers!**
1. Galactic Ice Cream Parlor
2. Pete's Pizza To Go
3. Milky Way Dry Cleaners
4. Go Anywhere Repair Service
5. Cosmic Book Store

Name ___Minnie Martian___

1. Galactic Ice Cream Parlor
   705-1239
   Page 58

2. Pete's Pizza To Go
   328-0080
   Page 171

Cosmos Telephone Directory

## Flipping Through The Yellow Pages

A discarded phone book makes a perfect alphabetizing center! Place the phone book, a supply of paper, and pencils at a center. Post a task card listing a series of business phone numbers that you would like your students to look up. On their papers, have the youngsters record the name of each business, its phone number, and the page of the phone book where the number was found. Provide an answer key if desired. Display a different task card each week and let the students' fingers do the alphabetizing!

Rebekah Howell—Gr. 2
Taylors Creek Elementary
Hinesville, GA

Come and practice your writing!

Aa Bb Cc Dd Ee Ff Gg Hh Ii Jj Kk Ll
Mm Nn Oo Pp Qq Rr Ss Tt Uu Vv Ww Xx Yy Zz

POEMS

Writing Tablet

## A Haven For Handwriting

Motivate your students to perfect their penmanship with a center that is strictly for handwriting practice. To attract students to the center, equip it with a desk pad, a fancy pencil that has a holder or a case for storage, and a small desk lamp. Also place at the center a binder containing a variety of kid-pleasing poems for copying, a handwriting model such as a laminated desk strip of alphabet letters, an assortment of crayons and markers for illustrating completed work, and supplies for evaluation purposes, such as stamps and stamp pads or stickers. In no time at all, this center will become a popular watering hole for handwriting enthusiasts.

Diane Afferton—Gr. 3
Chapin School
Princeton, NJ

## Keeping A Lid On Math Facts

This self-checking math center adds up to a lot of fun! Use Con-Tact® paper to cover a box and its lid. Then, using an X-acto® knife, cut several slits in the box lid approximately three inches apart. Make certain that a wooden craft stick can be inserted into each opening. Next duplicate a supply of seasonal shapes using the patterns on page 38. Program each shape with a math fact. Laminate the shapes and cut them out. Hot-glue each shape to one end of a wooden craft stick. Program the opposite ends of the craft sticks with the corresponding fact answers before inserting the sticks into the openings in the box lid. Place the completed project at a center along with a supply of paper and pencils. A student copies and answers the facts on his paper, checking his answers as he goes. Each month replace the facts with a new set.

Roxanne Rohlfing—Gr. 3
Immanuel Lutheran School
St. Charles, MO

## Pumpkin Tales

Harvest a crop of prizewinning writing at this seasonal center. Using a permanent marker, label four or five real pumpkins with different writing prompts. Display the pumpkins at a center along with crayons or markers, and a supply of story paper. A student chooses a writing prompt; then he writes and illustrates a pumpkin story. No doubt these pumpkin stories will be the pick of the patch!

Tonya Byrd—Gr. 2
William H. Owen Elementary
Hope Mills, NC

Write five tips for picking out a really cool pumpkin.

What if pumpkins could talk? Write a story about a talking pumpkin.

Last summer I lost a tooth. I put the tooth under the pillow. The next morning I found a pumpkin seed! At first I was mad. But then I got excited! What if the seed were magic? So I planted the seed right outside my bedroom window. You'll never guess what happened next! In only two...

## Bags O' Bones

Make no bones about it! This math center is everything it's cracked up to be! You will need a class supply of Brach's® Dem Bones™ tart and tangy candies in individual treat packs. Store the individual bags of candies in a plastic jack-o'-lantern or a Halloween gift bag; then display the container of candy at a center along with a class supply of page 40. A student uses a bag of candies to complete the reproducible activity. When his work is complete, he eats his bag of bones!

Kaye Langston & Glenda Potts
Spring Creek School
Seven Springs, NC

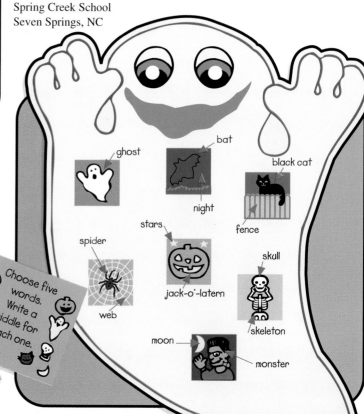

ghost • bat • black cat • night • stars • fence • spider • skull • jack-o'-latern • web • skeleton • moon • monster

## Nifty Word Banks

Stick with this idea and you'll have a center activity ready in a matter of minutes! To make a word bank with lots of kid appeal, attach a seasonal or thematic collection of colorful stickers to a poster-board cutout. Beside each sticker, write a word or phrase that describes it. Laminate the resulting word bank for durability and place it at a center along with assorted task cards, a supply of paper, and any other needed materials. A student uses the word bank to complete the task card of his choice.

Pauline R. Lawson—Gr. 1
Fuquay Elementary
Fuquay-Varina, NC

Write a Halloween story or poem.

Write the words in ABC order.

Choose five words. Write a riddle for each one.

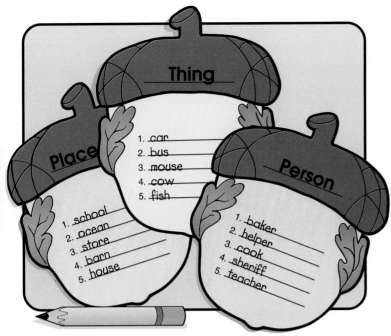

## A Phonics Factory

Sounds, sounds, and more sounds are sorted at this kid-run factory! To create a short-vowel center, you will need six sorting bins. Label one bin "Rejects"; then label one bin for each short-vowel sound. Next program a set of word cards to be sorted. Program five or more cards per bin. To make this center self-checking, code the backs of the cards that match with matching shapes. Store the cards in a decorated shoebox; then place the box and the sorting bins at a center. A student removes the cards from the box and sorts them into the appropriate bins. When she has finished sorting, she turns over the cards in each bin. If sorted correctly, the shapes on the backs of the cards will match.

Kristin McLaughlin—Substitute
Boyertown Area Schools
Boyertown, PA

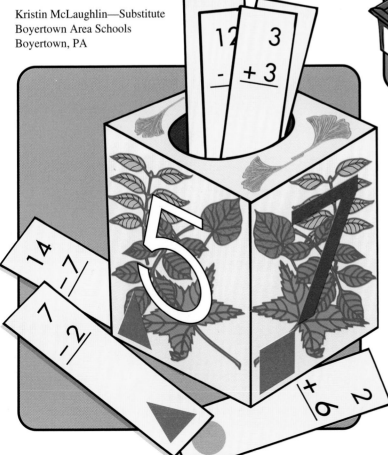

## Nutty About Nouns!

In a nutshell—this center is loads of fun! Using the patterns on page 39, duplicate three nuts and three nut caps per student. Place the patterns at a center along with scissors, glue, a dictionary, and crayons or markers. A student cuts out three nuts and nut caps. He labels the caps "Person," "Place," and "Thing"; then he glues each cap to a nut. Next he programs each nut with five appropriate nouns. He refers to the dictionary for correct spellings and to confirm that the words he has chosen are nouns. When his noun lists are finished, he colors the leaves on each nut. After all students have completed the center, display the students' work on a bulletin board entitled "Nutty About Nouns!"

Julie Decker—Gr. 2
Abbotsford Elementary, Abbotsford, WI

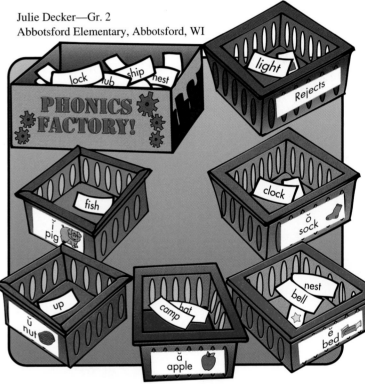

## It's A Fact!

It's a fact that this self-checking math center can be made in a jiffy! Carefully remove the plastic inset around the opening of an empty tissue box; then label each side of the box with a different fact answer and geometric shape. Cut out a supply of nine-inch poster-board strips. Write a different, unanswered math fact near the top of each strip. At the bottom of each strip, draw the geometric shape that appears on the box with the correct answer. Laminate the strips for durability; then stand them in the tissue box.

A student selects a strip and answers the fact. To check his answer, he finds his answer on the tissue box; then he removes the strip. If the shapes match, he lays the strip aside. If the shapes do not match, he returns the strip to the box. The student continues in this manner until he has correctly answered each math strip.

Mattie L. Burton—Gr. 1
Carver Primary School
Opelika, AL

### Summing Up The Season

Reinforce addition facts at this seasonal center. Write the numerals 1 through 9 on individual cards. Make a second set; then store both sets of number cards in a decorated container. Place the container of cards, several seasonal tracers, a supply of colorful construction paper, scissors, pencils, and glue at a center. A student traces a template on construction paper and cuts out the resulting shape. Next he removes two number cards from the container. Near the bottom of his cutout, he writes these two numbers in an addition sentence and supplies the missing sum. To check his work, he cuts out a set of shapes to represent each addend. The sets should be different colors. He then glues the shapes atop his seasonal cutout. If the total number of shapes on his cutout differs from the sum he wrote, he adjusts the sum to match.

Harriet Watson—Grs. 1 & 2
Hall-Woodward Elementary
Winston-Salem, NC

### Spelling Conversations

Spelling practice is loads of fun at this telephone center! You will need two disconnected or play telephones, a list of phone numbers that includes an assigned number for each student in the class, two notepads, several pencils, and a copy of the weekly spelling list. Students visit the center in pairs. To begin, one youngster dials his partner's number and makes a ringing sound. When his partner answers, the student asks him to spell a word from the weekly spelling list. The partner writes the word on his message pad; then he spells it aloud. The original caller checks the spelling against the provided list. If the word is spelled incorrectly, he notifies his partner of his mistake and asks him to respell the word. Then the students reverse roles and repeat the activity. Play continues in this manner until each student spells a predetermined number of words.

Kristin McLaughlin—Substitute Teacher
Boyertown Area Schools
Boyertown, PA

### Holiday Handicrafts

These no-mess holiday wreaths make a perfect art-center activity! Place a circular template, a bow-shaped template, red and green bingo-type markers (sponge-tipped bottles of colored ink that can be found at most craft and discount stores), white art paper, red art paper, crayons or markers for writing, glue, and scissors at a center. To make a wreath, a student lightly traces the circular template on white paper. He creates greenery by repeatedly pressing a green bingo marker around the circle outline. He uses a red bingo marker to create berries as desired. When the ink has dried, he uses a crayon or marker to write a holiday message inside the wreath; then he cuts out his project. Finally the student traces the bow-shaped template on red paper, cuts out the resulting shape, and glues it atop his wreath.

Roxanne K. Ward—Gr. 3
Greenwood Elementary School, Toledo, OH

### First-Class Recording Studio

Keep this oral reading center open year-round! Place a tape recorder and one cassette tape labeled for each student at the center. Each month stock the center with a different assortment of books in a variety of reading levels. A student visits the center at least once a month. He selects a book that he would like to record and prereads it. When he is ready to record, he places his cassette tape in the player, pushes "record," states the date and the title of the story he will be reading, and then reads the story in his best read-aloud voice. When he finishes, he rewinds the tape and listens to the recording he made. He then removes his tape from the recorder. The read-aloud tapes are fun for students to make, and they provide an excellent record of each student's read-aloud progress.

Donna Preston—Gr. 2
St. Mary Of The Assumption
Herman, PA

### State-Of-The-Art Sentence Builders

Students can show their stuff at this sentence-building center. Stock a center with glue, scissors, writing paper, and discarded newspapers and magazines. You will also need a variety of task cards like the ones shown. A student selects and completes one or more task cards. This activity is a great evaluation tool since students are both identifying and using different parts of speech. And your youngsters are sure to enjoy the hands-on approach to sentence building.

Kym Sitz—Gr. 3
Hay Branch Elementary
Killeen, TX

1. Cut out three verbs. Use each verb in a different sentence.

2. Cut out a noun and an adjective. Use the two words in a sentence.

3. Cut out two adjectives. Use the two words in a sentence.

Card 3

The **furry**, **black** puppy barked a lot.

Card 1

scored

TOLD

screamed

### Saving For A Snowy Day!

Cash in on money-counting skills with this center activity! Using the pattern on page 41, duplicate a supply of snow pals. Label each pattern with a different combination of coins using coin stickers, paper coins, or a stamp pad and a set of coin stamps. For added appeal, color the hats and scarves. Then laminate and cut out the snow pals. Use a permanent marker to program the back of each cutout for self-checking. A student calculates the total value of the coins shown on each snow pal, then flips the cutout to check his work.

Mary Taylor—Gr. 2
Sun Prairie, WI

56¢

# Spotlight on Centers

## Mending Broken Hearts

These broken hearts won't stay broken for long! Cut several heart shapes from construction paper. Label each heart with a pair of synonyms; then use a different jigsaw-style cut to separate the programming on each heart cutout. Store the cutouts in a heart-shaped candy box or other seasonal container. A student removes the cutouts from the container and mends the broken hearts by matching the heart halves. How sweet!

Cindy Corey—Gr. 1
Lealman Avenue Elementary
St. Petersburg, FL

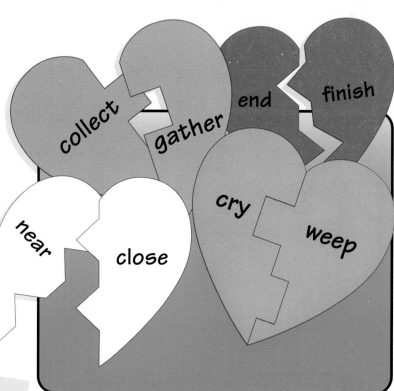

## All Smiles

Your youngsters will be all smiles as they complete this math and following-directions center. For each student, label a long, narrow paper strip with a series of ten happy faces. (Older students may draw their own.) Create a word bank that randomly features the number words one through ten written in ordinal form and program a set of directions for the students to follow. Laminate the word bank and directions for durability; then place the paper strips, word bank, and directions at a center along with pencils and crayons or markers. A student writes the corresponding ordinal number word above each happy face on his paper strip; then he carefully reads and follows the directions.

Gina Parisi—Gr. 2
Demarest Elementary School
Bloomfield, NJ

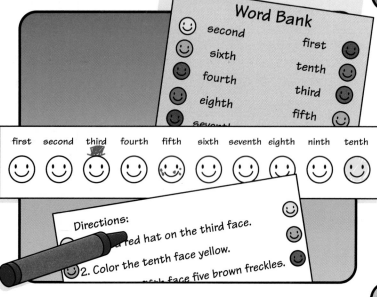

## Cereal Box Center

Enlist your youngsters' help in collecting empty (and clean!) cereal boxes for this high-interest reading center. Every other week, display a different collection of cereal boxes at the center along with a supply of paper, pencils, and a variety of task cards that can be used with any cereal box. A student selects a cereal box and completes one or more task cards. During the second week, place the students' papers that were completed the previous week at the center. Instruct each youngster to read and/or check a different classmate's paper, then write a positive comment on the work. Your youngsters are sure to enjoy this unique approach to reading!

Deanna Crisler—Gr. 2
Lafe Nelson School
Safford, AZ

The Big One
I had a bite. Boy, did I have a bite! My fishing pole was jumping all over the place. I lost my lucky fishing cap, then I lost my fish! But I didn't give up! And the next time...

## Shoe Swap

This writing center is a real "shoe-in"! Gather several pairs of high-interest adult-size shoes such as cowboy boots, ballet slippers, high-heeled shoes, snowshoes, fishing boots, ski boots, army boots, tap shoes, and high-top sneakers. Place the shoes, a supply of story paper, and crayons or markers at a center. A student slips her stocking feet into a pair of shoes and imagines her life as an adult in these shoes. Then she writes and illustrates a story about one of her adventures.

Krista K. Zimmerman—Gr. 3
Tuckerton Elementary School
Tuckerton, NJ

## Leprechaun Loot

If you can't catch the leprechaun, go for his loot! To make this seasonal center, use a 3 1/2-inch template to trace several circles onto gold construction paper. Label each resulting gold piece with a desired coin combination using coin stickers, paper coins, or a stamp pad and a set of coin stamps. For each piece of gold, program a construction-paper rectangle with the matching money amount and duplicate one black construction-paper pot (pattern on page 42). Attach the money amounts to the pots and embellish the pots with shamrock cutouts (patterns on page 42) if desired. Laminate the pots and the gold pieces; then cut them out. Use an X-acto® knife to make a slit along the dotted line on each pot. For self-checking, use a permanent marker to program the back of each gold piece with the corresponding money amount. Store the cutouts in a resealable plastic bag at a center. A student calculates the total value of the coins shown on each gold piece and slides it into the matching pot. To check his work, he flips the piece of gold.

Cindy Corey—Gr. 1
Lealman Avenue Elementary
St. Petersburg, FL

37¢

54¢

81¢

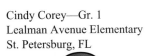

## Cookie Capers

There's no doubt that this versatile center will attract lots of student interest! Label a supply of seasonal cookie shapes for matching, sorting, or sequencing. Laminate and cut out the shapes; then attach a piece of magnetic tape to the back of each one. Store the cutouts in a nonbreakable cookie canister. Place the canister, a cookie sheet, and an answer key at the center. A student arranges the cutouts on the cookie sheet; then he uses the answer key to check his work. Delicious!

Mary Kay Gallagher—Gr. 1
Seton Catholic School
Moline, IL

# Spotlight on Centers

### Calling All "Eggs-perts"!

Youngsters will be eager to have a crack at this seasonal center! Write a numbered list of ten seasonal words on a tagboard strip labeled "Answer Key." Also number ten plastic eggs from one to ten. Copy each numbered word from the answer key onto one-inch graph paper; then cut the word apart—letter by letter—and place the resulting letters in the corresponding plastic egg. Store the plastic eggs in a basket filled with cellophane grass. Place the egg basket, the answer key, and a supply of paper at a center. A student numbers a paper from one to ten. Then he cracks open each egg, removes and arranges the letter cards to spell a seasonal word, and copies the word on his paper by the appropriate number. The student then puts the letter cards back inside the egg and returns the egg to the basket. When he has cracked all ten eggs, he uses the answer key to check his work! "Egg-ceptional"!

adapted from an idea by Sharon Weiss—Gr. 1
Oasis Elementary, 29 Palms, CA

Listen...
then choose one writing activity.

- Write several sentences that tell what the story was about.
- Write one sentence about each main character. In the sentence tell something about the character.
- Write several sentences that describe your favorite part of the story.
- Write a new ending for the story.
- Write a letter to the author. In your letter explain why you did or did not like the story.

Sam
1. April
2. spring
3. bunny
4. showers
5. cottontail
6.
7. hunt
8. basket
9. surprise
10. tree

### Listen And Write

Turning your listening center into a writing center is as easy as 1, 2, 3. *First* write a list of follow-up activities that are suitable for a variety of listening-center choices. *Second,* display the list of activities at your listening center. *Third,* stock the center with crayons or markers and a supply of paper. There you have it! A listening/writing center that's ready to use!

Krista K. Zimmerman—Gr. 3
Tuckerton Elementary School, Tuckerton, NJ

### Dig In!

Students dig into the dictionary at this high-interest center! Choose a class supply of words from a student dictionary that may be unfamiliar to your youngsters. Write each word at the top of a sheet of construction paper and store the labeled sheets in a file folder. Place the file folder, a student dictionary, crayons or markers, a hole puncher, a binder, a supply of paper, and desired instructions at a center. A student chooses a sheet from the file folder and follows the provided instructions. When her work is done, she hole-punches her project and places it in the binder in alphabetical order. The binder becomes a one-of-a-kind dictionary with plenty of kid appeal! If desired, leave this center in place for an extra week. Place a supply of blank construction paper at the center and invite each student to complete a second page for the student-made dictionary—this time choosing her own word from the provided student dictionary.

Dig In!
1. Find the word in the dictionary.
2. Illustrate the word.
3. In your own words, write what this word means.
4. Write your name on the back of your paper.

Lynx
no tail
It is a wild cat that doesn't have a tail. It has thick fur. Its ears are even furry!

## Pasta With Pizzazz

This partner math center has plenty of "pasta-bilities"! Fill a plastic bowl with three or more different kinds of uncooked pasta shapes. Attach a sample of each pasta shape to a length of laminated tagboard labeled "Pasta Values." Then, using a wipe-off marker, write a desired number value beside each piece of pasta. Place the resulting pasta code, the bowl of pasta, a small scoop, paper napkins, and a supply of blank paper at a center. Each student places a scoop of pasta on a napkin and uses the code to determine its total value. Next he trades pasta with his partner and repeats the activity. The two students then compare their pasta totals. If their totals match, they return the pasta to the bowl. If one or both of the totals do not match, the students together recalculate the value of the pasta scoop(s). To keep the center fresh, reprogram the pasta code each week!

*Gina Parisi—Gr. 2, Demarest Elementary, Bloomfield, NJ*

PASTA VALUES

=2
=3
=4
=5
=6

## Stick With It!

Recycle juice cans for this sorting center. Use colorful construction paper or Con-Tact® covering to cover two or more clean, empty juice cans. Number and label each can with a desired category; then program a supply of craft sticks with words to be categorized. For easy self-checking, code the backs of the craft sticks with numbers that correspond to the cans. Store the craft sticks in a basket; then place the basket of sticks and the labeled juice cans at a center. A student sorts the basketful of sticks into the proper cans. When the last stick is sorted, she checks her work.

## All Aflutter!

Watch your students' knowledge of math facts take flight with these colorful fliers. Using the patterns on page 43, duplicate a desired number of butterfly bodies and wings on colorful construction paper. Program each butterfly body with a different sum or difference; then program a set of wings with corresponding math facts. Laminate and cut out the shapes. Use a permanent marker to program the backs of the wing cutouts for self-checking. Place the cutouts at a center with a supply of scratch paper (for calculating math facts). A student matches a pair of wings to each butterfly body, then peeks under each wing to check his work. Now that's a flock of fancy fliers!

*Cindy Corey—Gr. 1*
*Lealman Avenue Elementary*
*St. Petersburg, FL*

## High-Flying Readers

Give your beginning readers a confidence boost at this nifty newspaper center. Place a supply of crayons and single newspaper pages at a center. A student chooses a newspaper page and uses a crayon to circle each word on the page that he can read. When the student has finished the page, he draws a black string from each circled word to create a balloon. Wow! Prepare for liftoff! These pages will definitely be a joy for your young readers and their parents to see!

Theodora Gallagher—Gr. 1, Carteret School, Bloomfield, NJ

## Here's The Scoop!

These ice-cream cones are piled high with skill reinforcement opportunities. Duplicate several construction-paper cones and ice-cream scoops. Label each cone shape with a math answer, a rhyming word, a pair of guide words, or a vowel sound. Then program three or four paper scoops to correspond to each cone. Laminate and cut out the pieces; then use a permanent marker to program the backs of the cutouts for self-checking. Store the cool cutouts in a resealable plastic bag at a center. A student sorts the scoops atop the cones, then flips the cutouts to check his work. Delicious!

Linda Anne Lopienski, Asheboro, NC

## Tasty Treasure

Ahoy, mateys! There's pirate treasure to be estimated, sorted, graphed, and tallied at this tasty center! Decorate a large box with a removable lid to resemble a treasure chest. Then, using sandwich bags and curling ribbon, package a treasure of 12–16 small assorted gumdrops (jewels) for each student, making certain that each treasure contains no more than six of any one color. Store the gumdrop treasures in the decorated treasure box; then place the treasure box, crayons or markers, and student copies of page 44 at a center. Each student chooses a bag of booty from the treasure box and uses it to complete the provided center activity. When his paperwork is done, the student asks a matey to check his calculations and sign the bottom of his paper in the space provided. Suggest that each student give his matey a few gumdrop jewels to thank him for his assistance. The rest of the booty is his to eat!

Jennifer Gibson, Pawleys Island, SC

## Toying With Cause And Effect

Simple toddler toys are the only items needed in this clever language arts center. Enlist your youngsters' help in gathering several toys that represent cause-and-effect relationships, such as a pull toy that makes noise, a jack-in-the-box, and any type of windup toy. Place the toys at a center along with a supply of paper. A student visits the center and plays with each of five different toys. On his paper, he describes each toy in a cause-and-effect sentence. Collect the students' papers. Later, when all students have completed the center, return the students' papers and, as a class, discuss the youngsters' sentences and observations. The result will be a much better understanding of cause and effect!

## Snapshot Memories

If you've been snapping photos of your students and other school-related events throughout the year, you can prepare this writing center in a snap too! On the first page of an inexpensive photo album, insert a title page that includes your name, the school's name, the dates of the school year, and the names of your students. Then on each left-hand album page insert one snapshot that you've taken during the school year. Leave the last page in the album blank. Prepare as many of these photo albums as you like; then place the albums at a center along with a supply of writing paper that has been trimmed to fit the album pages. A student flips through the albums and chooses one photograph that he would like to write about. Then he inserts his completed writing into the album page opposite the photo. After each student has had an opportunity to write about a different photo, invite students to revisit the center until each featured photograph has been written about. On the last day of school, look through the albums with your students and ask each student to read aloud his written contribution(s).

Karen Walden—Gr. 1, Ravenel Elementary, Seneca, SC

MY CLASS • 1996

A Day At The Orchard

We rode a bus. We saw lots of trees and apples. My apple was crunchy.

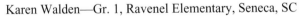

## Art Extravaganza

For an end-of-the-year art center that's long on usability and short on preparation time, try this earth-friendly idea. Gather together leftover or ready-to-discard greeting cards, wallpaper samples, construction-paper and gift-wrap scraps, buttons, stickers, canceled stamps, and other recyclable materials. Sort them into containers at a center that you've equipped with glue, scissors, crayons, 12" x 18" sheets of construction paper, and other desired art supplies. A student uses the materials at the center to create an original piece of artwork. Replenish the center with donations from co-workers who are also winding down the school year.

**Patterns** Use with "Very 'Apple-tizing'!" on page 26 and "Keeping A Lid On Math Facts" on page 27.

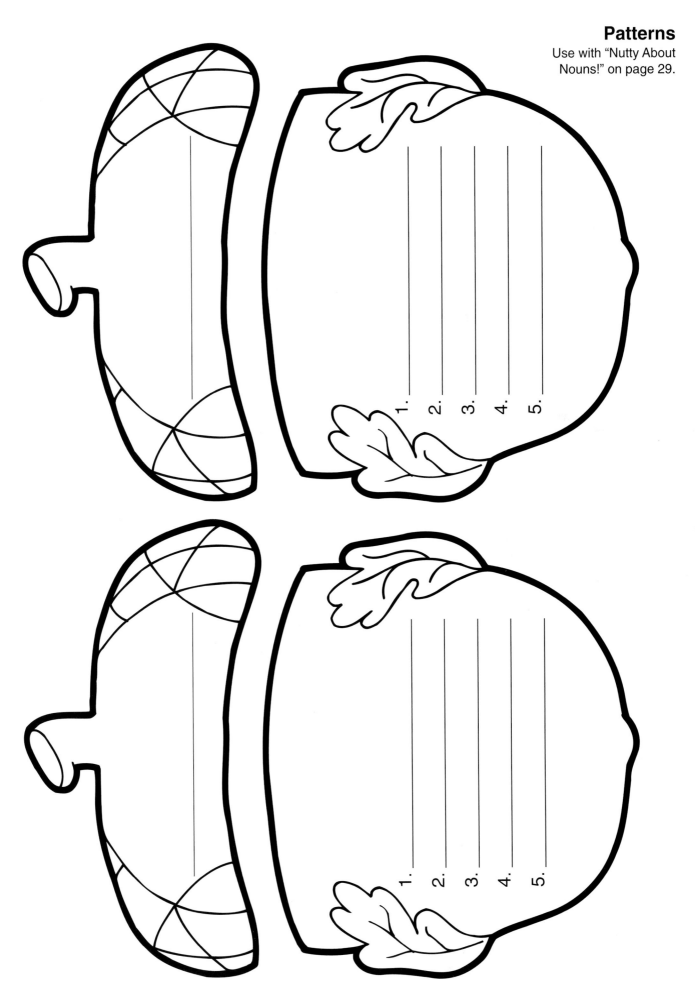

1.
2.
3.
4.
5.

1.
2.
3.
4.
5.

Name _____

# Bag O' Bones

Open a bag of candy bones.
Sort the candy on the matching shapes.

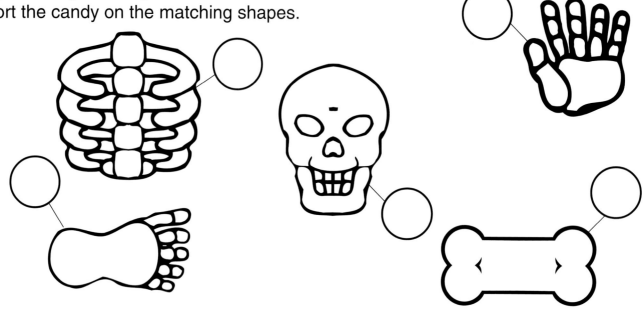

In each circle, write the number of candies on that shape.

## Answer the questions.

1. How many ⊂⊃ and 🦴 are there in all? _____

2. Do you have more 💀 or more 🦶 ? _____

3. How many ⊂⊃ , 💀 , and 🖐 in all? _____

4. How many 🖐 and 🦶 in all? _____

5. Which equals the most? Circle your answer.

   🦴 + 🦶        💀 + 🖐        🦶 + ⊂⊃

6. How many candy bones in all? _____

**Bonus Box:** Happy Halloween! You may eat your candy bones. Boo!

**Note To The Teacher:** Use with "Bags O' Bones" on page 28.

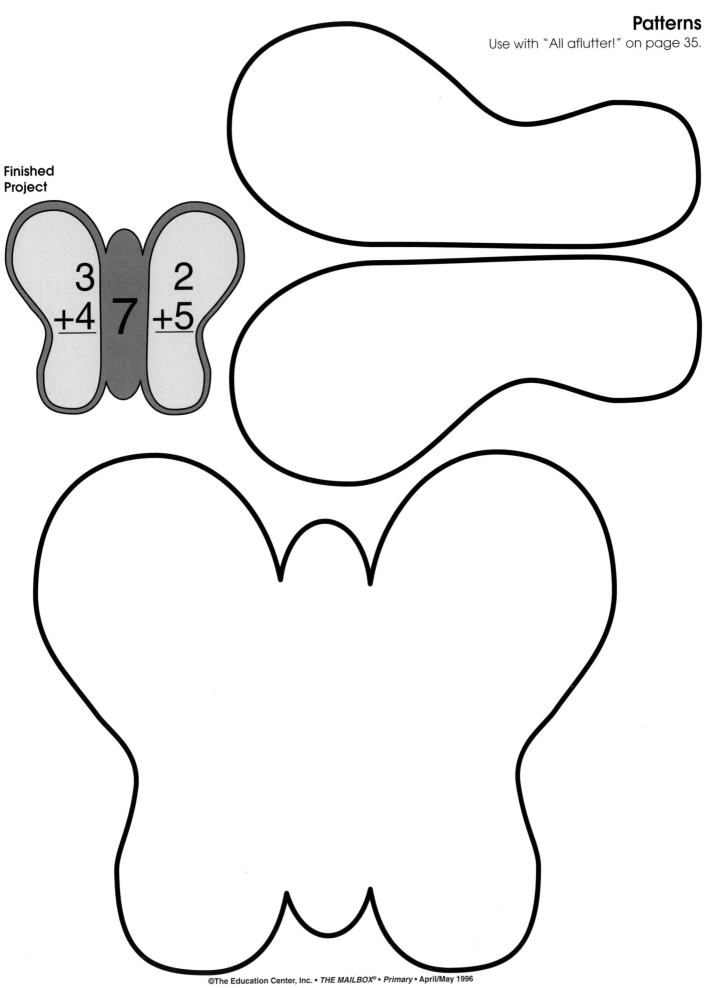

**Finished Project**

3
+4

7

2
+5

# Pirate Treasure

1. Look closely at your bag of treasure.
   How many gumdrop jewels do you think are in the bag?
   Write your estimate on the line. _____

2. Open your bag of treasure. Graph your gumdrop jewels.

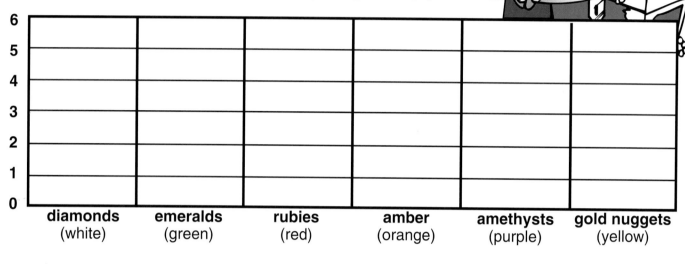

| | diamonds (white) | emeralds (green) | rubies (red) | amber (orange) | amethysts (purple) | gold nuggets (yellow) |
|---|---|---|---|---|---|---|
| 6 | | | | | | |
| 5 | | | | | | |
| 4 | | | | | | |
| 3 | | | | | | |
| 2 | | | | | | |
| 1 | | | | | | |
| 0 | | | | | | |

3. Use your graph. How many of each jewel do you have?

   _____ diamonds          _____ emeralds          _____ rubies

   _____ amber             _____ amethysts         _____ gold nuggets

4. Which jewel do you have the most of? _____

5. Which jewel do you have the fewest of? _____

**Find the sums.**

**a.** diamonds + emeralds = _____

**b.** gold nuggets + diamonds = _____

**c.** amber + gold nuggets = _____

**d.** rubies + diamonds = _____

**e.** amber + rubies = _____

**f.** rubies + emeralds = _____

**g.** amethysts + diamonds = _____

**h.** emeralds + amber = _____

Calculations checked by Matey _____.

**Note To Teacher:** Use with "Tasty Treasure" on page 36.

# Arts and Crafts

# Arts & Crafts

## Shapely Critters

Snip, snip, snip! Small pieces of colored construction paper make a big impact on these one-of-a-kind critters. First ask each child to picture in his mind an animal that he would like to design. Also ask the student to think of something the animal could be doing and to visualize the animal's surroundings. Once his mental picture is complete, the student is ready to begin his project. Working with a colorful assortment of construction-paper scraps, he cuts out small geometric shapes and glues them onto a 9" x 12" sheet of black construction paper in a desired fashion. Details can be added with markers. This project has endless possibilities and very shapely results!

## Edible Peanut-Butter Clay

Try this recipe for an afternoon of modeling fun and a tasty snack all in one! Mix your clay a day in advance so that it can be refrigerated overnight. To make enough clay for 25 to 27 students, mix 3 cups of peanut butter with 1 1/2 cups of honey. (Swirl 1 teaspoon of oil in the measuring cup before measuring the honey to keep it from sticking.) Stir in 4 1/2 cups of instant dry milk, a little at a time, until stiff. Knead the dough with your hands until well blended; then cover and store it in the refrigerator. The next day, give each youngster a piece of waxed paper and some peanut-butter clay. Each student molds his clay into a desired shape or shapes. Encourage students to view their classmates' peanut-butter sculptures; then let each child eat his own.

## Foil Fanfare

For lots of razzle-dazzle, get creative with foil and permanent markers. To make this project, crumple a piece of foil; then flatten it, leaving it somewhat crinkled. Using a black permanent marker, draw a large shape on the foil. Inside the shape, draw smaller, yet similar shapes. Color the shapes using permanent color markers. (If colorful permanent markers are not available, add a few drops of food coloring to each of several small containers of white glue. Paint each shape with a thin coat of tinted glue.) Cut out and mount the project on black construction paper; then trim the black paper to create an eye-catching border.

Darlene Hennessy—Substitute Teacher
Tacoma School District
Tacoma, WA

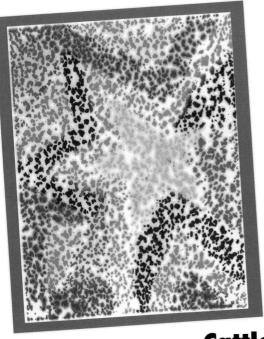

# Arts & Crafts

## Sandpaper Designs

Sandpaper and a creative flair set the stage for this impressive printing project. To make a print, color a design on a piece of coarse sandpaper. For the best results, color heavily atop the sandpaper, making sure that the entire surface is colored. Place the sandpaper, colored side down, atop a piece of white construction paper. Place the project between sheets of newspaper and gently press it with a hot iron. (This portion of the project should be completed only by an adult or by a child under close adult supervision.) When the project has cooled, remove the newspaper and carefully peel the sandpaper from the white paper. Trim around the resulting print and mount it onto a slightly larger piece of construction paper in a complimentary color.

Mary Jane Farrar—Gr. 1, Ridgemount Elementary, Hamilton, Ontario, Canada

## Cattle Crossing

Steer your youngsters into a creative frenzy with this dazzling project. Before you begin, inform students that herding cattle is an age-old occupation in western Africa. Some peoples, such as the Fulani, count a man's wealth by the number of cattle he owns. Begin with a colored paper plate or a white paper plate that has been spray-painted gold. Cut the center from the plate and trim the resulting rim to create horns. Trace a tagboard template of the head (see the pattern on page 70) on the remaining portion of the paper plate. Cut out the shape; then glue the horns onto the head as shown. Provide rhinestones, sequins, and colored foil for decorating the projects. Encourage each student to embellish his project to reflect a style all his own—much like the work of African artists. Though their inspirations stem from real objects, African artists do not try to be realistic in their interpretations.

Marsha Black and Michelle McAuliffe
Greensburg, IN

## Showy Sunflowers

Big and bold, these striking sunflower projects create a stunning display! Begin by cutting a six-inch circle from white construction paper. Using brown tempera paint, sponge-paint the resulting cutout and set it aside. Trace and cut out approximately 30 petal shapes from yellow paper. (If desired, use the patterns on page 70 to create tagboard templates for this purpose.) Glue a row of petals side by side around the back edge of the circle cutout. Glue a second row of petals behind the first, so that their tips can be seen between the existing row. Repeat a third time. To give the project dimension, fold some of the petals forward. Glue a long stem cut from green paper onto the back of the flower; then glue a desired number of leaf cutouts along the stem. Showcase the giant flowers side by side on a bulletin board or wall for an eye-catching garden display.

Rita Andreu—Gr. 3, Sabal Palm Elementary, Ponte Vedra, FL

## Jack-O'-Lantern Trio

By Jove! It is three jack-o'-lanterns! For this project, fold each of three 12-inch squares of orange construction paper in half. Make a half-pumpkin template similar to the one shown. Cut out the template and trace it on each folded square. Cut on the resulting lines; then unfold the squares to reveal three pumpkin shapes. From scrap paper, cut out desired facial features and stems. Glue the cutouts in place. When the glue has dried, refold the pumpkins, making sure that the artwork is folded to the inside.

To assemble the project, place one folded pumpkin shape on a tabletop. Apply a thin coat of glue on the upper paper surface. Lay one end of a crepe-paper streamer near the bottom edge. Then, lining up the edges, place another folded pumpkin shape atop the first one. Repeat the process, this time aligning the third folded shape atop the second one. Next cover the upper paper surface of the third pumpkin with glue. Position a crepe-paper streamer as before; then carefully pick up the project and bring together the top and bottom surfaces. Hole-punch the pumpkin stem; then thread and tie a few lengths of curled ribbon through the stem. Suspend the project from monofilament line. Now that's a handsome threesome!

Cynthia Goth—Gr. 1
Glen Elder Grade School
Glen Elder, KS

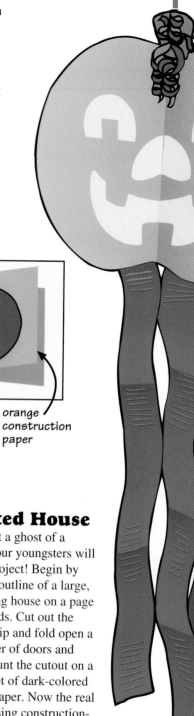

tagboard
template

orange
construction
paper

## Haunted House

There's not a ghost of a chance that your youngsters will boo this art project! Begin by sketching the outline of a large, spooky-looking house on a page of classified ads. Cut out the shape; then snip and fold open a desired number of doors and windows. Mount the cutout on a 12" x 18" sheet of dark-colored construction paper. Now the real fun begins! Using construction-paper scraps, glue, markers, crayons, and other desired supplies, create spooky scenery and a house full of ghoulish guests! Boo!

## Fall Leaf Banner

Enlist your students' help in collecting colorful autumn leaves for this project. To make a banner, fold a three-foot length of waxed paper in half; then unfold the paper. Brush one half of the paper with a layer of thinned white glue. Place pieces of torn tissue paper on the glue so that they overlap. Next arrange several fall leaves atop the tissue-paper design. Cover the project with the remaining half of the waxed paper. Sandwich the project between newsprint, and press it with an iron on low heat.

To display the project, fold a 9" x 12" sheet of construction paper lengthwise. Unfold the paper. Run a trail of glue from corner to corner as shown. Lay the midsection of a three-foot length of yarn in the crease of the paper so that equal lengths of yarn extend on the sides. Then refold the paper, tucking one narrow end of the waxed-paper project inside. Tie the yarn ends and suspend the resulting banner for all to see.

Linda Rabinowitz—Gr. 1
Torah Day School Of Atlanta
Atlanta, GA

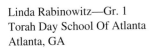

glue

yarn

## Colorful Corn

This year harvest a bumper crop of colorful Indian corn! Begin with a white construction-paper copy of the patterns on page 71. Using crayons, randomly color blue, purple, red, black, and brown kernels on each ear of corn; then color the remaining kernels different shades of yellow and orange. Cut out the ears of corn and set them aside. Open a brown paper lunch sack. Cut along the side seam; then cut away the bottom of the bag. Fold the resulting rectangle into thirds. Sketch a corn husk on the folded paper and cut on the outline. Slightly crumple the three resulting corn-husk shapes.

To assemble the project, stack the ears of corn. Place two corn husks on the bottom of the stack and one on top. Hold the lower edges of the cutouts together as you slightly fan the tops. When the desired look is achieved, staple the lower edges in place. If desired, fashion a bow from brown paper scraps or raffia, and glue it to the project as shown.

Robin Woodson—Gr. 3
James Poole Elementary
Gilmer, TX

## Roly-Poly Gobblers

Whether these bright, student-made gobblers are used as napkin rings or just for decoration, they add a festive touch to any Thanksgiving table. Roll a 3" x 9" strip of brown construction paper into a cylinder and glue it. Poke a brad through one end of several colorful feather cutouts before poking the brad through the back of the cylinder. Open the brad and fan the feathers as desired. For the turkey's head and neck, trim a 3" x 4" piece of brown paper into a shape like the one shown. From scraps of construction paper, cut out two eyes, a beak, and a wattle. Glue the cutouts to the turkey head. Use a fine-tip marker to add desired details; then glue the head in place. Attach construction-paper feet, and this gobbler is ready to strut his stuff!

49

# Holiday Gifts Galore

'Tis the season for gift-giving and here's our gift to you—12 adorable projects that can be made by students. Peruse this seasonal collection of easy-to-make gift ideas and get your little ones started today!

## Christmas Tree Ornament

**Materials For One Ornament:**

yellow tempera paint
paintbrush
1 wooden, star-shaped cutout
1 cinnamon stick
four 1/2" x 3" strips of green fabric
craft glue
pinking shears
4 small, multicolored buttons
one 5" length of narrow ribbon

**Steps:**

1. Paint the wooden star yellow. Set it aside to dry.
2. Tie a knot in the middle of each fabric strip. Starting 1/2 inch from the top of the cinnamon stick, glue the strips to the stick.
3. When dry, use pinking shears to trim the fabric strips to resemble a fir tree.
4. Glue a button on each fabric knot.
5. Loop the ribbon and glue the ends to the top of the cinnamon stick.
6. Glue the star cutout to the top of the stick, covering the ribbon's ends.

Kristy Osborn—Gr. 3, Abraham Lincoln Elementary
Indianapolis, IN

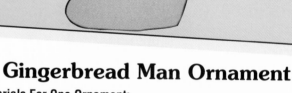

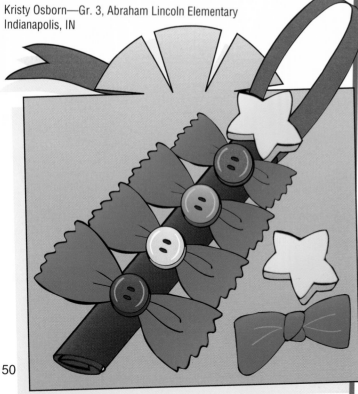

## Gingerbread Man Ornament

**Materials For One Ornament:**

1 gingerbread man template
   (approximately 4" x 5")
brown paper lunch bag
pencil
scissors
white tempera paint
paintbrush
red and black markers
two 8" lengths of narrow ribbon
craft glue
3 cotton balls
hole puncher
one 8" length of yarn

**Steps:**

1. Trace the gingerbread man template onto a brown paper lunch bag. Cut on the resulting outline to create two cutouts identical in size and shape.
2. Paint white wavy lines and buttons on one side of each cutout. Use the red and black markers to draw facial features and other desired details.
3. Fashion a bow from each ribbon length. Glue one bow to each cutout.
4. Position one cutout facedown. Squeeze a trail of glue around the perimeter of the shape, leaving the head unglued. Align the back of the second cutout atop the first one. Press the two cutouts together.
5. When the glue has dried, carefully stuff cotton balls into the opening. Glue the opening closed.
6. Punch a hole near the top of the ornament. Thread the yarn through the hole and tie the ends together.

Kristy Osborn—Gr. 3

# A One-Of-A-Kind Ornament

**Materials For One Ornament:**

three 9" x 12" sheets of construction paper—each a different color
one 3" circle (or other simple holiday shape) template

| | | |
|---|---|---|
| pencil | 1 heavy book | clear acrylic spray |
| glue | sandpaper | 1 paper clip |
| paintbrush | scissors | hot glue gun |
| waxed paper | glitter | one 5" length of ribbon |

**Steps:**

1. Trace the template onto each piece of construction paper six times. Cut out the shapes.
2. Making sure to cover the entire surface, paint a thin layer of glue on one side of one cutout; then align and press a second cutout of a different color atop the glue. Paint a thin layer of glue atop the newly placed cutout; then align and press a third cutout of a different color atop the glue. Repeat this process of painting and pressing until you have joined all of the cutouts.
3. Place the resulting ornament between two sheets of waxed paper. Set the heavy book on top of the project and allow the project to dry overnight.
4. Using a piece of sandpaper, sand both sides of the ornament. By sanding to various depths, you can achieve a wide variance in color. Continue rubbing until you have a desired design on each side of the ornament.
5. Paint a thin layer of glue over the entire surface of the ornament; then sprinkle the ornament with glitter.
6. In an open area, spray a coat of clear acrylic on the ornament. Allow drying time.
7. Use a hot glue gun to attach a paper clip to one side of the ornament.
8. Thread the ribbon through the paper clip. Tie the ribbon's ends.

Hope H. Taylor
Omaha, NE

# Thumbprint Ornament

**Materials For One Ornament:**

1 red or green, plastic shower-curtain ring
one 2 1/2" square of white construction paper
pencil
scissors
black ink pad
one 5" length of red or green narrow ribbon
one 2 1/2" square of self-sticking felt
black, pink, gray, red, and green fine-tip markers

**Steps:**

1. Lay the plastic ring on the white construction-paper square and trace around the inside of the ring. Cut out the resulting circle shape.
2. Use the ink pad to make a thumbprint in the center of the circle cutout.
3. Using fine-tip markers, draw features on the thumbprint so that it resembles a mouse. Sign and date your work.
4. Lay the plastic ring on the felt square. Trace the outside of the ring onto the felt. Cut out the resulting circle shape.
5. Remove the backing from the felt circle, center the artwork atop the adhesive, and press it in place. Position the plastic ring around the artwork, making sure that the top of the ring is at the top of the project. Press the ring into the adhesive.
6. Thread the ribbon through the top of the shower-curtain ring. Tie the ribbon's ends.

Michelle M. Dudley—Gr. 1
Boones Mill Elementary School, Boones Mill, VA

# A Gift Of Bread

## Pumpkin-Nut Bread
### Makes 4 miniloaves

**Ingredients:**

1 teaspoon baking soda
1/3 cup water
1 1/2 cups sugar
1/2 teaspoon salt
1 teaspoon cinnamon
1/2 teaspoon nutmeg

2 eggs, beaten separately
1/2 cup oil
1 cup canned pumpkin
1 3/4 cups sifted flour
1/2 cup raisins
1/4 cup chopped walnuts

Preheat oven to 350°. In a small bowl, dissolve the baking soda in the water. Set aside. In a large bowl, combine the sugar, salt, cinnamon, and nutmeg. Mix well. Add the eggs one at a time, then the oil. Beat well after each addition. Stir in the pumpkin and the baking soda solution. Add the flour in two parts; then stir in the raisins and the nuts. Spoon the batter into four greased miniloaf pans. Bake for 35–40 minutes.

**Materials Needed:**

supplies to make and bake pumpkin-nut bread (see recipe above)
wire rack
1 small, paper doily per child
plastic wrap
1 copy of the recipe per child (If desired, mount each recipe on
  construction paper and laminate it for durability.)
2 feet of curling ribbon per child
clear tape

**Steps:**

1. Prepare and bake the bread.
2. Allow the bread to cool for approximately 10 minutes; then remove it from the pans and set it on a wire rack to cool completely.
3. Center each cooled loaf on a small, paper doily; then use plastic wrap and curling ribbon to wrap the gift.
4. Tape the recipe to the gift.

Katherine Gartner—Grs. 1 & 2 Special Education
Oxhead Road Elementary School
Centereach, NY

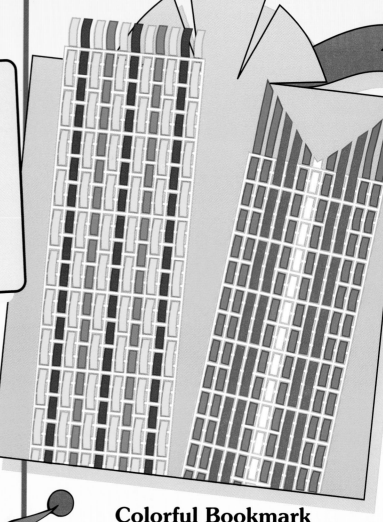

# Colorful Bookmark

**Materials For One Bookmark:**

one 1 1/2" x 6" strip of plastic needlepoint canvas
nine 12" lengths of lanyard (plastic lacing) in desired colors
scissors

**Steps:**

1. Determine the order in which you wish to weave the lengths of lanyard.
2. Weave each length of lanyard through the needlepoint canvas. If desired, use different weaving patterns such as "over one, under three, over one, under three" or "over two, under two, over two, under two."
3. When the project is completely woven, trim the ends of the lanyards as desired.

Margo Stocker—Gr. 3
Tonda Elementary
Canton, MI

## Bread Warmer

**Materials For One Bread Warmer:**

1 pound of earthenware clay*
waxed paper
1 sprig from an evergreen branch
1 toothpick
1 drinking straw
1 copy of "How To Use Your Bread Warmer"

hole puncher
one 10" length of curling ribbon
Optional: small pizza box, packing
peanuts, gift wrap, scissors,
tape, gift bow, gift tag
Access to a kiln

(*Earthenware clay is available in 25-pound blocks. For easy dispensing, cut the large block into six equal-size slices; then cut each slice into fourths.)

**Steps:**

1. Use your hands to shape the clay into a flat circle that is approximately 1/4-inch thick. Place the circle on a sheet of waxed paper.
2. Smooth the top surface of the clay circle and round the edges; then use your thumb to press a series of indentations around the edge of the clay.
3. Near the lower edge of the circle, carefully press the evergreen sprig into the clay. Remove the sprig.
4. To make the candle, press the side of your little finger into the clay. Then use the toothpick to outline the resulting candlestick and to draw a flame above it. Also use the toothpick to sign and date your artwork.
5. Using a drinking straw, poke a hole in the top of the project that is large enough to thread a length of curling ribbon through.
6. Peel the project off the waxed paper. To harden and dry the project, fire it in a kiln.
7. Punch a hole in your copy of "How To Use Your Bread Warmer." Then thread a length of curling ribbon through the hole and the hole in the project. Tie the ribbon's ends.
8. Optional: To prepare the gift for wrapping, place the bread warmer in a small pizza box between layers of packing peanuts. Wrap the package as desired and attach a gift label.

Jane Williams—Gr. 1
Milan Elementary
Bluewater, NM

## Trash-Bag Wreath

**Materials For One Wreath:**

1 wire coat hanger
scissors
7 white, plastic trash bags (13-gallon size), cut into 1" x 3" strips
1 decorative bow

**Steps:**

1. Reshape the wire coat hanger into a circle.
2. Securely tie each strip onto the hanger and push it toward the top of the wreath. Continue in this manner until the hanger is full.
3. Trim any ragged edges from the wreath.
4. Attach a decorative bow to the top of the wreath.

Helen Rogers—Gr. 1
Siler City Elementary
Siler City, NC

### How To Use Your Bread Warmer

Remove these directions and the ribbon that attaches them before using the warmer. To use, heat the bread warmer for 10 minutes in an oven set at 350°. Use tongs or a pot holder to remove the warmer from the oven. Place the heated warmer in a basket and cover it with a towel. (Do not set the warmer on a cold surface.) Fill the basket with breads or tortillas; then cover with a cloth and serve. The contents of the basket will stay toasty warm!

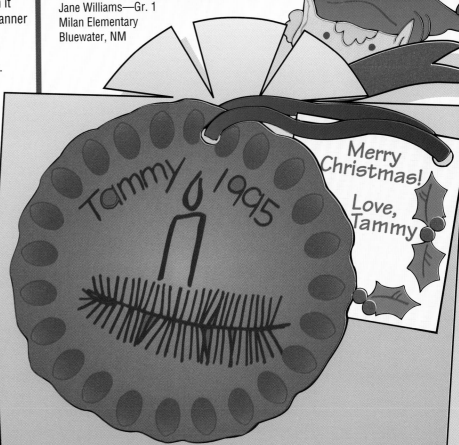

# Flowerpot Bell

**Materials For One Bell:**

one 2" clay flowerpot     paint pens
glue     one 18" length of ribbon
one 8" length of rickrack     1 jingle bell

**Steps:**

1. Invert the flowerpot. Then, using paint pens, embellish the pot (except for the rim) with holiday decorations.
2. When the decorations are dry, glue the rickrack around the rim of the pot.
3. Thread the ribbon length through the top of a jingle bell. Tie a knot in the ribbon about one inch above the bell.
4. Starting from inside the pot, thread the ribbon's ends through the drain hole. Pull the ends upward until the knot reaches the drain hole and stops the ribbon. Tie a second knot just above the hole.
5. Tie the ribbon's ends together.

Sonya Franklin
Springville, AL

Pam Crane

# Snowman Door Hanger

**Materials For One Door Hanger:**

1 wooden paint stir stick
1 wooden craft stick
white, black, and orange acrylic paints
paintbrush
toothpicks or a fine-tipped paintbrush
1 pencil with unused eraser

craft glue or hot glue gun
one 1" x 8" strip of fabric
2 wiggle eyes
raffia
1 small button
one 16" length of brown twine

**Steps:**

1. Paint the wooden stir stick white, stopping at the handle. Paint the handle of the stick black.
2. Paint the craft stick black.
3. When the paint dries, glue the craft stick to the base of the handle. Glue two wiggle eyes just below the craft stick.
4. Use a toothpick or a fine-tipped brush to paint an orange nose and a series of black dots that resemble a mouth.
5. About two inches below the mouth, paint three black buttons (circles). To create a nice, round button, apply the paint with an unused pencil eraser. Allow drying time.
6. Between the snowman's mouth and buttons, tie the strip of fabric around the stick. Secure the fabric to the stick with glue.
7. Fashion a bow from raffia and glue it to the snowman's hat. Glue a small button atop the bow.
8. Thread the twine through the hole at the top of the stick and tie the ends.

Suzann M. Shea—Grs. 3 & 4, Faris Elementary School, Hutchinson, KS

## Holiday Shirt

### Materials For One Shirt:
1 white sweatshirt
cardboard cut to fit inside the sweatshirt
green, yellow, and brown fabric paints
red and black, fine-tip fabric markers
scrap paper
pencil
1 plate

### Steps:
1. Insert the cardboard cutout inside the sweatshirt to prevent paint from bleeding through to the back of the shirt.
2. Using yellow fabric paint, paint a star at the top center of the shirt, just below the neckline.
3. On scrap paper, design a holiday thumbprint tree based on the number of students in your class. Using your design and a pencil, mark the shirt to indicate where each thumbprint should be.
4. Pour a small amount of green fabric paint onto a plate. Have each child press his thumb into the paint, then onto an indicated spot on the shirt.
5. To create the tree trunk, press your thumb into a small amount of brown fabric paint; then press it onto the shirt just below the last row of green prints.
6. When the paint dries, have each child add features to his thumbprint with a black, fine-tip fabric marker. Have him write his name next to his thumbprint with a red, fine-tip fabric marker. Add similar features to your brown thumbprint.

Cheryl Sergi—Gr. 2
Greene Central School
Greene, NY

**Happy Holidays!**

## Classy Calendar

### Materials For One Calendar:
1 duplicated calendar page for each month of the year
1 duplicated calendar cover          student snapshots
1 plastic binding ring or individual rings for binding
hole puncher
various craft supplies and colors of construction paper
scissors
glue

### Steps:
1. Using blank calendar pages or a computer program that creates calendars, program a calendar page for each month of the year and a calendar cover. Indicate important information such as school holidays and students' birthdays on the calendar pages.
2. On heavy paper, duplicate a 12-month set of calendar pages.
3. Create a border of students' snapshots around the calendar cover; then duplicate a class set on heavy paper.
4. Distribute the pages and covers. Have each child sequence his calendar, then embellish and personalize his calendar cover as desired.
5. Bind each calendar using a plastic comb binding system. Or hole-punch the pages and use individual rings.
6. Using colorful construction paper and a variety of craft supplies, have students create an illustration or design for each month of the year and glue their projects inside their calendars. (Each project should be glued to the back of the page that precedes the month for which it was designed.)
7. To prepare the calendars for hanging, have each child hole-punch the bottom center of each of his calendar pages.

Jane Williams—Gr. 1
Milan Elementary
Bluewater, NM

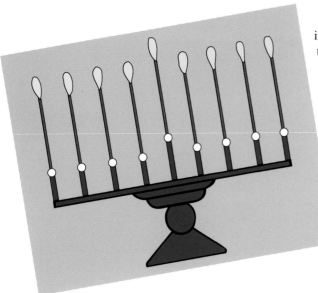

## Warm Reminder

Crafted by little hands, this menorah project casts an especially warm, inviting light during Hanukkah. In preparation for making a menorah, position a sheet of construction paper horizontally and draw a centered horizontal line about two-thirds of the way down a sheet of construction paper. Extending upward from the line, draw nine evenly spaced, short, vertical lines, making the fifth one a bit longer than the others. Attach a sticky dot at the upper end of each vertical line. Use a marker to draw a base beneath the horizontal line to complete the menorah. For imitation candles, trim one swab from each of nine Q-tips®. Color each swab stick with a marker; then dip each swab in yellow paint. When the paint has dried, glue each swab to the menorah to resemble a candle. The cheerful glow of this menorah is a warm reminder of the great miracle it represents.

Ellen M. Stern—Gr. 1, Alberta Smith Elementary, Midlothian, VA

## Darling Deer

Although your youngsters will want to create an entire herd of reindeer, the most popular one will likely be the most famous reindeer of all—Rudolph! To make a reindeer, begin by folding two sheets of light brown paper in half vertically. Cut one piece of construction paper to create a large heart shape when the paper is unfolded. Turn the heart upside down for the reindeer's head. Then similarly cut two smaller heart shapes from the remaining folded construction paper. Glue these hearts to the back of the head for ears. Fold a darker piece of construction paper in half, cut the paper to create antlers, and glue the antlers behind the reindeer's ears. Embellish this basic reindeer form with paper or button eyes, a circular nose, a drawn-on expression, a tissue-paper topknot, and cutouts to resemble a sprig of holly. Is it just my imagination, or can you actually hear the prancing and pawing of dozens of hooves?

D. Hautala—Gr. 3, Washington Elementary School, Ely, MN

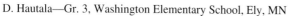

## Stepping To The Beat

Rat-a-tat-tat! Since classic holiday stories bring to mind playthings from a simpler time, you'll find these stiff and stately geometric soldiers are a refreshing change of pace. To make a soldier, you will need a red 2-inch square (jacket); two red 3" x 1/2" strips (sleeves); a red 2" x 1 1/2" rectangle (hat); a tan, brown, or pink circle cut from a 1 1/2" square (face); a blue 6" x 2" rectangle (pants); a black 1" x 2" rectangle (shoes); a white 9" x 6" sheet of construction paper (background); some glue; markers; and gold glitter glue or a gold marking pen. To make a soldier from the geometric pieces, vertically place the blue rectangle on the background paper. Placing the black rectangle on the blue one, align it with the bottom and sides of the blue shape. Similarly place the red square on the blue rectangle, aligning it with the top and sides of the larger shape. Place the two long, narrow strips beside the other shapes to resemble the soldier's sleeves. Position the circle and the remaining rectangle so that they resemble a soldier's hat and face. Glue all of the pieces in place before embellishing them with markers and a gold pen or glitter glue to add the finishing touches to the soldier design. Rat-a-tat-tat! Rat-a-tat-tat! Rat-a-tat-tat!

Sr. M. Henrietta, Villa Sacred Heart, Danville, PA

## First-Fruits Necklace

Kwanzaa is the African-American holiday reminiscent of traditional African harvests. Since the word Kwanzaa comes from a Swahili term meaning "first fruits," celebrate Kwanzaa this year by making first-fruits necklaces. To make a necklace, cut out three different fruit shapes from red construction paper and three more from green construction paper. From black paper, cut out the shape of Africa. Punch a hole near the tops of all seven shapes. If necessary, refer to a book such as *Kwanzaa* by Dorothy Rhodes Freeman and Dianne M. MacMillan (Enslow Publishers, Inc.) for the African terms, their translations, and the sequence in which they are introduced. Then write one of the principles of Kwanzaa and its translation on each of the seven shapes, putting the African term on one side and its translation on the other. (Since the first principle goes on the black cutout of Africa, either write the first principle and its translation with a white crayon or write them on small pieces of white paper and glue them on.) Tape the ends of a length of thick, black yarn to prevent raveling. Then, in the order shown, thread the labeled shapes onto the yarn along with red, green, and black beads or dyed pasta. Tie the ends of the yarn together, and wear the first-fruits necklace with pride.

### The Seven Principles Of Kwanzaa

Umoja—unity
Kujichagulia—being yourself
Ujima—helping one another

Ujamaa—sharing
Nia—having a goal
Kuumba—being creative

Imani—believing

## The Water's Fine!

Your youngsters will dive into this project with much the same enthusiasm that compels a penguin to plop blithely into frigid waters. To begin making the sky in this icy scene, use a wide brush to paint the upper half of a large sheet of art paper with water. Use thinned yellow tempera paint to make horizontal streaks in the wet area; then brush sweeping strokes of thinned red paint in some of the remaining moistened area. Observe as the colors bleed and mingle. Using the same wet-on-wet process, paint the entire lower half of the art paper with water first; then paint on streaks of thinned green and blue paint. When the paper has thoroughly dried, attach torn pieces of white construction paper with glue so that they appear to be icebergs floating in the water. Fashion a few penguins from construction paper and glue them to the scene. Mount the artwork on a larger sheet of blue paper. Wouldn't you just love to dive in?

Michelle Williams—Gr. 1
Meadow Lane School, Olathe, KS

57

# Arts & Crafts

## Northern Lights

As depicted in children's books—such as *A Northern Alphabet, A Northern Lullaby,* and *Mama, Do You Love Me?*—during the aurora borealis, beautiful streaks of light brighten the deep, dark polar skies. Share pictures or illustrations of the northern-lights phenomenon with your students. Then have each student create artwork inspired by the aurora borealis. Begin this project by outlining the shapes of the geographic features along what will be your horizon line. Above the horizon line, use tempera paints to paint streaks of various colors so that they resemble northern lights. Beneath the horizon, paint the darkened landscape. When the paper has dried, use a smaller paintbrush to draw black lines that separate each color from the other colors. Use Arctic animal tracers to create black cutouts that resemble silhouettes when placed on the painted background. Or have each student draw an Arctic animal outline on a sheet of black paper using chalk, then cut out the animal shape. Glue the shape onto the painted background; then mount the artwork on a larger sheet of black paper. These northern lights—much like the real thing—may be enough to take your breath away.

Rhonda Boychuk—Gr. 1, St. Augustine School
Humboldt, Saskatchewan, Canada

## Penguins With A Personal Touch

Have you ever had a personal connection with a penguin? No? Well, here's your chance! To make a penguin, begin by tracing the outline of your hand (fingers outstretched) and your shoe onto black construction paper. Cut along the resulting outlines. Position the cutout that matches your shoe's sole so that the heel of the tracing is at the top and will represent the penguin's head. Use white chalk to color the penguin's belly. Split the hand cutout by cutting downward between the index and middle fingers. Glue the part with the thumb and index-finger shapes to the penguin's body so that it resembles its foot. Attach the remaining part of the hand cutout to the body to represent a flipper. Trace the end of your thumb onto orange construction paper. Cut on the outline and glue the cutout to the penguin so that it resembles the penguin's beak. Finish this proper penguin by attaching an eye fashioned from paper. How about that? You now have a personal connection with a penguin!

Melissa Raleigh—Gr. 1
Whittier Elementary School
Amarillo, TX

## Parka Pals

When the temperature drops, slip into this parka project and watch students' interest go up and up. To make a parka pal, trace a circle template that's seven inches in diameter onto skin-toned paper. Cut on the resulting outline. Using markers, glue, scissors, construction paper, and assorted art supplies, decorate the circle to resemble your face. Glue the circle to a paper plate; then glue cotton balls along the outer rim of the plate. Trim to round two corners of a 9" x 12" sheet of construction paper, and draw two lines as shown to indicate the arms of the jacket. Glue this paper to the back of the plate. Complete this project by attaching buttons and/or cotton balls to finish the parka. It's cold outside, but you'd never know it snuggled deep down in your parka!

Deborah Burleson, Silverdale, WA

## A Furry Forecast

These wanna-be woodchucks are just in time for Groundhog Day!

**For each woodchuck you will need:**

— two 2" brown circles (ears)
— two 3 1/2" brown circles (cheeks)
— one 7" brown circle (head)
— two 1" pink circles (inner ears)
— one 1" x 2" white rectangle (teeth)
— two 1 1/2" white circles (eyes)
— one 1 1/2" black circle (nose)
— a black crayon or marker
— one wooden clothespin
— white glue
— craft glue
— scissors
— writing paper and a pencil

**Instructions:**

1. Glue each pink circle atop a 2-inch brown circle. Glue the resulting ears to the large brown circle (head). Set aside.
2. To make the cheeks, position the two 3 1/2-inch brown circles side by side so that they slightly overlap. Glue.
3. Glue the small black circle (nose) and the white rectangle (teeth) in place. Use the marker to add details to the teeth and cheeks.
4. Use craft glue to attach the clothespin to the back of the nose and teeth as shown. Allow drying time.
5. Position the cheeks atop the head; then use craft glue to secure the clothespin in the desired location. Allow drying time.
6. Pen a February forecast, a woodchuck-related tall tale, or another piece of creative writing; then clip your literary work in the woodchuck's mouth.

Laura Mihalenko—Gr. 2, Truman Elementary School, Parlin, NJ

**Wild Bill Woodchuck**

Wild Bill Woodchuck was the wildest woodchuck in the west. ...too. He could pop ... in a minute ... exactly what ... n. Wild Bill was ...ting tornadoes.

**Step 4.**

## Famous Folks

Get to the heart of the matter with this presidential project. Duplicate the patterns on page 72 onto black construction paper; then cut out each presidential profile. Mount each cutout on a 6" x 8" white construction-paper rectangle. Stack the rectangles and trim the edges to create two equal-sized ovals. Mount each oval on a 7" x 9" rectangle of blue paper. Trim each blue rectangle to create an eye-catching border. Cut a large heart shape from a 12" x 18" sheet of red construction paper; then mount one project on each side of the heart cutout. Punch a hole near the top of the project and suspend it from the ceiling.

Judy Goodman
Perryville Elementary
Perryville, MO

# Arts & Crafts

## Hearts Aflutter

These wings of love are just a heartbeat away! To make a butterfly, fold in half a 12" x 18" sheet of red, pink, or purple construction paper. Unfold the paper. Working atop newspaper, place several dollops of white tempera paint on one half of the paper. Refold the paper and gently rub the top of the folded paper with your open palm. Unfold the paper. When the paint has dried, refold the paper. Using a template like the one shown, trace a large heart shape on the folded paper. Cut on the resulting outline and unfold the paper. Attach a construction-paper body and bent pipe-cleaner antennae. Now that's a flamboyant flyer!

Elizabeth McDonald
Lincoln Elementary
Wichita, KS

template

Please Be Mine

## Twirls And Curls

Whether you're sending a heartfelt message or counting sheep, this art technique—called quilling—creates one-of-a-kind results. To make a quilled heart, cut a heart shape from construction paper; then cut a supply of 6" x 1/2" paper strips in a desired color(s). One at a time, wrap a paper strip around a pencil; then slide the strip off and glue it—standing on edge—to your heart cutout. Continue in this manner until the cutout is filled in. When the project has dried, mount it atop a folded construction-paper card. Add a heartfelt message; then present your handcrafted work to a loved one.

To make a sheep, cut out a construction-paper copy of one pattern from page 73. You will also need a supply of 6" x 1/2" white paper strips. Using the technique described above, quill a coat for the sheep. Add other desired details using construction-paper scraps or markers; then showcase the completed project at a seasonal display. Or mount it on construction paper to which you have added desired scenery.

Joan Mary Macey—Art Teacher, Benjamin Franklin School, Binghamton, NY

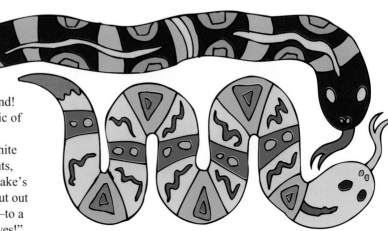

## Snakes Alive!

Legend has it that St. Patrick drove all the snakes from Ireland! Besides being fun to make, these colorful snakes are a great topic of conversation. So how did St. Patrick do that, anyway?

To begin, sketch the outline of a snake on a large sheet of white construction paper. Then—using colorful markers, tempera paints, chalks, or crayons—create a series of colorful patterns on the snake's body. Trace the outline of the snake with a black marker; then cut out the project and attach it—along with a piece of your best work—to a good-work display entitled "Snakes Alive! We've Outdone Ourselves!"

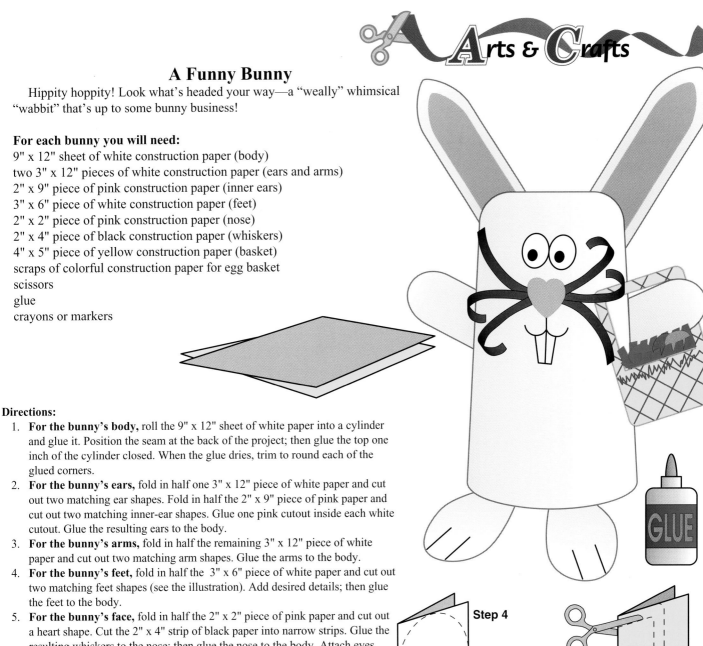
## A Funny Bunny

Hippity hoppity! Look what's headed your way—a "weally" whimsical "wabbit" that's up to some bunny business!

**For each bunny you will need:**
9" x 12" sheet of white construction paper (body)
two 3" x 12" pieces of white construction paper (ears and arms)
2" x 9" piece of pink construction paper (inner ears)
3" x 6" piece of white construction paper (feet)
2" x 2" piece of pink construction paper (nose)
2" x 4" piece of black construction paper (whiskers)
4" x 5" piece of yellow construction paper (basket)
scraps of colorful construction paper for egg basket
scissors
glue
crayons or markers

**Directions:**

1. **For the bunny's body,** roll the 9" x 12" sheet of white paper into a cylinder and glue it. Position the seam at the back of the project; then glue the top one inch of the cylinder closed. When the glue dries, trim to round each of the glued corners.

2. **For the bunny's ears,** fold in half one 3" x 12" piece of white paper and cut out two matching ear shapes. Fold in half the 2" x 9" piece of pink paper and cut out two matching inner-ear shapes. Glue one pink cutout inside each white cutout. Glue the resulting ears to the body.

3. **For the bunny's arms,** fold in half the remaining 3" x 12" piece of white paper and cut out two matching arm shapes. Glue the arms to the body.

4. **For the bunny's feet,** fold in half the 3" x 6" piece of white paper and cut out two matching feet shapes (see the illustration). Add desired details; then glue the feet to the body.

5. **For the bunny's face,** fold in half the 2" x 2" piece of pink paper and cut out a heart shape. Cut the 2" x 4" strip of black paper into narrow strips. Glue the resulting whiskers to the nose; then glue the nose to the body. Attach eyes made from construction-paper scraps, or draw them using crayons or markers.

6. **To make the basket,** fold the yellow paper in half and cut out a basket shape (see the illustration). Cut out construction-paper grass and eggs; then glue them in the basket. Slip the basket onto the bunny's arm.

**Step 4**

**Step 6**

## Cotton-Ball Blossoms

Greet the new season with a classroom full of pretty posies made from colored cotton balls. In preparation for designing a picture, cut each of several colored cotton balls into segments to create disklike shapes. Arrange each of the segments on a sheet of construction paper, along with tufts of cotton balls and construction-paper scraps to create an original, spring-flower picture. Glue the elements of the picture in place and enjoy the gardenlike view!

Virginia Mozden, South Lincoln Elementary School, Alliance, OH

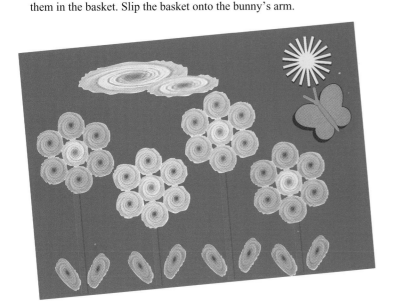

## Pond Life

Set the scene for this painting activity by reading aloud a pond-related book such as *In The Small, Small Pond* by Denise Fleming (Henry Holt And Company, Inc.; 1993), *All Eyes On The Pond* by Michael J. Rosen (Hyperion Paperbacks For Children, 1994), or *Good Morning, Pond* by Alyssa Satin Capucilli (Hyperion Books For Children, 1994). Then, working atop a paper-covered surface, use diluted watercolors to paint a desired pond scene. When the project dries, outline the pond life shown with a black marker. Embellish the project with construction-paper details as desired. The results are "pond-itively" striking!

Joan M. Macey, Binghamton, NY

## An Expression Of Love

The love that fills this Mother's Day greeting keeps growing and growing and growing!

### For each card you will need:

6" x 18" piece of construction paper (card)
3 1/2" x 5" piece of construction paper (flowerpot)
four 3" x 3" pieces of colorful construction paper (flowers)
1/2" x 12" piece of green construction paper (plant stem)
scraps of colorful construction paper for leaves and flower centers
scissors
crayons
glue

### Directions:

1. To make the flowerpot, fold and trim the 3 1/2" x 5" piece of construction paper as shown. Glue the cutout at the lower edge of the card.
2. Glue the green-paper stem to the card, tucking one end of the stem just below the surface of the flowerpot. Allow to dry.
3. Cut a flower shape from each 3" x 3" piece of paper. Decorate each flower shape as desired. Set aside.
4. Bend the top of the card forward until it is flush with the top of the flowerpot. Hold the paper in place; then flatten and fold it.
5. Repeat step 4, this time bringing the fold to the top of the flower pot.
6. Unfold the card. Starting at the top, fold the card forward at each crease.
7. With the card folded, glue a flower cutout above the flowerpot. In the top left-hand corner, use a crayon to write "My Love For You." In the lower right-hand corner of the folded paper, write "Just Grows,". Then unfold one section at a time and glue a flower on the folded paper above the stem. Each time write "And Grows," in the lower right-hand corner of the folded paper. When the card is completely unfolded, write "And Grows!" to the right of the flower. Add desired leaves to the stem.
8. Use a crayon to write "Happy Mother's Day!", the date, and your name on the flowerpot. Then refold the project to proudly present it to Mom!

Louis Lessor—Gr. 2, Westside Elementary, Sun Prairie, WI

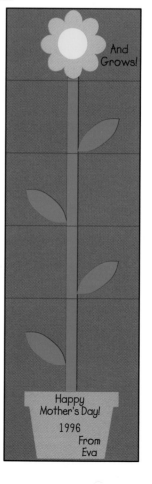

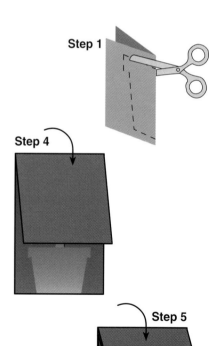

**Step 1**

**Step 4**

**Step 5**

**Finished Project**

# More Gifts Galore

This collection of gift-giving ideas is ready for the taking. Youngsters will enjoy the projects—and parents will enjoy the fruits of their labors!

## Poetic Planter

**Materials For One Planter:**

blank paper
1 pencil
1 arc-shaped construction-
 paper pattern (page 313)
fine-tipped markers
scissors
two 9-oz. clear plastic cups

clear tape
craft glue
1 spoon
1 cup potting soil
1 seedling
water

**Steps:**

1. Write a poem on the blank paper. (Use the writing suggestions provided with the pattern on page 313.)
2. Use markers to copy and decorate your poem on the arc-shaped pattern.
3. Cut out the pattern.
4. Wrap the cutout around the outside of one plastic cup so that it is approximately 1/4 inch from the cup bottom. Tape the ends of the cutout together.
5. Dab glue around the bottom rim of the cup; then securely set the cup inside the second cup.
6. Spoon the potting soil into the cup.
7. Plant the seedling in the soil; then sprinkle the soil with water.

Linda C. Buerklin—Substitute Teacher
Monroe Township, Williamstown, NJ

## A Recorded Keepsake

**Materials For One Recorded Keepsake:**

1 blank cassette tape
1 tape recorder with microphone
1 book selected by the student for reading aloud
1 brown paper lunch bag
1 shallow pan of red tempera paint
1 heart-shaped sponge
1 clothespin
hole puncher
one 18" length of red yarn

**Steps:**

1. Start the recorder.
2. Introduce yourself, state the date, and give the title of the book you will read aloud.
3. When you finish reading the book, sign off with a personal message for whomever you are making the tape; then stop the recorder.
4. Rewind the tape and set it aside.
5. Attach the clothespin to the sponge cutout.
6. Create a design on the paper bag using the sponge cutout and the red paint. Allow the paint to dry.
7. Place the cassette inside the decorated bag.
8. Fold down the bag top and punch two holes near the center of the folded portion.
9. Thread the ends of the yarn length through the holes; then tie the yarn and fashion a bow.

Krista K. Zimmerman—Gr. 3, Tuckerton Elementary School
Tuckerton, NJ

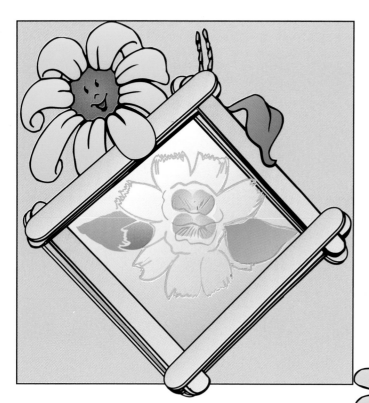

## Special Day Placemat

**Materials For One Placemat:**
one 12" x 18" sheet of white construction paper
fine-tipped markers
clear Con-Tact® covering or laminating film
scissors

**Steps:**
1. Trim to round the corners of the paper.
2. Create a colorful border around the paper. Write an appropriate greeting inside the border.
3. Sign and date the back of the project.
4. Cover the resulting placemat with clear Con-Tact® covering or laminate it for durability.

Fran Rizzo—Gr. 3, Brookdale School, Bloomfield, NJ

## Fun Suncatchers

**Materials For One Suncatcher:**
one 4 1/2" x 9" piece of clear Con-Tact® covering
flowers and/or leaves that have been picked, dried, and
   flattened by the student
8 craft sticks
craft glue
one 9" length of string or fishing line
scissors

**Steps:**
1. Fold the Con-Tact® covering in half and crease it. Unfold.
2. Lay the covering on a flat surface, backing-side up; then peel away the backing.
3. In the center of one half of the covering, arrange the dried items.
4. Fold the remaining half of the covering over the dried items, aligning the edges. Set aside.
5. Use four craft sticks to make a frame. To do this, arrange two sticks parallel to each other and about 4 1/2 inches apart. Place the two remaining sticks on top of—and perpendicular to—the other two sticks. Glue the sticks in place. Allow to dry.
6. To make a second frame, repeat step 5. Before gluing the sticks in place, loop and tie the length of string around one stick. This will be your hanger.
7. Glue the dried arrangement on top of the first frame. When the glue has dried, trim away any covering that extends beyond the frame.
8. Glue the second frame on top of the project, keeping the hanger free from glue.
9. To display the project, turn it diagonally and slide the hanger to one corner. Suspend the project in a sunny window.

Mary Lam Boardwine—Library Media Specialist
Montvale Elementary School, Montvale, VA

## A Flower Just For You

**Materials For One Flower And Card:**

scissors
one 3" square of green felt
one 4" square of floral fabric
1 cup from a polystyrene egg carton

1 green pipe cleaner
one 5" x 8" rectangle of white construction paper
markers or crayons
hole puncher

**Steps:**

1. Cut a heart-shaped leaf from the green felt; then cut a small slit in the pointed end of the heart.
2. Trim to round the corners of the fabric; then scallop the fabric's edges to create a flower shape. Cut a small slit in the center of the flower.
3. Thread the felt leaf onto one end of the pipe cleaner; then poke the pipe cleaner through the bottom of the egg cup. Next thread the fabric flower onto the pipe cleaner.
4. Extend the end of the pipe cleaner about one inch beyond the fabric flower.
5. Coil and flatten the one-inch end of the pipe cleaner to form the flower's center.
6. Fold the construction paper in half to make a card.
7. Use markers or crayons to decorate and write a desired message on the outside and inside of the card.
8. In the back of the card—near the fold—punch two holes.
9. Starting on the inside of the card, thread the long end of the pipe cleaner through the top hole and then through the bottom hole.
10. Close the card and adjust the position of the flower to your liking.

Leigh-Ann Hensal, Lockport, NY

## Homemade-Paper Hearts

**Materials For Homemade-Paper Hearts:**

2 sheets of dark pink tissue paper (cut into 1" squares)
2 sheets of light pink tissue paper (cut into 1" squares)
2 quarts water
2 teaspoons liquid starch
1 electric blender
1 wire coat hanger
1 large bowl
1 leg of a pair of discarded pantyhose
1 tray of rose-shaped plastic candy molds
one 8" length and one 10" length of narrow pink ribbon per project
craft glue
hot glue gun

waxed paper
paper towels

**Steps:**

1. Place the dark pink tissue paper, 1 quart of water, and 1 teaspoon of starch in the blender. Blend for one minute.
2. Make a strainer by stretching the pantyhose leg over the wire hanger. Place the resulting strainer over the large bowl.
3. Pour the contents of the blender through the strainer.
4. Gently squeeze the excess water from the paper pulp that remains atop the strainer; then press the pulp into the candy molds (will yield approximately six roses). Allow them to dry.
5. Prepare and strain a second batch of paper pulp using the light pink tissue paper, and the remaining water and liquid starch.
6. Gently squeeze the excess water from the paper pulp; then form the pulp into two heart shapes atop waxed paper. Transfer the hearts to paper towels and allow them to dry.
7. Glue a dried rose from a candy mold in the center of a dried heart shape.
8. Fashion a bow from the 8-inch ribbon length. Glue the bow to the heart.
9. Tie together the ends of the 10-inch ribbon length to make a loop for hanging. Using a hot glue gun, attach the loop to the back of the project.

Cynthia G. Besosa—Gr. 2, Tuloso-Midway Primary, Corpus Christi, TX

# Wooden Notepad Holder

**Materials For One Notepad Holder:**

one 5" x 7" piece of hard wood*
sandpaper
one 5" x 7" piece of white con-
    struction paper
crayons
1 black permanent marker
scissors
1 plastic cup
craft glue

water
1 craft stick
one 12" square of waxed
    paper
1 paintbrush
one 5" x 7" piece of felt
1 spring-type metal notepad
    holder and screws
1 screwdriver
a supply of 4" x 6" notepaper

**Steps:**

1. Use the sandpaper to smooth the top and edges of the board.
2. Illustrate a colorful picture on the construction paper. For best results color heavily.
3. Use the black marker to outline the different elements of your picture; then cut out each one.
4. In the plastic cup, mix together one part water and one part glue. Stir the mixture with the craft stick.
5. Place the wood atop the waxed paper; then paint the top and the sides of the wood with a coating of the mixture.
6. Arrange the colorful cutouts on top of the wood and press them in place.
7. Apply a second coat of the glue mixture to the top and sides of the wood. Smooth out any air bubbles trapped under the cutouts. Allow to dry.
8. Apply two or three more coats of the glue mixture to the top and sides of the project. Allow each coat to dry before the next application. A smooth finish should be achieved.
9. Glue the felt piece to the bottom of the project.
10. Use the screwdriver and screws to attach the notepad holder to the project.
11. Slip desired notepaper into the holder.

*Inquire about obtaining scrap pieces of wood from a local manu-facturer or a high-school woodworking class.

Betty Jean Kobes—Gr. 1, West Hancock Elementary School
Kanawha, IA

# Puzzle-Piece Picture Frame

**Materials For One Picture Frame:**

one 12" length of decorative tinsel wire or narrow ribbon
one 6" x 8" piece of clear plastic mesh
1 student photo
1 piece of clear Con-Tact® covering twice the size of the photo
one 8" x 10" piece of clear plastic wrap
70 to 80 jigsaw-puzzle pieces
craft glue

**Steps:**

1. Attach the tinsel wire to a short end of the plastic mesh by tying the ends of the wire to the outermost corners of the mesh.
2. Cover the student photo with the Con-Tact® covering.
3. Place the plastic mesh atop the piece of clear plastic wrap; then glue the photo in the center of the plastic mesh.
4. Glue a layer of puzzle pieces around the photo, creating a border.
5. Glue a second and a third layer of puzzle pieces around the photo until the edges of the photo and the plastic mesh can not be seen.

Linda Mates—Gr. 2, Public School 206, Brooklyn, NY

## Miniature Vase Of Flowers

**Materials For One Vase:**
one 5/8" wooden candle cup
one 6" square of waxed paper
light brown acrylic paint
1 paintbrush
1 small ball of clay (approximately 1")
2 small sprigs of silk flowers

**Steps:**
1. Working atop the waxed paper, paint the outer surface of the candle cup light brown. Allow the paint to dry.
2. Press the clay into the candle cup.
3. Insert the silk-flower stems into the clay.

Gerrie Gutowski, Sombra del Monte School, Albuquerque, NM

## Hats Off To Moms

**Materials For One Hat:**
1 paper plate
1 pencil
one 9" x 12" piece of floral-print wallpaper
three 9" x 12" sheets of white construction paper
scissors or pinking shears
glue
1 paintbrush
1 unopened can or lidded jar having a 3" diameter
one 12" length of wide ribbon
1 paper clip
hot glue gun
one 9" length of narrow ribbon

**Steps:**
1. Using the paper plate as a template, trace a circle on the wallpaper and each of the three sheets of white construction paper. Cut out the resulting circles.
2. Making sure to cover the entire surface, paint a thin layer of glue on one side of one construction-paper circle. Align and press a second construction-paper circle atop the glue. Paint a thin layer of glue atop the newly placed circle, and align and press the remaining construction-paper circle in place. Repeat the gluing process; then align and press the wallpaper circle atop the glue.
3. With the wallpaper circle on top, center the stack of cutouts over the can. Form the hat's crown and brim by shaping the project over the end of the can. Leave the project in place and allow it to dry.
4. Fashion a bow from the wide ribbon and glue it to the hat as shown.
5. Use a hot glue gun to attach the paper clip beneath the hat rim—opposite the bow.
6. Thread the narrow ribbon through the paper clip. Tie the ribbon's ends and suspend the project in a desired location.

Joan M. Macey, Binghamton, NY

## Dazzling Dinosaurs

Students can create these prehistoric beauties single-handedly, or for artistic inspiration they can first study Marcus Pfister's illustrations in *Dazzle The Dinosaur*. Working atop a paper-covered surface, use diluted watercolors to paint a desired background on a 9" x 12" sheet of white construction paper. Also paint an eight-inch, white construction-paper square with diluted watercolors. Overlap the colors for added interest. When the paint dries, use a template to trace a dinosaur shape onto the painted paper square. (See the patterns on page 74.) Outline the resulting shape with a permanent black marker; then cut along the outer edge of the black line. For a touch of razzle-dazzle, spread a thin layer of glue over a portion of the cutout and apply a coating of glitter. Shake off the excess glitter and glue the cutout onto the painted background. Use markers and/or construction paper to add desired details; then mount the project on a slightly larger piece of black paper. For additional ohhhs and ahhhs, laminate the masterpiece before show-casing it in a classroom gallery.

Glorianne Bradshaw—Gr. 1
Valley Elementary School
Crystal, ND

## All Aflutter!

These eye-catching butterflies can be created in just a flit and a flutter! Invert a small-size disposable soup bowl; then use colorful tempera paints to paint the bottom of the bowl. While the paint is drying, trim four 4 1/2" x 6" sheets of construction paper to resemble butterfly wings and two 2" x 4" strips of black construction paper to resemble butterfly antennae. Arrange the wing and antennae cutouts so that they achieve the desired results when the inverted bowl is in place. Glue together all overlapping surfaces of the wing and antennae cutouts, creating one large shape. Squeeze a trail of glue around the rim of the bowl; then invert the bowl on the construction-paper shape. Gently press on the bowl until the glue dries. Now that's a colorful flier!

Doris Hautala—Gr. 3
Washington Elementary
Ely, MN

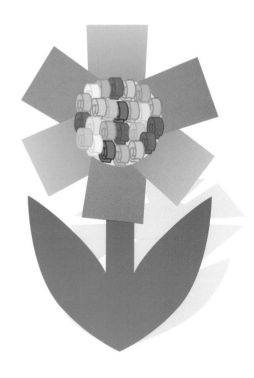

## Beauteous Blooms

When these colorful flowers take center stage, heads will turn! Cut leftover scraps of construction paper into narrow strips (approximately 1/2" x 3"). One at a time, roll each of several paper strips around a pencil, slide the rolled paper off the pencil, and glue one end of the strip to a four-inch construction-paper circle. Continue in this manner until the entire surface of the circle is covered. For best results glue the paper strips close together. Then trim six 3" x 4" pieces of colorful construction paper to resemble petals. Glue the petals side by side around the back edge of the circle cutout. Glue a stem cut from green paper onto the back of the flower; then glue a desired number of leaf cutouts along the stem. Showcase the flowers side by side on a bulletin board or wall for an eye-catching garden display.

Doris Hautala—Gr. 3

## Sunset Silhouettes

To make this impressive sunset, align an 8" x 11" piece of manila paper atop an 8" x 11" piece of white construction paper and staple the two top corners. At the bottom, tear off a narrow strip of the manila paper. Pressing heavily, draw a chalk line along the torn paper edge; then use a facial tissue to rub the chalk downward onto the exposed portion of the white paper. When this step has been completed, tear off another narrow strip of manila paper and repeat the process, using a different color of chalk and a clean portion of tissue. Continue in this manner until you have used the last strip of manila paper. Then remove the staples and the remaining manila paper. Smear the top chalk layer upward to cover any white space at the top of the page. Cut a desired silhouette from black paper and glue it on your colorful sunset. Mount the project on a 9" x 12" sheet of black construction paper.

Karen Saner—Grs. K–1
Burns Elementary School
Burns, KS

## Daffy Daisy Heads

So what would you do if a daisy sprang from the top of your head? Follow up an oral reading of *Daisy-Head Mayzie* by Dr. Seuss with this kid-pleasing project. To make a daisy head, adorn a three-inch Styrofoam® ball with a crop of yellow yarn hair, two wiggle eyes, and a red pipe-cleaner smile. Poke the stem of a plastic daisy into the top of the resulting head; then rest the daisy head atop a decorated toilet-tissue tube. For a related writing activity, ask each child to pen a story about his daisy head's latest adventure!

Peggy Auvil—Gr. 3
Espy Elementary
Nixa, MO

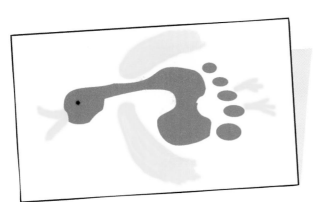

## Footprint Fowl

These one-of-a-kind fliers will bring your students to their feet! Protect an area of the classroom floor with newspapers. Into a dishpan pour a thin layer of tempera paint and liquid soap mixture. (Prepare one dishpan for each desired paint color.) To make the body of his bird, a youngster puts his bare foot into a dishpan of paint, then presses his paint-covered footprint onto the center of a sheet of white construction paper. Then, using a contrasting color of paint and a paintbrush, he creates his bird's wing(s) and any desired scenery. The following day, when the paint has dried, each student uses markers to draw details like eyes, a beak, and feet.

Janette E. Anderson—Substitute Teacher Grs. K–3
Fremont School District
Fremont, CA

**Patterns**

Use with "Cattle Crossing" on page 47.

Use petal patterns with "Showy Sunflowers" on page 47.

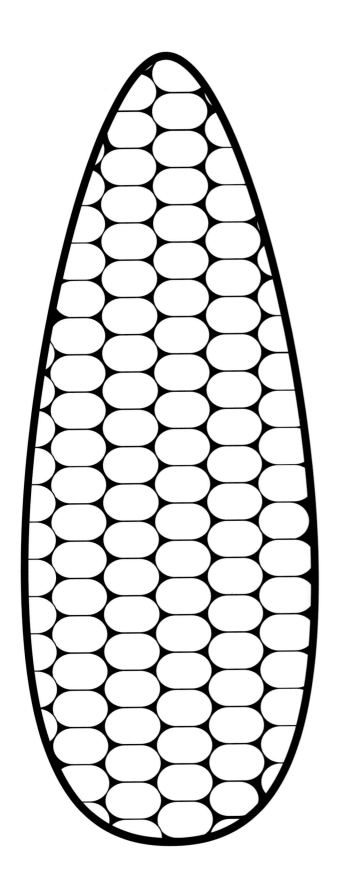
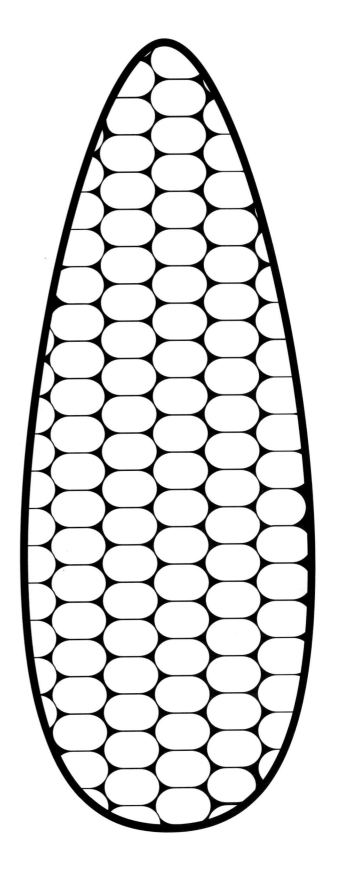

# Patterns

Use with "Famous Folks" on page 59.

# Patterns

Use with "Dazzling Dinosaurs" on page 68.

# AUTHOR UNITS

# Gerald McDermott

## A Master Of Storytelling And Illustration

### About The Author

Gerald McDermott is an internationally known author and illustrator who has created numerous books and animated films for children. A master of his craft, McDermott can spin and illustrate tales that represent the cultures of many peoples.

McDermott's career began at the young age of four when his parents enrolled him in art school. Until the age of 14, he attended classes at the Detroit Institute Of Art every Saturday morning. In the afternoons he explored the galleries. By the age of nine, McDermott knew he was destined to become an artist.

McDermott's innovative picture books have earned him several prestigious awards including the Caldecott Medal for *Arrow To The Sun: A Pueblo Indian Tale*, and Caldecott Honors for *Anansi The Spider: A Tale From The Ashanti* and *Raven: A Trickster Tale From The Pacific Northwest*. In addition to writing and illustrating, McDermott is Primary Education Program Director for the Joseph Campbell Foundation on mythology in education. A native of Detroit, Michigan, the author currently resides in southern California.

## Pick and choose from this sampling of McDermott's work and the related classroom activities.

### Anansi The Spider: A Tale From The Ashanti

*Anansi's six sons save their father from a terrible fate. Unable to decide which one son should be rewarded, Anansi enlists the help of Nyame—The God Of All Things.*

No doubt each of your youngsters will have an opinion about which son should receive the prize Anansi has found. Draw a graph on the chalkboard that lists the names of the six sons. In turn have each child express and defend his opinion, then color the corresponding space on the class graph. After students have interpreted the completed graph, use the graph to create an assortment of problem-solving activities.

*Arlene Levine—Gr. 1, Freeman School, Phillipsburg, NJ*

These moon-shaped journals are the perfect places for students to write additional tales about Anansi and his six sons. To make a journal, staple several blank, circular pages between two slightly larger yellow construction-paper covers. Students can write and illustrate a series of spider-related tales. Or they can write and illustrate stories that explain which son becomes the keeper of the moon.

*Arlene Levine—Gr. 1*

Stories
Of Anansi
by
Nikki Stamnos

## Arrow To The Sun: A Pueblo Indian Tale

*This adaptation of a Pueblo tale won the Caldecott Medal in 1975. Bright, bold graphics and few words tell the tale of how the spirit of the sun was brought down to the Pueblo people.*

Once at the sun, the Boy is challenged by four *kivas* (ceremonial chambers). Have students reexamine these illustrations and describe the inhabitants of each chamber as the Boy enters and as he exits. The Boy tames the lions, serpents, and bees instead of killing them. Ask your youngsters to propose ways to tame the inhabitants of kivas filled with bears, spiders, and crocodiles.

This book is a vivid visual reminder of the Indian reverence for the source of all life: the Solar Fire. Students—inspired by McDermott's bold illustrations—can produce bright paper-plate sunbursts of their own. To make a sun, sketch a desired design on a paper plate. Then use crayons, markers, or tempera paints to give color to your sun.

## The Stonecutter: A Japanese Folk Tale

*A foolish longing for power forever changes the life of a lowly stonecutter. This ancient Japanese fable is a tale of wishes and dreams—and consequences.*

Tasaku's continuous quest for more and more power becomes his ultimate undoing. Invite your students to talk about their wishes and dreams. Find out what they learned from Tasaku's experience and how they can apply this new knowledge to their pursuit of happiness. Next have each child copy, complete, and illustrate the following: "Happiness is…." Showcase the completed projects on a bulletin board featuring a large, mountain-shaped cutout and the title "Happiness Is…." Or bind them into a book bearing a similar cover.

## Papagayo: The Mischief Maker

*The noisy daytime habits of a mischievous parrot perturb the nocturnal creatures of the rain forest. But the nocturnal bunch has a change of heart when Papagayo's noisy ways save the day!*

You won't hear many squawks of protest when you unveil this follow-up art activity! In advance cover a bulletin board with bright blue paper. Attach a white moon-shaped cutout and the title "Papagayo's Rain Forest." As a class, admire the author's bright, bold, and colorful rain-forest artwork. Then challenge your students to create a similar scene. To do this, divide the class into small groups and assign each group a portion of the rain forest. For example, different groups could be responsible for the rain-forest vegetation, the nocturnal creatures, Papagayo, and the moon-dog. Each group uses bright, bold tempera paints or markers to illustrate its assigned topic on white art paper. Then each group cuts out its artwork and attaches it to the display. Wow! Wouldn't Mr. McDermott be impressed?

*Lisa Kelley—Gr. 1, James Walker Elementary, Blue Springs, MO*

## Daniel O'Rourke: An Irish Tale

*Hold on tight! This fast-paced and lighthearted fantasy about a young Irishman may sweep you off your feet—and that's no blarney!*

Daniel O'Rourke's ordeal creates a perfect setting for a bit of St. Patrick's Day creative writing. Discuss Daniel's adventures with your youngsters. Have students explain how each one related to a previous incident in Daniel's life. Challenge students to carry out this theme as they write and illustrate additional adventures for this likable Irishman. Be sure to set aside time for interested students to share their Irish tales. If desired bind the stories between booklet covers cut in the shape of an island. Title the book "Daniel O'Rourke's Island Adventures."

*Fran Palffy, Parma Park Christian Life Academy, Parma, OH*

It looks like green cheese, but does it taste like it? Students are sure to enjoy this green cheese look-alike!

### Green Cheese Delight

| | |
|---|---|
| 3-oz. package lime gelatin | 24-oz. container of cottage cheese |
| 1 cup boiling water | 12-oz. container of thawed Cool Whip® |
| 1 cup cold water | 1 cup miniature marshmallows |

In a large bowl, use the water to prepare the lime gelatin according to the package directions. Refrigerate the gelatin until it begins to thicken. In a second bowl, mix together the cottage cheese, the Cool Whip®, and the marshmallows. Fold this mixture into the thickened gelatin. Refrigerate until set. Makes approximately 25 to 30 small servings.

*Fran Palffy*

Step 1    Step 2

## Tim O'Toole And The Wee Folk: An Irish Tale

*Penniless Tim O'Toole teams up with the wee folk to trick the McGoons into giving him back his fortune.*

The luck of the Irish was with Tim O'Toole when he spied the wee folk in the light of day. But because Tim couldn't keep from boasting, his good fortune quickly turned into misfortune—more than once! Ask your youngsters how they feel about boasting. When do they think boasting is acceptable? not acceptable? What did they learn from Tim O'Toole's experience?

When your students make a troop of wee folk, the luck of the Irish is sure to find its way into your classroom!

### For each leprechaun you will need:
— three 3" green construction-paper squares (body)
— a 2" x 3" green construction-paper strip (hat)
— two 2" black paper squares (boots)
— two 2" skin-tone construction-paper squares (hands)
— one 2 1/2" skin-tone construction-paper circle
— scraps of black and yellow construction paper
— a fine-tip marker
— yarn for the beard
— scissors
— glue

### Directions:
1. Cut a heart shape from each green square. To form the body, glue the points of the heart shapes together as shown.
2. Use the marker to draw a face on the skin-tone circle. Glue the resulting face in place.
3. Trim the green rectangle into a hat shape. Glue the hat in place.
4. Stack the skin-tone squares. Cut out two matching hand shapes. Glue the hands in place.
5. Stack the black squares. Cut out two matching boot shapes. Glue the boots in place.
6. Cut a hat band and a hat buckle, a belt and a belt buckle, and two shoe buckles from paper scraps. Glue the cutouts in place.
7. Glue a yarn beard in place.

## Zomo The Rabbit: A Trickster Tale From West Africa

*Zomo the Rabbit isn't very big and he isn't very strong—but he's quite clever! Now he also wants to be wise. Can Zomo prove to the Sky God that he's worthy of wisdom?*

At the end of the story, Sky God warns Zomo about his shortcomings. Ask students to recall why Zomo stole from Big Fish, Wild Cow, and Leopard. Then ask the youngsters to explain why they do or do not think Zomo demonstrated true wisdom. Next divide the class into groups of five students each. Have each group member illustrate a different story character, then cut out and glue his character to a craft stick. Invite each group to use their puppets to reenact Zomo's story or to create a new adventure for Zomo, Sky God, Big Fish, Wild Cow, and Leopard.

### THE TRICKSTER TRIBUNE

Mr. Pond's Class    March 1996

**Skunk: A Trickster Tale From The Forest**
Long ago, Skunk was very popular. He smelled like sweet flowers. He felt happy most of the time. But many of his friends felt sad. He decided to help them, so…

**Whale: A Trickster Tale From The Ocean**
Whale was big and strong. Most of the time he was very happy. But today he is sad. He is worried about his home…

## Raven: A Trickster Tale From The Pacific Northwest

*When Raven came to the world, it was in total darkness. Can the wise and clever Raven find the gift of light, and then give it to the world?*

Raven felt sorry for the people who were living in the cold darkness, so he took it upon himself to find light for the world. Ask students to brainstorm things that trouble them—things in the world that they wish they could change. List the students' ideas on the chalkboard. Ask each child to choose a topic from the list and write and illustrate a trickster tale that explains how the problem is solved. Decorate the front page of a newspaper to show the title "The Trickster Tribune," the date, and a class byline. Mount your students' completed projects on the newspaper pages. Laminate the pages for durability; then place the newspaper in your class library for all to read!

## Coyote: A Trickster Tale From The American Southwest

*Coyote finds mischief and mayhem wherever he goes. This time it's Coyote's boastful ways that land him in a heap of trouble.*

Point out that stories such as Coyote's sometimes explain how something in nature came to be, or they teach a lesson or have a moral. Ask students why coyotes are no longer blue. Also find out if the youngsters think Coyote's tale taught a lesson or had a moral. For a fun writing assignment, ask each student to write and illustrate a legend that explains an occurrence in nature. Bind the students' stories into a class booklet.

*Lisa Kelley—Gr. 1, James Walker Elementary, Blue Springs, MO*

LEGENDS FROM NATURE

Ms. Kelley's First Grade Class

# Tony Johnston

## Teacher Turned Author

Pick and choose from this sampling of Tony Johnston's work and the related classroom activities.

### About The Author

As a youngster, Tony collected everything that crawled or flew. She even raised Monarch butterflies! But her childhood dream of becoming a veterinarian or a "bugologist" was replaced by other interests. Soon after graduating from Stanford University, Tony Johnston began teaching elementary school. Her love of writing was apparent in the stories that she wrote for her students. At the urging of a fellow teacher, Johnston investigated getting her stories published. It was an investigation that took time and energy, but one that young readers today are thankful for. To date, Johnston has published nearly 75 books and has plenty more on tap. She currently resides in California.

### *The Quilt Story*

Illustrated by Tomie dePaola

G. P. Putnam's Sons, 1985

*Follow a well-loved quilt through the years and across the miles as it provides warmth and comfort to those who love it.*

After reading this book aloud, discuss how the quilt helped both of the girls in the story. Share with students an example of something that brought you warmth and comfort as a child, such as a favorite quilt, blanket, stuffed toy, or special place. To make a class quilt that is overflowing with warm feelings, ask each child to illustrate his special item or favorite place on a nine-inch square of white construction paper. Mount the illustrations on a bulletin board covered with brightly colored paper, leaving about two inches between the illustrations. Then use a marker to draw stitches around the project. If desired, attach gathered crepe paper to the outer edges of the display for a quilt border.

### *Whale Song*

Illustrated by Ed Young

G. P. Putnam's Sons, 1987

*A procession of impressive whales sing their way through ocean waters, passing on to one another the numbers from one to ten.*

Could these gentle giants gliding through the world's oceans really be counting to one another? This poetic tale is sure to please your youngsters and invoke some creative thoughts as well. At the conclusion of the story, ask your youngsters to share what they know about whales and what they'd like to find out. Then make plans to study these one-of-a-kind mammals. For a fun writing activity, have each child write and illustrate a make-believe story about what else whales might be conversing about underwater. Compile the stories into a whale-shaped booklet like the one shown.

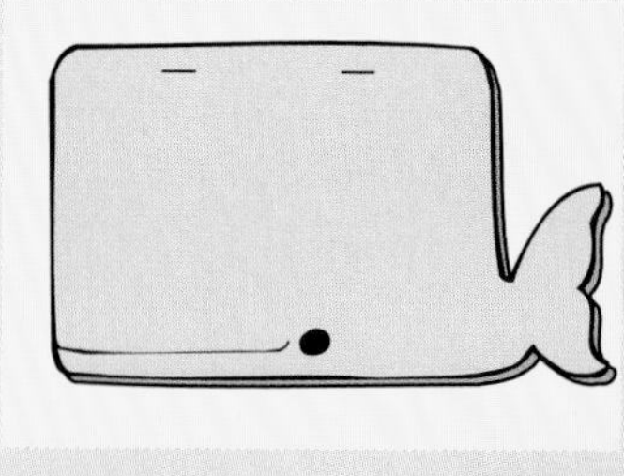

## Grandpa's Song

Illustrated by Brad Sneed

Dial Books For Young Readers, 1991

*Grandpa—a big, round man with a bellowing voice—is shaken when he forgets the words to his favorite song. But his grandchildren are there to carry the tune in a joyous expression of love that's as big and strong as Grandpa's voice.*

Like the hero of this story, Tony Johnston's grandfather once composed a song that everyone in the family had to learn! Discuss Grandpa and what a character he is. Ask students if they know of anyone who reminds them of Grandpa in one way or another. Also talk about why Grandpa has trouble remembering things; then ask students to suggest ways they can help older people who have similar problems. For a fun finale, have your students follow your lead as you assume Grandpa's singing stance. Then, as a class, belt out a few favorite tunes!

## The Cowboy And The Black-Eyed Pea

Illustrated by Warren Ludwig

G. P. Putnam's Sons, 1992

*In this clever parody of* The Princess And The Pea, *the wealthy daughter of a Texas rancher devises a plan to find a real cowboy among her many suitors.*

Follow up an oral reading of this story by reading aloud your favorite version of *The Princess And The Pea.* Divide students into small groups and ask each group to compare the two stories, then create a list of similarities and a list of differences. Compile the group lists into a class list. To conclude the activity, have students vote for the tale that they like the best.

*Karen Cast—Gr. 2, Ben Milam Elementary, Cameron, TX*

Saddle up for some superb storytelling with this creative-writing activity. First discuss the many qualities that a cowboy must have, like being strong, hardworking, and brave—as well as being sensitive to environmental concerns, and the needs of people and animals. Then have each student describe and illustrate her ideas for the most comfortable saddle in the world. Be sure to set aside time for students to share their inventions with their classmates.

*Carole Curcio—Gr. 1, Hampton School, Hampton, NJ*

## Slither McCreep
## And His Brother, Joe
Illustrated by Victoria Chess
Harcourt Brace Jovanovich, Publishers; 1992
*Slither, a young snake, is furious that his brother, Joe, won't share his toys. Determined to get even, Slither sneaks into Joe's room and squeezes Joe's toys until they break. However, instead of satisfaction, Slither feels remorseful about his squeezing rampage.*

When this project is complete, your youngsters can have a hissy-fit of giggles too! To make a Slither McCreep look-alike, each student draws a large snake shape on a sheet of 12" x 18" drawing paper. Then, following your oral directions, the student draws and colors a series of geometric shapes inside his snake outline. When the projects are complete, ask students to recall how Slither felt after his squeezing frenzy and how the two brothers came to terms with what had happened. Encourage students to talk about times they have done things that they later wished they hadn't.

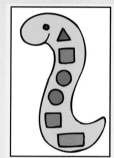

*Carrie Rensberger, Angleton, TX*

## Lorenzo, The Naughty Parrot
Illustrated by Leo Politi
Harcourt Brace Jovanovich, Publishers; 1992
*Wherever the action is—or wherever the cookies are—that's where you'll find Lorenzo. He's a watchdog pet parrot who gets into lots of trouble trying to protect his human family.*

Lorenzo is a busy parrot! With the help of your students, recap the events of each of Lorenzo's four adventures. Have students identify how Lorenzo finds trouble each time. Is it his curiosity that lands him in trouble? His tendency to be overprotective? Or both? Invite students to share pet-related stories that have landed other pets in trouble. Then have each child write and illustrate another adventure for Lorenzo. When the projects are complete, bind them into a classroom book titled "Lorenzo's Latest Adventures." A few days later, gather your youngsters around you and read the stories aloud while your youngsters munch on Lorenzo's favorite snack—cookies!

## The Tale Of Rabbit And Coyote
Illustrated by Tomie dePaola
G. P. Putnam's Sons, 1994
*If you think a man resides in the moon, look again! In this Zapotec retelling, Rabbit coaxes Coyote into a series of disasters—then scampers to the moon where he is safely out of reach.*

Poor Coyote! He's such a gullible pup that Rabbit outwits him time and time again. Read the story aloud a second time, stopping after each incident. Ask students what Coyote could have done to thwart each of Rabbit's clever plans. Next ask students how they think Coyote might be able to get Rabbit back from the moon. Brainstorm ideas as a class; then use the ideas to compose a class story. To make a big book titled "Clever Coyote," copy the resulting story text onto a series of large story pages. As a class, determine a color scheme for the book; then have students work together to illustrate the story pages before compiling them into a big book.

## Amber On The Mountain

Illustrated by Robert Duncan

Dial Books For Young Readers, 1994

*Amber's mountain is a beautiful yet lonely place until she meets Anna—a girl from the city. As a wonderful friendship unfolds between the two girls, Anna helps Amber realize that anything is possible "if you fix your mind on it"—and that includes learning to read and write.*

At the conclusion of this heartwarming story, discuss Amber's determination. Invite students to talk about times that they have set goals, and then—when the going got rough—gave up on their goals and themselves. Also discuss the challenges that Amber faced and the support she received from Anna. Then, on a strip of white construction paper, have each student write a goal that she is ready to fix her mind on. The goals may be personalized or anonymous. Mount the programmed strips on a bulletin board that students have decorated to resemble Amber's mountain paradise. Title the display "Our Minds Are Fixed!"

*Barbara Denlinger—Grs. K–2 Reading Teacher, Bergstrasse Elementary School, Ephrata, PA*

## The Old Lady And The Birds

Illustrated by Stephanie Garcia

Harcourt Brace And Company, 1994

*In her garden in Mexico, a weathered Mexican woman passes the hours in harmony with her garden. She is alone—but never forlorn—in this touching story of kindness.*

Tony Johnston lived in Mexico for 15 years. She spent many hours in beautiful enclosed gardens, watching birds and listening to fountains. No doubt these experiences influenced her as she wrote this touching tale. Have students recall the ways in which the old lady watches out and cares for the birds. Discuss the joy that she experiences from spending time in her garden and ask students if they think the woman feels alone there. Then have each child write a letter to the old lady in which he describes a beautiful, bird-filled garden that he would like for her to visit. In his letter the student can explain the kinds of things that the lady could see and do in the special garden. Students who finish early can illustrate the garden paradises that they've described!

## The Iguana Brothers

Illustrated by Mark Teague

The Blue Sky Press, 1995

*Dom and Tom, two iguana brothers living in Mexico, crawl through three laid-back adventures. After several bouts of thinking—followed by long hours of lazing in the sun—the duo discover that brothers make terrific best friends.*

What is a best friend? List your students' ideas on the chalkboard. Be sure that the student-generated list reflects friendship tips from the iguana brothers. For a fun follow-up activity, have each student design an eye-catching poster that includes three or more pointers for being a good friend. Display the friendship posters throughout your school. Wouldn't Dom and Tom be impressed?

# Bravo For Beverly Cleary!

Henry Huggins, Ramona Quimby, Ralph S. Mouse, and Muggie Maggie are just a few of Beverly Cleary's endearing storybook characters. Her books have become the favorites of many young readers, and in the classroom they rank as first-rate read-alouds. To complement your best-loved books from Cleary's outstanding collection, pick and choose from these classroom-tested suggestions.

## Meet The Author

As a child growing up in Oregon amidst two world wars and economic hardships, Beverly Cleary longed to read honest stories of real kids and their true-life experiences. Later, as a children's librarian, Cleary found herself frustrated in her search for interesting, easy-to-read books that would speak to the average, ordinary child. Finally she decided to fill the void by writing her own children's books. Her first book, *Henry Huggins*, was published in 1950. To date Cleary has penned more than 30 books for young readers.

For a most delightful and accurate portrayal of Beverly Cleary as a child, a teenager, an adult, and a writer, read her autobiography *Beverly Cleary: A Girl From Yamhill* (William Morrow And Company, Inc.; 1988).

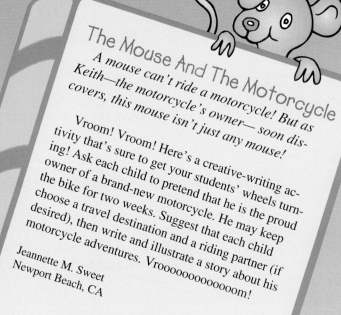

## The Mouse And The Motorcycle

A mouse can't ride a motorcycle! But as Keith—the motorcycle's owner— soon discovers, this mouse isn't just any mouse!

Vroom! Vroom! Here's a creative-writing activity that's sure to get your students' wheels turning! Ask each child to pretend that he is the proud owner of a brand-new motorcycle. He may keep the bike for two weeks. Suggest that each child choose a travel destination and a riding partner (if desired), then write and illustrate a story about his motorcycle adventures. Vroooooooooooooom!

Jeannette M. Sweet
Newport Beach, CA

Trying to choose a favorite scene from *The Mouse And The Motorcycle* may be the most difficult part of this follow-up activity! Once students have made their selections, ask each child to re-create his favorite scene in the form of a diorama. Give each child a small empty box (a shoebox works well), and make available an assortment of construction paper and craft supplies such as fabric scraps, glitter, sequins, and pipe cleaners. Set aside small portions of time on each of several days for students to work on their projects. When the dioramas are complete, invite each youngster to present and explain the scene he depicted in his diorama.

Betty Kobes—Gr. 1
West Hancock Elementary
Kanawha, IA

The Mouse And The Motorcycle diorama by Luke

## Ramona Quimby, Age 8

*There are trials and triumphs aplenty as Ramona Quimby, age 8, enters third grade.*

When a hard-boiled egg fad begins at school, Ramona joins right in! But she's soon sorry that she did! After reading this portion of the story aloud, discuss the term *fad* with your youngsters. Ask students to brainstorm trends that are currently popular. Record their ideas on a chart labeled "What's Hot!"; then discuss how and why certain fads become popular and others do not. Follow up this discussion by challenging each student to design a poster that introduces a new fad. On a given date, encourage each child to share his fabulous new fad with his classmates!

Laura Lee Powers & Lisa Donahoo—Gr. 3
Bryant Elementary
Mableton, GA

For a lively discussion, ask students to talk about Ramona's relationship with her teacher, Mrs. Whaley. Find out how your students think Ramona rates as a student and how Mrs. Whaley rates as a teacher. For added fun, find out how your students think Ramona would adjust to a classroom taught by teachers featured in other books, such as Ms. Frizzle (Magic School Bus series), Viola Swamp or Miss Nelson *(Miss Nelson Is Missing!),* or Mrs. Green *(The Teacher From The Black Lagoon).* Conclude the discussion by having students write and illustrate want ads seeking the perfect teacher for Ramona.

Laura Lee Powers & Lisa Donahoo—Gr. 3

☆ Wanted ☆
Nice, friendly teacher with lots of patience for an imaginative, high-spirited 8 year old!

After seeking advice from her father on how to "sell" her book to her class, Ramona decides to write her book report in the form of a television commercial. Your youngsters will enjoy selling their favorite books in the same way! Ask each youngster to create a poster that he feels will hook readers on his favorite book. Remind students that the name and author of the books they are selling must be featured on their posters. Display the resulting advertisements in a prominent location where passersby might also be "sold" on your youngsters' reading suggestions!

Tracy Hutcheson—Gr. 2, Featherstone Elementary
Woodbridge, VA

Don't be a Fruit Loop! Read Ramona by Beverly Cleary

Ramona can provide plenty of writing motivation for your youngsters! Her experiences are fun, yet so true-to-life that children easily relate to them. The following prompts are sure to get your youngsters writing!

- After reading about Ramona's first day of third grade, ask students to write about their most recent first-day-of-school experiences. You may find that your youngsters' impressions of their first day of school are somewhat different than you recall!
- Follow up chapter three by asking students to write about their most embarrassing moments.
- When Ramona and Beezus prepare Sunday dinner for their parents, it turns into quite an experience. Ask students to write about a time they tried to prepare a meal for their families. Or have students plan meals (with cooking instructions) that they would like to prepare for their families.
- At the conclusion of the book, the Quimbys are astounded by the kindness of an older gentleman. Ask the students to write about a time that an act of kindness took them by surprise, or about a time that they have surprised others with an act of kindness.

Barbara Rumsey
John Kennedy Elementary
Batavia, NY

## Ramona And Her Father

When Mr. Quimby unexpectedly loses his job, Ramona takes an active hand in the challenges that develop.

Your students are sure to get down to business when you present them with this creative challenge! To begin ask students to recall Ramona's desire for a million dollars—an amount of money that was sure to solve all of her family's financial problems. Then challenge each student to create a make-believe business that she thinks would earn her a million dollars. Have each child design a 4" x 8" business card for her million-dollar business. Explain that each business card should include the name of the business, a catchy slogan that explains what the business produces or what service it provides, the student's name, and a business phone number. Then in turn have each entrepreneur display her business card as she explains her enterprise to her classmates.

Jennie Mehigan—Gr. 3
St. Hilary School
Akron, OH

When Ramona crafts a crown from burrs, she ends up in a very sticky situation. But when your youngsters create these crowns, they'll end up with one-of-a-kind headpieces and a better understanding of some real-life math skills. In advance set up a classroom store from which crown decorations (such as sequins, feathers, ribbon, lace, and imitation jewels) will be sold. To make a crown, a student colors and cuts out a construction-paper copy of the crown pattern on page 88. He then takes a predetermined amount of play money to the store and buys the crown-making supplies he desires. (Each student should tally his purchases and determine the amount of change he is due.) Then he adorns his crown cutout with his purchases. Help each youngster secure his crown to the center of an 18" x 1 1/2" tagboard strip. Adjust the ends of the headband until the crown fits snugly on the child's head; then remove the crown and staple the headband ends in place. There you have it! A crown like no other!

Peggy Wolke—Gr. 1
Graham North Elementary
Rosewood, OH

## Ramona Forever

Ramona is back! And she has lots of surprises headed her way—a new job for her father, a wedding, and a new little Quimby!

What would be the perfect name for the newest Quimby? No doubt your youngsters will have an idea or two! On chart paper, record a student-generated list of names, sorting them into girl names and boy names. Narrow the list of names to the top five favorites in each category. Then, for added fun, ask student volunteers to find the meanings of the listed names in a book of baby names. Keep the class list of names posted until the name of the newest Quimby is revealed in the final chapter of the book.

Fran Rizzo—Gr. 3
Brookdale School
Bloomfield, NJ

## Muggie Maggie

Maggie is far from thrilled about having to learn cursive writing. In fact, she decides she absolutely won't do it! Will Maggie ever change her mind?

Mrs. Leeper devises a plan! She writes cursive notes about Maggie; then she asks Maggie to deliver them to other teachers. Just as Mrs. Leeper had hoped, Maggie's curiosity gets the better of her and she peeks at the notes. Like Maggie, your youngsters are likely to be curious about the notes that you and other teachers write to one another. Build on that curiosity by asking each student to choose a teacher and write a note that he feels the selected teacher might write to a colleague. Increase the challenge by asking students to exchange and respond to each other's notes.

Kelli A. Thomas—Gr. 3
Otis Elementary School
Fremont, OH

Dear Ms. Thomas,
You won't believe what happened! Jason's pet snake got loose this morning! The kids went wild. Remember play practice at 1:00.
Mrs. Leeper

Oops! Maggie didn't mean to spell her name "M-u-g-g-i-e." It was just her awful handwriting. But when her classmates see her mistake, they begin to call her "Muggie Maggie." If only she had written more carefully! Help your students learn the value of writing their own names carefully by having them purposely write their names carelessly. Ask each student to write various letters within her name incorrectly. For example, Sally might make her *a* look like an *i*. Then she would write her name as "Silly Sally." Plan to let students share their mistaken identities aloud.

Kaye Schilling—Gr. 3
Lake Cable Elementary
Canton, OH

To reinforce cursive skills, get students reading your cursive writing! Each morning write an intriguing question or comment on the chalkboard. Ask the students to read the sentence to themselves; then ask a volunteer to read the sentence aloud. If desired invite students to respond to the sentence in their journals. As students begin to improve their own cursive writing and reading abilities, leave cursive notes of praise on their desktops.

Pam Williams—Gr. 3
Dixieland Elementary
Lakeland, FL

Wow! I can read this!

## A Tour Of The Neighborhood

Through her wonderful stories, Cleary re-created her childhood neighborhood, moved it several blocks to Klickitat Street, and peopled it with lovable yet true-to-life characters. The result is a high-interest neighborhood that's perfect for reinforcing the concepts of neighborhood and community. Once your students are familiar with several of Cleary's books, have them work together to create a mural-size map of the neighborhood featured in Cleary's books. When the class project is complete, students can conduct neighborhood tours in which they share favorite events and humorous anecdotes about the neighborhood.

Patricia White—Librarian & Susan Gerritz—Gr. 3
Ventura Park Elementary School
Portland, OR

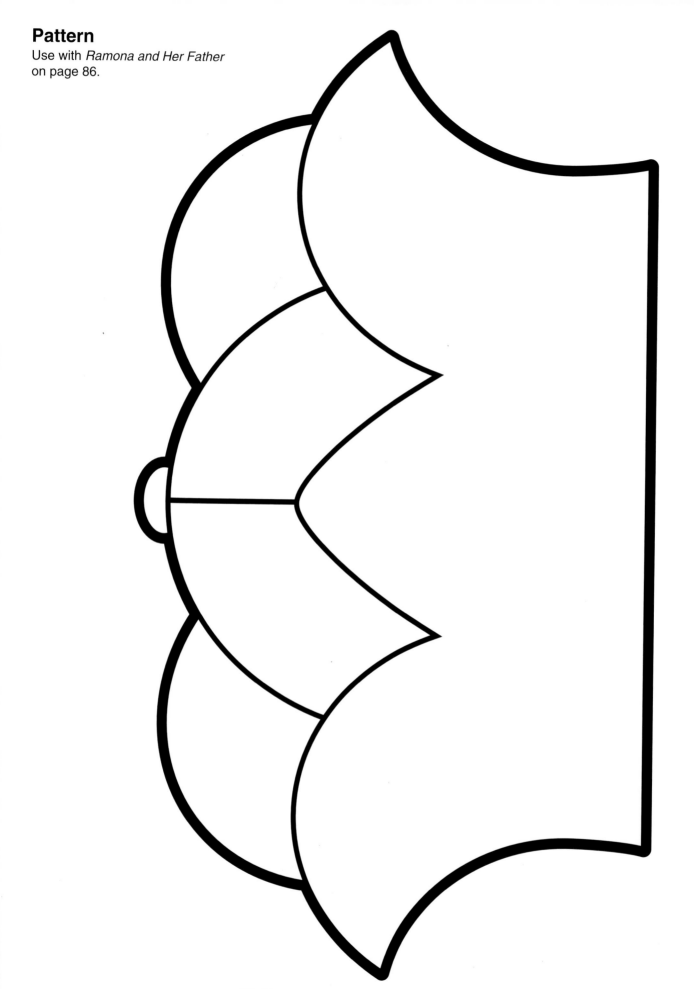

# Back To School With Kevin Henkes

Kevin Henkes took a brave step at a young age. Carrying three portfolios filled with artwork and a children's book that he'd written and illustrated, the college freshman flew to New York City in search of a publisher. His search was short and sweet—his first official appointment landed him a book contract. Not bad for a 19-year-old kid from Wisconsin!

Kevin, the second-youngest in a family of four children, showed an interest in art at an early age. Drawing on anything from tiny scraps of paper to the backs of discarded envelopes, Kevin enjoyed creating pictures, and others enjoyed his creations. He also loved to read and looked forward to the regular trips he made with his family to the local library. His love for children's books resurfaced during high school when he became interested in writing. As soon as he realized that children's books were a combination of the two things that he most enjoyed—illustration and writing—he knew without a doubt what his career goal would be.

Henkes modestly attributes a large amount of his success to the support he continues to receive from his family and friends, and to the guidance he receives from a top-notch editor who asks all the right questions. This is from a man who seeks perfection and pushes himself to attain it, an author and illustrator who captures with his words and pictures the hurdles and triumphs of childhood, and a kid-at-heart who has a delightful sense of irrepressible humor.

Henkes is currently working on his 21st children's book. His advice to aspiring writers is: "Everyone has stories to tell. If you want to write, look at your own experiences. Don't worry about creating masterpieces. Don't worry if your work is not perfect. Rewrite and keep working. Just because someone is published does not mean it comes easily. Enjoy what you are doing. Have fun!"

*And having fun is exactly what's in store for you and your youngsters! Use the ideas on the next five pages to follow up several of Kevin Henkes's stories. We feel certain a good time will be had by all.*

*ideas contributed by Theresa Ives Audet*

## Bailey Goes Camping

Greenwillow Books, 1985

*What does a little bunny named Bailey do when his older brother and sister go on a Bunny Scout camping trip and leave him behind? After a bit of bunny pouting and some encouragement from his folks, he has a terrific time eating hot dogs, fishing in the bathtub, and roasting marshmallows!*

If this story were to continue, Bailey would eventually write and illustrate a delightful children's book about his camping adventures as a youngster. That's what author Kevin Henkes did! You see, the story *Bailey Goes Camping* is based on a childhood memory of being left behind while two older brothers went camping. Many of your students with older siblings will empathize with Bailey. Even students without older siblings have probably fallen victim to the "You're just too young," and "When you get a little older…," explanations that adults often offer as to why certain requests cannot be honored. For a fun follow-up to this story, enlist your students in mixing up a batch of trail mix (any combination of raisins, peanuts, cereal, dried fruit, and candy pieces). As students munch on servings of this tasty camping snack, invite them to talk about things they have asked to do, that their parents wouldn't be talked into. Have the students evaluate why they felt their requests should have been granted. Also ask students to recall the antics that they used to try to convince their parents to agree to their requests. Have students brainstorm how they might make the best of these disappointing situations in the future—now that they've heard Bailey's story.

## Grandpa & Bo

Greenwillow Books, 1986

*This heartwarming story is a gentle reminder of the important role grandparents play in children's lives. While Bo spends the summer with his grandpa, the twosome do many things together. They fish, take long walks, and even celebrate Christmas! And when at last the youngster and his grandpa spy a shooting star, it seems perfectly natural that their wishes would be exactly the same.*

Close by or faraway, grandparents love without restrictions and with endless patience. Their experiences and wisdom open the past to the eager ears and open hearts of a younger generation. Invite students to talk about special times that they have spent with their grandparents or other older adults. Follow up the discussion by having each student design a brag book about a favorite older person. To do this, give each child a construction-paper mini-booklet containing four to six blank pages. The student decorates and personalizes the front cover of his brag booklet. On the first booklet page, he writes a dedication to the person to whom he plans on giving the completed mini-booklet. On each of the following pages, he describes a special trait of the older adult or he writes about a special memory that the twosome have shared. The recipients of these projects will thank their lucky stars to have such thoughtful young admirers.

The topic of shooting stars—those streaks of light that have long fascinated sky watchers—is sure to evoke an enthusiastic response from your youngsters. Ask students to share their knowledge and questions about shooting stars. Then inform students that some people believe that a wish made upon a shooting star is a wish that will come true. For a fun writing activity, have each youngster design a page for a class booklet of shooting-star wishes. To make a booklet page, fold a sheet of 9" x 12" construction paper in half and glue the outer edges to form a pocket. Draw and color a night sky scene on the front of the pocket, and personalize the back of the pocket. Then, on a slip of paper, have each student write and personalize his wish for a shooting star and tuck it inside the pocket. Bind the pockets between a construction-paper cover labeled "Shooting-Star Wishes." Place the completed project in your classroom library for all to enjoy.

## A Weekend With Wendell

Greenwillow Books, 1986

*Things run amok when Wendell, a mischievous mouse, spends the weekend at Sophie's house. From making all the rules (none of which are fair) to giving Sophie a new shaving-cream hairdo, Wendell is up to no good. Even Sophie's parents are dismayed at the rebellious rodent. But in the end, Sophie surprises Wendell with a trick of her own, and a new friendship unfolds.*

After reading this story aloud, poll your class to find out which students have been on sleepovers. Invite students to talk about their sleepover experiences. What do they think are the most fun parts of a sleepover? The scariest parts? Then have each student pack a bag for an imaginary sleepover. To do this, have each child fold and cut a 9" x 12" sheet of construction paper as shown to create a suitcase cutout. Staple four sheets of writing paper inside the suitcase. Have the students label their sheets with the following headings: "Things I Must Pack," "A Scary Story I'll Tell," "Three Things I Must Remember To Do," and "Three Things I Must Remember Not To Do." Allow plenty of time for students to complete their pages and decorate the outsides of their suitcases. Then have each youngster label a piece of 2" x 3" construction paper with his name and address and attach the tag to his suitcase handle using a hole puncher and a length of ribbon. Students will enjoy sharing these projects with their classmates and their families.

## Once Around The Block

illustrated by Victoria Chess
Greenwillow Books, 1987

*Annie is bored, so her mother tells her to take a walk around the block. This wise advice starts Annie on a journey that fills her afternoon with fun and excitement.*

Most youngsters can easily recall times when they have felt bored and could think of nothing to do. This easy-to-make project puts a stop to boredom! To begin, divide students into small groups. Ask each group to brainstorm a list of things that children their ages can do by themselves. When the allotted time is over, have each group share its ideas. Compile the ideas on the chalkboard and entitle the resulting list "Boredom Busters." Next give each child five to ten large index cards. Ask each student to choose his favorite Boredom Busters from the list and write each one on a different index card. To record additional Boredom Busters, suggest that students use the backs of their cards. Finally give each child two large index cards to personalize and decorate for front and back covers. To complete the project,

have each student hole-punch the upper left-hand corner of each of his cards and thread a metal ring or something similar through the holes. Encourage students to take their projects home and store them for safekeeping. When boredom strikes, who are they going to call? The Boredom Busters!

## Sheila Rae, The Brave

Greenwillow Books, 1987

*Sheila Rae is brave. She is fearless. But when she tries to walk home from school a different way than usual—she is lost! The unexpected heroine in this tale of two mice is none other than Sheila Rae's scaredy-cat little sister. In this adorable story, two mouse sisters learn about bravery, each other, and themselves.*

Once students have heard Sheila Rae and Louise's story, they'll most likely be eager to talk about times when they have felt afraid. Encourage students to share their experiences and explain how they dealt with their fears. Then, using a comic-strip format, have each student create a personalized story about bravery. To make a comic strip, fold a 12" x 18" sheet of construction paper in half and crease it. Repeat this two more times; then unfold the paper to reveal eight rectangles. To complete his comic strip, a student illustrates a sequence of events that tells a story in which he faces— and then overcomes—a fearful situation. Once students have shared their completed projects with their classmates, collect the comic strips and publish them in a newspaper format. To do this, cut and fold several lengths of bulletin-board paper to resemble blank newspaper pages. Decorate the front page to show the title "Special Edition: Overcoming Fears," the date, and a class byline. Mount your students' completed projects, two per page, on the folded paper. Laminate the pages for durability; then place the resulting newspaper in your class library for all to read. Extra! Extra! Read all about it!

## Chester's Way

Greenwillow Books, 1988

*Chester has a certain way of doing things. His friend Wilson does things just like he does, and that makes Chester happy. Then Lilly, a one-of-a-kind mouse, moves into their neighborhood. She doesn't do anything like anyone else, and that makes Chester very uncomfortable. Eventually Chester learns to embrace Lilly's uniqueness and actually finds himself changing under her zany influence. It isn't hard to understand how Lilly has become one of Kevin Henkes's favorite characters. Her self-assuredness and eccentricity are endearing. Henkes breaks stereotypes by giving the female character the derring-do and unabashed courage to break conventions.*

After reading aloud *Chester's Way,* ask students to recall the things that Lilly and Chester taught one another. Also ask students to think of things they've learned from friends who have enriched their lives. Help students understand that people (and mice!) learn from each other. Then plan a day on which each student demonstrates for her classmates a special skill, talent, or interest that she has. For example a child might demonstrate how to tie a double knot in a shoestring, braid hair, fold paper to make shapes, or do the splits. For a surprise treat at the conclusion of the demonstrations, provide the supplies needed to make peanut butter–and–jelly sandwiches. And don't forget to bring some cookie cutters! Your youngsters can cut shapes from their sandwiches with the cookie cutters, just as Lilly would do. Your children will see that they too can learn from the irrepressible Lilly.

Chester learns that he should not judge others just because they do things differently than he does. In fact, he discovers that making friends and learning new things are loads of fun. With this in mind, find out how your students think Chester and his pals will embrace Victor, the newest member of their neighborhood. For writing motivation, show students the final illustration in the book; then have each child write a sequel to *Chester's Way* that stars Victor as the new kid on the block. Suggest that students describe Victor's unique traits and talents; explain how Chester, Wilson, and Lilly meet Victor; and tell about an adventure the foursome share.

## Julius, The Baby Of The World

Greenwillow Books, 1990

*The irrepressible Lilly is back and this time she's kicking up her red boots over the latest addition to her family—her brother Julius. Before the baby arrives, Lilly is the best big sister in the world. But after Julius—the baby of the world—is born, Lilly decides her new brother is indeed the biggest pain in the world. This hilarious story of intense sibling rivalry was actually inspired by Henkes's real-life nieces. Imagine that!*

At the conclusion of the story, ask students how they feel about Lilly's experience. Did they learn anything from Lilly? Have they ever felt similar feelings? If so, how did they cope with their feelings of jealousy? When the students have finished sharing their ideas, they'll be ready to complete this "Best In The World" project. Enlarge a globe pattern to a desired size; then duplicate a class supply on white construction paper. On the chalkboard write

"[student's name], The _____ Of The World." Ask each child to decide how to complete the title. For example, a child might choose to be the sister, brother, student, helper, or athlete of the world. Then distribute the globe patterns, and ask each student to copy and complete the title and illustrate himself in the role he chose (see the illustration). After adding any other desired decorations, have students cut out and mount their projects onto black construction paper. Display the completed projects on a bulletin board entitled "The Best In The World!"

Joey Smith
The Basketball Player
Of The World

# Chrysanthemum

Greenwillow Books, 1991

*Chrysanthemum absolutely loves her name—until her first day of school! As soon as Chrysanthemum's classmates hear her name, the teasing begins. Though her parents assure their daughter that her name is as perfect as she is, the teasing continues and the young mouse is mortified. When it seems as if there's no hope for a mouse with a flower name, Mrs. Delphinium Twinkle enters the picture.*

*An afternoon jog provided Henkes with the inspiration for Chrysanthemum's story. It was near the end of his run that the author observed a young girl being teased by her peers. The forlorn look on the young girl's face reminded Henkes of a kindergarten memory of his own. These experiences materialized into the young mouse's story.*

After reading the story aloud, ask your students to share what they know about their names. Do they know who named them or whom they were named after? For a fun, family-centered homework activity, ask students to interview their parents to find out more about their names. Then invite each student to share two or three facts that he learned about his "absolutely perfect" name!

Even children who love their names may wonder what it would be like to have a different name. Why not let them find out for themselves? Tell students that for one day they may change their names. Encourage students to choose names that they feel match their personalities and interests. Then, on a strip of construction paper, have each student design a nametag that reflects his new name. For added fun, collect the nametags and display them one at time, challenging the students to guess whom each new name belongs to. Then have the students attach their nametags to their desks for the day. For a fun graphing activity, create a class graph that shows how many students

chose to name themselves for famous people, relatives, colors, flowers, or friends. What's in a name? Plenty of opportunities for learning!

# Owen

Greenwillow Books, 1993

*Owen has a favorite blanket. He has loved it, stained it, and worn it threadbare. And he refuses—much to his parents' disdain—to discard it. Finally, Owen's mom finds a comforting way to solve the blanket dilemma. Owen's story will be reassuring to those youngsters who find it difficult to give up favorite items.*

After reading the story to your class, tell students about a favorite blanket, stuffed toy, or other object that you had as a child. Describe the item and explain to students why it was important to you. Then invite students to talk about their most-loved items. Follow up the discussion with a quilt-making activity that would make Owen proud! On a nine-inch square of drawing paper, have each student illustrate a much-loved item that he hopes to have forever. Collect the squares and mount them on a bulletin board covered

in yellow paper, leaving approximately two inches between the illustrations. Then use a marker to draw "stitches" around the projects. If desired, attach gathered crepe paper to the outer edges of the display for a quilt border, and add the title "Our Favorite Things."

Put your students' creative-thinking skills to the test with this small-group activity. Read *Owen* to your class a second time, stopping just after Owen's mother has "an absolutely wonderful, positively perfect, especially terrific idea." Challenge each group of students to brainstorm ideas for redesigning the blanket into a more acceptable form. Then have each group choose its favorite idea and present it to the class. If desired, take a class vote to find out the favorite blanket-transforming idea. Who knows? You may find that your youngsters' ideas are just as handy as the handkerchiefs!

# Introducing...
# Virginia Kroll
## Author Extraordinaire

Virginia Kroll has won the hearts of numerous children, teachers, and adults by sharing her gift of writing. The following pages feature only a few of her outstanding books, but that's not a concern. As Ms. Kroll's fans know—it only takes one!

*by Donna C. Kester Phillips*

## About The Author

As a former elementary school teacher, a mother of six children ranging in ages from eight to 26, a grandmother, and an author of 22 children's books to date—Virginia Kroll understands children! A recreational writer of poetry and greeting cards, Virginia first tried her hand at writing articles and short stories for publication in 1984. It wasn't until five years later that she ventured into writing children's books.

Virginia's books are based on her experiences and those of her family and friends. But Virginia says that she draws her insight and guidance from what she calls her "word angels." These visions are what allow her to use her writing as an instrument to achieve her mission in life. Virginia's mission, she says, is to change lives. Through her work she hopes to show children how much the people of the world are alike—bridging the cultural differences that are present in what Virginia calls our "global village."

Virginia reads to her children each morning as they eat their breakfast. This, she believes, is the most important thing that she can do for her children. Her love of children and animals (she has 29 pets with more guinea pigs on the way!) are the center of her work. In Virginia's own words, "My greatest reward is receiving letters from the children who read my books." These letters let her know that her books really do help to change lives.

## Masai And I

Illustrated by Nancy Carpenter
Four Winds Press, 1992

*In* Masai And I, *Virginia Kroll tells the story of what it might be like to be a child of the Masai people of Africa. As the young girl goes through her day, she imagines what she would be doing if she lived with the Masai. Through this comparison of daily activities, youngsters learn that people are much the same, even though lifestyles and cultures greatly differ. The author believes this to be her best book to date.*

This account provides a wonderful link to community and/or cultural studies. Challenge each student to imagine what life would be like if he had been born in another country or culture. Then have students create a class big book or individual booklets using the format shown below. After the booklet pages have been illustrated, compile them between student-decorated covers. If a class big book results, invite neighboring classes to your room for an oral presentation of the story. If the product is individual booklets, set aside time for students to share their work with their classmates.

If I were _____, my house would be…
If I were _____, I would get my water and food…
If I were _____ and I wanted dessert, I would…
If I were _____, at night I would…
If I were _____, I would go to bed…
If I were _____, my pets would be…
If I were _____, I would wear…
If I were _____ and going to a party, I would…
If I were _____, I would travel by…
If I were _____, I would love and respect my…
If I were _____, my name might be…

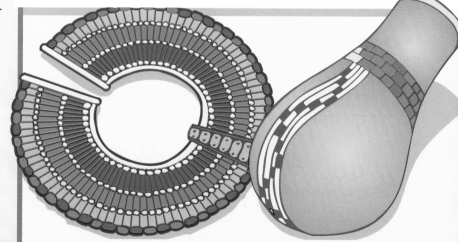

# Pink Paper Swans

Illustrated by Nancy L. Clouse
William B. Eerdmans Publishing Company, 1994
*Janetta, intrigued by the paper animals that her neighbor Mrs. Tsujimoto makes, learns the art of origami and becomes Mrs. Tsujimoto's hands when her arthritis makes it difficult for her to continue.*

Virginia Kroll's favorite place to visit as a child was a Japanese store where Mrs. Tsujimoto taught the art of origami. Although Virginia was fascinated by the paper folding and worked hard to master it, she never did. So she decided to write a story about a child who was successful! There's little doubt that your students will be eager to try their hands at origami. Although directions for making a paper swan are included at the end of the book, you may want to choose simpler projects for your beginning paper folders. There are many good books that provide directions for folding frogs, fish, cats, giraffes, crabs, birds, and scores of other creatures. To display the students' origami projects, cover the lower half of a bulletin board with green paper and the upper half with blue paper. Enlist your students' help in creating appropriate habitats for their folded critters. Then, using straight pins, display the projects in the appropriate environments. Now that's impressive!

# Sweet Magnolia

Illustrated by Laura Jacques
Charlesbridge Publishing, 1995
*The author's sister was the inspiration for this story that takes place in the bayous of Louisiana. When six-year-old Denise visits her grandmother, a wildlife rehabilitator, she helps heal and free an injured baby bird. Sprinkled with images and words of Cajun and Creole culture, this book will enlighten and enrich the lives of the children who experience it.*

The rich illustrations and the poetic language of this sweet story are a treat for the eyes and ears. These elements set the stage for children to investigate the wild animals of the bayou and learn about these animals' special needs. Start by having the children generate a list of the animals that are named or illustrated in the story. Then have each child choose an animal from the list that she would like to have for a pet and illustrate it on the top half of a sheet of drawing paper. Next have each child fold and unfold a second sheet of paper to create two columns. In the left column, she lists reasons why she would like to have the animal she illustrated. In the right column, she lists reasons why it would be unfair to make this animal her pet. Conclude the activity by asking each youngster to illustrate a domesticated animal that is somewhat similar to the wild animal, but that would make a good pet.

Set aside time for students to share their work with their classmates. This activity will enrich the children's book experience and do justice to the intent of the author—which is understanding the importance of respecting animals in the wild.

## Jaha And Jamil Went Down The Hill: An African Mother Goose

Illustrated by Katherine Roundtree
Charlesbridge Publishing, 1995
*Through her poetry Virginia Kroll introduces children to African customs, traditions, and cultures. Each page of rhymes and illustrations represents a different African country and is referenced by a map at the end of the book.*

Thanks to Virginia, the fun and learning never stop in this book. From the rhythm of the rhymes to the knowledge gained about Africa and its people, this book will make a difference in the lives of your children. To make the most of this experience, enlarge and display a map of Africa like the one shown at the back of the book. Laminate a sheet of poster board and display it next to the map. Use one pushpin to attach one end of a yarn length near the blank poster. Insert a second pushpin nearby. Every few days copy a different poem from the book onto the blank poster and use the extra pushpin to secure the unattached yarn end to the appropriate African country. Encourage students to practice reading the rhyme. Also challenge them to recall the original Mother Goose rhyme on which it is based. If desired, instruct students to copy each posted rhyme for handwriting practice. Have each student keep his handwriting papers in a personalized folder. When appropriate each student can illustrate his papers and compile them between a self-decorated construction-paper cover.

Barry Slate

## Hats Off To Hair!

Illustrated by Kay Life
Charlesbridge Publishing, 1995
*It's a celebration of hair! How many ways can it be cut, combed, or colored? Virginia Kroll has a pretty good idea! Through the rhythm and rhyme of her words, readers discover a lot about hairdos. In the process vocabularies are enriched and a greater understanding of celebrating differences is achieved.*

Who hasn't at some point in his or her life longed for someone else's hair? For a fun follow-up activity to this delightful romp, give each child a piece of tagboard in which you have cut a circle large enough to reveal a child's face. Then—using yarn, felt, ribbon, markers, crayons, or any other desired medium—have each child create a new "do." Ask students to name their new hairdos, too. Students may wish to refer to the glossary of hairdo terminology at the back of the book for inspiration. When the projects are finished, set aside time for students to take turns modeling the different do's for their classmates. If a large mirror is available, tape several of the projects to the mirror. Students can take turns looking into the mirror and seeing themselves sporting a variety of original hairdos!

## Writing To The Author

Virginia Kroll would love to hear from your students. She prefers class letters and she asks that the letters be sent to her in care of the publisher of the book about which you are corresponding. The address of the publisher is listed inside the book—either at the front or the back.

# LITERATURE-RELATED UNITS

# Bess's Log Cabin Quilt

*Written by D. Anne Love*
*(Holiday House, Inc.; 1995)*

Bess Morgan longs for the day when her papa will come back home to her and her mama in Oregon. He's supposed to be leading a wagon train of settlers westward on the Oregon Trail, but he should have returned over a month ago. Ever since Mama got sick with swamp fever, ten-year-old Bess has been tending the farm single-handedly. And now a man who says Papa owes him money is trying to take the farm away! What can Bess do? This endearing story is sure to capture your youngsters' attention as well as their hearts!

*ideas by Lisa Leonardi*

## Pioneers: Past And Present

At the conclusion of chapter one, investigate the meaning of *pioneer* with your students. Guide students to understand that pioneers are people who courageously try new things and who pave the way for others to follow in their footsteps. Ask students what made Bess Morgan and her family pioneers, and how the efforts of pioneers like the Morgan family influenced the development of our country. Discuss present-day pioneers so students will understand that pioneers are an important part of our country's past, present, and future. Then ask students to name traits they have that pioneers must have too—such as determination, courage, curiosity, and knowledge. To help students realize that they, too, can be pioneers, label a length of bulletin-board paper "The Pioneers Of Tomorrow." Provide colorful markers and ask each child to sign the paper. Display the resulting banner for all to see!

## A Different Way Of Life

Your youngsters will quickly realize that Bess's life is different than their own. Invite students to talk about things that Bess does that they would or would not like to do. Ask students what they think Bess might think about life today. Find out how many students think they could enjoy living like Bess did. For an up close look at the similarities and differences between Bess's lifestyle and that of your students, have the students complete the reproducible activity on page 101 after reading chapter two.

## Learning About Quilts

Quilts were cherished keepsakes that most families brought with them on their journey westward. In addition to providing warmth, the quilts were treasured for the memories that they represented. In fact it has been said that a woman's quilting patterns were one of the most cherished things in a family's covered wagon! Explain to students that inspiration for quilt patterns often came from the world surrounding the pioneers. Patterns such as Log Cabin, Turkey Tracks, and Weather Vane are evidence of this. Then give each child a 5" x 6" piece of one-inch (or 1/2-inch) graph paper. Ask each child to design a colorful quilt pattern that she feels reflects something about her life. Mount the completed projects on a large piece of bulletin-board paper to create a class quilt.

## A Ten-Year-Old Trooper

As Bess's story unfolds, many sides of her character are revealed. For example, Bess is responsible, brave, hardworking, determined, and fun-loving. She also experiences a variety of feelings that include fear, frustration, and loneliness. On the chalkboard write a student-generated list of words that describe Bess. Then have each child create a character web. To do this, a child illustrates Bess in the center of a 12" x 18" sheet of drawing paper. In each corner he draws a large circle. Near the top of each circle, he writes and underlines a word that describes Bess. Then, below the word, he describes how and when Bess displays this trait or feeling in the story. Set aside time for students to share the character webs they have woven.

## Unwanted Visitors

When Indians pay Bess and her mama a visit in chapter five, the mother and daughter are terrified for their safety. While the visit is short and uneventful, it is packed with emotion. And it could possibly leave your youngsters with a negative image of Native Americans. At the conclusion of the chapter, discuss the incident. Ask students why they think the pioneers' relationships with some Native Americans were unpredictable. Remind students that Native Americans played an important role in helping the first settlers in America survive. Also remind youngsters that the pioneers were settling on land that Native Americans had called home for centuries. When the white man began taking over the land—sometimes without concern for the wildlife and the people who already inhabited it—some Native Americans began to take measures to protect what was rightfully theirs. Invite students to share their thoughts on this part of our country's history. What suggestions would the youngsters have today for the pioneers and Native Americans of the 1800s?

## Winning Isn't Everything

Mrs. Fairchild removes her quilt from the contest to better Bess's chances of winning. Ask students to explain Mrs. Fairchild's actions. Find out if the students were surprised by what Mrs. Fairchild does, and if so, why. Discuss Mrs. Fairchild's statement—"There are some things in life more important than winning." Ask students what Mrs. Fairchild feels is more important than winning the quilting contest. Lead students to understand that while Mrs. Fairchild does not win a contest prize, she is a winner in many other ways.

For a fun follow-up activity, have the students design a ribbon for Mrs. Fairchild and one for themselves! On a white, construction-paper copy of page 102, ask students to copy and complete the following sentences, one on each ribbon: "Mrs. Fairchild is a winner because…" and "I am a winner because…." After students have decorated the ribbons to their liking and cut them out, have each youngster securely tape his ribbon to the side of his desk. Ask students to take home Mrs. Fairchild's ribbon and use it to help them tell their families about *Bess's Log Cabin Quilt*.

Mrs. Fairchild is a winner because... she cared more about helping Bess than she cared about herself.

## Story Quilts

Unlike the real thing, these story quilts can be made in a jiffy—and the results are quite impressive! Have each student use a pencil to draw one horizontal and two vertical lines to visually divide a 9" x 12" sheet of drawing paper into six equal-size sections. Then ask each child to choose his six favorite parts of the story and sequentially illustrate the story parts on his paper. When his illustrations are complete, the child chooses an 11" x 14" sheet of colorful paper on which to mount his project. With his paper selection made, he can now use an appropriate color to trace over his pencil lines and add stitch marks. Then he centers and mounts his project on the colorful paper. Now that's impressive handiwork!

*Papa already paid Mr. Trask, so what should I do with the money?*

## Dear Liza

Talk about a happy ending! Bess wins second prize in the quilting contest, which earns her 100 dollars—and Papa comes home! And since Papa has already paid his $100 bank note, all of Bess's winnings belong to her—maybe. As a class, review the final events of the story. Remind students that Bess is undecided as to whether to keep all of her winnings for her school fund or to share the money with Mrs. Fairchild. Invite students to share and explain their opinions about what Bess should do with her earnings. Then ask each student to pretend that a week has passed and Bess has decided to write her good friend Liza a letter and tell her all that has happened since she saw her last—from winning the quilting contest, to Papa's return, to what she did with her $100 earnings and why. Bind the letters in a class booklet entitled "Dear Liza" and place the project in your class library for your students' reading enjoyment!

## The Pioneer Spirit

Helping each other was a way of life for pioneers. They worked alongside one another building homes, clearing land, and sowing seeds. Have students recall examples from the story of pioneers helping other pioneers. Discuss the positive effects of this pioneer spirit of helpfulness. Then challenge students to get into the pioneer spirit by declaring a Pioneer Spirit Day. Encourage helpfulness and camaraderie between your classmates and everyone they come in contact with throughout the day. Plan activities that have students working with partners, in small groups, and in a large group. Near the end of the day, write a class list of the acts of helpfulness and kindness that were shared. Then, with the help of a parent volunteer or two, surprise your youngsters with an end-of-the-day ice-cream social.

# Bess And Me

Read each sentence about Bess.
On the lines describe how your life is
   the same or different.
Use the code to color the quilt patches.

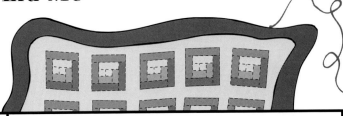

Bess lives in a log cabin.

I live _____

_____.

Bess eats food grown on
her family's farm.

I eat food _____

_____.

Bess wears plain, brown
dresses.

I wear _____

_____.

Bess sleeps in a featherbed.

I sleep _____

_____.

Bess is schooled at home
by her mama.

I am schooled _____

_____.

Bess rides a horse for
transportation.

I ride _____

_____.

Bess is learning to quilt.

I am learning to _____

_____.

Bess likes to dance for fun.

I have fun _____

_____.

Bess milks the cow and
feeds the chickens.

One chore of mine is _____

_____.

Bess hoes and weeds the
garden.

Another chore of mine is

_____.

**Color
Code**

If you like the way Bess lives best, color the patch blue and green.
If you like the way you live best, color the patch yellow and green.

©The Education Center, Inc. • THE MAILBOX® • *Primary* • April/May 1996

**Note To Teacher:** Use this activity after completing chapter two.

101

# Patterns
Use with "Winning Isn't Everything" on page 99.

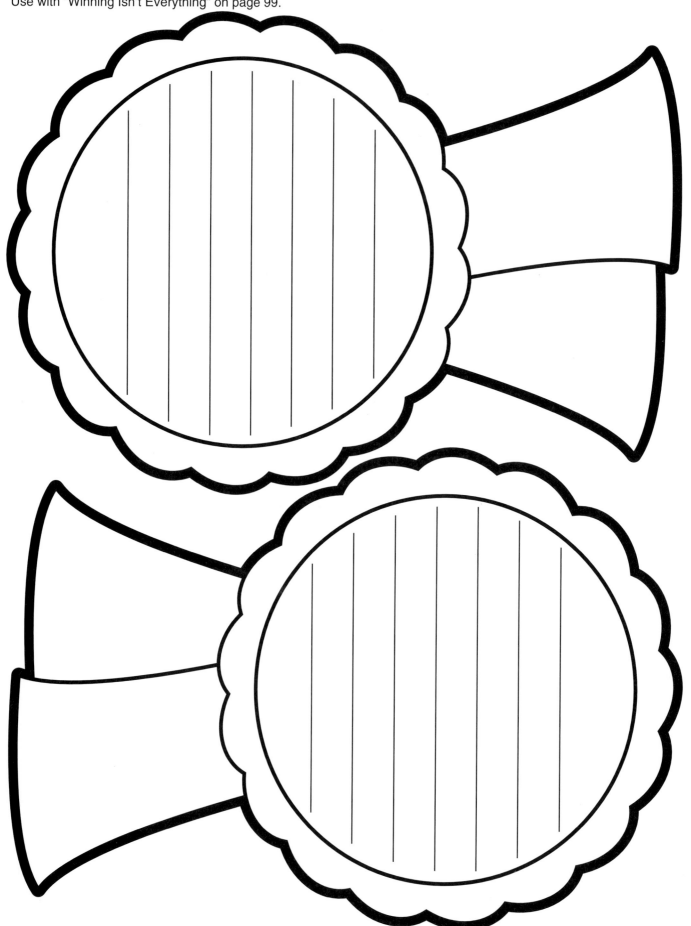

# Amber Brown
## Is Not A Crayon

*Written by Paula Danziger & Illustrated by Tony Ross*
*(G.P. Putnam's Sons, 1994)*

Best friends—that's what Amber Brown and Justin Daniels are. They know how to have fun and they know how to help each other out. But now disaster has struck. Justin has to move and third grade has turned into a total nightmare for Amber. How things change from worse to better is what this delightful read-aloud tale is all about.

*ideas contributed by Karen Gibson*

## Meet The Author

Paula Danziger loves to write for and about kids. Drawing her inspiration from children she knows or has met, the author writes stories that appeal to young and old alike. And her personal passions—which include a love for life, travel, people, and pinball—make her as interesting as the characters she creates!

Born in Washington, D.C., and raised in New York, Danziger knew from second grade on that she wanted to be a writer. She began her career as a teacher, but the success of her first book, *The Cat Ate My Gymsuit,* encouraged Danziger to write full-time. And it has been nonstop for the author ever since! Though she has written and published several books for older readers, *Amber Brown Is Not A Crayon* is Danziger's first chapter book for seven- to nine-year-olds. She has since published *You Can't Eat Your Chicken Pox, Amber Brown.* The third book in the series, tentatively titled *Amber Brown Goes Fourth,* is due for release this fall. No doubt Danziger has even more escapades in mind for Amber Brown!

## Friendship Crayons

The beginning of the school year is the perfect time for a discussion about friends and friendships. Set the stage for this story by asking students to brainstorm characteristics that they feel are important for their friends to have. Write the students' ideas on the chalkboard and encourage group discussion. Then have each child make a set of friendship crayons. Provide a 4" x 9" strip of tagboard and a white construction-paper copy of the crayon patterns on page 105 for each child. To make a crayon holder, a student folds up and creases the tagboard strip to make a pocket like the one shown. He entitles the pocket "Friendship Crayons" and adds desired decorations before gluing the outer edges of his pocket together. To make a set of crayons, the student chooses his five favorite friendship characteristics from the chalkboard and copies each one on a different crayon. Then he colors the crayons, cuts them out, and slips them inside his crayon holder. As you read Amber's story to your students, keep a supply of crayon patterns on hand. Students may find that they'd like to add a few more friendship crayons to their collections.

## What's In A Name?

Having a name like Amber Brown isn't easy, especially since some of Amber's "goofball" classmates can't resist teasing her about it. Amber no longer wishes that her parents had named her differently. In fact she likes her unusual name—but she could do without the name-needling. Give your youngsters the opportunity to show off and share a few inside secrets about their names with this art project.

To make a name banner like the one shown, fold a 12" x 18" sheet of construction paper in half widthwise. Use your ruler to draw a faint line approximately 1 1/2 inches from the open end; then cut a series of 1 1/2-inch-wide wavy lines from the fold to the pencil line. Unfold the resulting loom and set it aside. Next draw a set of 1 1/2-inch-wide wavy lines across the width of another 12" x 18" sheet of construction paper. Number the strips and cut them apart. Then tightly weave the strips through the loom in order. On the last strip that will fit in the loom, trim one side to a straight edge. Discard the extra strips and glue the ends of each woven strip in place. To personalize the banner, trace and cut out the letters needed from a third color of construction paper. Glue the letters in a pleasing arrangement on the woven banner. When the students have completed their projects, ask each one in turn to hold up his banner and share one or two things about his name. Then display the eye-catching banners around your classroom.

## Being An Only Child

In chapter three Amber wishes that she had a little brother or sister. Since she's an only child, she doesn't have a younger sibling to tease. On the other hand, that means that she doesn't have a little brother or sister to tease her! Using a simple Venn diagram labeled as shown and a supply of sticky dots, students can learn about their classmates' siblings. In turn, have each student attach a dot to the diagram in the appropriate location. When all of the dots have been gathered, evaluate the diagram to determine how many students have brothers, sisters, brothers and sisters, and neither brothers nor sisters. Ask those students without brothers or sisters to share their feelings about not having siblings. This discussion may create interest in a second Venn diagram labeled "I wish I had... [brothers, sisters, brothers and sisters, none]."

**Do You Have A Brother Or A Sister?**

Brother   Sister

Both

None

## A Giant Ball Of Chewing Gum

It won't take your youngsters long to start talking about the giant ball of chewing gum that Amber and Justin compiled. Collected for a year and half, this unique object takes on a major role in the story when Justin announces that he's going to throw the project out. Find out if your students agree with Justin and think that Amber is making a big deal out of nothing, or if they feel Justin is being insensitive.

For a fun follow-up, ask each child to bring to school a wrapper from her favorite gum. Students can collect and record data to determine favorite gum brands and flavors, how many students prefer sugar-free or regular chewing gum, and how often gum is chewed. The gum wrappers could even be used to create a large pictograph that represents your students' favorite gum flavors.

## Not Talking

Rather than talking to Amber about his move, Justin acts as if everything is the same. Amber finds this extremely frustrating and hurtful. Ask your students why they think Justin is choosing to act this way, and discuss the consequences of his actions. Invite students to talk about times when they have felt like Justin or Amber. Then ask each child to write a friendly letter to either Justin or Amber. In his letter the student should note his understanding of the situation, share encouraging thoughts, and offer a positive suggestion that might help rejoin the two friends. Invite interested students to share their letters with their classmates.

## Making Friends

At the start of chapter eight, Amber is trying to choose a new best friend by studying a list of her classmates. But by the end of the chapter, Amber realizes that "getting a best friend isn't like making a shopping list." Ask students to describe what Amber learned in this chapter. Then invite students to share their tips for making friends.

You can nurture friendships and writing skills when you buddy up your students for this activity. Assign or randomly pair buddies; then instruct the students to write biographies about their buddies. Suggest that students interview their buddies to learn about their families, special interests, secret talents, and future dreams before they start writing. Later ask each student to share the biography that he wrote.

## More About Making Friends

Another way to promote new friendships and build self-esteem is to have each student create and share a "Me Bag." Build interest in this activity by decorating a lunch-size paper bag to reflect your own interests. Inside the bag place a few carefully selected items. During a group time, remove the items one at a time from the bag. Tell the youngsters why each item is important to you, and answer any questions they have about your items. Then ask each student to create a Me Bag for himself, to be filled at home with a few select items that reflect his interests, activities, and family life. Set aside time for each student to share and explain his bag and its contents. Classmates can easily identify mutual interests, and each student has an opportunity to emphasize his individual strengths.

## Crayon Patterns
**Crayon Patterns** Use with "Friendship Crayons" on page 103.

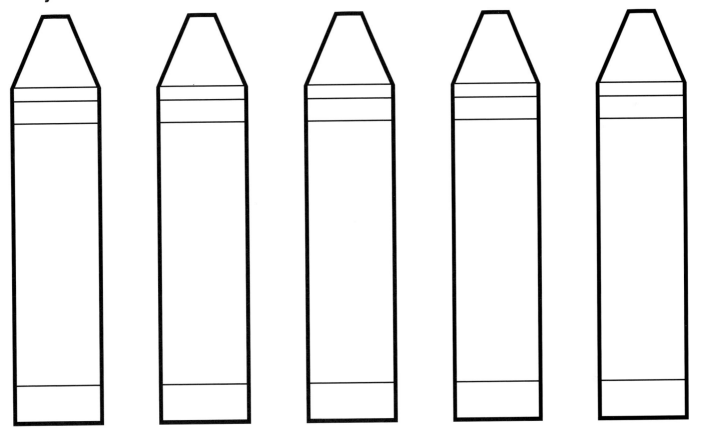

Name _____

# Best Friends

Think about Amber and Justin.
Use the color code to outline the boxes.

| | | |
|---|---|---|
| is very messy | has a great imagination | lives in New Jersey |
| is helpful | is good at fractions | has a best friend |
| is an only child | is in third grade | **Color Code** |
| sometimes feels sad | is moving | describes Amber = red |

**Color Code**
describes Amber = red
describes Justin = blue
describes both = purple

**Note To Teacher:** Use this activity after completing chapter two.

# Fun With Fractions

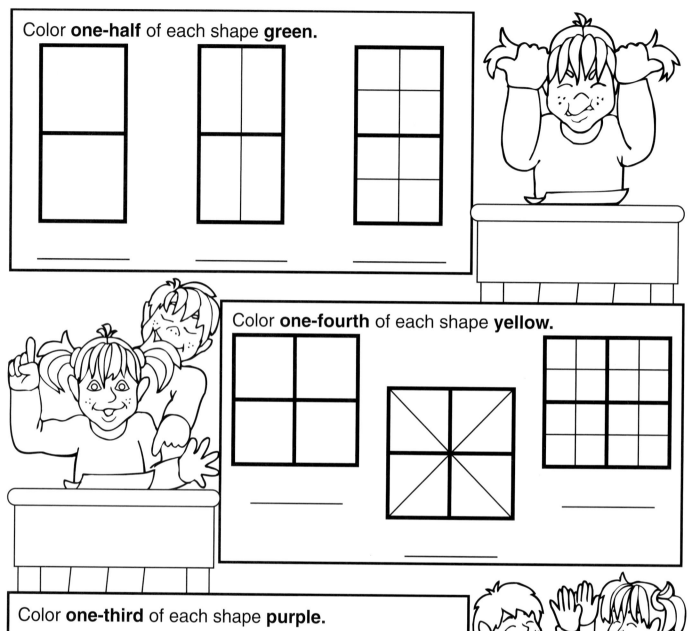

Color **one-half** of each shape **green**.

Color **one-fourth** of each shape **yellow**.

Color **one-third** of each shape **purple**.

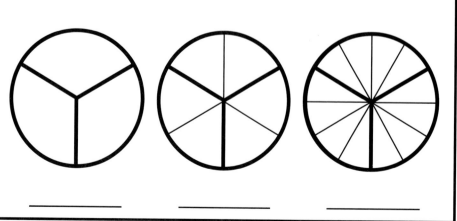

Look at the colored part of each shape. On the line, write a fraction that describes this part. You **may not** use the same fraction more than once!

©The Education Center, Inc. • THE MAILBOX® • Primary • Aug/Sept 1995 • Key p. 312

**Note To Teacher:** Use this activity after completing chapter six. To encourage fraction-related friendships, allow students to work with partners as they each complete their own activity sheet.

Name _____

# Hold The Anchovies!

Read each sentence.
Decide if it is a fact or an opinion.
Circle the letter in the matching column.

|  | fact | opinion |
|---|---|---|
| **1.** | U | I |
| **2.** | S | M |
| **3.** | R | E |
| **4.** | E | N |
| **5.** | W | V |
| **6.** | F | P |
| **7.** | G | O |
| **8.** | N | P |
| **9.** | D | C |
| **10.** | I | E |
| **11.** | R | T |
| **12.** | H | F |

1. Mr. Cohen is the best third-grade teacher ever.

2. Justin is moving to Alabama.

3. Amber has trouble with fractions.

4. Justin and Amber invent their own games.

5. Justin's little brother is a brat.

6. Amber and Justin collect chewed gum.

7. Their chewing-gum ball is the best one ever made.

8. Justin's dad moved because of his job.

9. Some things are hard to talk about.

10. Pizza is the best food ever invented.

11. Amber and Justin will miss each other.

12. It's easy being a best friend.

**Which words best describe Amber and Justin?**
**To find out, write the circled letters in the matching boxes below.**

| 12 | 11 | 1 | 4 | 8 | 9 | 2 |
|---|---|---|---|---|---|---|

| 6 | 7 | 3 | 10 | 5 | 4 | 11 |
|---|---|---|---|---|---|---|

**Note To Teacher:** Use this activity after completing the story.

# The Young At Heart

## Celebrating Grandparents

Call them Nonnie and Pup-Pup, Meemaw and Pappy; they could be Granny and Gramps, or Nana and Boompa. They answer to whatever trips from the tongue of the first grandchild and sticks as a title. Their names only serve to honor the parents of the parents—who share a very precious place in the lives of their grandchildren. Perhaps it is because they really come from a different world: from 50, 60, or 70 years in the past. They speak a vocabulary with some forgotten phrases; they remember past wars and presidents, and the origins of quilt pieces.

Close by or faraway, grandparents love without restrictions and with endless patience. They share a bountiful harvest of experiences and wisdom. This unique relationship that spans three generations is lauded in the picture books that follow.

*books reviewed by Deborah Zink Roffino*

## ❀ Grandmothers ❀

### Apple Juice Tea
*Written & Illustrated by Martha Weston*
*Clarion Books, 1994*

Families may be far-flung these days, and a grandparent's visits can be infrequent. It's often difficult for all three generations to acknowledge the adjustment it takes for a child to learn to love a virtual stranger during a two-week vacation. This book confirms that it is normal to be apprehensive about a new relationship and that it may take a bit of time for love to grow. Soft watercolors capture the peace and patience of a grandmother willing to wait for the trust of her grandchild.

### Pot Luck
*Written by Tobi Tobias & Illustrated by Nola Langner Malone*
*Lothrop, Lee & Shepard Books; 1993*

Gram is called to entertain an old friend on short notice and she promises a simple potluck supper, but instead she delivers a feast! Just elbow-high, her granddaughter Rachel watches in amazement. Rachel scrambles to keep up with the highly animated Gram, and learns a few things about old friends and good food. Warmth radiates from Gram's oven; her love and humor permeate the story.

### Up The Tracks To Grandma's
*Written by Judith Hendershot & Illustrated by Thomas B. Allen*
*Alfred A. Knopf, Inc.; 1993*

Set in the hollow of an Ohio coal town, this story beautifully underscores the deep friendship between a child and her grandma. When Grandma must go away for just a few days, she leaves her granddaughter in charge of feeding the chickens and weeding the garden patch. This old country grandma with her steaming chicken soup and blue-flowered chapeau is full of old-fashioned affection.

### Gramma's Walk
*Written & Illustrated by Anna Grossnickle Hines*
*Greenwillow Books, 1993*

She sits in the sunroom, confined to her wheelchair. From what could be the saddest setting, this resourceful gramma takes her grandson magically soaring over the world. They travel on imagination and take long walks on a whim. Today they wander the seashore searching for treasures. Seemingly hand in hand, they wiggle their toes in the sand, build a castle, and watch a ferry glide by. The message comes through clearly—there are no barriers for those who love.

### Grandma's Shoes
*Written by Libby Hathorn & Illustrated by Elivia Little, Brown and Company; 1994*

Grief becomes the painful cost of loving a grandparent in this rich, imaginative account. Unprepared at any age for the sorrowful day, this book focuses on the granddaughter's sorrow. The world seems emptier without a grandma who was so full of stories, poise, and peace. At the family gathering, the inevitable question rings out: "Who could ever step into such a woman's shoes?" The answer comes from this child who loved her grandma so much. She pledges to fill her grandma's shoes for those who missed out by being too young to know Grandma.

# Grandfathers

## Grandaddy And Janetta

*Written by Helen V. Griffith & Illustrated by James Stevenson*
*Greenwillow Books, 1993*

This short chapter book touches on the insecurities of traveling alone and the hollow fear of homesickness. However, the real focus is the gentle relationship between a youngster and her grandaddy when she arrives to spend a peaceful summer at his home in Georgia. Stevenson's wispy watercolor sketches carry the chatter and laughter like soft southern breezes.

## Grandaddy's Highway

*Written by Harriet Diller & Illustrated by Henri Sorensen*
*Boyds Mills Press, Inc.; 1993*

Grandaddy was a trucker who'd start his route just east of Pittsburgh, crossing this wide and wonderful country to the Pacific Ocean. Now his driving days are in the past, but his memories sing like the tires on the highway. When the night comes and it's time to tell stories, his granddaughter knows just what she wants to hear. Realizing the value of an older person's experiences will enrich every child's life. This granddaughter gets a priceless driving lesson.

## A Day's Work

*Written by Eve Bunting & Illustrated by Ronald Himler*
*Clarion Books, 1994*

*Abuelo* speaks no English, so young Francisco accompanies his grandfather as the old one seeks day work. A job comes, but only after Francisco bends the truth. The price is high. Even with the two of them laboring, the gardening on this golden California hillside is not done to satisfaction. For the gray-headed abuelo is not a yardman—he is a carpenter. Grandfather's integrity mutes the fury of the employer and offers Francisco a compelling lesson of honor.

## Grandpa's Face

*Written by Eloise Greenfield & Illustrated by Floyd Cooper*
*Philomel Books, 1988*

Children resist change. When Grandpa must transform his facial expressions while rehearsing for a theater production, his granddaughter worries about the man behind the new face. Patience and understanding dispel the fear in this luminous story of love and friendship across generations. The book also underscores a child's inclination to misbehave as a means of dealing with fear or confusing emotions.

## Grandad Bill's Song

*Written by Jane Yolen & Illustrated by Melissa Bay Mathis*
*Philomel Books, 1994*

Seeking to fill the emptiness he feels when his beloved grandad dies, a youngster questions family members looking for comfort in their memories of the man. Warm, strong colors suggest the deep emotions of Grandad's friends and family. The pages hold lyrical couplets full of gentle grieving expressions; the pictures suggest a scrapbook created out of love. These soothing messages may help explain to a grieving youngster the hollow spaces that threaten to crush an aching heart.

## Grandpa's House

*Written & Illustrated by Harvey Stevenson*
*Hyperion Books For Children, 1994*

Every child should have a place to fly to where the rules are different. For this youngster, it is Grandpa's house. Ideally located, Grandpa lives near the woods, on a lake, and not far from the seashore. Likable, silly, and unpredictable—the youngster doesn't quite know what to make of this guy who is not at all like the other adults he knows. Illuminated with soft watercolor art, this celebration of a relationship proves that the young and the old can meet comfortably somewhere in the middle.

---

## National Grandparents Day

Turn the spotlight on your students' grandparents and older adult friends in honor of National Grandparents Day: the first Sunday following Labor Day. Or plan a special day during October or November. Any time is ideal for recognizing the importance of a loving relationship between the elderly and the youth of our society. Your guests of honor will enjoy hearing books that are featured in this collection, as well as stories that their young counterparts have written in their grandparents' honor. For added fun, invite your visitors to reminisce about the school days of long ago. And last, but not least, invite your guests to return to your classroom. Whether listening to students read or helping students practice math facts, these special visits will be looked forward to by all. And your students will be taking advantage of one of society's most valuable resources.

# A Treasury Of Favorite ABC Books

**Snuggle up with this collection of ABC books and related activities. Straight from our subscribers to you—these classroom favorites promise to please.**

## A: My Name Is Alice
### Written by Jane Bayer & Illustrated by Steven Kellogg
### Dial Books For Young Readers, 1984

The alliterative text of this alphabet book is sure to capture your students' attention—as will the parade of animals that grace the book's pages. From *A* to *Z*, animal couples are introduced by their names, their point of origin, and the wares they sell. The text is based on a playground game the author played as a child. If you really want to impress your students, demonstrate the playground game. All you'll need is a rubber ball and a bit of ball-bouncing prowess! Then follow up by asking each student to create an alliterative verse that features his name and that follows the pattern established in the book. These verses can be written, illustrated, and compiled into a classroom book. Or they can be chanted on the playground as part of ball-bouncing, hand-clapping, or jump-rope games.

*Theodora Gallagher—Gr. 1, Carteret School, Bloomfield, NJ*
*Shirley Gillette—Reading Specialist, Lafe Nelson School*
*Safford, AZ*

## Alphabears: An ABC Book
### Written by Kathleen Hague & Illustrated by Michael Hague
### Holt, Rinehart and Winston; 1984

In this delightful book, rhyming text and adorable teddy bears introduce students to the letters of the alphabet. To make an endearing display or a charming classroom version of the book, begin with student copies of the teddy-bear pattern on page 116. Have each student cut out and glue a bear pattern on story paper. Then using scraps of construction paper, wallpaper, and fabric; yarn; crayons or markers; and other arts-and-crafts supplies, have each student dress up his bear and create background scenery. Suggest that students create artwork that reflects their personal interests. Next ask each child to write about this teddy bear that shares his name. Younger students can dictate the information to an adult. Display the projects with the title "Meet Our Alphabears!" or bind your students' work into a "bear-y" special ABC book.

*Maggi Eichorn—Gr. 1, Parker School, Tolland, CT*

To reinforce rhyming skills, challenge students to create rhyming verses for an ABC book entitled "Alphakids." In turn, have each child share her special qualities and interests with her classmates. This can be in a large-group or small-group setting. After each child's turn, the group members work together to create a rhyme for that child. When each child in the group has a rhyme written on story paper, the group members illustrate their own rhymes. Alphabetically compile the completed projects into a class book.

*Rosemary A. Shannon—Gr. 1, Wyomissing Hills Elementary,*
*Wyomissing Hills, PA*

## The Extinct Alphabet Book
### Written by Jerry Pallotta & Illustrated by Ralph Masiello
### Charlesbridge Publishing, 1993

Each page of this intriguing alphabet book features information about a creature that no longer exists. And as if that isn't interesting enough—the author and illustrator have included a few more surprises! For example, on the *B* page the trees spell a two-word message that challenges the reader to find the author. (His photo is neatly camouflaged on a later page.) Or turn the *U* page upside down and find the profile of a rock-and-roll legend. Without a doubt, this book merits several careful readings and examinations.

This ABC book also packs a powerful message about extinction. Discuss extinction and how it might be prevented in the future. To draw your students' attention to creatures that are nearing extinction, have each child create a page for "An Endangered Alphabet Book." Or have students create a research-based ABC book on a current topic of study such as rain-forest animals or famous Americans.

*Ritsa Tassopoulos—Gr. 3, Oakdale Elementary, Cincinnati, OH*

## Dr. Seuss's ABC

*Written & Illustrated by Dr. Seuss*
*Random House, Inc.; 1963*

Just what the doctor ordered—an ABC book that's fun through and through! After a few oral readings of this Beginner Book, students will be ready to create alphabet books of their own. Before students begin to write, have them identify adjectives in the text. Discuss how the descriptive words enhance the doctor's story. Then give each student a blank, 28-page booklet in which to compose his alphabetical masterpiece. To make a 28-page booklet, fold 14 sheets of blank duplicating paper in half; then staple the folded paper between construction-paper covers. If desired, have students use crayons or markers to underline the adjectives in their stories.

*Suzanne Albaugh—Gr. 2, Wintersville Elementary*
*Wintersville, OH*

## Handsigns: A Sign Language Alphabet

*Written & Illustrated by Kathleen Fain*
*Chronicle Books, 1993*

This one-of-a-kind book is both an alphabet book and an introduction to American Sign Language. The easy-to-follow format presents 26 full-color illustrations, each revealing at least one animal that begins with the featured alphabet letter. On each alphabet page, an inset picture of a human hand shows how to sign the letter. A foreword provides information on the history of sign language and how it is used today, and a glossary gives information about each animal shown. Students will enjoy signing the alphabet letters and learning about a colorful menagerie of animals.

*Elouise Miller, Lincoln School, Hays, KS*

## On Market Street

*Written by Arnold Lobel & Illustrated by Anita Lobel*
*Greenwillow Books, 1981*

A day spent on Market Street results in 26 very interesting purchases—from apples to zippers! After a few readings of the book, put your students' memories to the test! Read the story again, but this time read just the alphabet letters and let the students recall the merchandise that was purchased. Some students may even be up to the challenge of recalling all 26 purchases!

For a fun writing and drawing activity, have each child create his own alphabetical shopping spree along a street of his own choosing. With unlimited budgets, students are likely to make some unusual purchases!

*Christy Meyer, Honolulu, HI*

## A Little Alphabet

*Written & Illustrated by Trina Schart Hyman*
*Morrow Junior Books, 1993*

In this tiny volume, each letter of the alphabet is illustrated with a child playing with or using objects that begin with the featured letter. For example, sharing the spotlight with the letter *A* is a child *artist,* the *arm* of the artist, *acorns,* an *apron,* an *avocado, apples,* an *artichoke,* an *anemone,* and an *ant.* Students will love the challenge of naming all of the pictured items. List the words on tagboard strips—one strip for each alphabet letter. (A glossary provides the items pictured on each page.) When you have completed one strip for every letter, distribute them to your students. Ask each youngster to use the words on his strip to craft a story about the child pictured on the alphabet page. When the students have completed their writings, revisit the book and have each student read his story aloud when the appropriate alphabet letter is displayed.

*Agnes Tirrito—Gr. 2, Kennedy Elementary School, Texarkana, TX*

# Chicka Chicka Boom Boom

*Written by Bill Martin, Jr., and John Archambault*
*Illustrated by Lois Ehlert*
*Simon And Schuster Books For Young Readers, 1989*

This lively alphabet rhyme—in which all the letters of the alphabet race each other up a coconut tree—proved to be a favorite among our subscribers!

Acting out this alphabet rhyme is a must! Have each child cut out and decorate a different alphabet letter. Or have each child design a large poster-board letter that can be worn. During an oral reading of the story, each child stands and displays her artwork when her letter is mentioned. When all of the letters tumble from the tree, the students chant, "Chicka chicka boom boom!" and drop to the floor. At the end of the story, have students trade letters and repeat the activity. Before long students will be retelling the story without any help from their teacher. Chicka chicka boom boom!

*Justine A. White—Gr. 1, Southside Elementary, Cleveland, TX*
*Marcia Dosser—Gr. 1, University School, Johnson City, TN*

This coconut caper is a great way to evaluate your students' knowledge of the alphabet. Display a large coconut-tree cutout on a bulletin board entitled *"Chicka Chicka Boom Boom."* Staple 26 coconuts in the tree—each one bearing a different lowercase letter. Along the bottom of the display, staple 26 more coconuts—each one bearing an uppercase letter. As you point to each of the lowercase letters, ask a different student to point to the corresponding capital letter.

*Kelley Russell—Interim Teacher, Rogersville City School*
*Rogersville, TN*

Boom! Boom! A few bumps, bruises, and other minor injuries result when the alphabet letters fall to the ground. Read the story to your youngsters and draw their attention to the condition of the letters after they tumble from the tree. For a fun art activity, have each child choose a different alphabet letter. Then—using colorful paper, markers or crayons, and scissors—each youngster creates a cutout of his slightly shaken letter. For added fun, give each child a small bandage to use. When the projects are done, have each student mount his letter in the top of a classroom coconut tree! Chicka! Chicka!

*Linda Stroik—Gr. 1, Bannach Elementary School, Stevens Point, WI*

Imagine the view from the top of a coconut tree! That's what youngsters do as they complete this follow-up activity. On light green construction paper, duplicate student copies of the treetop on page 116. Distribute the copies and have each student write a different alphabet letter in the first blank. Then ask each student to finish his sentence. The word(s) he writes must begin with his assigned letter. Next give each student a strip of brown construction paper and a 9" x 12" sheet of construction paper. A student cuts out his treetop; then he cuts a tree trunk from the brown paper. He glues both cutouts on the sheet of construction paper. Next he uses crayons or markers to embellish his tree and to illustrate what his letter saw. Compile the personalized projects in alphabetical order between a poster-board cover entitled *"Chicka Chicka Boom Boom* retold by _____'s Class."

*Maxine Bergman—Gr. 1, Loretto Elementary School*
*Jacksonville, FL*

From coconuts to continents! For a unique geography lesson, label one coconut cutout for each alphabet letter. Divide students into small groups. Give each group a world map or atlas and an equal number of coconuts. Challenge the groups to write on each coconut the name of a country that begins with the programmed letter. On the back of the coconut, the group writes the continent where the country is located.

To display the students' work, label a paper palm tree for each of the seven continents. Mount the trees on a bulletin board entitled "From Coconuts To Countries To Continents." Then, beginning with coconut A and proceeding in alphabetical order, have different group members present the programmed coconuts. To do this, a student names the country on the coconut, finds the country on a world map or globe, and attaches the coconut to the appropriate tree.

*adapted from an idea by Marcia Dosser—Gr. 1*

# Q Is For Duck: An Alphabet Guessing Game

*Written by Mary Elting and Michael Folsom*
*Illustrated by Jack Kent, Clarion Books, 1980*

Actually *Q* is for quack—but since ducks quack, that means *Q* is for duck! It won't take long before your youngsters will be experts at figuring out this zany book. As you can tell, this ABC book reinforces more than just beginning sounds. It's great for building logical-thinking skills as well. After reading the book with your class, charge them with the enjoyable task of developing a book that is similarly patterned. Younger students can create sentences and illustrations for individual letters. These projects can be compiled alphabetically into a class book. Older students can create individual books by writing and illustrating sentences for each alphabet letter. As the lesson draws to a close, you may find that students are dedicating a letter to you: *F* is for teacher because teachers make learning *fun!*

*Michelle Higley—Gr. 2, St. Thomas Aquinas, Lansing, MI*

# Alligator Arrived With Apples: A Potluck Alphabet Feast

**Written by Crescent Dragonwagon**
*Illustrated by Jose Aruego and Ariane Dewey*
*Macmillan Publishing Company, 1987*

From Alligator's apples to Zebra's zucchini, a multitude of alphabetical animals and foods celebrate Thanksgiving with a grand feast. After students have heard this deliciously entertaining story, they'll be hungry to create a class version of the tale. To do this, have each child design a page that features his name and the food he is bringing to the feast. Challenge students to maintain the alliterative pattern the author used. Compile the completed pages into a one-of-a-kind class booklet.

*Betsy Meyer—Gr. 1, Pulaski Academy, Little Rock, AR*

# Old Black Fly

*Written by Jim Aylesworth & Illustrated by Stephen Gammell*
*Henry Holt And Company, Inc.; 1992*

The old black fly may pester the characters of this book, but he'll undoubtedly win quite a few fans in your class. As you read the book to your students, invite them to join in on the refrain: "Shoo fly! Shoo fly! Shooo!" For a high-interest verb lesson, have students identify the verb used on each alphabet page. List these verbs and ask students to examine the completed list for a common factor; then guide them to discover that the verbs are all past tense. Next have the students provide the present tense of each listed verb. Then reread the story with your students. In addition to supplying the refrain, have them supply a present-tense verb for each alphabet page.

*Judy Chunn—Grs. 2–3, Westminster School, Nashville, TN*

Keeping up with a busy fly can be challenging! But when this project is completed, students will have no trouble at all! Give each child a small construction-paper booklet containing 30 blank pages. Ask each student to write "Old Black Fly retold by [student's name]" on the front cover; "Buzz, buzz, buzz" on the first page; and "It's been a very bad day" on the second page. In the top, outside corner of the third page, the student writes "A." Then on the page she draws and colors an apple pie, writing the words "apple pie" below her illustration. On the fourth page she writes "B" in the top, outside corner; then she draws and colors a baby on the page and writes the word "baby" beneath her illustration. The student continues in this manner for each of the remaining alphabet letters. Then she writes "Buzz, buzz, buzz" on the first of the two remaining pages and "Swat!" on the final page. Suggest that students refer to their books as they retell the fly's story for their friends and family.

*adapted from an idea by Linda C. Buerklin—Substitute Teacher*
*Monroe Township Schools, Williamstown, NJ*

# More To Come!

We had such a great response when we asked our subscribers to tell us how they used their favorite ABC books in the classroom that we were unable to feature all of the ideas we received. Look for more ABC books and related activities in your December/January issue.

# More Favorite ABC Books

Just as we promised, we're back with more of our subscribers' favorite ABC books and related activities. We hope that this alphabetical collection suits you to a T!

## Have You Ever Seen...? An ABC Book

*Written & Illustrated by Beau Gardner*
*BGA Publishing, Inc.; 1994*

What do you get when you cross the alphabet with a hefty dose of imagination? An ABC book that's filled with improbable creations ranging from an *antlered alligator* to a *zippered zebra!* After a few oral readings of this book, your students will be eager to create some crazy combinations of their own! To make a big-book version, have each student write a different alphabet letter in the upper left-hand corner of a 12" x 18" sheet of construction paper. Write the phrase "Have you ever seen…?" on the chalkboard. Each student completes the phrase on his paper and creates a corresponding illustration. Bind the resulting pages in alphabetical order into a one-of-a-kind book titled "Have You Ever Seen…?"

*Peter Tabor—Gr. 1, Weston Elementary School, Schofield, WI*

## The Ocean Alphabet Book

*Written by Jerry Pallotta & Illustrated by Frank Mazzola, Jr.*
*Charlesbridge Publishing, 1986*

This information-packed alphabet book is quite a catch! Read the book aloud to reel in an interest in ocean life. Once your students are hooked, have each one choose a favorite ocean inhabitant to research and illustrate. Set aside time for students to share their completed projects with their classmates. To create a unique underwater display, mount your students' work on a bulletin board covered with blue paper. Provide markers and crayons; or construction-paper scraps, scissors, and glue; then invite students to add desired details to the underwater display.

*Robbin Hair—ESL Grs. 1–5, Conder Elementary, Columbia, SC*

## Animalia

*Written & Illustrated by Graeme Base*
*Harry N. Abrams, Inc.; 1986*

Take a trip from *A* to *Z* through an animal world that is nothing short of spectacular! You'll find animals—exotic and familiar; everyday things in strange settings; and a wealth of hidden objects and ideas. No doubt your students will ask to have this book read to them again and again. Besides being lots of fun, this book is a wonderful example of alliteration. For a fun writing activity, have each student write an alliterative sentence on a 12" x 18" sheet of white construction paper. Then, following Graeme Base's example, have each student illustrate his sentence, add details that begin with the letter he has alliterated, and hide a self-portrait somewhere on his paper. Mount the completed projects on a bulletin board entitled "Alliteration And More!" or alphabetically compile them into a book for your class library.

*Melanie Cadmus—Gr. 3, Ferris Intermediate, Ferris, TX*

## A Prairie Alphabet

*Written by Jo Bannatyne-Cugnet*
*Illustrated by Yvette Moore*
*Tundra Books Of Northern New York, 1992*

Life on the prairie unfolds between the covers of this exquisitely illustrated book. From *A* to *Z*, different facets of the prairie are visited. At the end of the book, the information presented on each page is explained further. After students have learned about life on the prairie, find out what other topics they'd like to explore. List all students' suggestions; then take a vote to determine which one will become the theme of a class-created ABC book. Next help students brainstorm words and phrases related to the chosen topic. Finally distribute the paper of your choice, and have each child write and illustrate an alliterative sentence for a different alphabet letter. Alphabetize the resulting pages and bind them into a first-rate thematic ABC book!

*Marty Suter—Gr. 3, Cleveland School, Elkhart, IN*

## The Cow Is Mooing Anyhow: A Scrambled Alphabet Book To Be Read At Breakfast

*Written by Laura Geringer & Illustrated by Dirk Zimmer*
*HarperCollins Publishers, 1991*

Most everything about this alphabet book is unusual! What begins as an ordinary breakfast turns into a rowdy affair when a menagerie of animals representing the letters of the alphabet drop by for a bite to eat. And to add to the confusion, the animals appear out of alphabetical order! The book is a fun way to introduce students to several less familiar animals. After reading the book aloud, challenge students to recall the animals that dropped by. Then have the students alphabetize the animal names and/or sort them into animal groups. Encourage interested students to research and report on the animals they find most intriguing.

*Kathy Seals, Park Lane Elementary, Lawton, OK*

## Alpha Bugs: A Pop-Up Alphabet

*Written & Illustrated by David A. Carter*
*Little Simon, 1994*

Youngsters will be eager to get their hands on this delightful pop-up book! As tabs are pulled, lifted, and turned, an assortment of imaginative alphabet bugs come to life and make learning as easy as ABC. These adorable sock puppets are guaranteed to extend the learning fun! To make his puppet, each student needs an adult-size sock, scissors, craft glue, and access to a variety of craft supplies including buttons, yarn, felt and fabric scraps, and sequins. Each student also needs a different alphabet letter cut from fabric or felt. Have the students attach the letters to their puppets, then choose puppet names that begin with these letters. Make plans for the students to use their puppets for a variety of alphabet-related activities. For a fun debut, invite each "puppet" to present his page in *Alpha Bugs*.

*Betty Jean Kobes—Gr. 1, West Hancock Elementary, Kanawha, IA*

You can count on your students going buggy over this follow-up activity! Keeping with the bug theme, have students stand in line single file and begin marching around the classroom. Tell the students that they have formed a *soundapede*—a bug that is excellent at identifying beginning and ending sounds. Review the sounds of the alphabet with the soundapede before asking different segments of the bug to identify the beginning and ending sounds of select words. Make sure that each soundapede segment has an opportunity to participate. Then make arrangements for the soundapede to perform for a younger audience. Have students design simple masks and wrist decorations to be worn during the presentation. The expertise and visual appeal of this soundapede is sure to make a *big* impression!

*Betty Jean Kobes—Gr. 1*

# Patterns

Use with *Alphabears: An ABC Book* on page 110.

Use with *Chicka Chicka Boom Boom* on page 112.

_____
_ _ _ _ _ _ _ _   climbed to the top
of the coconut tree to see

_____
_ _ _ _ _ _ _ _ _ _ _ _ _ _ _ _ _ _ _ _ _
_____ .

# Spooky Stories For Halloween

One of the oldest types of tales—ghost stories—is especially popular at this time of year. Most primary-age students are eager to take hold of the silliness of the supernatural and be tickled by ever-so-eerie tales. So if you dare—pop some corn, dim the lights, and tease your students' imaginations with these spooky tales. Boo!

*books reviewed by Deborah Zink Roffino*

## Beneath The Ghost Moon

*Written by Jane Yolen & Illustrated by Laurel Molk*
*Little, Brown and Company; 1994*

Preparing for an innocent Halloween party, a company of sweet mice have their home invaded by a band of mean, green, creepy crawlies. In spite of this threatening scenario, hazy watercolor illustrations depict the critters and the abandoned old house as cuddly and cozy. The importance of fortitude, forgiveness, and friendship comes to light in this book of rhyme.

## The Horrible Spookhouse

*Written by Kicki Stridh & Illustrated by Eva Eriksson*
*Carolrhoda Books, Inc.; 1994*

Alone in a deep, dark forest, a little girl comes upon a house full of witches, ghosts, and slimy monsters who are most delighted to have a visitor. Pages full of bug-eyed, bony, long-nosed harpies proceed to concoct all manner of toil and trouble in an effort to petrify the child. However, this child is undaunted by the events—which leaves the spooks of the house more than a bit bewildered!

## Ghost Train: A Spooky Hologram Book

*Written by Stephen Wyllie & Illustrated by Brian Lee*
*Dial Books, 1992*

Three mischievous spirits find themselves out of work when the roof falls in on old Ravenswick Castle. Wandering the countryside in search of a place to haunt, they float by an amusement park. Here the threesome spots a ghost-train ride that is desperately in need of some haunting. Ghostly books are the perfect place for gimmicks, and this imaginative tale includes several holograms for viewing pleasure.

## Faces In The Dark: A Book Of Scary Stories

*Compiled by Chris Powling*
*Illustrated by Peter Bailey*
*Kingfisher, 1994*

This collection offers ten haunting stories to choose from—each one written by a different children's book author. There are monsters, good and ugly; witches, cold and goose-bumped; and ghosts as sheer as smoke. Many cultures are represented in the colorful illustrations found throughout the book.

## Diane Goode's Book Of Scary Stories & Songs

*Illustrated by Diane Goode*
*Dutton Children's Books, 1994*

Humor and spookiness blend in this collection of stories, poems, and songs from around the world. Ghosts, ghouls, and goblins drift among the pages, with a narrative tone that turns the ridiculous to matter-of-fact. This deliciously spooky book is perfect for reading aloud.

# A Spooky Story by

**Note To Teacher:** After you've tickled your youngsters' imaginations with some ever-so-eerie tales (see the suggested reading list on page 117), duplicate copies of this page and have students pen their own spooky stories. If desired, add lines before duplication. Or white-out the programming and use the sheet for seasonal stationery or other holiday-related activities.

# A Feast Of Thanksgiving Reading

Journey into the past with this banquet of books. You'll find several servings of Pilgrim life and the first Thanksgiving. A book stuffed with tasteful ideas for a present-day celebration is also included.

*books reviewed by Deborah Zink Roffino*

## The First Thanksgiving

*Written by Jean Craighead George*
*Illustrated by Thomas Locker*
*Philomel Books, 1993*

Appealing to the natural imagination, intellect, and fairness of children—this picture book is an unparalleled account of the history leading up to the first Thanksgiving feast. Stunning oil paintings provide a panoramic perspective on the beautiful land called New England. Packed with well-researched but little-known details, the story and illustrations leave a lasting impression.

## N. C. Wyeth's Pilgrims

*Written by Robert San Souci*
*Chronicle Books, 1991*

Robert San Souci has created a spirited narrative to accompany the famous murals of N. C. Wyeth. In challenge to the customary view of Pilgrim life, Wyeth chose to portray the peace that the religious wayfarers came to know in the New World. He infused the pictures of their lives with the colors of the land, the sea, and the rich golden harvest. Young readers will easily capture the joy and love that was surely a part of Pilgrim life.

## The First Thanksgiving Feast

*Written by Joan Anderson*
*Photographed by George Ancona*
*Clarion Books, 1984*

Black-and-white photographs of real people give this chronicle of the *Mayflower* voyagers a "you were there" atmosphere. Actually the characters are portrayed by the authentic-looking actors at the Plimouth Plantation—an outdoor living-history museum in Plymouth, Massachusetts. With bona fide tools and implements filling the scenes, the reader is reminded that the Thanksgiving story is not simply an American fairy tale—but an account of real people who struggled and sacrificed for freedom.

## Sarah Morton's Day: A Day In The Life Of A Pilgrim Girl

*Written by Kate Waters*
*Photographed by Russ Kendall*
*Scholastic Inc., 1989*

## Samuel Eaton's Day: A Day In The Life Of A Pilgrim Boy

*Written by Kate Waters*
*Photographed by Russ Kendall*
*Scholastic Inc., 1993*

The color photographs in both books were shot on location in Plimouth Plantation. Using first-person narration, the author takes readers through a typical day of chores and events for a Pilgrim girl and boy. The children portrayed in these two books—Sarah Morton and Samuel Eaton—were real children. Sarah was nine years old in 1627. She is mentioned in several Pilgrim journals, although there is no clear date of her death. Samuel was age seven in 1627. He lived to be 64 years old.

## My Very Own Thanksgiving: A Book Of Cooking And Crafts

*Written by Robin West*
*Carolrhoda Books, Inc.; 1993*

If you're planning a Thanksgiving party or celebration, this book is a must. You'll find a collection of easy-to-make recipes and crafts, accompanied by information about the holiday, in this user-friendly book. Cute graphics and clear instructions are a bonus.

# Charlie And The Chocolate Factory
## Written by Roald Dahl

The one thing Charlie Bucket longed for more than anything was a Golden Ticket that would entitle him to a tour of Willy Wonka's Chocolate Factory and a lifetime supply of chocolate. "Many wonderful surprises await you!" read the invitation on the much-coveted Golden Tickets. And that is exactly what's in store for Charlie Bucket and your youngsters!

*ideas by Lisa Leonardi*

## The Man Behind The Story
## Roald Dahl: 1916–1990

It's interesting to note that Roald Dahl did not intend to become a writer. His writing career began quite accidentally when a reporter from *The Saturday Evening Post* arranged to interview Dahl about his experiences as a World War II fighter pilot. Dahl had jotted down his ideas in the form of a story, and it was Dahl's story that appeared in print. This incident launched Dahl's writing career.

Much of Roald Dahl's writing reflects adventures he experienced as a boy. In writing *Charlie And The Chocolate Factory*, Dahl drew upon memories of a neighborhood sweetshop, and recollections of testing and rating chocolate inventions for a well-known chocolate manufacturer. To learn more about Dahl's childhood adventures—and misadventures—read *Boy: Tales Of Childhood* (Puffin Books, 1986).

## Five Golden Tickets

However slim Charlie's chances were, he was lucky enough to find a Golden Ticket. Use this exercise to explore the concept of probability with your youngsters. You will need two gift bags labeled "Bag 1" and "Bag 2," ten gold construction-paper tickets, and 75 white construction-paper tickets. Under the watchful eyes of your youngsters, place five gold tickets in each bag. Then place 25 white tickets in Bag 1 and 50 white tickets in Bag 2. Scramble the tickets in each bag.

First ask students to decide from which of the two bags they think they would have a better chance of drawing a golden ticket and why. Lead students to understand that since Bag 1 has the same number of golden tickets as Bag 2, but it has less tickets in all, the chances of drawing a golden ticket from Bag 1 are greater. Then let each student take a turn drawing a ticket from each bag. Record the results on graphs. (Be sure the tickets are returned to the proper bags and the contents of each bag are scrambled after every turn.) When the exercise is complete, help students analyze the results.

## Spoiled Rotten

Augustus Gloop, Veruca Salt, Violet Beauregarde, and Mike Teavee were all spoiled children who, with the help of their parents, routinely got their own way. Ask your students if they think it's possible for a child to have everything he wants. Then ask each child to think of five things he really wishes he could have. Next ask the youngsters if these are the same things they would have wished for last year. Discuss why a person's wants change. Invite students to share their opinions about whether youngsters should or should not be able to have their way all or most of the time.

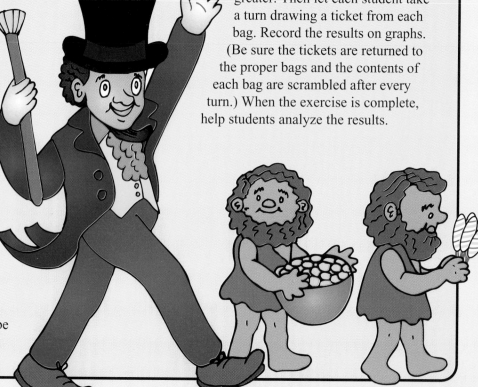

## Revolting Recipes

Listening to candy names like Toffee-Apple Trees, Lickable Wallpaper, Eatable Marshmallow Pillows, and other creative confections will have your youngsters wishing for a taste of the sweet stuff. You can make their wishes come true with *Roald Dahl's Revolting Recipes* (Penguin Books, 1994). This unique cookbook features 31 recipes from Dahl's books, and ten of those tasty treats are referenced to *Charlie And The Chocolate Factory*. So whether your class is in the mood for Willy Wonka's Nutty Crunch Surprise or Hot Ice Cream For Cold Days, you're bound to find at least one revolting recipe to whet your youngsters' appetites!

## Willy Wonka's Glass Jar

Sweeten up your classroom estimation jar by renaming it Willy Wonka's Glass Jar. Fill the jar with one kind of candy. Give the candy a Wonka name such as Everlasting Gobstoppers, Exploding Candy, or Rainbow Drops. After all students have submitted their estimations for the number of candies in the jar, count the candy and determine which student had the most accurate estimate. Then give each student one piece of candy and send the remaining candy home with the winner. Refill the jar with a different kind of candy—one that has a Willy Wonka name, of course!

## Keeping Ahead Of The Competition

It will be very challenging for Charlie to fill the shoes of Mr. Willy Wonka. He'll need to be very clever, indeed! Find out if your youngsters think they could keep the chocolate factory one step ahead of its competition. Working in pairs, challenge students to create new candy machines for the factory that would produce never-before-heard-of, savory, sweet confections. Students can illustrate their machines on drawing paper or construct models of the machines using modeling clay, cardboard boxes and tubes, craft sticks, pipe cleaners, and other building materials. Also ask each student pair to develop an advertisement for its new candy invention. When the twosomes are ready to unveil and "sell" their new candy creations, invite a neighboring classroom to share in your youngsters' sweet success!

## From Cacao Beans To Chocolate

If you're looking for a rich research project, try investigating chocolate! *Chocolate* by Jacqueline Dineen (Carolrhoda Books, Inc.; 1991) offers an excellent look at the history of chocolate, where it comes from, and how it's made. *Let's Visit A Chocolate Factory* by Catherine O'Neill (Troll Associates, 1988) also provides youngsters with a firsthand look at a real-life chocolate factory. Let your youngsters show off their chocolaty knowledge on a classroom cacao tree. Display a large tree cutout on a bulletin board entitled "Flavorful Facts About Chocolate." Add several green leaves near the top. Next to the display, provide a supply of red, yellow, gold, and light green construction paper and a tagboard tracer cut into the shape of a cacao pod. Invite students to record facts about chocolate on pod cutouts; then attach their facts to the tree.

## Oompa-Loompas

Wonderful workers, musical, and mischievous—that's how Willy Wonka described the Oompa-Loompas. What he didn't mention is that they sing exactly what's on their minds! Talk about each of the four songs the Oompa-Loompas sang. Use the songs to discuss the unflattering characteristics of each of the children who left the chocolate factory in disgrace. Lead a friendly class debate about the author's motives for these characterizations. What was he trying to say about gum chewers? spoiled children? overeaters? television addicts? children not minding their parents? rudeness to others? Ask students to explain why Charlie was chosen to inherit the factory. Then divide students into small groups and have each group create an Oompa-Loompa song about either Charlie, Willy Wonka, or Grandpa Joe. After the songs are written, have a sharing time for the student groups to read their songs. Or for fun, ask each group to sing its song to a familiar tune!

## Book Versus Video

Invite your students to an afternoon at the movies! The video *Willy Wonka & The Chocolate Factory* is just as scrumptious to watch as the book is to read, yet offers several differences from which to build an exciting activity on comparing and contrasting. After listing the differences between the book and the video, ask students why they think these differences exist. Students may be surprised to discover that Roald Dahl wrote the screenplay for the movie, too.

## "Wonkamania" Day!

As a culmination to this appetizing read-aloud, plan a "Wonkamania" Day! A day or two in advance of the event, present each youngster with a golden ticket invitation. Inform students that they must have their tickets with them to participate! Then gather a top hat and a gold-topped walking cane (or something similar) and work your magic by integrating sweets into activities you've planned for the day. Here are a few savory suggestions you might like to consider:

- Have students write and illustrate an ABC book of candy inventions.
- Complete a taste comparison between three or four different candy treats; then create a class graph that shows which of the four candy treats was most favored by your youngsters.
- Let your students finger-paint with chocolate pudding.
- Brainstorm a class-generated list of foods that are made from or with chocolate. Have each youngster choose his top ten favorites and list them in alphabetical order.
- Have each student write and illustrate a news article about the greatest chocolate story ever told.
- Make a chocolate cookbook. Ask each student to contribute one wacky recipe.
- Set aside some time for singing! Invite students to choose songs they think the Oompa-Loompas might enjoy.

*A Golden Ticket Invitation*

Entitles you to admittance to "Wonkamania" Day
Date: February 9, 1996
Place: Your classroom
Time: 8:15 AM
*Many wonderful surprises await you!*

## More Chocolaty Read-Alouds

***Chocolate-Covered Ants*** by Stephen Manes (Scholastic Inc., 1990)

Two brothers make a bet about eating chocolate-covered ants in this hilarious account of one boy's recipe for disaster.

***Mary Marony And The Chocolate Surprise*** by Suzy Kline (G. P. Putnam's Sons, 1995)

Second-grader Mary Marony resorts to cheating to be sure that she gets a golden ticket in her candy bar. The results of her dishonesty surprise Mary and the whole second-grade class. A perfect follow-up to *Charlie And The Chocolate Factory*.

***The Chocolate Touch*** by Patrick S. Catling (Bantam Books, Inc.; 1984)

John Midas discovers that his sweet dream come true (being able to turn everything his lips touch into chocolate) has its bitter side.

***Chocolate Fever*** by Robert Kimmel Smith (Dell Publishing Company, 1994)

Henry Green loves eating chocolate—morning, noon, and night. But a case of chocolate fever teaches Henry that there can be too much of a good thing!

# Picture-Perfect

Make a picture chart.
Read each clue; then draw the matching
  picture on the chart.
Color your drawings.

|  | A | B | C | D |
|---|---|---|---|---|
| **3** |  |  |  |  |
| **2** |  |  |  |  |
| **1** |  |  |  |  |

## Clues

In C-1, draw what the Bucket family eats for breakfast.

In D-3, draw what the Bucket family eats for dinner.

In B-1, draw what Charlie gets every year for his birthday.

In A-2, draw what is made at the factory where Mr. Bucket worked.

In D-2, draw what Mr. Bucket read to find out about the Golden Tickets.

In C-3, draw what Charlie wants to find in his candy bar.

In A-1, draw what Augustus eats all day.

In C-2, draw what Veruca's father shelled at his factory.

In B-2, draw what Violet puts behind her ear at mealtimes.

In A-3, draw what Mike watches day and night.

In B-3, draw what Grandpa Joe gave Charlie.

In D-1, draw what Charlie found in the snow.

**Note To Teacher:** Use this activity after completing chapter ten.

# Two More Tickets!

Pretend that two more Golden Tickets were found.

Think about the characters that Roald Dahl created.
Think about what happened to them at the chocolate factory.

Create a character for each new Golden Ticket holder.
Write about the character.
Draw what you think the character would look like in the box.

### Golden Ticket Number Six

Name:_____

Annoying Habit:_____

_____

Description: _____

_____

_____

_____

What happens to this character? _____

_____

_____

### Golden Ticket Number Seven

Name:_____

Annoying Habit:_____

_____

Description: _____

_____

_____

_____

What happens to this character? _____

_____

_____

**Bonus Box:** On the back of this page, design a Golden Ticket that you would like to find. Be sure to write on the ticket exactly how it can be used.

©The Education Center, Inc. • *THE MAILBOX® • Primary •* Feb/Mar 1996

124    **Note To Teacher:** Use this activity after completing the story.

# The Royal Palace Presents
# Nutritious Reading
## A Menu For Good Health

Enhance your study of food and nutrition with this appetizing assortment of notable picture books. Each book is served with a delectable activity that should satisfy the taste buds of even the pickiest primary-aged youngster. Now that's a feast fit for royalty!

*books reviewed by Deborah Zink Roffino*

## This Is The Way We Eat Our Lunch
### A Book About Children Around The World
*Written by Edith Baer & Illustrated by Steve Björkman*
*Scholastic Inc., 1995*

Here's an adventure in eating that beats the school cafeteria! A quick trip across America and then to several points abroad shows children of many cultures and their lunchtime preferences. Pulling information from Björkman's dynamic watercolors and a descriptive couplet, readers learn the menu and the milieu that makes lunchtime special.

At the conclusion of the book, use the provided map to locate the home of each child mentioned in the story. Challenge students to recall the different lunches that the youngsters ate; then use the "Did you know that..." information at the back of the book to answer questions your students have about the different food fares. For a fun booklet-making project, give each child a paper lunch sack and a sheet of white construction paper. Ask each student to illustrate his favorite lunch foods on the construction paper and his favorite lunchtime eating location on the front of his folded lunch sack. Instruct each child to cut out the lunch foods he drew and store the resulting cutouts inside his folded and personalized lunch sack. Set aside time for the youngsters to share their projects; then bind the projects into a one-of-a-kind booklet.

## Dinosaurs Alive And Well: A Guide To Good Health
*Written & Illustrated by Laurene Krasny Brown & Marc Brown*
*Little, Brown And Company; 1990*

Snaggle-toothed characters with bright chartreuse skin provide a bounty of guidelines for kids to follow for good health. Topics include exercise, nutrition, first aid, and even stress management. Fitness facts presented cover the essentials. A profusion of text packed with new vocabulary and valuable information enhances the lively drawings.

These big, bold banners are fun to make and carry important reminders for practicing good health. To make a banner, a student uses a tagboard template to trace the outline of a large banner shape on light-colored bulletin-board paper. Using letter templates, he traces the letters of his name on a contrasting color of paper. Next he cuts out the letters and the banner; then he glues the letters on the banner so that they spell his name. Finally he uses colorful markers and glitter pens to embellish his banner with good health tips. Suggest that each student share his banner with his family members, then request permission to exhibit his artwork in a location where it will benefit the people he cares about the most.

*Get plenty of exercise!* *Deal with your feelings!* **DUDLEY** *Eat right!* *Keep yourself clean!*

From the home office in Camelot, here's the Veggie Top Ten List...

## Vegetables
*Written by Susan Wake & Illustrated by John Yates*
*Carolrhoda Books, Inc.; 1990*

Ten delicious chapters, a glossary, and an index make this compact reference book an excellent resource for any study of nutrition. Photographs and diagrams explain the growing, harvesting, processing, cooking, and enjoying of the veggies of the earth. This colorful introductory book is one in a series of other tasty offerings. Other books in the Foods We Eat series include *Apples, Beans And Peas, Bread, Butter, Cheese, Chocolate, Citrus Fruits, Eggs, Fish, Meat, Milk, Pasta, Potatoes, Rice,* and *Sugar.*

With your youngsters' help, gather and prepare an assortment of veggie vittles. In a note to parents, request that interested parents send a vegetable plate or dish to school on a designated day. Then have your students sort the vegetable offerings by plant parts—plant leaves, fruits and seeds, stems, and roots. Encourage students to try several different vegetables. Based on the results of the vegetable tasting, create a classroom list of students' top ten favorites.

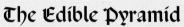

## The Edible Pyramid
**Good Eating Every Day**
*Written & Illustrated by Loreen Leedy*
*Holiday House, Inc.; 1994*

Escort your youngsters to The Edible Pyramid, a restaurant that specializes in nutritious offerings. Restaurant customers learn how many daily servings should be sampled from each of the different food groups according to the United States Department Of Agriculture's Food Guide Pyramid. Nutrition has never been so much fun!

Students put their nutritional knowledge to the test when they begin writing healthful food orders. Give each youngster a blank page from a restaurant order pad (or something similar) and challenge her to write an order for a well-balanced meal. Once her order has received a nutritional stamp of approval from another classmate, she invents a price for each ordered item and tallies the food bill. Order up!

*idea by VaReane Heese, Omaha, NE*

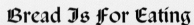

## Bread Is For Eating
*Written by David and Phillis Gershator*
*Illustrated by Emma Shaw-Smith*
*Henry Holt and Company, Inc.; 1995*

It's on most grocery lists around the world and it comes in many shapes and sizes. What is it? Bread, of course! In this story from Guatemala, rich with full-page native artwork in harvest colors, Mamita does more than insist that her little one finish the bread on his plate. Mamita proceeds to trace the bread from seed to table. When youngsters learn the effort folks have made just to put a single slice of bread in their hands, they too may sing, "¡El pan es bueno!"

Bread *is* for eating! Ask each youngster to list the different breads he has eaten during the past two days. Then have the students evaluate their lists to determine if they are eating between 6 and 11 bread servings per day. Invite students to discuss their findings. Conclude the activity by having each student write and/or illustrate steps that show how one bread from his list made it from a seed to his tummy!

# The Vegetable Show

*Written & Illustrated by Laurene Krasny Brown*
*Little, Brown and Company; 1995*

This look at veggies could probably pop the eyes of a potato! Starring in their own sideshow, these vegetables do a bit of vaudeville in an attempt to make their way to youngsters' dinner plates. It's definitely corny—but sure to grow on you!

There's little doubt that this book will be favored by your youngsters. Tasty performers such as Bud the Spud, the Tip-Top Tomato Twins, and Lotta Root (a singing carrot) are just too good to miss! As a follow-up to the book, challenge students to create additional acts for The Vegetable Show. Working in pairs, ask the youngsters to design posters that announce their performing vegetables. Encourage the students to incorporate vegetable facts into their work. Then have each twosome present its poster to its classmates. Who knows? You might have some students who are interested in creating simple vegetable costumes and performing for the live audience!

Fruit Follies? Turn to the last story page of the book and direct your students' attention to the sign bearing these two words. Then take the author's lead and begin production on *next week's* show!

# D. W. The Picky Eater

*Written & Illustrated by Marc Brown*
*Little, Brown and Company; 1995*

Arthur's little sister is typical of so many children who never want to try new foods. In this expansion of the ever-popular adventures of the bespectacled aardvark, D. W. demonstrates that sometimes it's better to not know exactly what's on your plate until it's down the hatch!

When your youngsters' gasps and giggles have subsided, talk about foods that your youngsters feel are intolerable. Invite them to explain why they dislike (or think they dislike!) certain foods. Does the smell, texture, or appearance of a food make a difference? Next ask each student to choose the food that he dislikes the absolute most, then write his name and the name of the food on a slip of paper. Collect the paper slips and redistribute them, making sure that no one receives his own. Then, remembering D. W.'s experience, challenge the youngsters to write and illustrate stories that describe how the classmates named on their paper strips end up eating (and enjoying!) the foods they like the least!

If you're looking for some unique recipes, consider *Acorn Pancakes, Dandelion Salad And 38 Other Wild Recipes* (HarperCollins Publishers, 1995). In this eye-opening book, naturalist and children's author Jean Craighead George shares recipes made from what most youngsters would figure to be weeds. Pancakes from cat-o'-nine-tails? Fried fern fiddleheads? How about a big bowl of lemon daylilies for lunch? Some extraordinary classroom cooking is sure to evolve as well as newfound knowledge about our earth's edible offerings.

## What Food Is This?
*Written & Photographed by Rosmarie Hausherr*
*Scholastic Inc., 1994*

This photographic explanation with clear, concise text establishes the origination of some common foods. Carrots, cauliflower, fish, walnuts, and even sausage are investigated. A question is posed along with a close-up of a particular food, then answered on the following page. Basic nutrition is reviewed and lots of fine family dinner trivia is offered.

Continue the question-and-answer format of this book in a classroom rendition. Write a student-generated list of food-related questions. Ask each youngster to choose a different question from the list and research its answer. Provide assistance as needed. To complete his booklet page, a youngster writes and illustrates his food-related question on one side of a 9" x 12" sheet of white construction paper. Then, on the remaining blank side of his paper, he writes and illustrates the corresponding answer. Compile the student pages into a one-of-a-kind "What Food Is This?" booklet. Each day set aside time for one or more students to share their pages from the classroom booklet. When each booklet page has been presented, place the volume in your classroom library for further perusal.

## Grandpa's Garden Lunch
*Written & Illustrated by Judith Caseley*
*Greenwillow Books, 1990*

From tilling and planting to eating salad, Sarah helps her grandpa grow lunch. Honoring the rewards and benefits of gardening, this simple picture book introduces a whole field of new vocabulary as it emphasizes that care and patience have some delectable rewards.

As a prereading activity, ask each child to list what he ate for lunch on that day or the previous one. Then have the students set their work aside. At the conclusion of the story, ask the students to evaluate their lists to determine which foods began as seeds. This activity will no doubt shed some light on the variety of foods that are "garden grown"!

For a fun follow-up, ask each child to decorate a 4" x 5" card to resemble a seed packet. Use the completed projects for a border on a bulletin board entitled "[your name]'s Garden Cafe." Each day select a different student to post the daily special. Each daily special should include a garden beverage, a lunch entree or sandwich, and a dessert. Encourage creativity!

# MATH UNITS

# Math About Me!

Did you know that there are many numbers that describe you?
Use numbers to answer these questions about yourself.
If you need help, ask an adult in your family to help you.

1. What month, date, and year were you born? _____

2. How much do you weigh? _____

3. How tall are you in inches? _____

4. How many people are in your family? _____

5. What is your telephone number? _____

6. What is your favorite number? _____

7. How many pets do you have? _____

8. What numbers are in your street address? _____

9. What was your birth weight? _____

10. What is your zip code? _____

11. How many eyes do you have? _____

12. How old are you? _____

13. What year did you start school? _____

14. What is your library card number? _____

15. How many books do you own? _____

**Bonus Box:** On the back of this paper, write three more numbers that describe you. Next to each number, write what the number tells about you.

**Note To Teacher:** Use with "Math About Me!" on page 131.

# Math About Me!

This child-centered back-to-school math activity brings a whole new meaning to math. In addition to learning a lot about one another in positive, nonthreatening ways, students experience the role that math plays in everyday life. And when the poster activity has been completed, you'll have everything you need to create a first-rate bulletin board or class booklet. Mathematically speaking, it adds up to the perfect start to a new school year!

*Beth Haugeto—Basic Skills Math: Grs. 3 & 4, Merriam Avenue School, Newton, NJ*

## Materials Needed To Make A Poster:
a completed copy of page 130
one sheet of 9" x 12" tagboard
one sheet of 9" x 12" construction paper (provide several colors)
a school picture or similar photo
markers
scissors
glue

## To Prepare For The Poster-Making Activity:
1. Ask students to name the ways that numbers are a part of their lives. If they seem to be stumped, guide them along by pointing out that there are numbers in their addresses, ages, and phone numbers—even their classroom has a number! After several ideas have been shared, distribute page 130.
2. Tell students that you would like them to complete the "Math About Me!" activity as homework. Suggest that each child have a parent review his work for accuracy. Encourage the students to list additional number-related facts about themselves on the backs of their papers. Ask that all papers be returned the following school day for a special math project.

## Directions For Making A "Math About Me" Poster:
1. Fold the 9" x 12" sheet of construction paper in half and crease it. Repeat two more times; then unfold the paper to reveal eight rectangles.
2. Cut out the eight rectangles; then trade rectangles with several classmates until you have a colorful assortment.
3. Using a marker(s), personalize one rectangle. Then write a different math fact about yourself on each of the remaining rectangles. Use your activity sheet as a guide.
4. Arrange the construction-paper rectangles on the 9" x 12" sheet of tagboard as desired. Be sure that you have room for your picture!
5. Glue the construction-paper rectangles and your picture in place.
6. Laminate the completed project for durability.

Invite each child to share his work with his classmates. Then either mount the projects on a bulletin board entitled "Math About Us," or compile the projects into a class booklet. To do this, hole-punch the projects and a decorated cover; then thread metal rings through the holes.

Barry Slate

# UNDER CONSTRUCTION

## BUILDING A FOUNDATION OF MEASUREMENT SKILLS

So, how *do* your youngsters' measurement skills measure up? Create a blueprint for success using these classroom-tested tips and hands-on activities.

### PARTNERS IN MEASUREMENT!

Pair students for this undercover measurement mission. Give each twosome a different set of written measurement clues, such as "Quietly sneak up to the chalkboard. Measure the wooden pointer stick, one chalkboard eraser, and the piece of blue chalk. Write the name of each item and its measurement on your paper. Carefully sneak back to your desks and wait quietly." After each pair has completed its measurement mission, have each twosome trade measurement clues with another pair. Repeat the activity. Then have the student pairs who traded clues compare their measurement results and explore any discrepancies. Collect the measurement clues to use again later.

Ann E. Scheiblin, Bloomfield, NJ

This room is over 1200 peanuts long!

Premium Packing Peanut Perimeter Placement Purveyor

**BARRY SLATE**

### EXPLORING PERIMETER

To introduce perimeter, give each youngster a supply of packing peanuts or paper clips. Ask students to use the manipulatives to measure the perimeters of their desks, library books, and school supplies. After a bit of practice, ask students to predict which of two objects will have the larger perimeter. Then have the youngsters measure to prove or disprove their predictions. Practicing perimeter is fun!

Betty Kobes
West Hancock Elementary
Kanawha, IA

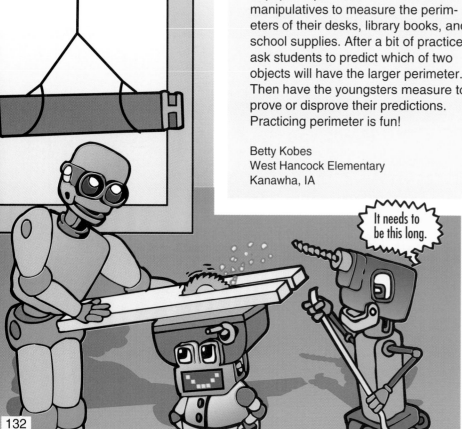

It needs to be this long.

### A FAMOUS FOOTPRINT!

When the unit of measurement is the school principal's footprint, all of a sudden measurement takes on a whole new meaning! Invite the school principal to your classroom. Trace the outline of his or her foot onto a piece of tagboard and cut out the resulting shape. Then have each child use the template to create a construction-paper replica. As a class, brainstorm a list of items that could be measured using the principal's footprint. On provided paper, have each student illustrate a different item from the list. Then, working with a partner, each youngster measures the item he chose and records his findings on his paper. Compile the students' work into a booklet entitled "In Step With [your principal's name]." No doubt your youngsters will be eager to repeat the activity using their own footprints!

Kelly A. Wong—Gr. 2, Berlyn School
Diamond Bar, CA

132

# MONSTROUSLY FUN!

Creating monsters to measure is a measurement activity in itself! Ask each youngster to illustrate a monster on drawing paper. Before students begin drawing, explain that the illustrated monsters will be used as measurement activities. Ask each child to provide five measurement questions that relate to his illustrated monster along with a corresponding answer key. Encourage students to decide what monster parts they plan to incorporate into their measurement activities so that they can accurately draw their monsters. Collect the completed projects. Each day post a different monster project at a measurement center. Students complete the activity on provided paper, then use the student-created answer key to check their work.

Merle Goess—Special Education
Albany Avenue Elementary School
North Massapequa, NY

# OUTJUMP THE TEACHER!

You'll get an enthusiastic response to this measurement activity. Create an indoor or outdoor standing-long-jump site. All you need is a starting line and a cushioned landing area. With your toes behind the starting line, leap forward. Ask two students to mark your landing, and another couple of youngsters to measure the total distance of your jump. Display the measurement near the long-jump site. Then challenge students to out-jump the teacher! Have students rotate positions—from markers, to measurers, to jumpers—making the jumping portion optional. Wow! What a jump!

Suzanne Franzen—Gr. 2
Jacksonville Elementary School
Phoenix, MD

# MEASUREMENT MAN

It's a bird! It's a plane! No, it's Measurement Man! With this dude on display, your worries about teaching liquid measurement will quickly evaporate! Gather the following clean and empty paper milk cartons: one gallon, four quarts, eight pints. Design and decorate a construction-paper head to your liking; then assemble the head and the cartons as shown. It's been said that Measurement Man lingers in the minds of youngsters for many years to come!

Linda Moore—Gr. 1
MacArthur Park Lutheran School
San Antonio, TX

# MARSHMALLOW MEASUREMENT

Sweeten your youngsters' measurement skills with this partner activity. Place two resealable plastic bags of miniature marshmallows at a center along with a list of items for students to measure (such as their pencils, their thumbs, a library book, the tabletop) and a canister of regular-size marshmallows. Before using the miniature marshmallows to measure each listed item, both youngsters estimate its marshmallow length. After they've measured the items, they compare their estimations to the actual measurements. When the center activity is completed, each youngster helps himself to a marshmallow from the canister. Yummy!

# "DINO-MITE" MEASUREMENT!

Make a BIG impression on your youngsters with this measurement activity. Label each of several cards with the name and length of a different dinosaur (shark, whale, etc.). Pair the students and give each twosome a labeled card, a stick of chalk, and a ruler—then head outdoors to a large, paved area. Instruct each twosome to draw a line that equals the length of the dinosaur named on its card, then write the dinosaur's length and name near the line. Ask that each pair have its work verified by another pair of students. No doubt the results of this measurement activity will be a hot topic of discussion during the next outdoor recess!

Grace K. Savoie—Gr. 3, Belle Rose Primary School, Belle Rose, LA

# DOUBLE THE FUN

Students get twice the practice and twice the fun with this measurement activity! Place a numbered sticky dot on each classroom item that you want measured. Ask each student to measure the length, width, height, or perimeter of a predetermined number of items—each time recording the item number, the name of the item, and its measurement on his paper. When the students have finished their measurement task, create a master list of measurements by compiling the students' data. If an inconsistency arises, choose two students who measured the item in question to remeasure it. Several days later, write several measurements from your master list on the chalkboard and challenge students to locate the corresponding classroom items. It's a scavenger hunt!

Kelly Malandra
Lorane Elementary School
Exeter Township, PA

# A HODGEPODGE OF HEIGHTS

The Shaq is *how* tall? For a star-studded measurement activity, enlist your youngsters' help in finding out the heights of a variety of famous folks. Write each person's name and height on a star cutout; then mount each star on a designated classroom wall at the height listed. As much as possible, involve your youngsters in the measurement process, keeping safety your foremost concern. Next have each youngster personalize a star. Pair the students by height so that each student can measure the height of his partner. After the students have listed their heights on their star cutouts, have them mount the stars on the display at the appropriate heights. The stellar results of this activity can be used for a variety of problem-solving challenges.

Ritsa Tassopoulos—Gr. 3
Oakdale Elementary
Cincinnati, OH

# THE KILOMETER CHALLENGE

Calibrating a kilometer is a hefty challenge, but one that most youngsters are eager to pursue. Students can measure the perimeter of their school or school grounds until the distance of one kilometer is reached. Or they can measure a specified playground area, then as a class calculate how many trips around the area would equal one kilometer. As a finale to your youngsters' measurement feat, invite a neighboring classroom to join your students in a one-kilometer walk. At the finish line, present measurement awards and serve refreshments!

Kelly Bransom—Gr. 3
Poolville Elementary
Poolville, TX

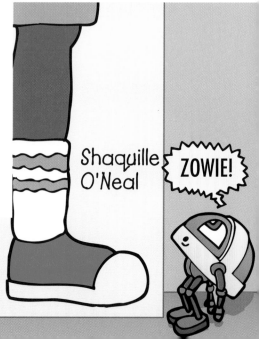

## MEASURING AND MUNCHING

Add a delicious dimension to your measurement activities! When introducing linear measurement, have students measure string licorice. To reinforce that there are 12 inches per foot, give each student a one-foot length of string licorice. Then have each child attempt to eat his lace in 12 one-inch bites. Ask the students to measure their strings of licorice after each bite. Students are bound to remember the number of inches per foot after that sweet experience!

Jodi Tuskowski—Gr. 2, Madison Elementary, Stevens Point, WI

## DRINKING UP MEASUREMENT

Measurement becomes meaningful—and drinkable—during this weekly activity! Each week provide the necessary ingredients and supplies for mixing and serving a classroom beverage. Vary the recipes and the portion sizes. Ask a different group of youngsters to mix and serve the beverage each week. As the students sip their liquid refreshments, pose a variety of problem-solving situations for the students to solve. If you have a quart of Frosty Fruit Surprise, how many one-cup servings do you have?

Kristin L. Moyer—Gr. 2
Weigelstown Elementary, Dover, PA

## CUDDLY CALIBRATIONS

For a warm and fuzzy measurement activity, ask each student to bring to school a favorite stuffed animal. Be sure to bring in a personal favorite of your own! Younger students can use Unifix® cubes or another nonstandard unit of measurement to determine the lengths of their fuzzy friends' ears, feet, legs, arms, etc. Have all students use string to determine circumference. The resulting string lengths can then be measured using the chosen unit of measurement. For added fun, have each student create a minibooklet like the one shown in which to record his fuzzy friend's measurements.

Kelly A. Wong—Gr. 2
Berlyn School, Diamond Bar, CA

## FOR GOOD MEASURE

Encourage creative thinking by using this measurement activity. To begin have youngsters estimate designated distances across the classroom, using their shoes as units of measure. When the predictions are in, have students take turns measuring the distances. As the measurements are recorded, note any discrepancies in the collected data. Help students determine that the differences in shoe sizes and methods of measurement have affected the measurement outcomes. After agreeing upon a standard unit of measurement and a measurement technique, have students remeasure the distances and compare their results.

Bear Measuring
by Zepod Mertlemax

1 1/2 inches
Ear

## INCHING YOUR WAY HOME

Motivate your youngsters to practice linear measurement with this easy-to-make activity. Prepare a set of task cards by drawing a simple house on one end of each card. Place a vehicle sticker on the other end of the card. Then use a ruler to measure and draw three connected line segments between the vehicle and the house. Vary the lengths of the segments on each card. To make the card self-checking, write the total distance of the line segments on the back of the card.

Label each card with a letter. Laminate the cards for durability; then hole-punch the top left-hand corner of each card and use a metal ring to fasten the cards together. To use the task cards, a child measures the segments on each card with a ruler, writes each measurement on a piece of paper, and then adds the lengths together to find the total distance. The activity is great for a math center or to send home for extra measurement practice.

## SQUARE INCHES

Use this tasteful approach to teaching area! Give each student a two-inch paper square, a three-inch paper square, a four-inch paper square, and 16 Wheat Thins® (or another cracker that measures 1" x 1"). To teach area, have the students cover the smallest paper square with a layer of crackers, then count the squares to determine the area in "square inches." Repeat the activity using each of the remaining paper squares. Then invite students to munch on their crackers as you pose additional area-related problems for them to solve.

Sara Fakoury—Gr. 2
Camden Primary School, Camden, SC

## EXPLORING WEIGHT

This cooperative learning project carries its own weight! Give each group of four students a scale and a collection of objects to be weighed. To begin have each student list his group's objects on his paper and write an estimated weight for each one. Next have each group member assume one of the following roles: *item selector* (places each item on the scale), *scale reader* (reads the scale to determine each object's weight), *scale checker* (verifies the weight of each object), or *recorder* (records the weight of each object). When all of the objects have been weighed, have each group member list the actual weights on his paper. Then have the members of each group critique the weight estimates that they made.

TA-DAAAA!

# Sweet Solutions
## A Math Center

**General Directions:**

1. Make a copy of the Answer Keys below; then mount the copy onto construction paper.
2. Copy the cards on pages 138 and 139, then mount the copies onto construction paper.
3. Laminate the cards and the Answer Keys.
4. Cut the cards and the Answer Keys apart.
5. Display the cards at a center along with a supply of the open student page on page 140, pencils, crayons or markers (pink, red, green, yellow, orange, and purple), and an envelope containing the Answer Keys.

| **Answer Key Card #1** | **Answer Key Card #2** | **Answer Key Card #3** | **Answer Key Card #4** |
|---|---|---|---|
| **a.** 16—red | **a.** 97—green | **a.** 5—yellow | **a.** 52—orange |
| **b.** 12—red | **b.** 98—red | **b.** 6—green | **b.** 34—orange |
| **c.** 7—pink | **c.** 56—red | **c.** 7—yellow | **c.** 11—yellow |
| **d.** 9—pink | **d.** 96—red | **d.** 9—yellow | **d.** 42—orange |
| **e.** 5—pink | **e.** 75—green | **e.** 2—green | **e.** 33—yellow |
| **f.** 6—red | **f.** 84—red | **f.** 8—green | **f.** 13—yellow |
| **g.** 8—red | **g.** 98—red | **g.** 3—yellow | **g.** 24—orange |
| **h.** 13—pink | **h.** 79—green | **h.** 4—green | **h.** 52—orange |
| **i.** 10—red | **i.** 89—green | **i.** 1—yellow | **i.** 12—orange |
| **j.** 14—red | **j.** 87—green | **j.** 4—green | **j.** 21—yellow |
| **k.** 15—pink | **k.** 48—red | **k.** 8—green | **k.** 23—yellow |
| **l.** 11—pink | **l.** 67—green | **l.** 7—yellow | **l.** 26—orange |

| **Answer Key Card #5** | **Answer Key Card #6** | **Answer Key Card #7** | **Answer Key Card #8** |
|---|---|---|---|
| **a.** 22—purple | **a.** 59—purple | **a.** 57—red | **a.** 334—purple |
| **b.** 89—green | **b.** 54—pink | **b.** 23—red | **b.** 666—purple |
| **c.** 57—green | **c.** 8—pink | **c.** 98—green | **c.** 123—red |
| **d.** 59—green | **d.** 38—pink | **d.** 63—red | **d.** 275—red |
| **e.** 99—green | **e.** 39—purple | **e.** 31—red | **e.** 509—red |
| **f.** 28—purple | **f.** 17—purple | **f.** 82—green | **f.** 810—purple |
| **g.** 68—purple | **g.** 37—purple | **g.** 78—green | **g.** 548—purple |
| **h.** 97—green | **h.** 49—purple | **h.** 75—red | **h.** 777—red |
| **i.** 68—purple | **i.** 27—purple | **i.** 43—red | **i.** 992—purple |
| **j.** 79—green | **j.** 29—purple | **j.** 84—green | **j.** 198—purple |
| **k.** 69—green | **k.** 43—purple | **k.** 42—green | **k.** 563—red |
| **l.** 46—purple | **l.** 36—pink | **l.** 79—red | **l.** 342—purple |

Subtraction facts to 18

## A Sweet Treat

Copy each problem on your paper.
Solve.

| a. 7<br>−2 | b. 10<br>−4 | c. 13<br>−6 | d. 12<br>−3 | e. 11<br>−9 |

| f. 15<br>−7 | g. 12<br>−9 | h. 8<br>−4 | i. 6<br>−5 | j. 4<br>−0 |

| k. 13<br>−5 | l. 14<br>−7 |

Color the candies
on your paper:
green = even answer
yellow = odd answer

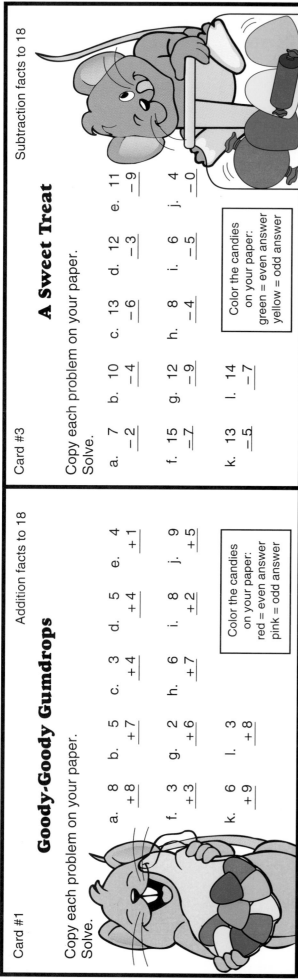

Comparing two-digit numbers

## Gumdrops Galore

Write the greatest number on your paper.

| a. 51 36 57 | b. 23 16 10 | c. 94 49 98 | d. 37 63 59 | e. 29 31 14 | f. 73 69 82 |
| g. 72 78 68 | h. 57 75 47 | i. 33 43 34 | j. 82 81 84 | k. 42 28 40 | l. 67 79 69 |

Color the candies on your paper: green = even answer   red = odd answer

Addition facts to 18

## Goody-Goody Gumdrops

Copy each problem on your paper.
Solve.

| a. 8<br>+8 | b. 5<br>+7 | c. 3<br>+4 | d. 5<br>+4 | e. 4<br>+1 |

| f. 3<br>+3 | g. 2<br>+6 | h. 6<br>+7 | i. 8<br>+2 | j. 9<br>+5 |

| k. 6<br>+9 | l. 3<br>+8 |

Color the candies
on your paper:
red = even answer
pink = odd answer

Two-digit addition: no regrouping

## Sugarcoated Sums

Copy each problem on your paper.
Solve.

| a. 11<br>+11 | b. 36<br>+53 | c. 26<br>+31 | d. 42<br>+17 |

| e. 71<br>+28 | f. 15<br>+13 | g. 47<br>+21 | h. 55<br>+42 |

| i. 56<br>+12 | j. 39<br>+40 | k. 14<br>+55 | l. 23<br>+23 |

Color the candies
on your paper:
purple = even answer
green = odd answer

Two-digit subtraction: no regrouping

## Sweet Subtraction

Copy each problem on your paper. Solve.

a. 75
− 23

b. 67
− 33

c. 34
− 23

d. 88
− 46

e. 59
− 26

f. 28
− 15

g. 49
− 25

h. 86
− 34

i. 63
− 51

j. 95
− 74

k. 73
− 50

l. 38
− 12

Color the candies on your paper:
orange = even answer   yellow = odd answer

---

Two-digit addition: no regrouping

## Mmm! Mmm! Good!

Copy each problem on your paper. Solve.

a. 63
+ 34

b. 53
+ 45

c. 35
+ 21

d. 73
+ 23

e. 42
+ 33

f. 24
+ 60

g. 45
+ 53

h. 11
+ 68

i. 63
+ 26

j. 72
+ 15

k. 24
+ 24

l. 42
+ 25

Color the candies on your paper: red = even answer   green = odd answer

---

Comparing three-digit numbers

## Colorful Candies

Write the greater number on your paper.

a. 321
334

b. 666
656

c. 123
116

d. 257
275

e. 499
509

f. 808
810

g. 548
539

h. 747
777

i. 992
949

j. 198
189

k. 356
563

l. 234
342

Color the candies on your paper:
purple = even answer   red = odd answer

---

Two-digit subtraction with regrouping

## Mouthwatering Memories

Copy each problem on your paper. Solve.

a. 81
− 22

b. 73
− 19

c. 47
− 39

d. 66
− 28

e. 98
− 59

f. 35
− 18

g. 64
− 27

h. 86
− 37

i. 72
− 45

j. 53
− 24

k. 70
− 27

l. 85
− 49

Color the candies on your paper: pink = even answer   purple = odd answer

# Sweet Solutions

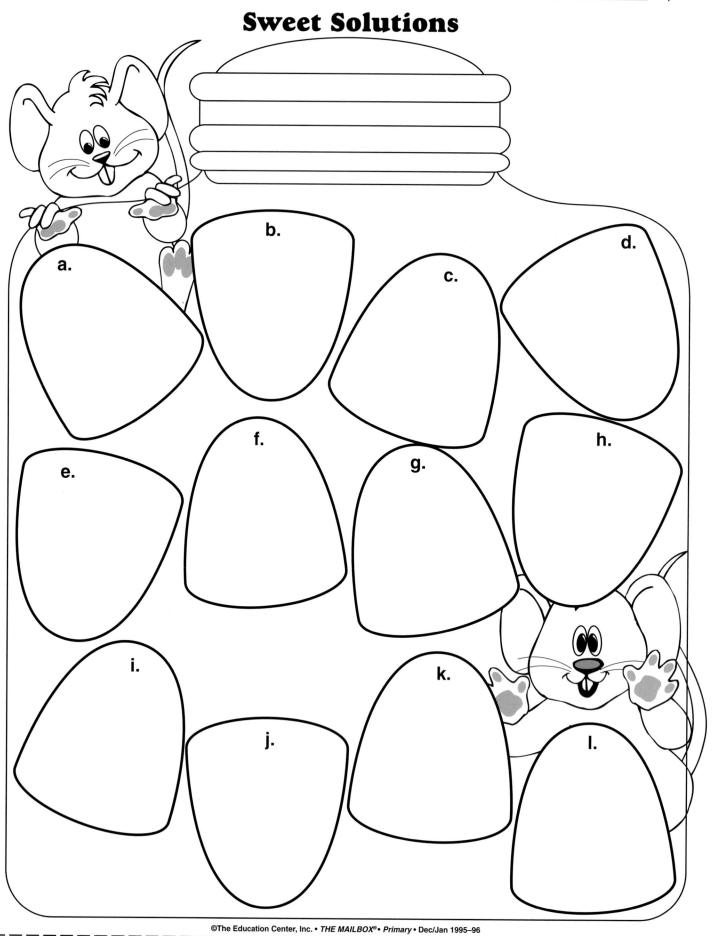

**Note To Teacher:** See page 137 for how to use.

# "Purr-using" Catalogs

## Fun Activities To Reinforce Calculator Skills

Catalogs, calculators, gift-giving occasions, and shopping—the "*purr*-fect" combination for loads of fun, real-life math practice. Now that's a mathematical bargain you mustn't pass up!

*Idea contributed by Shirley VanderTuig—Grades 2 & 3, Callaway Hills Elementary, Jefferson City, MO*

### 'Tis The Season...

For catalogs and shopping! Collect several seasonal catalogs from large department stores such as Sears, JCPenney, and Montgomery Ward. Ask your students to bring catalogs from home too. You will need one catalog and a calculator for each pair of students.

### Catalogs Close-Up

Distribute a catalog to each student pair. Have each pair find its catalog's index. Discuss how an index helps shoppers locate categories of merchandise, as well as individual items, in the catalog. Give several examples of items for students to find in their catalogs by using the index.

### Turning On Calculators

Model for students how to use a calculator for finding money sums and differences. Do several addition and subtraction examples. Remind students that dollars and cents are entered in a calculator the same way that they are written: number of dollars, followed by a decimal point, and two numbers that represent cents. Divide students into pairs and give each twosome a calculator. Have the partners take turns entering a variety of money amounts in their calculator as you say the amounts aloud. Help students understand that the word *and* means "decimal."

**You have $100 to spend!**

Write the name of the person you will shop for on the line.
_Dad_

Cut out the catalog items that you want to buy for this person.

Glue the pictures below. Near each item, write its price.

Total cost of the items = $80.87
Money left over = $19.13

**You have $100 to spend!**

Choose an outfit that you would like to buy for yourself.

Cut out the clothing items from the catalog.

Glue the pictures below. Near each item, write its price.

Total cost of your outfit =
Money left over

$27.95    $11.00    $4.95
$16.98    $19.99

**You have $500 to spend!**

Choose three items that you would like to buy for your bedroom.

Cut out each item from the catalog.

Glue the pictures below. Near each item, write its price.

Total cost of the items =
Money left over

**Unlimited Spending!**

Pretend you could furnish a dream playroom.

Choose five items for the playroom.

Cut out the five items from the catalog.

Glue the pictures below. Near each item, write its price.

Total cost of the items =

### Now Let's Go Shopping

Provide each student with a 12" x 18" sheet of construction paper, a copy of page 142, scissors, and glue. Ask each student to fold his sheet of construction paper in half two times, then unfold it to reveal four equal-size sections. Next have every student cut out each gift box on his copy of page 142 and glue each one in a different section of his construction paper. Instruct students to complete the activities presented on the gift boxes in the corresponding sections of their papers. Since students will be sharing a calculator and a catalog with a partner, remind them of the importance of working together.

# You have $100 to spend!

Write the name of the person you will shop for on the line.

_____

Cut out the catalog items that you want to buy for this person.

Glue the pictures below.
Near each item, write its price.

Total cost of the items = _____
Money left over          = _____

# You have $100 to spend!

Choose an outfit that you would like to buy for yourself.

Cut out the clothing items from the catalog.

Glue the pictures below.
Near each item, write its price.

Total cost of your outfit  = _____
Money left over               = _____

# You have $500 to spend!

Choose three items that you would like to buy for your bedroom.

Cut out each item from the catalog.

Glue the pictures below.
Near each item, write its price.

Total cost of the items = _____
Money left over            = _____

# Unlimited Spending!

Pretend you could furnish a dream playroom.

Choose five items for the playroom.

Cut out the five items from the catalog.

Glue the pictures below.
Near each item, write its price.

Total cost of the items = _____

# Lookin' For Loot!

Ahoy, mateys! If you're searching for ways to reinforce money skills, you'll find this booty of swashbuckling subscriber ideas as precious as gold!

### A Penny A Day

A penny per day is a great investment in your youngsters' money skills. For this daily money activity, you will need a supply of play money and six resealable plastic bags. Label one bag "Pennies." Label the remaining bags "Nickels," "Dimes," "Quarters," "Half-dollars," and "Dollars." Beginning with the pennies bag, staple the plastic bags in order near your calendar display. Make certain that each bag can easily be opened and closed. Each day ask a different student to add a penny to the pennies bag; then as a class evaluate the contents of the bags and determine if coin exchanges are in order (for example, exchanging five pennies for a nickel or exchanging five pennies and a nickel for a dime). Conclude the activity by enlisting your youngsters' help in determining the value of the bagged money. As the year progresses, your students' money skills will grow right along with the amount of play money in the bags!

Barbara Turner—Gr. 2
North Central Schools
Pioneer, OH

### Bags Of Money!

Money skills are in the bag at this kid-pleasing free-time center! Place a supply of play money at a math center; then for each student label one side of a paper lunch bag with eight or more different money amounts. Distribute the bags and have each student personalize his bag. When a student has free time, he circles one money amount on the side of his bag; then he goes to the center and fills his empty bag with a matching amount of play money. At the end of the day, have those students who completed the free-time activity exchange money bags. If the amount of play money inside the bag equals the circled amount, a student draws an X over the circle; then he returns the play money to the center and the empty bag to its owner. If the money amounts do not match, the student returns the bag of play money to its owner. When all the money amounts on a student's money bag have been crossed out, reward the student with a special privilege or a small prize; then present him with a new money bag!

Tamsin Monnoleto—Grs. 3 & 4
John Glenn School
Pine Hill, NJ

### Spill The Beans

With this easy-to-make partner game, students practice their money-counting skills using lima beans. To make the game, give each student ten lima beans in a lidded container. Have each student use markers to program one side of his beans as follows: four beans with a blue dot, three beans with a red dot, and three beans with a green dot. Explain that a blue dot equals one cent, a red dot equals five cents, and a green dot equals ten cents. Then, playing with a partner, each student takes a turn shaking his container of beans, spilling them on the floor or a table, and determining the total value of the beans that have colored dots showing. The student who has the higher money value earns one point for the round of play. Students continue playing in this manner until a predetermined number of points are scored or game time is over. To increase the difficulty of the game, have each student label additional beans to represent quarters and half-dollars.

Donna Tobey—Gr. 1, Gulliver Academy, Coral Gables, FL

## A Booming Business

Enhance your math program, foster community awareness, and build responsibility in your students—all by forming a classroom stationery company! As a class agree upon a company name; then make samples of the note cards and stationery that will be offered for sale. Every few days review the state of the company and discuss decisions that need to be made, such as buying supplies and filling orders. Each month, after the students have determined the amount of profit their company has made, have them donate a portion of the profits to a charity or organization. For example, students may decide to buy food for the needy or adopt a zoo animal. Use the remainder of the profits to purchase books for the students' reading enjoyment.

Maria D. Morris—Gr. 2
Tulsa, OK

## Classroom Garage Sale

Culminate your money unit by having each child donate toys and books for a classroom garage sale. Display the items after labeling each one with a price tag. Position a toy cash register (or something similar) containing play money near the display. Give each student a resealable plastic bag of coin manipulatives. The manipulatives may vary, but the total value of the coins must be the same. Invite each student to shop for one item. After a student selects her item, she goes to the cash register where she pays the teacher or another classmate for her purchase. Repeat the activity again, inviting each student to shop for a second item. Students who have money remaining after their second purchases may return to the sale to spend the rest of their money. Children will love this shopping experience and gain a better understanding of money value. Store unpurchased items for a later sale or donate them to a local charity.

Linda Stiefel—Gr. 1
Walter Hall Elementary
League City, TX

## Coupon Math

Inspire youngsters to write creative story problems with the help of grocery-store coupons. Give each child two coupons and challenge him to write a story problem about his trip to the store. In his story, the child tells the price of each item he buys, how much money he spends, and how much money he saves by using the coupons. Below his story problem, the student shows the math calculations that gave him the answers in his story. Then he glues the coupons to the back of his paper.

adapted from an idea by Cathy Pace—Gr. 2
Mount Pleasant Elementary
Mount Pleasant, NC

144

# SCIENCE UNITS

# A Pocketful Of Science

## Exploring Yeast

Looking for a few hands-on activities to make your students bubble over with excitement? Rise to the occasion with this super collection. You'll find plenty of food for thought!

*ideas by Ann Flagg*

## Activity 1: Baking Bread

**You will need:**

a 4-loaf package of frozen bread dough
4 bread pans
nonstick cooking spray
4 tea towels
4 rulers
oven

**What to do:**

Early in the day, spray each bread pan with nonstick cooking spray and place the frozen loaves in the pans. Divide students into four groups and give each group a bread pan, a ruler, and a tea towel. Explain that the bread dough was made in advance and frozen. Ask students to share what they know about bread and bread preparation. Write a student-generated list of bread ingredients on the chalkboard. Next have each group measure the height of its bread dough. Record the resulting measurements by group. Then have each group use its tea towel to cover its bread dough. Store the projects in a desired classroom location. Allow the bread to rise according to the package instructions. Periodically ask the groups to observe and remeasure their projects. Record the results. Discuss any changes in the bread dough that the students observe. Then, when appropriate, bake the bread and enjoy!

**Questions to ask:**

1. What kinds of changes did you observe in the bread dough?
2. How did the temperature of the bread dough change?
3. Why do you think the size and smell of the dough changed?

### This is why:

Enriched white bread and whole-wheat bread provide us with important vitamins. The type of bread that you made today is called yeast bread. About 95 percent of commercially made bread in the United States is this type. Most yeast breads contain flour, salt, water, oil, sugar, and yeast. As the temperature of the frozen dough rose, the yeast in the bread was activated. This created a slight odor and caused the bread to rise. Other types of bread include flat breads (tortillas and pita bread) and quick breads (most muffins and biscuits).

## Activity 2: On The Rise

**For each small group you will need:**

a serving tray
4 clear plastic cups
masking tape
1 tbsp. each: flour, cooking oil, salt
a small thermos filled with warm water (approximately 115°)
1 tsp. each: yeast, sugar
4 stir sticks
a fine-tipped marker
a slice of sandwich bread

**What to do:**

Prepare a serving tray for each group. To do this, fill the four cups as follows: one tablespoon of flour in the first cup, one tablespoon of cooking oil in the second cup, one tablespoon of salt in the third cup, and one teaspoon each of yeast and sugar in the fourth cup. Place a stir stick in each cup. Arrange the thermos, marker, bread slice, and cups on the tray. Attach a small strip of masking tape on the tray in front of each cup.

Divide students into small groups and distribute the trays. Ask students to recall bread-making ingredients and help them identify the substances in the cups as such. Then, using the marker and masking-tape strips provided, have each group label its cups. Provide assistance as needed. Instruct one member of each group to fill each cup half full of warm water. Have the remaining members thoroughly stir the cups' contents. Have all group members observe the cups.

**Questions to ask:**

1. What happened when you mixed water into the flour (oil, salt)?
2. What happened when you mixed water into the sugar and yeast?
3. What ingredients do you think cause bread to rise? Why?
4. How might bubbles cause bread dough to rise?
5. Look closely at a slice of bread. What might have caused the tiny holes?

### This is why:

Yeast is an important bread-making ingredient. Yeast helps bread rise through a process called fermentation. During this process, yeast breaks down sugar into alcohol and carbon-dioxide gas. Gas bubbles, like the ones you saw today, are trapped by a substance found in bread dough called gluten. As the gas expands, the gluten stretches and causes the bread to rise. The alcohol that is produced during fermentation evaporates during baking. Baking also destroys the yeast, but the tiny holes in a slice of bread prove that yeast was present.

## Activity 3:
## The Power Of Sugar

**For each group you will need:**
a serving tray
2 stir sticks
a clear plastic cup labeled "Y"
a clear plastic cup labeled "Y + S"
one package of dry yeast
1 tsp. of sugar plus 1 tsp. more
thermos of warm water (approximately 115°)

**What to do:**
Prepare a tray for each group. To do this, pour one-half package of dry yeast into the cup labeled "Y." Pour the remainder of the yeast and 1 tsp. of sugar into the cup labeled "Y + S." Place a stir stick in each cup; then set the cups and the thermos of warm water on the serving tray.

Divide students into small groups and distribute the trays. Ask one member in each group to fill each cup half full of warm water. Enlist two more group members to thoroughly stir the contents of the cups. As a large group, compare and contrast what is happening in the different cups. Set the trays aside. Every few minutes, have the groups check the contents of their cups and report their findings. Next ask the students to predict what might happen if more sugar were added to the cups. Then have each group stir an additional teaspoon of sugar into one of its cups and observe the results.

**Questions to ask:**
1. Why do you think the ingredients of the two cups reacted differently?
2. What did you learn about yeast?
3. What happened when additional sugar was added to the yeast? Why?

### This is why:

Yeast is a living substance. It belongs to a group of simple organisms known as fungi. Yeasts reproduce rapidly, and they grow especially well in substances containing sugar. In breadmaking a commercial yeast called baker's yeast is used to make bread dough rise. Baker's yeast is manufactured in two forms—as a moist, compressed cake containing live, active yeast cells; and as dried grains. Because the yeast cells in dried yeast are alive but not active, the yeast must be mixed with warm water before it will begin to grow. Adding sugar to dried yeast provides the yeast with additional food, which increases its reproduction and growth.

## Activity 4:
## A Yeast Feast

**You will need:**
clear plastic cups
stir sticks
dry yeast
a pitcher of warm water (approximately 115°)
food for yeast (Suggestions include artificial sweetener, molasses, syrup, apple slices, honey, powdered milk, flour, coffee, and anything else you wish to try!)

**What to do:**
Review with students what they learned in "Activity 3." (Sugar gives yeast the energy it needs to grow and reproduce.) Challenge students to brainstorm other substances that might provide food for yeast. Make a list of student suggestions on the chalkboard. Combine this list with the supplies you have on hand. If possible, gather any missing items; then let the experimenting begin. Divide students into small groups. Give each group one or more cups—each containing a stir stick and a small amount of yeast. Next distribute the materials to be tested, making sure that a group is testing a different substance in each of its cups. Fill each group's cups half full of warm water. Instruct the groups to stir the contents of their cups and observe the results. Then have each group, in turn, report its findings.

**Questions to ask:**
1. Which of the items tested contain some type of sugar? How do you know?
2. Where you surprised by any of the test results? Why or why not?

### This is why:

Yeast can reproduce rapidly if it has sugar to fuel its process. Evidence of this growth is seen in the bubbles the yeast produces. Sugar can come from a variety of natural sources such as fruits, grains, honey, and molasses. Artificial sweetener may cause yeast to bubble a bit, but it does not contain enough nutritive sugars for yeast to thrive.

Pam Crane

147

# Dinosaur Days!

Fasten your seat belt! Hold on tight! You're about to travel back in time—and back to school—with this "dino-mite" collection of activities and reproducibles. It's the perfect cure for any Jurassic jitters your youngsters might be experiencing.

*ideas by Michele Converse Baerns & Lisa D. Reep*

## Hot Off The Press!

Even your most bashful brontos will find this back-to-school activity irresist-ible! Pair students and deem them pal-osauruses. Ask each student to inter-view her pal to find out about her family, special interests, favorite book, favorite food, and so on. Using the form on page 154, have each child write a short article about her pal. When the articles are written, instruct the pals to exchange papers. Then have each student create a dinosaur name for herself that includes her real name (such as Saratops or Meganasaurus). Then, in the box on her paper, she writes her prehistoric name and illustrates herself as a dinosaur. When she's finished, she cuts out her project on the bold lines.

Decorate the front page of a newspaper to show the title "Dino Times," the date, and a class byline. Mount your stu-dents' completed projects on the newspaper pages. Laminate the pages for durability; then place the newspaper in your class library for all to read. Extra! Extra! This one-of-a-kind prehistoric publication is hot off the press!

## We're BIG On Books!

This eye-catching bulletin board will be an enormous hit with your readersauruses! Mount a large dinosaur cutout onto your bulletin board that stretches from the floor to the ceiling. (See the patterns on page 153.) Add the title "We're BIG on Books!" Nearby keep a supply of drawing paper. For each book a youngster reads or has read to him, he copies the title of the book on a sheet of drawing paper, then illustrates his favorite part of the book. Display the completed projects on the bulletin board. Every few days, recognize each new addi-tion to the board and invite the appropriate readersaurus to tell about the book he read.

Laura Gill-Williams—Gr. 1
Hawthorne Elementary
Tulsa, OK

## Colossal Collages

What's on your menu for back-to-school success? Here's a meal plan that's sure to create a HUGE appetite for dinosaurs! Gather a supply of discarded magazines, and enlarge each of the three dinosaur patterns on page 153 onto a length of color-ful bulletin-board paper. Cut out the enlarged patterns and temporarily display them on a classroom wall. Invite your students to tell what they know about the eating habits of dinosaurs. Lead students to understand that all dinosaurs belonged to one of the following groups: *herbivores*—plant eaters; *carnivores*—meat eaters; or *omnivores*—meat and plant eaters. Then divide students into three groups. Armed with a stack of discarded magazines, scissors, glue, and one of the three dinosaur cutouts, have each group create a colossal collage by covering its dinosaur with magazine pictures show-ing the kinds of foods (meat, plants, or both) that its dinosaur would have eaten. As students are working, share additional facts about dinosaurs and their eating habits (see "Feast On These Facts!"). Display the completed projects in your class-room or school library. Challenge students to discover more facts about the eating habits of dinosaurs.

### Feast On These Facts!

- Meat-eating dinosaurs ate anything that moved, including other dinosaurs, insects, and birds.
- Plant-eating dinosaurs had to eat large amounts of plants to fuel their large bodies.
- Many of the plants that dinosaurs ate can be seen in gardens and parks today.
- Meat eaters often had short, powerful necks and big heads.
- Plant eaters often had long necks so that they could reach the treetops.
- There were many more herbivores than carnivores.
- Some herbivores had up to 960 teeth!
- Most carnivores walked on their back legs, leaving their front limbs free for catching and holding prey.

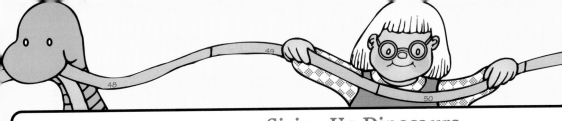

## Sizing Up Dinosaurs

Help your students conceptualize just how big dinosaurs were with this measurement activity. Cut a large supply of 1" x 13" newspaper strips. Divide students into groups and give each group the length of two dinosaurs. The members of each group glue newspaper strips end-to-end to create the actual length of each of their two dinosaurs. Explain to students that the precut newspaper strips measure 13 inches each, but when they are glued together end-to-end with a one-inch overlap, each strip will measure one foot. Suggest that the groups use markers to number the strips as they glue them together. Next have each group brainstorm three or four items in or around the school that might equal the length of each completed strip the group creates. After each group has tested its ideas, set aside time for the groups to report their findings to their classmates. If desired, mount the completed strips in a school hallway, gym, or cafeteria. Have each group design a poster to accompany each of its strips. Each poster should include a labeled illustration of the featured dinosaur and its length in feet. An illustration of something that compares in size to the dinosaur could also be shown.

*How Big Were The Dinosaurs?* by Bernard Most (Harcourt Brace & Company, 1994) is an excellent literature connection for this activity. In this colorful picture book, the sizes of several dinosaurs are described by comparing them to more familiar objects like a school bus, a basketball court, and a bowling alley.

## Not "Eggs-actly"!

Dinosaurs must have laid HUGE eggs, right? Not "eggs-actly"! Scientists know that the eggs laid by small- and medium-sized dinos were only about the size of chicken or turkey eggs! You see, if dinosaurs had laid eggs in proportion to their size, all the eggs would have broken unless they had very thick shells. And a baby dinosaur could never have chipped its way out of an egg like that. As for the shape of the eggs, fossils indicate that they were either egg-shaped, long and thin, or pointed at one end.

This dinosaur-egg project is sure to "egg-cite" your youngsters! To begin, have each child inflate a round or oblong balloon to about ten inches—the size of the largest dinosaur eggs ever found. Using strips of newspaper and a mixture of equal parts glue and water, have each student cover his entire balloon in papier-mâché. When the first layer has dried, have the students add a second layer. Provide a colorful assortment of tempera paints and invite students to decorate their dried eggs. Scientists can't be sure what color(s) the eggs of different dinosaurs were, so encourage your paleontologists to create spectacular egg specimens!

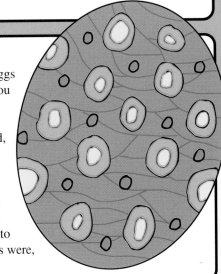

## Egads! More Eggs!

Just in case your youngsters' math skills have become extinct over summer vacation, here's a tasty way to revive them! Fill a large transparent container with dinosaur eggs (jelly beans) and display it in a prominent location. Ask the students to study the container of eggs during the next few days. When appropriate have each student complete a copy of the "Prehistoric 'Eggs-timate' Form" on page 154. Collect the forms; then divide the students into small groups. Distribute the dinosaur eggs among the groups, and give each group one or more copies of the graph on page 155. Working as a team, have each group sort its eggs on the graph and determine how many of each color it has. Pose a series of questions that could include "Which color of egg did you have the most (least) of?", "Did you have more red eggs or more green eggs?", and "How many eggs were either pink or orange?" Have each group use its graph to supply answers to the questions. Next find out how many eggs were in the jar. To do this have each group count its eggs, then combine the counts to determine the grand total. As each group is dividing its eggs among its members, return the "Prehistoric 'Eggs-timates'." Give the student with the most accurate estimate a HUGE round of applause; then let the egg-munching begin!

## Designer Dinosaurs

No one really knows what colors dinosaurs were. Even though a few fossilized pieces of skin have been found, scientists know that any color would have faded from the skin long before it was discovered. Since many present-day reptiles are gray or green, we know dinosaurs might have been gray or green, too. But there are also reptiles that have brightly colored skin—even some that have stripes and spots. Who know? Maybe dinosaurs had stripes and spots, too!

These colorful, prehistoric masterpieces are certain to be showstoppers! In advance, thin glue with water. Gather a variety of dinosaur templates and a class supply of art paper. In addition to paintbrushes, pencils, glue, and scissors, students will need access to a supply of colorful tissue paper, construction paper, and wallpaper. To begin, a student brushes the thinned glue onto a sheet of art paper. Then he places pieces of tissue paper on the glue so that they overlap, creating a sky-and-landscape background. Another layer of thinned glue may be applied if necessary. Next the student traces and cuts out several dinosaur shapes from construction paper or wallpaper, and glues them on top of the tissue-paper background.

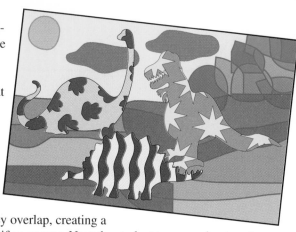

## Dinosaur Duds

The following poem makes a fun choral-reading project. If you decide to take the show on the road, ask each student to illustrate a decked-out dinosaur. Have youngsters hold their drawings facedown until the last line of the poem is read or recited; then have them display their dinos for all to see. The poem is also a fun choice for handwriting practice. After students have copied the prose in their prettiest penmanship, they'll be eager to illustrate their work.

### Decked-Out Dinosaurs
What kind of skin
Did a dinosaur wear?
Did it have some feathers?
Did it have some hair?

What were the colors
It wore in those days?
Were they bright reds and pinks
Or cool blues and grays?

How did it feel
To touch dinosaur skin?
Was it bumpy and thick
Or slick, smooth, and thin?

How do we know
What a dinosaur wore?
We imagine and color—
That's what crayons are for!

*by Lucia Kemp Henry*

## Plenty Of Prehistoric Humor

"Why did the Stegosaurus wear his spikes to the party? Because he was a sharp dresser!" … "What do you call a dinosaur telephone? A rep-dial!" These are only two of the many dinosaur riddles that fill the pages of *Tyrannosaurus Wrecks: A Book Of Dinosaur Riddles* by Noelle Sterne (Thomas Y. Crowell, 1979). The riddles in this humorous book are sure to have your young paleontologists rolling with laughter and eager to dig up their own prehistoric riddles. The results will be a mixture of clever word play, scientific fact, and lots of laughter. Consider displaying three or four student-created riddles each day during your dinosaur unit. At the end of the day, reward those students who answer the riddles correctly with dinosaur stickers.

Andrea M. Troisi—Library Media Specialist, Niagara Falls, NY

## Snacking On A Snackasaurus!

Perfect as a culminating activity, these yummy snackasauruses are easy and fun to make. Combine several packages of refrigerated sugar-cookie dough; then divide the dough into six parts. Knead food coloring into each portion to create red, green, blue, yellow, purple, and orange dough. Give each child a piece of foil and two portions of differently colored dough. Working atop his foil, the student shapes a dinosaur body from one color of dough; then he adds details such as horns, plates, and claws using his second dough color. Leaving the dinosaur creations on the foil, arrange the projects on a cookie sheet(s). Bake the cookies at 350° for 8 to 12 minutes. When the cookies are cool, they can be enjoyed with a carton of dinosaur milk (regular milk) or any flavor of prehistoric punch (fruit juice or drink mix). As students munch on their snackasauruses, encourage them to discuss dinosaurs—what they've learned and what else they hope to find out!

# For "Readersauruses" Only!
## Books About Dinosaurs

Tantalizing theories attempt to explain the possible causes for their disappearances, but have the dinosaurs ever really vanished? Those cold-blooded Mesozoic reptiles have managed to shake the sand from their fossilized remains and spring to life in books, toy stores, and even the movies! Books about dinosaurs are far from extinction—but we think this collection will bring a herd of readersauruses racing to your bookshelves!

*books reviewed by Deborah Zink Roffino*

## Just-For-Fun Fiction

### Dinosaur Bob And His Adventures With The Family Lazardo
*Written & Illustrated by William Joyce*
*HarperCollins Publishers, 1988*

Great green nonsense rules in this delight of a storybook. Stylized and smooth, Dr. Lazardo and his flawless family trek to Africa. After a triumphant journey, they return to home-sweet-home with an endearing, unassuming, most agreeable pet dinosaur named Bob. His enormity is a pure asset and a tremendous diversion for the snazzy little town of Pimlico Hills.

### Dinosaur Days
*Written by Linda Manning & Illustrated by Vlasta Van Kampen*
*BridgeWater Books, 1993*

A dino a day creates one wild week for the little girl who lives in this house! From a dinosaur sliding down a drainpipe, to a dive-bombing dino that enters through the bathroom ceiling—mayhem flies through the pages of this fanciful book. It's a review of the days of the week that is nearly effervescent. Text and pictures constitute a buoyant enticement for beginning readers. A manageable glossary of dinosaur names is also included.

### Dazzle The Dinosaur
*Written & Illustrated by Marcus Pfister*
*Translated by J. Alison James*
*North-South Books, 1994*

This winsome tale introduces two tiny dinosaurs, one of whom turns his distinction into the stuff of heroes. Young Dazzle sports a reflective, iridescent spine that severely cuts down on camouflage. That does not stop the resourceful critter and his pal from reclaiming a cave for his new family. Friendship and adventure support an endearing story line that features a full range of prehistoric characters and a soft palette of watercolor purples, blues, and greens.

### Time Flies
*Illustrated by Eric Rohmann*
*Crown Publishers, Inc.; 1994*

Turn the pages of this 1995 Caldecott Honor book and take a journey that thrills the eye and sets loose the imagination. In this wordless tale, a bird swoops and flutters its way around a dinosaur exhibit. Its seemingly innocent venture takes a turn for the worse when one dinosaur appears to be interested in making a meal of the bird. Brilliantly executed oil paintings bring life to the dinosaurs and flying reptiles featured.

### Can I Have A Stegosaurus, Mom? Can I? Please!?
*Written by Lois G. Grambling & Illustrated by H. B. Lewis*
*BridgeWater Books, 1995*

A youngster could lie in bed and dream terrible nightmares about a large intruding reptile—or a more inventive mind might catalog the incredible benefits of having a dinosaur at one's disposal. Of course, while the parades, Halloween, football games, and life in general would be infinitely better with a pet dinosaur, Mom might still need a bit of convincing.

## Dinosaurs! Strange And Wonderful

*Written by Laurence Pringle & Illustrated by Carol Heyer*
*Boyds Mills Press, 1995*

Like postcards from prehistory, the many pages carry torn-edged pictures with enormous reptiles. This overview of Mesozoic inhabitants discusses dinosaurs that walked, climbed, swam, and flew. With many literal translations of their Latin and Greek names, the dinosaurs in this book roam dense, primitive landscapes with murky, methane-saturated skies. Familiar names like *Triceratops* and *Stegosaurus* blend with more outlandish designations, such as the chicken-size *Compsognathus* and the wolflike hunter *Velociraptor*.

## An Alphabet Of Dinosaurs

*Written by Peter Dodson & Illustrated by Wayne D. Barlowe*
*Scholastic Inc., 1995*

The alphabet epithet might mislead. This novel examination of 26 types of creatures challenges minds and vocabularies. Primeval, shadowed paintings face a page of large-size text with definitions, short facts, and a skeletal sketch. Archeologists keep digging up more fossilized beasts, and "dinophiles" can surely add to their store of data with this set of creatures. A concluding chart summarizes the study. This picture book could come with a guarantee to turn on new, reluctant, or picky readers.

## You Can Name 100 Dinosaurs!

*Written by becker&mayer! and Illustrated by Randy Chewning*
*Scholastic Inc., 1944*

Forget the fact that there is no story line; this book will be a popular choice in any library. Small, detailed drawings distinguish 100 dinosaurs. Identified by bones and fossil footprints nearly 150 million years old, these extinct hulks demonstrate powerful persistence in the hearts of children. With this sturdy board book, students can trace, research, and learn to spell and pronounce the tortuous names in this collection. The dinosaurs are grouped into Triassic, Jurassic, and Cretaceous period dwellers.

## Notable Nonfiction

### The Big Book Of Dinosaurs

*Written by Angela Wilkes & Illustrated with photographs*
*Dorling Kindersley, Inc.; 1994*

For scrutiny or browsing, for tracking teeth of terror, or for utter amazement—direct young minds to this big book. Irresistible photos of museum dinosaurs and actual skeletons command attention across full-page displays. Parts are labeled and factoids pop up in every space. The photos permit close-up examination of leathery hides, mighty jaws, and spiky claws. The finale is an in-scale composite picture that compares the sizes of the dinosaurs in this research book.

### Triceratops: On The Trail Of The Incredible Armored Dinosaur
### American Museum Of Natural History Series

*Written by William Lindsay; Mark Norell, Consultant*
*Dorling Kindersley, Inc.; 1993*

The *ceratoids* or horned dinosaurs may have deflected predators with their conspicuous spiky protrusions, but after several million years the appendages only seem to attract youngsters. Exploration is encouraged in this comprehensive investigation of one family of prehistoric creatures. Other books in this spectacular series by a British paleontologist enable readers to find models, facts, fossils, and skeletons of *Barosaurus, Tyrannosaurus,* and *Corythosaurus*. All volumes feature maps and real photographs from famed expeditions and dinosaur digs.

# Dinosaur Patterns

Use with "Colossal Collages" and "We're BIG On Books!" on page 148.

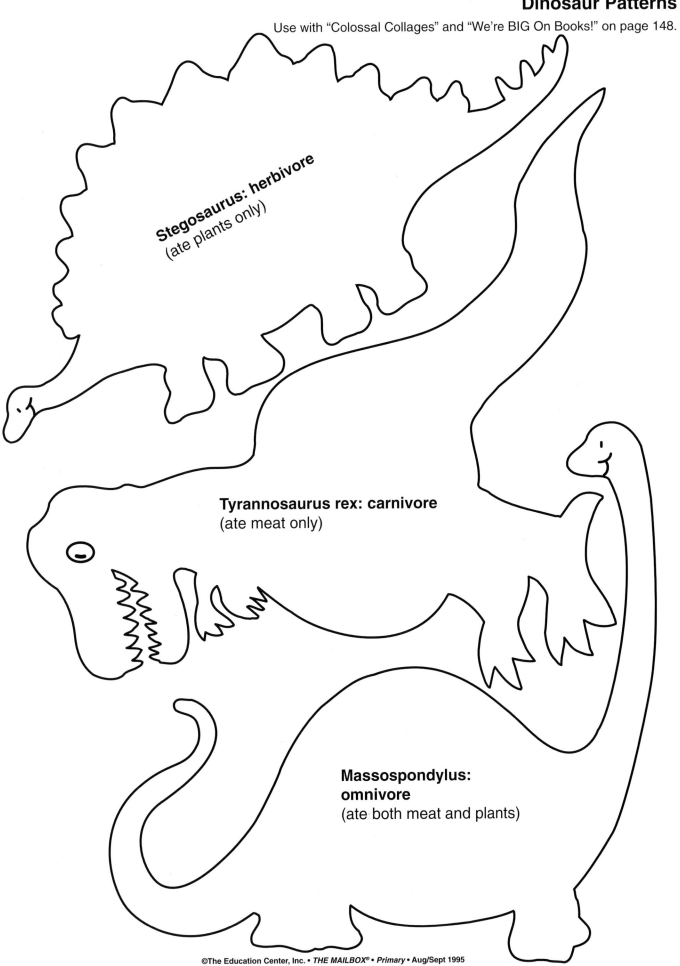

**Stegosaurus: herbivore**
(ate plants only)

**Tyrannosaurus rex: carnivore**
(ate meat only)

**Massospondylus:
omnivore**
(ate both meat and plants)

## Forms

Use the newspaper form with "Hot Off The Press!" on page 148.

*Dino Times* _____

[picture box]

_____
_____
_____
_____
_____
_____
_____
_____

Use the form below with "Egads! More Eggs!" on page 149.

Name _____

# Prehistoric "Eggs-timate"

 I think there are _____ eggs in the jar.

| purple | yellow | green | red | white | orange | black | pink |

# MOUNTAINS OF FIRE

## An Inside Look At Volcanoes

Volcanoes are natural events that happen all over the world. Use the following activities and reproducibles to get the inside scoop on a very hot topic!

*ideas by Ann Flagg*

## Activity 1: The Inside Story

**You will need:**
a globe        a paring knife
a hard-boiled egg in its shell

**Each student needs:**
a copy of page 158        a pencil
crayons        scissors        glue
a 9" x 12" sheet of construction paper

**What to do:**
Display the globe. Ask students how scientists would gather the information needed to make such an accurate model of the earth. Then ask students how scientists would learn about the inside of the earth. Explain that scientists aren't positive what's inside the earth because they can't see or visit there. However, scientists do have ways of gathering information about the inside of the earth. Tell students that scientists believe that the earth has three main layers, like an egg. Display the hard-boiled egg; then slice the egg in half and hold up one cross section for student viewing. Explain that the earth has a thin *crust* similar to an eggshell. Beneath this crust lies a layer of hot rock called the *mantle* (the egg white), and beneath the mantle lies the *core* (the egg yolk). Tell students that scientists also believe that the earth's core has two parts—an inner core and an outer core. The inner core is solid rock. The outer core is *magma* or melted rock.

**Questions to ask:**
1. Why do scientists believe the earth has three main layers?
2. What other items can you think of that have three main layers?

*This is why:*
No drill hole has ever reached as deep as the earth's mantle. However, sometimes when magma rises to the top of the earth (during a volcanic eruption), it tears off fragments of the mantle along the way. These fragments of very heavy mantle rock are then found in lava flows. The density and chemistry of the mantle fragments confirm the present theories that scientists have about the inside of the earth. Some items that have three main layers are apples, pears, and peanut M&M's® candies.

**Next:**
Distribute the student materials listed above. Have each student make a model of the inside of the earth.

## Activity 2: A Hot Escape

**You will need:**
a hot plate        a pot of boiling water
a spoon        a raw egg

**What to do:**
Hold up the raw egg. Remind students that the egg—like the earth—has three main layers. Tell students that scientists believe that the earth's crust is made up of several huge *plates* or sections. Make a few cracks in the eggshell by gently tapping the egg on a hard surface. Show students the resulting cracks in the eggshell. Explain that the solid areas of the shell are similar to the plates in the earth's crust. Then use the spoon to lower the egg into the boiling water. Have students gather around to watch what happens to the egg as it heats up.

**Questions to ask:**
1. What happened to the egg? the eggshell?
2. Where did the liquid ooze out of the shell? Why?
3. Where might hot liquid ooze out of the earth?
4. Why is a volcano like a window to the inside of the earth?

*This is why:*
When the liquid inside the raw egg heated up, it expanded and eventually pushed its way through the weak points in the shell—the cracks. In a similar manner, hot liquid rock inside the earth pushes its way out of the earth through a weak spot in the earth's crust. These weak spots are along the edges of the earth's plates. When a volcano occurs, it enlarges an opening in the earth's crust. By studying these openings and the materials that erupt from them, scientists learn about the inside of the earth.

# Activity 3: Pushy Plates

**Each student needs:**

a copy of page 159                    a pencil

**What to do:**

Distribute page 159. Ask students to identify the continents and the oceans shown on the map. Next review "Activity 2: A Hot Escape" from page 156, in which students learned that the earth's crust is made up of several large plates. Explain that this map shows some of these plates. Ask students to locate the Pacific plate and color it orange. Then have each student use his finger to trace the edge of this crust plate. Tell students that this area is called the Ring (or Circle) Of Fire. Then have the students use their maps to answer the following questions:

**Questions to ask:**

1. Where do you think the most volcanoes are?
2. Are all volcanoes on land?
3. Why do you think the edge of the Pacific plate is called the Ring Of Fire?
4. Can you find any volcanoes that are not near the edge of a crust plate?

*This is why:*

Volcanoes can occur on land and in water, anywhere on Earth. However, they are more common in some parts of the world than in others. This is because most volcanoes occur where two of the earth's plates—or sections of crust—meet. When the plates respond to forces and movements inside the earth, they may grind past each other, move apart, or even collide. This can result in intense geological activity such as a volcano or an earthquake.

Of all the active volcanoes in the world, over three-fourths are in the Ring (or Circle) Of Fire. However, some volcanoes—including those in Hawaii—are located far from plate boundaries. Scientists believe that these volcanoes develop when a huge column of hot magma rises from inside the earth. In some cases this plume of melted rock comes close enough to the earth's surface to break through the crust and form a volcano.

**Next:**

Have students complete page 159.

# Activity 4: Blast Off!

**You will need:**

two large bottles of seltzer water (unsweetened carbonated beverage)
a class supply of clear plastic cups
a sink or similar container

**What to do:**

Distribute the clear plastic cups. Open one bottle of seltzer water and pour a small amount of liquid into each child's cup. Ask students to observe the bubbles in their cups and describe what happens. (The bubbles move upward and eventually disappear.) Next display the unopened bottle of carbonated water. Explain that the bottle of water is like the inside of a miniature volcano. The bottle represents the liquid rock inside the earth. The neck of the bottle is like a small tunnel or vent that forms as hot rock pushes upward toward the earth's surface. The lid represents a weak spot or opening in the earth's crust. Next vigorously shake the bottle for one minute. Ask students to predict what would happen if you removed the bottle's lid. Then—holding the bottle away from you and over a sink or other similar container—unscrew the lid for a dramatic eruption.

**Questions to ask:**

1. What happened when the bottle lid was opened?
2. How does this activity show us what happens before and during a volcanic eruption?
3. Why did the eruption from the plastic bottle stop?
4. Why do you think a volcanic eruption stops?

*This is why:*

When rock melts deep inside the earth, it produces a gas. Carbonated water is simply water mixed with a gas (carbon dioxide). When carbonated water is poured into a cup, the gas bubbles rise to the top. In much the same manner, gas-filled rock moves upward because it is lighter than the rock surrounding it. When a bottle of carbonated water is shaken, the gas is forced out of the water and it rushes upward to escape. But since the gas cannot escape the airtight bottle, pressure builds inside. When the lid is loosened, the gas rushes out, causing an eruption of gas and liquid.

When volcanoes erupt a similar thing happens. As hot, gas-filled magma rises toward the earth's surface, it forms a chamber or reservoir a few miles beneath the earth's surface by melting surrounding rock. The gas-filled magma is under great pressure. If this pressurized, liquid rock finds a weak spot in the earth's surface, it blasts through with great force. When hot gases and rock escape above the ground, it is called a volcanic eruption. But just like the bottle of carbonated water's brief explosion, a volcanic eruption lasts only until all the gases have escaped.

Name _____

## The Inside Story

Make a model of the earth's layers.
Use the code to color the circles.
Cut out the circles.

**Color Code**
inner core = red
outer core = orange
mantle = yellow
crust = brown

Stack the circles to show the
    layers of the earth.
Glue.

**Bonus Box:** Glue your project on a sheet of construction paper. On the construction paper, copy the names of the earth's layers that are listed in the Color Code. Draw an arrow to connect each name to its layer of the earth.

**Note To Teacher:** Use with "Activity 1: The Inside Story" on page 156.

Name _____

# Mountains Of Fire

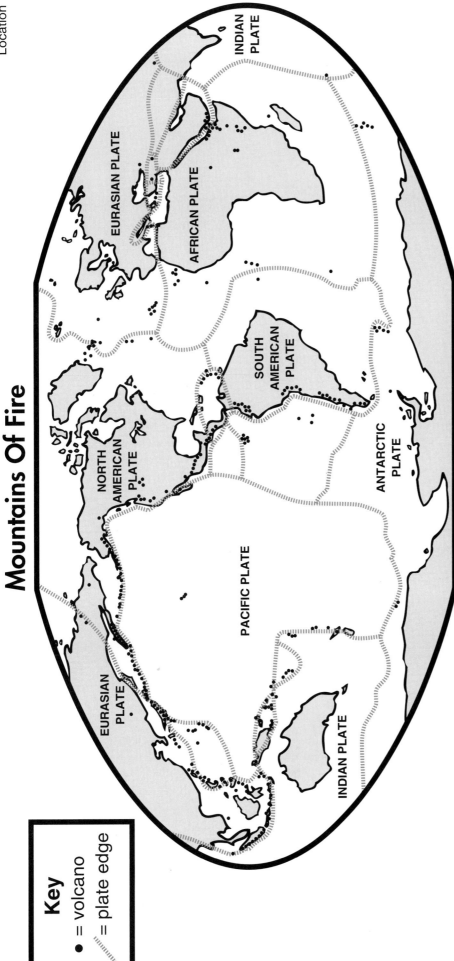

**Key**
● = volcano
░ = plate edge

EURASIAN PLATE

AFRICAN PLATE

INDIAN PLATE

NORTH AMERICAN PLATE

SOUTH AMERICAN PLATE

ANTARCTIC PLATE

PACIFIC PLATE

EURASIAN PLATE

INDIAN PLATE

**Write "true" or "false" in each blank. Use the map.**

1. All volcanoes occur on land. _____

2. There are no volcanoes in Africa. _____

3. Volcanoes only happen in warm climates. _____

4. Scientists think the earth's crust is divided into plates. _____

5. Most volcanoes are found in the center of a plate. _____

6. There are volcanoes all over North America. _____

7. The edge of the Pacific plate is called the Ring Of Fire. _____

8. Australia has very few volcanoes. _____

**Note To Teacher:** Use with "Activity 3: Pushy Plates" on page 157.

# MIND OVER MATTER

## Getting A Grip On The Basics Of Matter

So what's the matter? Has the thought of teaching your students the basics of matter turned you topsy-turvy? If that's the case, then it's time to get a grip—on matter, that is! Use this collection of hands-on activities and teaching ideas to help students understand that *matter* really matters!

*ideas by Sue Boulais and Ann Flagg*

### Learning About Matter

Give meaning to matter with this simple classroom activity. Tell students that matter is anything that takes up space and has weight; then challenge them to find matter within the classroom. After each child has named at least one item, ask students to survey the room again—but this time looking for items that are *not* matter. Guide students to determine that almost everything that can be seen and touched is matter.

### What About Air?

Air is matter—though youngsters may find this idea difficult to grasp. These quick demonstrations will help students get a grip on air. Ask each child to place her palms on her chest as she takes a few deep breaths. Have a student describe what happens to her chest when she breathes in air. *(It expands to make room for the air.)* Next have students observe you inflating a balloon. This time ask students what is inside the balloon. *(Air.)* Lastly capture some air inside a plastic produce bag; then seal the bag with a twist tie. Ask questions like "What do you see inside the bag?" and "How do you know something is inside the bag?" To further illustrate that air takes up space, place the inflated bag on a table and balance a book or other solid object atop it. Ask students to describe what is keeping the object from touching the table.

### Taking Up Space

This small-group activity makes it clear that not all things take up space. Give each small group of students a permanent marker, a golf ball, and a large plastic cup half-filled with water. Ask one student in each group to draw a line on the outside of his group's cup to mark the water level. (This reading should be taken at eye level.) Then ask each group to predict what will happen when a golf ball is placed in the cup. When the predictions are made, have one student from each group gently drop a golf ball into the group's cup. Then ask another student in each group to mark the new water level. Discuss how this activity proves that a golf ball is matter. *(It takes up space.)* Then ask students if they think *light* is matter. In turn, shine a flashlight on each cup of water. Allow time for the groups to check their water levels, then take a vote—is light matter? Students will see firsthand that because light does not take up space, it is not matter. (Examples of other things that are not matter are sound, shadows, thoughts, feelings, and dreams.)

### Matter Really Matters

Matter is very important;
It makes up the things that we see.
Without it, all things as we know them
Would simply just not even be!

We wouldn't have fish in the ocean;
We wouldn't have clouds in the air.
No people in houses, no grass on the ground.
Why, the ground wouldn't even be there!

Matter is very important—
Especially to you and to me.
Everyone's made up of matter…
Without it, we just wouldn't be!

*by Sue Boulais*

(MATTER REALLY MATTERS *by Sue Boulais. Copyright ©1995 by Sue Boulais. Reprinted by permission of the author. Teachers may reproduce for classroom use.*)

160

# Properties Of Matter

When you explore properties of matter with the ever popular pogs, be warned—your students could go "pog" wild! For this activity each child needs a pog, paper, a pencil, and crayons. Explain that scientists describe matter using physical properties such as weight, color, hardness, shape, and size. When applicable, scientists also describe matter by its taste and smell. To begin have each child list physical properties of his pog. Encourage students to list properties that would help other scientists differentiate their pogs from the rest of the pogs. Next collect the papers and the pogs. Redistribute the papers, making sure that each student receives a paper other than his own; then scatter the pogs on a tabletop. In turn have small groups of students approach the table and try to identify the pogs described on the papers they hold. When a student thinks he has a match, he consults the classmate who created his list of properties. If the classmate does not confirm his pog identification, the student keeps looking. When most of the pogs have been identified, ask students to describe the properties that most pogs share. Also find out why they think some pogs are more difficult to identify than others. Then if desired display the pogs at a center. Students who visit the center can sort and classify the pogs by common properties.

# Matter In A Bag

Solid, liquid, or gas? This partner activity has students identifying physical states of matter. Prepare a matter bag for every two students by placing different matter in each of several resealable plastic bags. (Inflate a few bags with air to represent gases. For liquids consider tinting water in a variety of colors. Be sure to avoid any liquids that might stain in the event of an accidental spill.) You will also need two or three sets of balance scales displayed around the room. Pair students and give each twosome a matter bag, a copy of the gameboard on page 165, and a game marker. Demonstrate how to use the gameboard; then let the fun begin. When pairs identify their matter, have them trade matter bags with other pairs who are finished and repeat the activity.

# Solid, Liquid, *And* Gas?

Up to this point, students probably haven't considered that matter can change states or forms. For example a solid can become a liquid, and vice versa. This quick demonstration shows students how a solid turns into a liquid and then into a gas! Gather students around a preheated electric skillet. Students should be able to observe the skillet, but not touch it. Place an ice cube in the center of the skillet. As the ice melts, ask students to describe what is happening to the solid matter in the skillet. Then, as the liquid matter begins to boil and *steam,* ask the students what is happening to the matter. Conclude the demonstration when all evidence of the matter is gone. Challenge students to ponder other examples of changing matter in their everyday lives.

# More Changing Matter

Students see three states of matter in this exciting demonstration. Using a funnel, pour vinegar (a liquid!) into a two-liter soda bottle. Stop pouring when the level of vinegar rises above the bottle's plastic base. Remove the funnel and set the bottle aside. Wipe the funnel clean; then use it to pour baking soda into a large balloon. When the balloon is half-full of baking soda, remove the funnel. Walk around the room and ask students to feel the lower half of the balloon—verifying that the matter inside is a solid. Then, being careful not to spill the baking soda into the bottle, secure the neck of the balloon over the bottle's mouth. When the balloon is securely attached to the bottle, lift the rest of the balloon over the bottle, causing the baking soda to drop into the two-liter bottle and the vinegar. Give the balloon momentary support as a resulting chemical reaction produces a gas inside the bottle and quickly inflates the balloon. What a *gas!*

# Amazing Matter

Youngsters are sure to enjoy concocting these two recipes. The mixtures are unique because each one has properties of both solids and liquids. Lead students to understand that these types of matter are very difficult for scientists to categorize—but lots of fun for students to make! After each recipe is made, have students conduct a series of tests (see "Testing, Testing" below) on the resulting mixture to see if they can determine whether each substance is most like a liquid or a solid.

## Solquid

**Each student needs:**
a paper-covered work space
a 9-oz. plastic cup
4 tablespoons of cornstarch
2 tablespoons of water
a wooden craft stick

Combine the cornstarch and the water in the plastic cup. Stir the mixture with the craft stick. The mixture should appear to be solidifying. If it does not, stir in a bit more cornstarch; then remove the craft stick. When the stick is removed, the substance should appear to be a liquid. But when the mixture is poked, stirred, or handled, it has properties of a solid.

## Goop

**Each student needs:**
a paper-covered work space
a 9-oz. plastic cup
1 tablespoon of liquid starch
2 tablespoons of white glue
food coloring (optional)
a wooden craft stick

Combine the liquid starch, glue, and food coloring in the plastic cup. Stir until well mixed; then let the mixture stand for approximately five minutes. Stir the mixture again and let it stand for five more minutes. Repeat the stir-and-stand process once more; then handle the goop and enjoy its properties.

- Pour the mixture from one hand to another. What happens?
- Poke the mixture with your finger or the craft stick. What happens?
- Roll the mixture into a ball; then try to hold the ball. What happens?

## Testing, Testing

Encourage students to use these methods and others of their own to test the properties of Solquid and Goop. Are these substances solids or liquids—or both?

## The Basics Of Matter

This booklet project can be completed at school or at home. Make construction-paper copies of pages 163 and 164 for each student. After each child has cut out his booklet pages and cover, give him three more blank booklet pages. Ask the student to stack his booklet pages so that a blank booklet page follows each duplicated page; then have him place his cover on top of the stack before stapling the booklet together. To complete the booklet, the student cuts pictures that represent the states of matter from discarded magazines, newspapers, and catalogs. He then glues the cutouts on the appropriate booklet pages. Each blank page should be covered with cutouts representing the matter introduced on the previous booklet page. The student also decorates and personalizes the cover of his booklet to his own liking. Students will enjoy looking at their classmates' completed projects. By golly, matter is everywhere!

# The Basics Of Matter

by _____

 **Solids**

A solid's a solid.
It doesn't change shape.
It can't move around;
It stays in one place.

Your desk is a solid
And so is your chair.
Just look in your classroom—
Wow! They're everywhere!

## Gases

Air is a gas.
We can't see it, that's true;
But often we feel it
In things that we do.

It keeps up a kite.
Air fills up a bubble.
Without it to breathe,
We would be in BIG trouble.

## Liquids

A liquid moves smoothly.
We say that it flows
From one place to another—
How quickly it goes!

We know that most liquids
Are easy to see.
With no shape of their own,
They're not like you and me.

Names _____

# Matter In A Bag

Place your marker in the first box.
Follow the directions. Use your bag of matter.

---

**1.**

Does your matter
take up space?

**Yes**—go to box 12.
**No**—go to box 8.

**2.**

Lay down your bag.
Gently press your hand
on the bag.
Can you make your matter
fill the whole bag?
**Yes**—go to box 6.
**No**—go to box 5.

**3.**

Gently squeeze your matter.
Can you change the shape
of your matter with
a squeeze?

**Yes**—go to box 2.
**No**—go to box 7.

---

**4.**

Are you sure?
When you fold down the top of
your bag, the size of your matter
changes from  to ☐.

Go back to box 6.
Think about the question again.

**5.**

Poke your matter with
your finger.
Does your finger go
through the matter?

**Yes**—go to box 10.
**No**—go to box 9

**6.**

Now try this!
Fold down the top
of your bag.

Did you change the size
of your matter?
**Yes**—go to box 11.
**No**—go to box 4.

---

**7.**

Squeeze your matter again.
Does it change shape?

**Yes**—go to box 6.
**No**—go to box 5.

**8.**

*Whoops!*
Go back to box 1.
All matter takes
up space!

**9.**

Your matter
is a
**solid!**

---

**10.**

Hold your bag of matter like this:

Now hold it like this:

Did the size of your matter change?

**Yes**—go to box 15. **No**—go to box 14.

**11.**

Your
matter
is a
**gas!**

**12.**

Place your bag of matter
on a balance scale.
Does it weigh more than
the empty bag?

**Yes**—go to box 3.
**No**—go to box 13.

---

**13.**

Good try, but you must go
back to box 12.

All matter will make the
scales tip because all matter
has weight.

**14.**

Your
matter
is a
**liquid!**

**15.**

Think again!
The size of your matter
didn't change.
Only its shape changed!

Go back to box 10
and choose "No."

---

**Note To Teacher:** Use with "Matter In A Bag" on page 161.

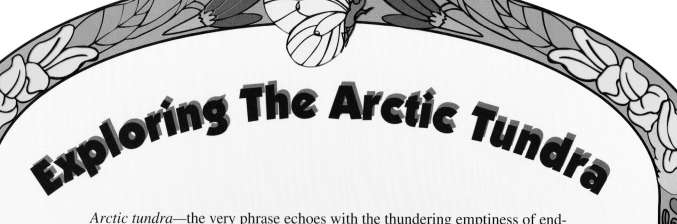

# Exploring The Arctic Tundra

*Arctic tundra*—the very phrase echoes with the thundering emptiness of endless stretches of vast, frozen wasteland. But take another look! The earth's tundra is not as desolate as it first appears. In fact, it's a fragile ecosystem that supports an intricate web of life. Use this collection of activities to visit a biome that beckons to be explored.

*ideas contributed by Laura Horowitz*

## Where Is It?

The tundra is a rolling plain that spreads across the northernmost edge of each continent surrounding the Arctic Ocean. It begins wherever the great forests of the North end. From there it continues to the Arctic Coast and the islands offshore. The tundra covers much of the coast of Alaska, and in Canada it reaches south of the Arctic Circle deep into North America. Use the mapping activity on page 172 to introduce your youngsters to the tundra. When this activity has been completed, turn the maps into journal covers by following the directions in "A Treeless Wonder?"

Amazing, But True!

Facts About The Tundra
by Eli Jetson

## A Treeless Wonder?

The word *tundra* means "treeless," and that pretty much describes this chilly northern location. The few trees that do grow on the tundra are either growing in sheltered valleys or are not recognizable. Why? Because a 100-year-old tree on the tundra can be less than one foot tall! Your study of the tundra is sure to reveal many more amazing facts. Have students record this tundra fact and others in journals entitled "Amazing, But True! Facts About The Tundra." To make these "tundra-rific" journals, have each child cut out his completed map project from page 172 and mount it on a 9" x 12" sheet of construction paper. After each child has titled and personalized his journal cover, have him staple several sheets of blank paper between his cover and a second sheet of 9" x 12" construction paper. Ready, set, write!

## Tundra Talk

Set the stage for lots of Arctic antics by inviting your students to choose tundra-related names for team and small-group activities. Suggest names like *Cool Caribou, Eager Ermines, Wise Wolves,* and *Magnificent Musk Oxen;* then invite students to brainstorm additional names. The thematic names could also be assigned to rows or clusters of student desks: "The Happy Hares may now line up!"

# The Changing Seasons

The seasons of the year on the tundra are probably very different from the seasons your youngsters normally experience. Travel to the tundra, and briefly step into each of its seasons with this activity. Give each student four 3 1/2" x 9" strips of white construction paper, and ask him to write the name of a different season at the top of each one. As a class talk about each tundra season. (If desired, begin your discussion by sharing the seasonal information below.) Conclude each discussion by asking the students to illustrate the season on their appropriately labeled strip. To complete this project, have each youngster mount his four illustrations in seasonal order on a 12" x 18" sheet of black construction paper. Display the eye-catching projects on a bulletin board entitled "A Year On The Tundra."

**Fall:** Autumn on the tundra is very brief. Animals are busy feasting on the remaining seeds and berries. By the end of September, there is snow on the ground. The ground squirrel begins to dig its winter den, and the caribou gather in herds to start their trip back into the forest. The air turns colder and colder. Winter is almost here.

**Winter:** The tundra looks deserted, but wait! Even in the bitter cold, the white-coated Arctic foxes and wolves must search for food. A snowy owl is preparing to swoop down on a little, white-furred lemming. The nights gradually get longer until—for more than a week—the sun doesn't even shine! Brrr! It's 50° below zero!

**Spring:** March, April, and May—it should be *spring!* But on the tundra there is still snow on the ground. The days are getting longer. The animals can feel the snow softening. Soon there will be lots of melted snow. Geese begin to arrive. So do ducks, swans, and millions of other birds. They are coming to the tundra to build their nests. Caribou also begin their trek to the tundra.

**Summer:** At last the snow is gone and the tundra is coming alive! Plants are pushing up out of the soil; flowers are beginning to bloom. Insects that were frozen are now searching for food. Many Arctic animals are losing their winter coats and growing lighter coats for the summer. Caribou, foxes, wolves, bears, and ermines are having babies. Look! There's a butterfly! The days are long, sunny, and cool.

# A Tundra Tune

Adapt these Arctic lyrics to the tune of "My Bonnie Lies Over The Ocean." For even more frosty fun, invite your tundra explorers to compose additional verses.

There are bears and hares on the tundra,
Musk oxen and Arctic wolves, too.
They roam on the plains of the tundra,
With deer that are called caribou.

*Chorus:*
*Arctic tundra—a cold place without many trees!*
*Arctic tundra—a cold place without many trees!*

A fox hunts its food on the tundra.
A lemming escapes underground!
Some creatures that live on the tundra,
Are often not there all year round.

*Chorus*

The winter is cold on the tundra.
There's darkness all the day through.
When summer comes to the tundra,
The sun shines all day—it's true!

*Chorus*

It never gets warm on the tundra.
The temperature's cold all year.
If you plan to visit the tundra,
Dress warmly and cover your ears!

# Animals Of The Arctic

When students complete this booklet project, Arctic animals will be popping up everywhere! To make each booklet page:

1. Color and cut out a picture of an Arctic animal (patterns on pages 174). Set the cutout aside.
2. Fold in half a 9" x 12" sheet of construction paper.
3. Center a 1 1/2" x 2 1/2" tagboard rectangle on the fold and draw two 2 1/2" lines.
4. Remove the rectangle and cut on the resulting lines.
5. Unfold the paper to a 90° angle. Pull the narrow strip forward and crease it in the opposite direction from the fold.
6. Glue the cutout from step 1 to the front of the protruding strip; then write a fact or two about the animal below the picture.

The musk ox's fur has two layers. The inner, woolly fur keeps in body heat, and the long, outer hairs keep out wind and water.

To compile the pages into a booklet, stack the pages so that the folds are aligned. Starting with the top two pages, glue the pages back-to-back, making sure that the folds stay in line. To make a cover, fold in half a 10" x 14" piece of construction paper. Slip the glued booklet pages inside the folded cover, and glue them in place. Decorate the booklet cover as desired.

# Arctic Plants

Here's a fun way to explore plant life of the tundra. Duplicate page 173 for your students and yourself. As your youngsters prepare their lotto gameboards, cut apart the plants on your copy of the page and place the cutouts in a container. Give each youngster 20 miniature marshmallows or yogurt-covered raisins to use as game markers. To play, announce the type of game to be played such as "Three in a row," "Four corners," or "Five in a row." Then, one at a time, draw a cutout from the container and name the featured plant. Each student places a marker on the corresponding square on her gameboard. If desired, have the winner of the first game become the caller of the second game and so on. At the conclusion of the activity—while students are munching on their game markers—talk about plant life on the tundra. Discuss how the tundra's short growing season affects plant life; then challenge your tundra explorers to dig up other interesting information about Arctic plants!

# Projects Aplenty!

Pull on your parkas; it's cold in the Arctic! For a fun art activity that has students dressing likenesses of themselves in warm and fuzzy parkas, see page 58 of this annual. On that same page, you'll find the perfect follow-up project for a discussion of the *aurora borealis* (northern lights). Wow! Learning about the Arctic tundra is loads of fun!

# A Very Cool Life

Take a class vote to find out how many students think they would enjoy living on the tundra. Invite youngsters to share what they think would be the advantages and disadvantages of such a life. Students may be surprised to discover that many groups of people live on the Arctic tundra. Some of these people have always lived in the Arctic and are called *natives*. Many others have moved to the Arctic.

*An Arctic Community* by Bobbie Kalman and William Belsey (Crabtree Publishing Company, 1993) is an excellent reference for learning about the current lifestyle of Arctic dwellers. This resource is packed with interesting information and appealing photographs. Students will enjoy finding the similarities and differences between their own lifestyles and those of youngsters their age who live in the Arctic.

# Postcards From The Tundra

Culminate your study of the tundra with this postcard-writing activity. Cut a supply of postcards from tagboard. Each card must be of legal mailing size—from 3.5" x 5" to 4.25" x 6". Have each youngster illustrate the front of his tagboard postcard with a tundra scene or a favorite tundra animal. Then—on the back of his card—in the upper left-hand corner, ask him to write a brief, informative caption about his illustration. Next have each youngster write a message to a family member or a friend in which he tells about his "visit" to the tundra. Help the students address their cards; then collect the cards, affix the proper postage, and place the cards in the mail. The recipients of these cards are sure to feel extra special indeed!

# Top-Of-The-World Reading

Bundle up and journey north to explore the Arctic tundra through the pages of children's literature. The weather outside will be frightful, but we feel certain that you'll find these books most delightful!

*books reviewed by Deborah Zink Roffino*

## Notable Nonfiction

### One Small Square: Arctic Tundra

*Written by Donald M. Silver*
*Illustrated by Patricia J. Wynne*
*W. H. Freeman And Company, 1994*

Part of a phenomenal science series that investigates small squares of our earth, this reference book is a first-rate choice for your tundra unit. It's packed with informative facts that are sure to pique your youngsters' interest in the Arctic tundra's strange and wonderful ecosystem. Carefully sketched life-forms grace the pages. Several experiments and a comprehensive index add to the appeal of an already superb book.

### The Arctic World Series

*Created by Bobbie Kalman*
*Crabtree Publishing Company, 1993*

Each of the four books in this outstanding series is packed with Arctic facts. The titles included are *The Arctic Land, Arctic Animals, Arctic Whales & Whaling,* and *An Arctic Community.* Invest in this series of books and you'll have a bounty of teaching information right at your fingertips! Diagrams, maps, and enlightening photographs embellish the pages.

### A Picture Book Of Arctic Animals

*Written & Illustrated by Kellie Conforth*
*Troll Associates, 1991*

This slim paperback holds a wealth of data on 16 tundra inhabitants. All of the animals are accurately represented and appealingly illustrated in their habitats. New vocabulary is italicized and used in clear context. And there are plenty of fascinating facts about the animals that are sure to enchant your youngsters.

### Tundra Swans

*Written & Photographed by Bianca Lavies*
*Dutton Children's Books, 1994*

Not all tundra inhabitants stay in the harsh Arctic environment year-round. Tundra swans—also called whistling swans—actually wing their way from the Arctic Circle to the waters of the Chesapeake Bay to spend their winters. These wild yet docile creatures of legend are examined in depth between the covers of this book. Rare, compelling photographs and sophisticated text blend to offer youngsters an inside look at scientists interacting with nature to protect this threatened species.

### Vanishing Cultures: Frozen Land

*Written & Photographed by Jan Reynolds*
*Harcourt Brace & Company, 1993*

Focusing on the Inuit caribou hunters who live at the northernmost section of Hudson Bay, Jan Reynold's award-winning blend of photography and simple clarification exposes a human world so foreign to most children that it can barely be envisioned. The titanic nature of the icy land and the humanity of the folks who make it their home is astounding. It is important to note that the Inuit culture is ever changing. This is a look at a culture that is quickly vanishing, yet still offers a valuable lesson in the importance of the relationship people have with their natural surroundings.

## To The Top Of The World: Adventures With Arctic Wolves

*Written & Photographed by
Jim Brandenburg
Walker And Company, 1993*

Join award-winning wildlife photographer Jim Brandenburg on the adventure of a lifetime! For one summer, Brandenburg had the unique privilege of being adopted by an Arctic wolf pack. Living near the Arctic Circle, side by side with the legendary white wolves, he captured on film a wealth of information about these often misunderstood animals. The result is a superb resource for an in-depth look at Arctic wolves.

## Habitats: Where The Wild Things Live

*Written by Randi Hacker
and Jackie Kaufman
John Muir Publications, 1992*

Although the tundra is but one of ten habitats explored in this resourceful paperback, the book is valuable for the vast number of facts packed on four pages. And the contrast that can be made to other environments supplies an additional attraction. The emphasis is on conservation. A map that delineates the tundra and timberline provides an excellent view of the northern portion of the globe.

## Vanishing Cultures: Far North

*Written & Photographed by Jan Reynolds
Harcourt Brace & Company, 1992*

Travel to the northern land called Finmark (also called Lapland), where the Samis live. For thousands of years, the Samis have followed the migration of the reindeer. They believe—and they have proven—that by following the natural cycle of seasons, nature will care for them. But this ancient way of life is disappearing. Today the landscape is dotted with new roads and towns. Helicopters and snowmobiles replace the Samis' traditional methods of reindeer herding. Take a look at the Samis' way of life—one that is in harmony with nature—before it vanishes forever.

## Fiction And Folklore

### The Bear On The Moon

*Written by Joanne Ryder
Illustrated by Carol Lacey
Morrow Junior Books, 1991*

"At the top of the world, a winter night lasts a long time" begins this piece of folklore from the North. It is the tale of a very curious and ambitious polar bear that sets out to answer some questions that have baffled its species for all time. This is a creation tale—one with an uncommon reverence for the polar bear and the iceberg world. Silvery scenes capture the cold as the narrative—nearly poetic in beauty—weaves an enchanting tale that manages to warm in spite of the chilly surroundings. The moon may never look the same to your young cubs!

### Ka-ha-si And The Loon: An Eskimo Legend

*Written & Adapted by Terri Cohlene
Illustrated by Charles Reasoner
Watermill Press, 1990*

This well-crafted and fascinating retelling of an Eskimo legend is sure to embrace your students. Known as the lazy one, Ka-ha-si spends every day sleeping on a warm caribou hide in his igloo. Only his mother believes that one day the young lad will be an important man. With the help of a loon, Ka-ha-si proves that his mother knows best. Following the story of Ka-ha-si, readers are treated to a short history of Arctic natives that includes a timetable and photographs.

### The Seasons And Someone

*Written by Virginia Kroll
Illustrated by Tatsuro Kiuchi
Harcourt Brace & Company, 1994*

The natives of Alaska, Greenland, and Canada squander nothing as they pass through the seasons. Watch in wonder as the distinct features of each Arctic season—captured here in glorious oil paintings—pass in beauty. The book's title comes from the Eskimo belief that it is wiser to refer to oneself as "Someone," thus avoiding the bad luck of speaking one's own name aloud.

## A Sled Dog For Moshi

*Written by Jeanne Bushey*
*Illustrated by Germaine Arnaktauyok*
*Hyperion Books For Children, 1994*

Tension is thick as Arctic snow in this riveting picture book. Two young girls are caught out on the tundra in a whiteout—a blizzard so blinding and dense that all sense of direction is lost. Jessica is a transplant from New York City, but Moshi is a native of Iqaluit and remembers the survival techniques that her father has taught her. Her sharp skills and a lead sled dog save the girls from the deathtrap of the cold. The Inuit artist has created color-pencil illustrations that chill the pages and add frosting to a sweet piece of fiction.

## Whale Is Stuck

*Written by Karen Hayles*
*Illustrated by Charles Fuge*
*Simon & Schuster Books For Young Readers, 1992*

Welcome to midsummer in the Arctic Ocean. Ice floes patch the blue-green waters, populated with a plethora of plump, appealing creatures. This menagerie of Arctic animals—luminous and lifelike in texture and color—is enlisted in a colossal effort to free a winsome whale that is pathetically stranded on a fragment of frozen ice. Animated expression and a fast-paced narrative hook the reader right to the climatic break from Mother Nature.

## Nessa's Story

*Written by Nancy Luenn*
*Illustrated by Neil Waldman*
*Atheneum, 1994*

Here's an enchanting and rare peek at summer on the tundra. Soft watercolors and easy text combine in this story of an Inuit girl who happens upon a giant, white egg and is privileged to witness its hatching. The creature that emerges is a baby *silaq*—a legendary animal found in the lore of Arctic cultures.

## Where The Great Bear Watches

*Written by James Sage*
*Illustrated by Lisa Flather*
*Viking, 1993*

Here is a joyful vision of life and nature in the Far North. A young Inuit boy paddles his kayak and sings a song to the birds above, the fish below, and the great bear on shore. It is a celebration of unity between man and nature.

## Arctic Spring

*Written by Sue Vyner*
*Illustrated by Tim Vyner*
*Viking, 1992*

Simple, straightforward text and vivid illustrations capture the excitement, beauty, and drama of this special season in the North. Spring in the Arctic brings new activity among the fox, seals, and other animals—but the polar bear has a very good reason for hovering near her den.

## Here Is The Arctic Winter

*Written by Madeleine Dunphy*
*Illustrated by Alan James Robinson*
*Hyperion Books For Children, 1993*

Breathtaking illustrations capture with stunning realism the cold, dark winter season of the Arctic. The lyrical, cumulative text introduces Arctic animals that are strong enough to survive this cold and bleak season, and describes how each one is linked to the others in an intricate chain of life.

## Call Me Ahnighito

*Written by Pam Conrad*
*Illustrated by Richard Egielski*
*A Laura Geringer Book, 1995*

A huge meteorite describes how it lay half-buried in the frozen Arctic ground until it was discovered and excavated by members of a Peary expedition. Based on a true story, the unique delivery of this one-of-a-kind tale is sure to capture your students' interest. Today the huge meteorite is on display in the American Museum of Natural History in New York City.

## The Hungry Giant Of The Tundra

*Retold by Teri Sloat*
*Illustrated by Robert and Teri Sloat*
*Dutton Children's Books, 1993*

Travel north to autumn in Alaska where adventurous Yupik children have a skirmish with *Akaguagankak*, the nasty child-eating giant. His great, hairy arms and unshaven face make him a brute to avoid. He is a favorite of Yupik storytellers who use the threat of his existence to warn young children never to roam far from the safety of their village. The children bound across the burnished tundra through a blaze of glorious colors, just before the first snows—and a few leaps ahead of the monster!

Arctic tundra
Map skills

# Touring The Tundra

Use the code to color the map.

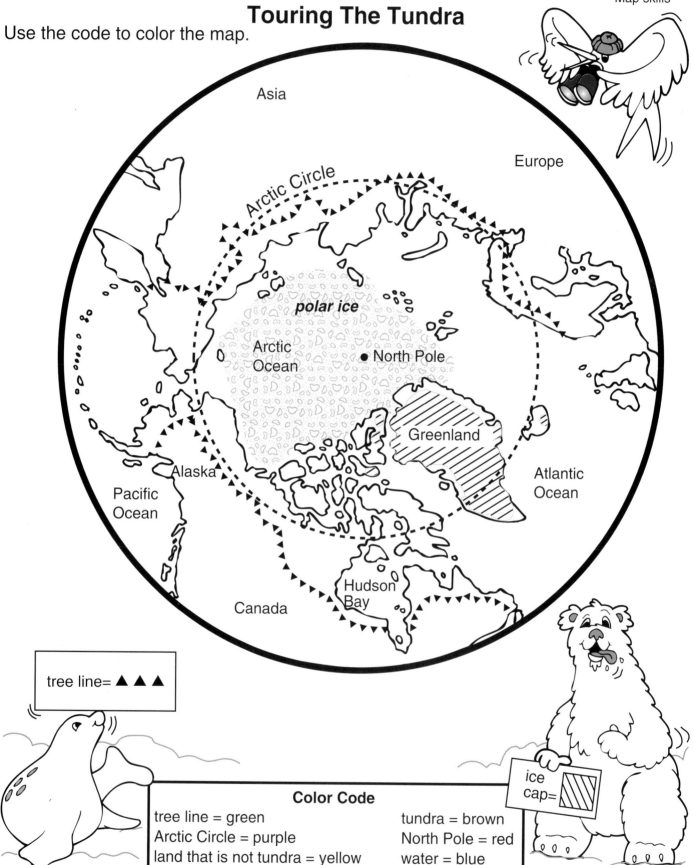

tree line= ▲ ▲ ▲

ice cap=

### Color Code

tree line = green
Arctic Circle = purple
land that is not tundra = yellow

tundra = brown
North Pole = red
water = blue

**Note To Teacher:** Use with "Where Is It?" and "A Treeless Wonder?" on page 166.

# Summertime Plants

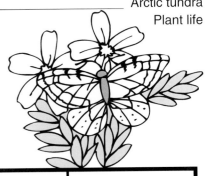

Name _____

Arctic tundra
Plant life

Make a lotto gameboard.
Color and cut out the plants.
Mix up the plants; then glue each one on the gameboard.

| | | | | |
|---|---|---|---|---|
| | | | | |
| | | | | |
| | | | | |

©The Education Center, Inc. • THE MAILBOX® • Primary • Dec/Jan 1995–96

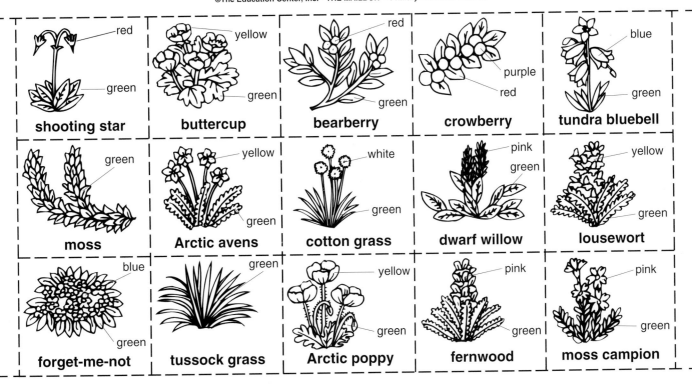

shooting star — red, green
buttercup — yellow, green
bearberry — red, green
crowberry — purple, red
tundra bluebell — blue, green
moss — green
Arctic avens — yellow, green
cotton grass — white, green
dwarf willow — pink, green
lousewort — yellow, green
forget-me-not — blue, green
tussock grass — green
Arctic poppy — yellow, green
fernwood — pink, green
moss campion — pink, green

**Note To Teacher:** Use with "Arctic Plants" on page 168.

173

# Patterns

Use with "Animals Of The Arctic" on page 167.

caribou

Arctic wolf

musk ox

polar bear

lemming

ptarmigan

Animals are not drawn to scale.

# A Pocketful Of Science

## Science Mysteries

Sharpen your students' scientific sleuthing skills with the following classic demonstrations. Students can use the principles they learn from the first and third mysteries to help them solve the second and fourth ones.

*ideas by Ann Flagg*

### Mystery 1: The Dry Napkin

**You will need:**
a clear drinking glass          a paper napkin
a fish tank or a large glass bowl filled with water

**What to do:**
With great fanfare, pick up the napkin and drinking glass. Ask a student to inspect the napkin and verify that the inside of the glass is empty. Then wad up the napkin and stuff it into the bottom of the glass. Ask students to predict what will happen to the napkin when the glass is submerged. When all the predictions are in, invert the glass and push it under the water. (Be careful to hold the glass straight up and down. If the glass tilts, the air inside the glass will escape and water will rush in to take its place.) Hold the glass underwater for a few seconds before pulling it straight out. With a flourish, remove the dry napkin from the glass and display it for all to see!

**Questions to ask:**
1. Did water fill the glass?
2. What stopped the water from entering the glass?
3. Was the glass ever really empty?

#### This is why:
Air is all around. It takes up space even though you can't see it, smell it, or taste it. Air was taking up space inside the glass. When the glass was pushed straight down into the water, the air was trapped inside. Water could not enter the glass because the glass was already filled with air. The air provided a barrier between the water and the napkin.

### Mystery 2: The Suspended Water

**You will need:**
two funnels                          modeling clay
a small container               a pitcher of blue-tinted water
an empty waterproof container or a sink
a glass jar in which one funnel fits snugly

**Each student will need:**
a copy of lab sheet A on page 177          a pencil
crayons or markers

**In advance:**
Snugly fit one funnel into the glass jar. Use the modeling clay to seal the open area between the rim of the jar and the funnel. (See the illustration below.) To assure that the seal is airtight, pour a small amount of water into the funnel. If the water stays in the funnel, the seal is airtight. If it does not, remove the water from the jar; then reseal the jar and funnel by adjusting the clay or adding more. Continue in this manner until the seal is airtight. Remove any water that remains in the funnel.

**What to do:**
Distribute lab sheet A and review the concepts listed. To demonstrate how a funnel works, ask a student to hold the loose funnel over the waterproof container as you pour blue-tinted water into it. Next show students the jar and funnel that you prepared. Point out the airtight seal. Tell students that you plan to pour some blue-tinted water into this funnel. On their lab sheets in the box labeled "My Guess," ask students to illustrate what they think will happen. Then slowly pour the water into the funnel. Then have students record what actually happened.

**Questions to ask:**
1. How is this demonstration similar to "The Mystery Of The Dry Napkin"?
2. Why did the water stay in the funnel?
3. What do you think would happen if you removed a portion of the clay? Why?

**Next:**
Have students complete their lab sheets.

#### This is why:
The mystery of the dry napkin demonstrates that air takes up space. Just like the drinking glass, the jar is full of air. When water is poured into the funnel, the air inside the jar prevents the water from entering. In fact, the air actually pushes on the water and holds it inside the funnel. If the airtight seal formed by the clay is broken, the air inside the jar can escape through the opening, making room for water in the jar.

Pam Crane

## Mystery 3:
## The Growing Balloon

**You will need:**
an empty bowl
a thermos of very hot water
a bowl of ice water
a thick glass bottle with a narrow mouth
a balloon (Its lip must fit over the mouth of the bottle.)

**What to do:**
As you stretch the balloon over the mouth of the bottle, ask students what is inside the bottle *(air)*. Then ask the youngsters to describe the appearance of the balloon. Next pour the hot water into the empty bowl and set the bottle in the bowl. After a few moments, the balloon will partially fill with air and stand straight up. Have the students describe how the appearance of the balloon has changed. Then ask students what they think might happen if you take the bottle from the hot water and set it in the bowl of ice water. When the students have shared their ideas, move the bottle into the ice water. The balloon will deflate and be sucked inside the bottle.

**Questions to ask:**
1. How do you normally inflate a balloon?
2. When did this balloon inflate? Where do you think the air came from?
3. When did this balloon deflate? What do you think happened to the air?

### *This is why:*

Air causes a balloon to inflate. Warm air takes up more space than cool air. (Liquids, gases, and many solids expand when they are heated and contract when they are cooled.) When the bottle was placed in hot water, the air inside the bottle heated up, expanded, and moved upward into the balloon. When the bottle was placed in the ice water, the air cooled down and contracted. The balloon was sucked into the bottle because the air had become cooler than room temperature, which resulted in its taking up less space than when the activity began.

## Mystery 4:
## The Disappearing Water

**You will need:**
a clear, thick glass, long-necked vase
a thermos of very hot water (tinted blue)
a rubber band
plastic wrap or a cork that fits the vase
a shallow bowl filled with ice and water

**Each student will need:**
a copy of lab sheet B on page 177     a pencil
crayons or markers

**What to do:**
Amaze students by proclaiming that you can make water disappear! Under the watchful eyes of your youngsters, carefully pour hot, blue-tinted water into the vase. Ask a student to feel the outside of the vase and confirm that the water inside is hot. Wrap the rubber band around the vase to indicate the water level. Use a cork or plastic wrap to seal the top of the vase. Stand the vase in the bowl of ice and water. Distribute lab sheet B and review the concepts listed. In the box labeled "My Guess," ask students to illustrate what they think will happen to the water inside the vase. After about 15 minutes, have students check the vase's water level. Then in the remaining box on their lab sheets, have the youngsters record what actually happened.

**Questions to ask:**
1. How do you know that some of the water in the vase disappeared?
2. What happened to the temperature of the water in the vase?
3. What could be done to make the water reappear?

**Next:**
Have students complete their lab sheets.

### *This is why:*

Like air, water expands when it heats up and contracts when it is cooled. This is because water molecules move more rapidly when heated. The faster the molecules move, the farther apart they spread, taking up more room. As the hot water in the vase cools, the water molecules slow down and take up less space, which causes the water level to drop. To make the missing water reappear, place the vase in a bowl of very hot water. As the temperature of the water in the vase rises, the molecules will speed up and scatter, causing the water to expand.

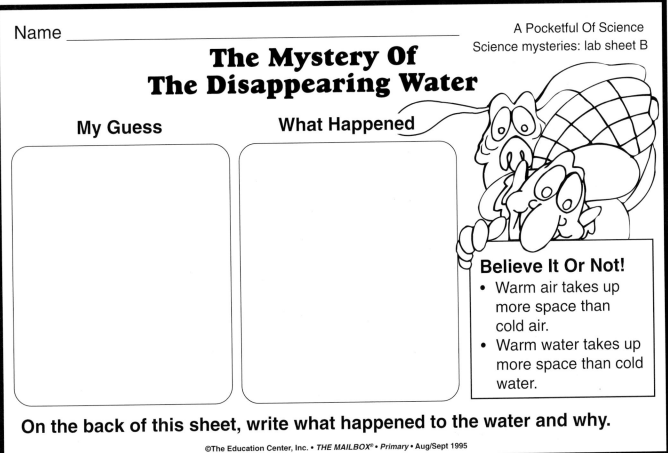

Name _____

# The Mystery Of
# The Suspended Water

**My Guess**

**What Happened**

**Believe It Or Not!**
- Air is all around.
- You cannot see, taste, or smell air.
- Air takes up space.

**On the back of this sheet, write what happened to the water and why.**

©The Education Center, Inc. • *THE MAILBOX* • *Primary* • Aug/Sept 1995

---

Name _____

# The Mystery Of
# The Disappearing Water

**My Guess**

**What Happened**

**Believe It Or Not!**
- Warm air takes up more space than cold air.
- Warm water takes up more space than cold water.

**On the back of this sheet, write what happened to the water and why.**

©The Education Center, Inc. • *THE MAILBOX* • *Primary* • Aug/Sept 1995

**Note To Teacher:** Use lab sheet A with "Mystery 2: The Suspended Water" on page 175. Use lab sheet B with "Mystery 4: The Disappearing Water" on page 176.

# This Place Is Dry!

## Exploring The Desert

The desert is definitely dry, but that doesn't mean it's a dry topic of study! Use this collection of activities and reproducibles to investigate an intriguing ecosystem that's home to some unique plants and animals. You're sure to have a hot time!

## What Is A Desert?

Most scientists agree that for an environment to be a true desert, it must receive less than ten inches of precipitation per year and have a high rate of evaporation. The following ditty is a fun way to acquaint your youngsters with the desert environment. Post the lyrics; then adapt them to the tune of "Oh! Susanna." Invite students to create additional verses as they learn more about the desert.

### Welcome To The Desert

Oh, the days are hot; the nights are cold;
The weather it is dry.
With rocks and sand and lots of space.
Sometimes the wind blows by.

*Chorus:*
*Come see the desert—it's a pretty place to be!*
*Just keep your cool and watch your step,*
*For you may have company!*

Look, there's a giant cactus tree.
Saguaro is its name.
It stores water for dry times,
And you should do the same.

*Chorus*

When the sun goes down, the air turns cool.
More critters start to roam.
They're hungry and they search for food.
The desert is their home.

*Chorus*

The centipedes and scorpions
Are poisonous as can be.
So keep your distance—don't you touch!
There's plenty more to see!

## Meet The Desert!

- No two deserts are exactly the same.
- Not all deserts are hot.
- Many desert animals hide during the day.
- Some desert animals do not drink.
- Birds nest in a saguaro cactus.

## A Bloomin' Cactus!

It only takes a minute to turn tissue-paper squares into colorful cactus blossoms. To make one blossom, stack four 6-inch squares of tissue paper. Fold the stacked squares in half and in half again; then staple the folded corner. Trim to round each unstapled corner. Gently pull the tissue paper apart to open the blossom. Use the colorful blooms to decorate the research project described in "A Prickly Approach," the cactus folder described in "A Barrel Of Vocabulary" on page 179, and other cactus-related projects.

## A Prickly Approach

Take this prickly approach to desert research and earn rave reviews! You will need one large cactus-pad cutout labeled "Meet The Desert" and a supply of small cactus pads—all cut from green paper. Mount the labeled pad at the lower edge of a large display area. Each time a new desert fact is discovered, a student writes the fact on a cactus pad cutout and attaches the programmed pad to the display. In no time your prickly pear cactus will be growing by leaps and bounds. At the conclusion of your unit, have each youngster craft a cactus blossom and attach it to the display. (See "A Bloomin' Cactus!") Toothpick spines can also be added. Keep this striking project on display as a reminder of your desert studies.

*Michele Converse Baerns—Gr. 2, Sevierville Primary School, Sevierville, TN*

## A Barrel Of Vocabulary

Create a thirst for desert-related vocabulary with cactus-shaped vocabulary folders. To make a folder like the one shown, begin with a 12" x 18" sheet of green construction paper. Fold and crease the paper to create a pocket; then trim the folded paper into the shape of a barrel cactus. (If desired, provide a tagboard template for students to trace.) Glue the outer edges of the pocket together. Personalize the pocket; then glue a tissue-paper blossom (see "A Bloomin' Cactus!" on page 178) and toothpick spines to the project.

Securely staple the completed folders to a bulletin board and provide a supply of blank construction-paper strips. Each morning post a different vocabulary word at the display. A student copies the word onto a blank strip, researches the meaning of the word, and writes and/or illustrates its meaning on the blank side of her word strip. She then stores her completed vocabulary project in her cactus folder. Your youngsters' desert vocabularies are sure to blossom!

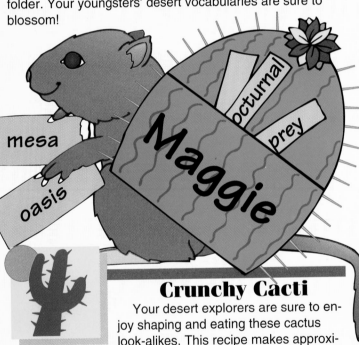

## Where Are The Deserts?

Deserts cover about one-fifth of the world's land, but where are they? Using the reproducible map on page 185, take students on a desert discovery mission. Introduce the map key and color code. Review what makes an environment a desert, and have students ponder the meaning of *semidesert.* Then help students conclude that a semidesert region is very much like a desert except that it receives a little more rainfall. This additional precipitation means a greater number of plants and animals can grow and survive there.

To complete the mapping activity, lead students from continent to continent. As students color their maps, share related facts from "Did You Know?" Point out that the Arctic region and the continent of Antarctica are not shown on the map. Explain that some scientists call these areas deserts because they have less than ten inches of rainfall a year. However, other scientists disagree, arguing that a true desert must also have a high rate of evaporation—something that these two areas do not. When the maps have been completed, challenge students to find out on which deserts the pictured wildlife can be found (see page 313 for locations).

## Crunchy Cacti

Your desert explorers are sure to enjoy shaping and eating these cactus look-alikes. This recipe makes approximately 15 to 20 crunchy cacti.

**Ingredients:**
1 12-oz. package butterscotch chips
2 tablespoons peanut butter
green food coloring
1 6-oz. can chow mein noodles
waxed paper

**Directions:**
1. Melt chips over low heat, stirring occasionally.
2. Stir in peanut butter and desired amount of green food coloring.
3. Add chow mein noodles and stir until well coated.
4. Remove from heat. Allow the mixture to cool until it is safe to handle.
5. Working atop waxed paper, have each child fashion a golf-ball-size portion of the mixture into a cactus shape.
6. When the projects have hardened, have each student peel his cactus from the paper and chow down!

*Michele Converse Baerns—Gr. 2, Sevierville Primary School Sevierville, TN*

## Did You Know?

Share these facts with your students as they complete the mapping activity described in "Where Are The Deserts?"

- The Sahara Desert in northern Africa is about the size of the United States. It is the largest desert in the world.
- The Gobi Desert in eastern Asia is the coldest desert in the world.
- Almost half of Australia is covered by desert.
- The sandiest desert in the world is the Arabian Desert.
- The Atacama Desert in South America is the driest desert in the world—some of its areas haven't had any rainfall for over 13 years!
- South America's Patagonian Desert is one of the least studied deserts because it is very difficult to reach.
- North American deserts are home to many plants, animals, and people. An air force base is located in the Mohave Desert!

# Cactus Country

Cacti are the most well-known desert plants, but other plants grow in deserts too. All desert plants have one thing in common—a method of gathering and storing water so that they can survive without regular rainfall.

A cactus uses its roots to gather and store water. Show students a picture of a barrel cactus and explain that this cactus also stores water in its stem. To show how this happens, have students stand side by side in a circle formation and imagine that they are part of a large barrel cactus. Ask the students to use their voices to create the sounds of rain; then instruct them to make slurping sounds as if the cactus is soaking up water through its roots. Next have the students join hands, then slowly and carefully step backward until their arms are extended. Ask the students to describe how this demonstration compares to a barrel cactus storing water; then have the students act out what will happen to the cactus after several weeks of hot, dry weather.

# Amazing Animals

The bodies of many desert animals are designed for life on the desert. The camel is a perfect example. Bushy eyebrows and long eyelashes protect a camel's eyes from the sand and sun. Its nostrils close between breaths so that sand does not enter its nose. A camel's broad feet keep it from sinking in the sand. And what about that hump? Well, it doesn't contain water as it was once believed. Instead it stores fat that breaks down into food when no food is available to eat. Students will enjoy investigating desert animals to discover how their bodies help them cope with desert life. Record students' findings on a chart like the one shown. Then, using the knowledge they have gained, have each student illustrate a make-believe desert animal and in a written paragraph explain how this animal copes with life in the desert. Be sure to set aside time for students to share their unique creations with their classmates!

*Denise Donahue, Berlin, MD*

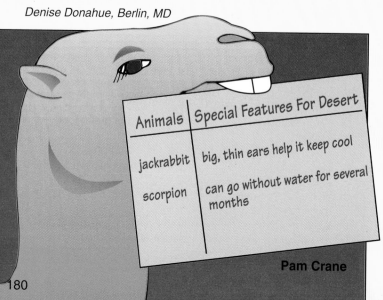

| Animals | Special Features For Desert |
|---|---|
| jackrabbit | big, thin ears help it keep cool |
| scorpion | can go without water for several months |

**Pam Crane**

# Beating The Heat

Desert animals have different ways of coping with the extreme desert heat. Some animals can tolerate high desert temperatures and seek shade only during the hottest part of the day. Other animals escape the heat by hiding in burrows, dens, or protected shelters. As the sun sets and the desert begins to cool, these animals come out of hiding and begin their search for food. Use the project on page 189 to introduce students to three *diurnal* (daytime) and three *nocturnal* (nighttime) desert animals.

Duplicate page 189 on white construction paper and have each youngster color a copy. To complete his project, a student cuts out patterns A and B on the bold lines. Then he cuts along the dotted lines to create one large window and three small ones in cutout A. (Provide assistance as needed.) Next the student stacks cutout A atop cutout B, aligns the edges, and pokes a brad through the black dots, joining both cutouts. To view diurnal animals, the student positions the daytime sky in the large window. When the nighttime sky is featured, nocturnal animals are on display.

## A Colossal Cactus

The saguaro cactus—which can grow to be 50 feet tall—is very impressive! The more water it stores, the heavier it becomes. In fact a saguaro cactus can weigh as much as an elephant! The cactus is covered with very sharp spines, and if the plant has "arms," it must be at least 50 years old. During its life span of approximately 200 years, the cactus is alive with activity, providing food and shelter for a variety of desert wildlife. *Desert Giant* by Barbara Bash (see page 183) provides an in-depth look at this colossal cactus.

For a fun follow-up project, have each student design a desert scene featuring a saguaro cactus. First have each child trace his hand and forearm on a 9" x 12" sheet of green construction paper to create a shape similar to the one shown. A student cuts on the outline and mounts the resulting saguaro shape on a 12" x 18" sheet of construction paper. He then uses construction-paper scraps, toothpicks, and crayons or markers to create his desert scene.

*Karen Faas Marovich, Erie, PA*

## A One-Of-A-Kind Dessert

Looking for a tasteful way to wrap up your desert studies? Try this cake-decorating idea! You will need a large, frosted yellow sheet cake and a variety of decorating supplies like crushed vanilla wafers for sand, whole vanilla wafers for desert landforms, a batch of blue Jell-O® Jigglers™ for an oasis, popped popcorn or caramel corn for tumbleweeds, small sweet pickles for cacti, stick pretzels and green icing for palm trees, gummy candies (snakes, lizards, spiders, etc.), and animal crackers (camels, coyotes, rabbits, etc.). Be creative!

As a class, design a desired desert scene on the chalkboard. Then, after everyone has washed and dried his hands, have each student in turn contribute to decorating the frosted cake—creating the desert scene designed by the class. Now that's a dandy desert dessert!

*Karen Walden—Gr. 1, Ravenel Elementary, Seneca, SC*

## A Walk In The Desert

This booklet-making project takes students on a stroll through the desert! Each youngster needs a tan construction-paper copy of the desert tortoise pattern on page 186, and white construction-paper copies of pages 187 and 188. Distribute pages 187 and 188. After each student has personalized and decorated his booklet cover, read and discuss the information presented on each booklet page before students complete their independent work. Then have each child cut out his booklet cover and pages on the dotted lines and stack them in sequential order. Distribute page 186, and instruct each student to color and cut out the desert tortoise pattern. Then help each youngster staple his booklet project to the cutout as indicated.

*Karen Faas Marovich, Erie, PA*

# A Literary Oasis

The deserts of the world may be dry, but this expansive selection of desert-related literature certainly isn't! Use these hot books to introduce and enhance your study of an extraordinary ecosystem.

*books reviewed by Deborah Zink Roffino*

## Fun-To-Read Fiction

### Alejandro's Gift

*Written by Richard E. Albert & Illustrated by Sylvia Long*
*Chronicle Books, 1994*
The furrows in Alejandro's ancient brow match the primal creases in the dry, desert earth. Alejandro lives alone in a small adobe house on a lonely desert road. His burro is his only companion. To pass the lonely hours, Alejandro plants a garden that—much to his surprise—cultivates a powerful lesson about nature and friendship. This beautifully illustrated story will prompt children to look at the world around them in a new way. An illustrated glossary, featuring some of the desert wildlife presented, adds to the appeal of this already superb book.

### The Three Little Javelinas

*Written by Susan Lowell & Illustrated by Jim Harris*
*Northland Publishing Company, 1992*
This chili-flavored adaptation of *The Three Little Pigs* is definitely hot! Scurrying from a tumbleweed shack to a saguaro-rib hut to an adobe-brick house, three little *javelinas* (wild pigs of the Sonoran Desert) try to outwit a huffing, puffing, big, bad coyote. Dressed in cowboy duds and prepared for life in the rugged desert, these three little piglets are more than this coyote bargained for!

### The Moon Of The Wild Pigs

*Written by Jean Craighead George & Illustrated by Paul Mirocha*
*HarperCollins Publishers, 1992*
Against the forbidding backdrop of Arizona's Sonoran Desert, the adventures of a wild piglet uncover the mysteries of weather, plants, and animals in this unique biosphere. This longer story for more advanced readers swells with environmental information, dangerous encounters, and a sweet resolution. Insightful and believable, the personification of this appealing little peccary results in a superb animal tale.

# Notable Nonfiction

## Here Is The Southwestern Desert

*Written by Madeleine Dunphy & Illustrated by Anne Coe*
*Hyperion Books For Children, 1995*
Here is a read-aloud masterpiece with gallery-caliber artwork! The story reveals the elements that build the chain of life in the Sonoran Desert. Cumulative text threads alongside breathtaking landscapes in energetic hues. The result is an unforgettable, factual tale that is a visual and linguistic treat!

## Look Closer: Desert Life

*Written by Barbara Taylor & Photographed by Frank Greenaway*
*Dorling Kindersley, Inc.; 1992*
There are plenty of strange-looking critters roaming the deserts of the world, and this striking examination brings youngsters nose to nose with some of the most outrageous. Splendid photos overwhelm the pages, capturing the slimy, spindly, craggy, gnarly hides that are detailed in the primary text. Sure to get a reaction from young readers, this volume is memorable, informative, and highly entertaining.

## Desert Giant: The World Of The Saguaro Cactus

*Written & Illustrated by Barbara Bash*
*Little, Brown And Company; 1989*
Intense colors brighten the pages of this fascinating Reading Rainbow® book. The giant saguaro cactus—stalwart symbol of the Sonoran Desert—is superbly introduced as the cactus that can grow as tall as 50 feet, weigh up to several tons, and live for 200 years! Readers learn that appearing barren and forlorn is only this cactus's public persona. In truth this colossal cactus is alive with activity! Youngsters will, without a doubt, come away with a better understanding of—and a lasting respect for—this desert giant.

## Vanishing Cultures: Sahara

*Written & Photographed by Jan Reynolds*
*Harcourt Brace & Company, 1991*
Author and photographer Jan Reynolds traveled to the largest desert on Earth to capture on film the Tuareg's unique way of desert life. A nomadic people, the Tuareg have lived in the heart of the Sahara for centuries. Now—because of outside influences—their ancient way of life is rapidly disappearing. Reynold's dramatic photographs and simple text beckon readers to experience the vanishing culture of a fascinating desert people.

## Where The Buffalo Roam

*Adapted & Illustrated by Jacqueline Geis*
*Ideals Children's Books, 1992*
Youngsters explore the diverse life and landforms of the Southwest through an expanded verse of the well-known song "Home On The Range." Soft watercolor paintings feature the varied faces of the American Southwest from the wide, grassy plains; through the harsh-yet-lovely desert; to the Rocky Mountain foothills. An abundance of protected, threatened, and endangered species are featured.

## One Small Square: Cactus Desert

*Written by Donald M. Silver & Illustrated by Patricia J. Wynne*
*W. H. Freeman And Company, 1995*
Part of a phenomenal science series that investigates small squares of our Earth, this reference book is an excellent choice for your desert unit. Cutaways, close-ups, and panoramic vistas show off the details of the desert. The text and sketches overflow with data, while the sidebars suggest experiments. It's the ultimate desert field trip. Young desert researchers will appreciate the desert life classifications and comprehensive index located at the back of the book.

## Watching Desert Wildlife

*Written by Caroline Arnold & Photographed by Arthur Arnold*
*Carolrhoda Books, Inc.; 1994*
A brief introduction to the deserts of the world is followed up by a journey of discovery that takes readers through the deserts of North America. Stunning photographs uncover a variety of desert wildlife. The somewhat lengthy text reveals some of the techniques that these plants and animals employ for survival in their harsh and arid environments. An excellent reference for research projects.

Pam Crane

## The Desert Alphabet Book

*Written by Jerry Pallotta & Illustrated by Mark Astrella*
*Charlesbridge Publishing, 1994*
Life on the desert unfolds between the covers of this vibrant book. From *A* to *Z*, a kid-pleasing assortment of desert wildlife and terms are explored. The traces of humor that are woven into the easy-to-read text reflect the author's understanding of the audience for whom he writes. A perfect learning tool for youngsters studying arid lands.

## Discover My World: Desert

*Written by Ron Hirschi & Illustrated by Barbara Bash*
*Bantam Books, 1992*
Explore the mysterious desert world and meet some of the animals that live there. The lyrical text of renowned environmentalist Ron Hirschi invites youngsters to guess the identity of the desert dweller that is being presented on each colorful spread. A boxed clue provides visual assistance. Additional information about the discovered desert dwellers can be found at the back of the book.

## Imagine Living Here: This Place Is Dry

*Written by Vicki Cobb & Illustrated by Barbara Lavallee*
*Walker And Company, 1989*
What might it be like to live on the Sonoran Desert in Arizona? This colorful paperback is packed with information describing the living conditions of this dry place. Meet Americans who live among the snakes, spiders, roadrunners, and cacti of this southwestern desert. Imagine that!

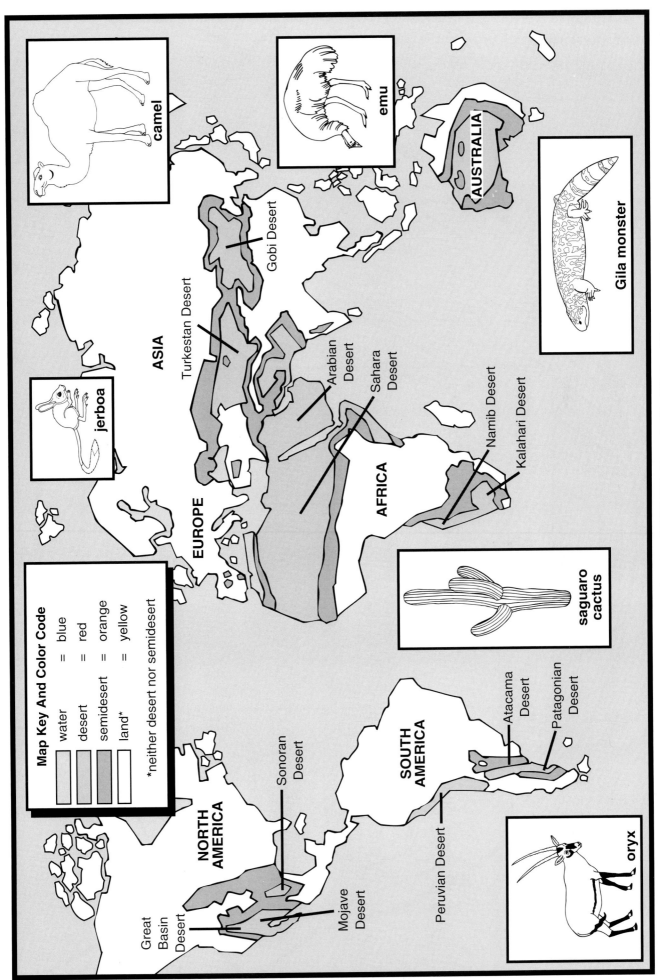

**Map Key And Color Code**

| | | | |
|---|---|---|---|
| | water | = | blue |
| | desert | = | red |
| | semidesert | = | orange |
| | land* | = | yellow |

*neither desert nor semidesert

camel

emu

AUSTRALIA

Gila monster

jerboa

ASIA

Gobi Desert

Turkestan Desert

Arabian Desert

Sahara Desert

EUROPE

AFRICA

Namib Desert

Kalahari Desert

saguaro cactus

NORTH AMERICA

Great Basin Desert

Sonoran Desert

Mojave Desert

SOUTH AMERICA

Atacama Desert

Patagonian Desert

Peruvian Desert

oryx

# Pattern

Use with "A Walk In The Desert" on page 181.

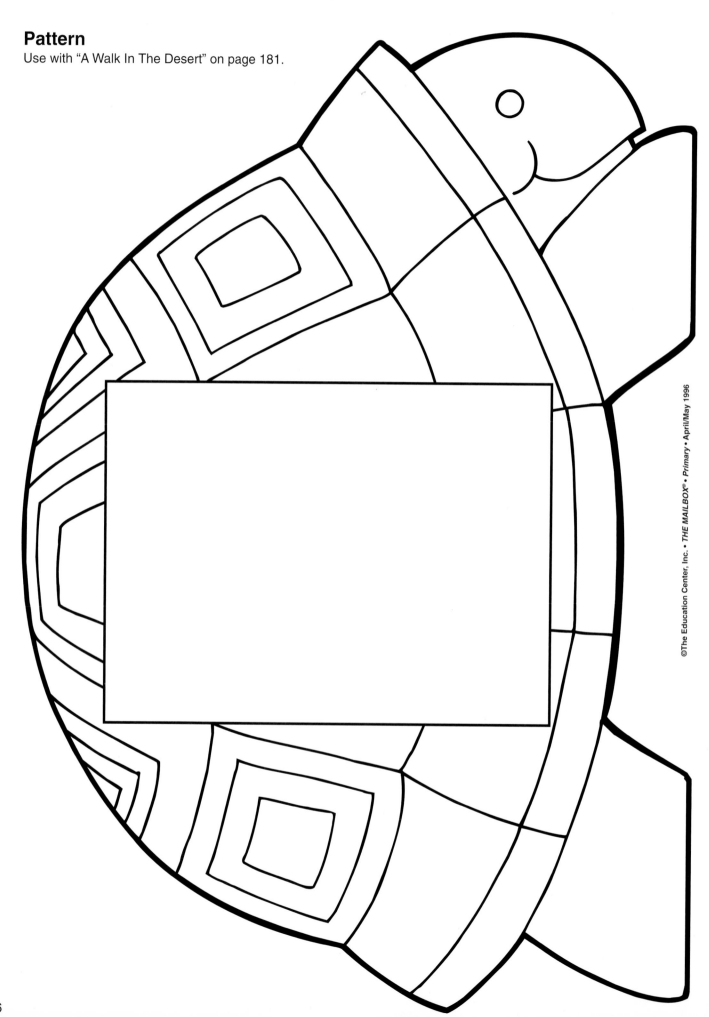

# A Walk In The Desert

by

_____

A desert is a very dry place. This is a picture of a desert.

1

A desert has many kinds of plants. This is a picture of my favorite desert plant.

It is a _____.

2

A desert has many kinds of animals. This is a picture of my favorite desert animal.

It is a _____.

3

**Note To Teacher:** Use with "A Walk In The Desert" on page 181.

187

This is a picture of an animal that hunts during the day.

It is a _____.

4

This is a picture of an animal that hunts at night.

It is a _____.

5

Deserts can be very different. This is me on a desert in

_____.

6

I think the desert is an interesting place because _____

_____

_____

_____

_____

_____

_____

_____

_____

_____.

7

**Note To Teacher:** Use with "A Walk In The Desert" on page 181.

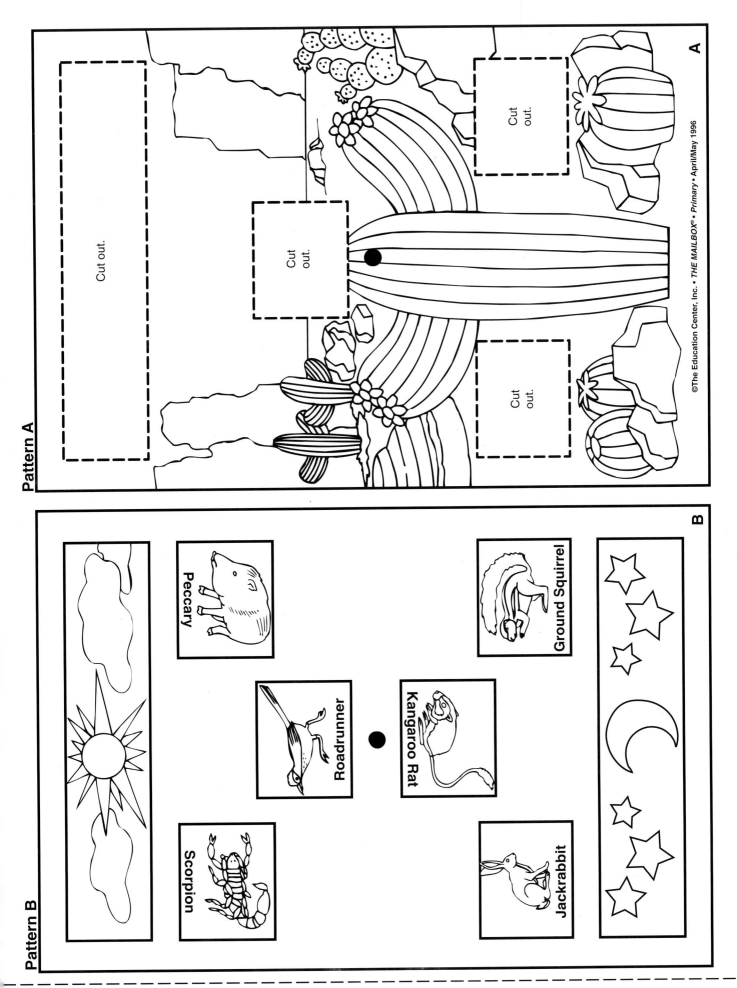

**Pattern A**

A

Cut out.

Cut out.

Cut out.

Cut out.

©The Education Center, Inc. • *THE MAILBOX*® • *Primary* • April/May 1996

**Pattern B**

B

Peccary

Ground Squirrel

Roadrunner

Kangaroo Rat

Scorpion

Jackrabbit

**Note To Teacher:** Use with "Beating The Heat" on page 180.

189

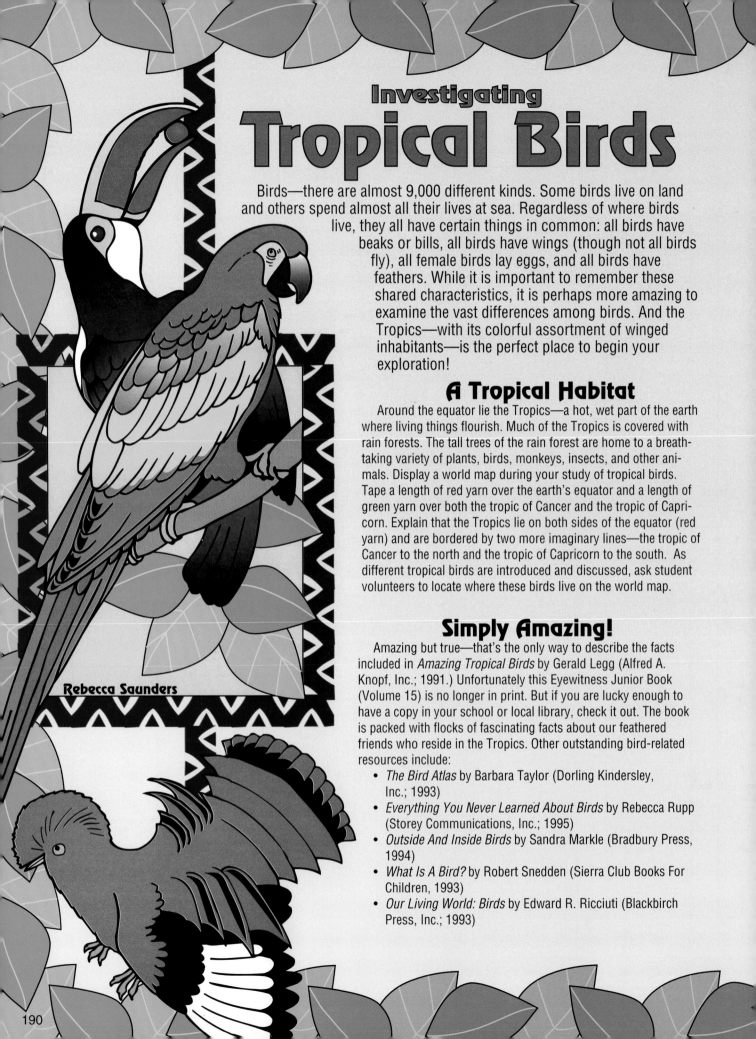

# Investigating
# Tropical Birds

Birds—there are almost 9,000 different kinds. Some birds live on land and others spend almost all their lives at sea. Regardless of where birds live, they all have certain things in common: all birds have beaks or bills, all birds have wings (though not all birds fly), all female birds lay eggs, and all birds have feathers. While it is important to remember these shared characteristics, it is perhaps more amazing to examine the vast differences among birds. And the Tropics—with its colorful assortment of winged inhabitants—is the perfect place to begin your exploration!

## A Tropical Habitat

Around the equator lie the Tropics—a hot, wet part of the earth where living things flourish. Much of the Tropics is covered with rain forests. The tall trees of the rain forest are home to a breath-taking variety of plants, birds, monkeys, insects, and other animals. Display a world map during your study of tropical birds. Tape a length of red yarn over the earth's equator and a length of green yarn over both the tropic of Cancer and the tropic of Capricorn. Explain that the Tropics lie on both sides of the equator (red yarn) and are bordered by two more imaginary lines—the tropic of Cancer to the north and the tropic of Capricorn to the south. As different tropical birds are introduced and discussed, ask student volunteers to locate where these birds live on the world map.

## Simply Amazing!

Amazing but true—that's the only way to describe the facts included in *Amazing Tropical Birds* by Gerald Legg (Alfred A. Knopf, Inc.; 1991.) Unfortunately this Eyewitness Junior Book (Volume 15) is no longer in print. But if you are lucky enough to have a copy in your school or local library, check it out. The book is packed with flocks of fascinating facts about our feathered friends who reside in the Tropics. Other outstanding bird-related resources include:

- *The Bird Atlas* by Barbara Taylor (Dorling Kindersley, Inc.; 1993)
- *Everything You Never Learned About Birds* by Rebecca Rupp (Storey Communications, Inc.; 1995)
- *Outside And Inside Birds* by Sandra Markle (Bradbury Press, 1994)
- *What Is A Bird?* by Robert Snedden (Sierra Club Books For Children, 1993)
- *Our Living World: Birds* by Edward R. Ricciuti (Blackbirch Press, Inc.; 1993)

Rebecca Saunders

## For The Birds

When a student completes this booklet project, she'll have the inside scoop on six different tropical birds and a map of the Tropics, too! Duplicate student copies of page 193 and the fact cards on page 312. Cut a 6" x 30" strip of light-colored bulletin-board paper for each student; then prefold each paper strip into thirds. Have each student use a yellow crayon to color the tropic region on her world map. Next read aloud each of the following descriptions so that students can accurately color the tropical birds on the page. When the coloring is completed, have students cut out the pieces on both pages.

- Bird #1 is a Resplendent Quetzal. It is mostly bright green except for its deep red belly.
- Bird #2 is a Northern Jacana. It is mostly brown. The wattle between its eyes is yellow. Its beak is yellow too.
- Bird #3 is a Toucan. Toucans are very colorful! Different kinds of toucans have different colors of beaks and faces. Color the beak of this toucan either bright green with a red tip or bright red with a blue tip. The area around its eye can be yellow or blue. Color the rest of its feathers black.
- Bird #4 is a Red-Fan Parrot. It has a brownish head and a green body. Its fan of feathers is red!
- Bird #5 is a Harpy Eagle. It is dark gray with a white belly, a black breast band, and a gray face.
- Bird #6 is a Three-Wattled Bellbird. It has a white head and a brownish body. Its three wattles are black.

To assemble the booklet, place the folded paper strip in front of you. Fold the top flap in half, bringing the paper end to the fold. Pull out the flap that is tucked in the center; then fold this flap in half in a similar manner. (See the illustration.) Keeping the booklet folded, glue the two halves of the world map in place. Unfold the booklet. Match each bird to a fact card. Glue the matching cutouts in the booklet as desired. In the remaining area, write "...The Tropics by [student name]. For a finishing touch, squeeze a trail of glue on the map along the equator. Position one ten-inch length of yarn on each map half so that the extra yarn remains at the center of the booklet. Allow the glue to dry; then fashion a bow from the yarn ends.

**(prefolded paper)**

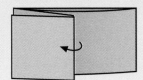

A Peek Inside...

A Peek    ...The Tropics    Inside...
by Robin Quetzal

## Songs And Calls

One of the ways birds communicate is through *birdsong*. There are two types of birdsong: *calls*—short and simple noises that deliver information, and *songs*—a more complicated and musical type of communication. Birds are born knowing how to call, but a bird must be taught how to sing. Tropical birds have a wide variety of calls and songs. For fun, divide students into small groups and have each group simultaneously repeat one of the following tropical bird's calls!

| Bird | Call |
|------|------|
| Black-Headed Parrot | "KLEEK! KLEEK!" |
| Toco Toucan | a deep croaking sound |
| Red-Billed Toucan | a series of rhythmic yelps |
| Jamaican Tody | a short "cherek" |
| Hyacinth Macaw | a harsh screech |

# A Peek At Beaks

The shape of a bird's beak (or bill) provides clues about how or what a bird eats. This student-made booklet project gives youngsters an up close look at the beaks of five different tropical birds. Duplicate student copies of page 194. To make the booklet shown, stack three 4 1/2" x 12" sheets of white construction paper. Slide the top sheet upward about one inch and the bottom sheet downward about one inch. Fold all three paper thicknesses forward to create six graduated pages and staple the resulting booklet close to the fold. Set the booklet aside. Color the birds on your copy of page 194 by referring to the provided color code. Then write your name where indicated and cut on the dotted lines. Glue the title to the top booklet flap. Match each beak description to a tropical bird; then glue the corresponding cutouts in the booklet as shown. Now take another peek at five fabulous beaks!

*Shari Abbey—Gr. 3, Abilene Elementary School*
*Valley Center, KS*

# Eating Like A Bird

Give your students the inside track on an often misused phrase! The phrase "eats like a bird" is commonly used to describe a light eater. But the fact of the matter is that birds have enormous appetites. Most birds eat one-quarter to one-half of their body weight in food each day! Just imagine if people did that! The diets of tropical birds vary a lot. Many tropical birds eat fruits, nuts, and/or seeds. Other tropical birds feast on insects or flower nectar—or find their food in an ocean, a lake, or a stream. And a few, like the huge Harris's hawk, prey on monkeys and other small animals. So if your students really want to eat like birds, invite each of them to bring to school a serving of dried fruit, sunflower seeds, or a favorite nut. Then mix the ingredients together and let the students senselessly stuff their faces for a few minutes. Now that's eating like a bird!

# Fowl Play

In the past 300 years, at least 44 species of birds have become extinct. The greatest threat to birds is pollution and habitat destruction by humans. Many tropical forests are being destroyed at the rate of 100 acres per minute, some environmentalists estimate. Another threat to tropical birds is the growth of the illegal pet trade. Parrots are often captured illegally because they can be sold for large amounts of money. Unfortunately, only about 10 out of each 100 captured parrots live long enough to become pets. Ask students what they think could be done to help save the lives and homes of tropical birds. Then, as a class, investigate what is being done. There are many groups dedicated to helping save the world's rain forests. The Rainforest Action Network (450 Sansome Street, Suite 700, San Francisco, CA 94111) organizes letter-writing campaigns for rain forest preservation. If desired, write a class letter requesting information about a letter-writing campaign in which your students could participate.

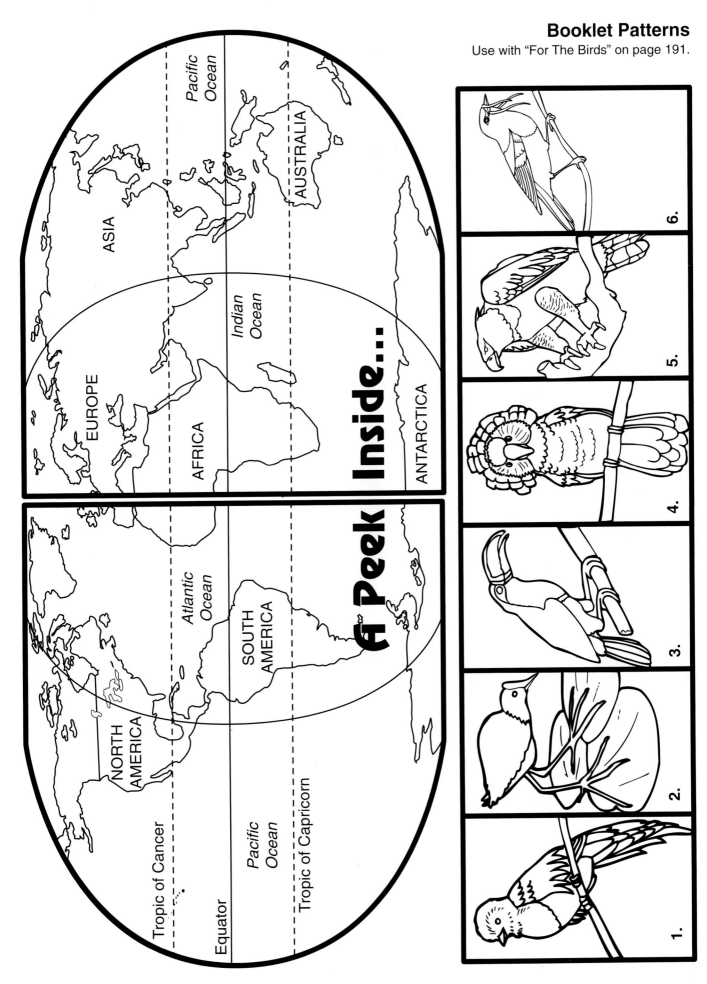

A Peek Inside...

Pacific Ocean

ASIA

AUSTRALIA

EUROPE

AFRICA

Indian Ocean

ANTARCTICA

NORTH AMERICA

Atlantic Ocean

SOUTH AMERICA

Pacific Ocean

Tropic of Cancer

Equator

Tropic of Capricorn

1.
2.
3.
4.
5.
6.

# Booklet Project

Use with "A Peek At Beaks" on page 192.

I reach inside flowers with my long, curved bill. I find sweet nectar there.

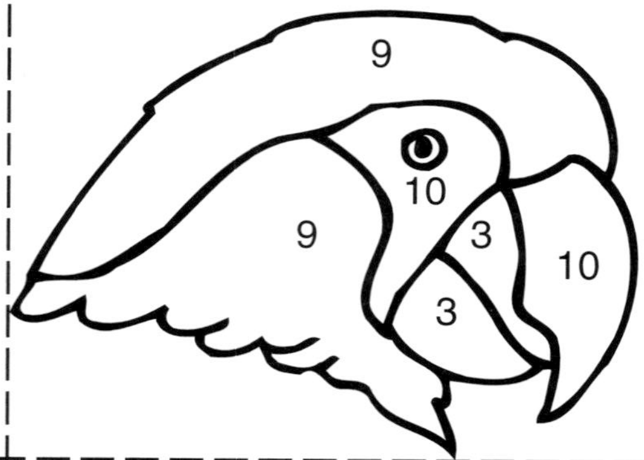

My long, straight beak is perfect for snapping up insects.

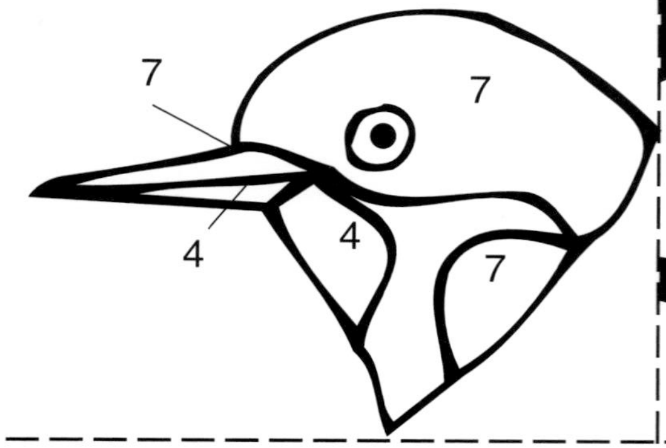

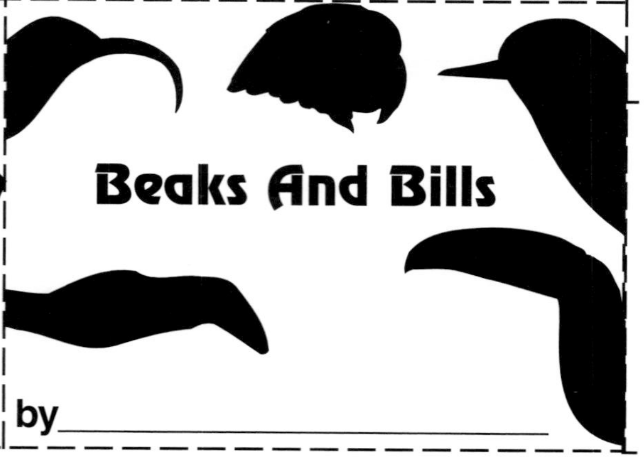

I reach out with my long bill to pluck berries and seeds from trees.

My bill looks like it has been broken in half. I find my food underwater.

My beak is short and powerful! I use it to crush seeds and nuts.

## Color Code

1 = pink
2 = white
3 = black
4 = orange
5 = blue

6 = yellow
7 = green
8 = brown
9 = red
10 = gray

## Toco Toucan

## Scarlet Macaw

## Beaks And Bills

by _____

## Greater Flamingo

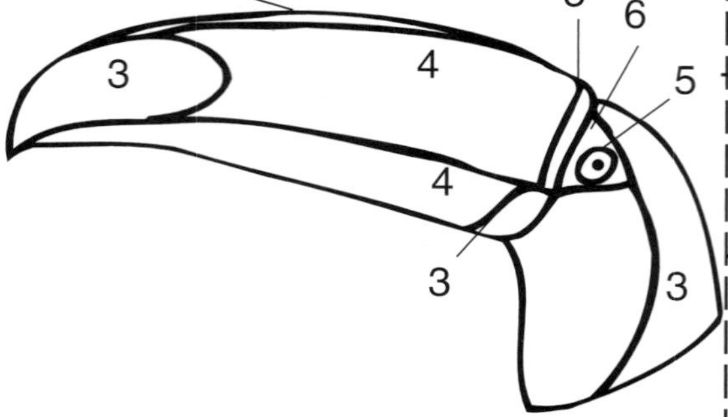

## White-Tipped Sicklebill

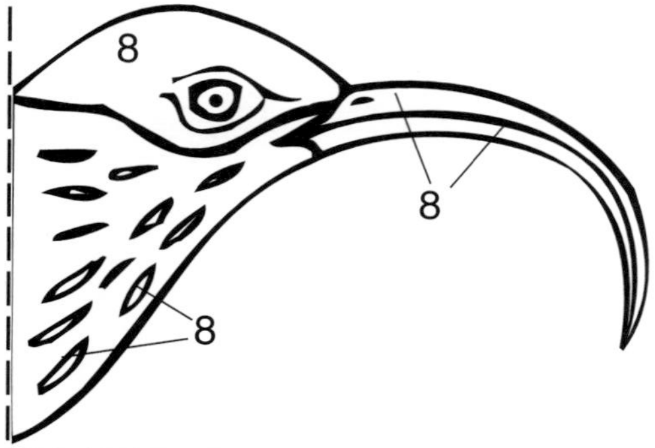

## Puerto Rican Tody

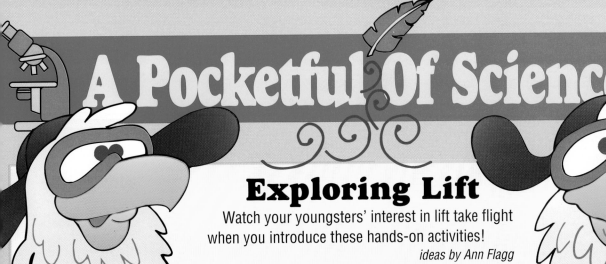

# A Pocketful Of Science

## Exploring Lift

Watch your youngsters' interest in lift take flight when you introduce these hands-on activities!

*ideas by Ann Flagg*

## Activity 1: Air Power

**Each student will need:**

a small spool of thread
a four-inch square of plastic wrap
a rubber band
a sharpened pencil
a thumbtack
a three-inch tagboard square

**Directions for the student:**

Use the plastic wrap to cover one end of the thread spool; then use the rubber band to secure the plastic in place. Gently poke a sharpened pencil into the middle of the spool—through the plastic. Use one hand to hold the covered end of the spool up to your mouth. Position your other hand at the opposite end of the spool. Blow air into the center of the spool.

**Question to ask:**

1. What happened?

**Next:**

Demonstrate how to gently poke the thumbtack into the center of the tagboard square, invert the tagboard, and set the uncovered end of the spool over the protruding end of the thumbtack. When students have completed these steps, ask them to predict what will happen when they blow into their spools. Record their predictions. Then have each student place his lips over the plastic-covered end of his spool and blow as hard as he can as he slowly lifts his head. Surprise! Thanks to air power, the tagboard square rises with the spool!

**More questions to ask:**

1. Did the tagboard square behave differently than you expected? How?
2. Where did the air go when you blew into the spool?

### This is why:

*Moving air exerts less pressure than still air. The air that you blow through the spool is dispersed at the bottom of the spool—over the tagboard square. This moving air exerts less air pressure than the still air below the tagboard. The still air pressing on the bottom of the square creates an upward force called lift.*

## Activity 2: More About Moving Air

**Each student will need:**

a 2" x 11 1/2" paper strip

**What to do:**

Hold one end of the paper strip just below your lower lip. Ask students what they think will happen when air is blown across the paper. Find out how many students think the unattached end of the paper will move upward (downward). Then have each student hold her paper strip as you have modeled and blow hard across the top of the strip.

**Questions to ask:**

1. How would you describe the air above (below) the paper strip?
2. How is this paper strip similar to the tagboard square in Activity 1?
3. Using your knowledge of air power, or *lift,* how do you think lift affects the flight of birds? Airplanes?

### This is why:

*The moving air above the strip causes a decrease in air pressure and the still air below pushes the unattached end of the strip upward—creating lift. It is air flowing over the wings of a bird that keeps the bird aloft. Birds flap, or move, their wings forward to make air flow over them. The curved wings of an airplane help it to sustain lift because the curve forces the air above the wing to travel faster than the air below the wing. The principle of lift was first discovered by Daniel Bernoulli. Bernoulli's principle states that the pressure of a liquid or a gas decreases as its speed increases.*

Pam Crane

## Activity 3:
## Winging It

**Each student will need:**
a golf-ball-size portion of play dough

**What to do:**
Challenge each student to use his play dough and his knowledge of lift to mold an airplane wing that—based on its shape—could create lift. Remind students that the air on top of the wing must be forced to move more quickly than the air on the bottom of the wing.

**Questions to ask:**
1. How does your wing design enable air to move faster on top of the wing than on the bottom of the wing?
2. How do you think people learned about wing design? Why?

### This is why:

*Students who understand Bernoulli's principle are more likely to design a curved wing. The wing of a bird or an airplane is curved on top and flat on the bottom. The curve on top of the wing forces air to flow up and across the top of the wing. As a result this air must travel farther in the same amount of time as the air traveling beneath the flat bottom of a wing. The faster moving air decreases the air pressure above the wing and lift results. The leading edge of a bird or airplane wing is also thicker than the trailing edge. The thick leading edge causes air to move aside. The thinner trailing edge lets air slip by with less resistance. After people discovered that it is the curved shape of a bird's wing that creates lift, people began to build airplane wings that were slightly curved.*

## Activity 4:
## The Wonder Of Wings

**Each student will need:**
one wing pattern from page 197    a pencil    scissors
tape    crayons

**What to do:**
Ask each student to color and cut out his wing pattern, fold it on the thin line, and tape the ends of the resulting wing together. Next have each student slide his wing onto his pencil. The taped ends of the wing should hang below the pencil and the curved wing surface should face away from his body. Then, as he grasps each end of his pencil in a different hand, instruct each student to hold the pencil slightly below his lower lip and blow hard across the top of the curved wing surface. Repeat the activity, but this time have each child position his wing so that he blows across the flat wing surface.

**Questions to ask:**
1. What happened?
2. Why is it important for an airplane wing to be curved on top and flat on the bottom?
3. What else does an airplane (bird) need for flight?

### This is why:

*Students will discover that blowing across the curved wing surface creates lift, and blowing across the flat wing surface does not. An airplane with inverted wings could not achieve lift. Four basic forces govern flight: lift, gravity (weight), thrust (the power which boosts the bird or plane into the sky), and drag (air resistance, the opposing force of thrust). A correctly designed airplane needs speed and engine power to boost it into the air. A bird relies on its powerful chest muscles to thrust it into the air. However, a heavy bird such as a swan also needs a long runway to build up enough speed to take off.*

**Note To Teacher:** Use with "Activity 4: The Wonder Of Wings" on page 196.

# A Pocketful Of Science

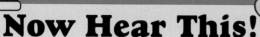

## Now Hear This!

What makes sound? Where does it come from? What does it look like? These are questions that youngsters often ask about this mysterious topic. Use these hands-on activities to learn about sound. Your youngsters will be all ears!

*ideas by Ann Flagg*

### Activity 1: Listen Up!

**You will need:**
a poster-board or cardboard divider
items that can be used to make distinctive sounds such as a bell, a plastic grocery bag, inflated balloons (and a pin), a stapler (and paper), a rubber band, a pair of scissors (and paper), and dice.

**What to do:**
Set up the divider on a table at the front of the room. Conceal the sound-making items behind the divider. Explain that you will be making several different sounds. Encourage students to listen carefully. Repeat each sound two or three times; then invite your students to identify the sound.

**Questions to ask after each new sound is made:**
1. How do you think this sound was made?
2. What word do you think best describes this sound?
3. What other sounds do you think resemble this sound?

### This is why:

*Sounds are all around us. The human ear can hear a wide range of sounds, but there are many sounds that it cannot hear. There are also sounds that our bodies tune out. For example, people do not hear most of the sounds that their bodies make. This is because the human body has a mechanism that screens out its own sounds. This enables people to hear the sounds that stimulate their brains. There are also many sounds in our environment that we constantly hear, but rarely listen for. Learning to listen carefully is important when exploring sound. Sounds carry information. The sounds around us connect us to our environment.*

### Activity 2: Exploring Vibrations

**For each student you will need:**
one fine-toothed comb
a rectangle of waxed paper that can be folded over the teeth of the comb

**What to do:**
Lay three fingers across your Adam's apple. Ask your youngsters to cover their throats in a similar manner. When the students' fingers are in place, have them join you in singing a familiar song. Then, as a class, have the students use their voices to make a variety of sounds.

**Questions to ask:**
1. What did you feel with your fingers when you sang and made noises with your voice?
2. How can you make the feeling stop? change? start again?

**Next:**
Distribute the combs and the pieces of waxed paper. Show students how to fold the waxed paper over the teeth of their combs. Then demonstrate how to play the resulting hummer. To do this, slightly pucker your lips and hold the teeth of the comb up to your mouth so that the waxed paper just touches your lips. Keeping the hummer in place, hum a familiar song with your youngsters.

**More questions to ask:**
1. What did you feel when you hummed into the hummer?
2. How did this feeling compare to what you felt when you sang?
3. How is making sounds with your voice similar to making sounds with the hummer?

### This is why:

*All sounds are caused by vibrations. The vibrations the children feel on their throats and lips are the sources of the sounds they hear. These vibrations create wavelike disturbances in the air called sound waves. The movement of a sound wave from its vibrating source allows us to hear sounds. Sound waves cannot be seen; however, our eardrums sense the vibrations in the air and send messages to our brains.*

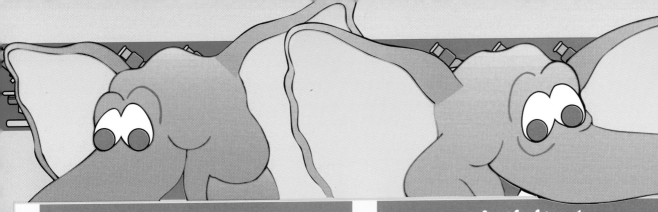

## Activity 3:
## It's All In Your Voice

**You will need:**
an empty, plastic soda bottle
a sharp knife
a balloon
scissors

**What to do:**

In advance cut away the bottom of the soda bottle just above its base. Snip off the neck of the balloon; then stretch the balloon over the large opening at the end of the bottle. Be sure the balloon fits snugly around the bottle.

Hold the neck of the bottle to your lips after asking each of two student volunteers to lay one finger across the balloon-covered opening. Using a strong voice, speak loudly into the neck of the bottle. Ask the volunteers to describe what they felt. If time permits, repeat the activity so that each student may take a turn.

**Questions to ask:**
1. What do you think you felt when I spoke into the bottle?
2. Do you think the feeling would change if I whispered or sang into the bottle? Why?
3. How is the balloon similar to the hummer you made?

### This is why:

The vibrations felt on the balloon surface were the result of sound waves. When you spoke into the neck of the bottle, vibrations were created. These vibrations traveled in waves through the air inside the bottle. When the sound waves struck the balloon, the balloon vibrated just like the waxed paper did when you used the hummer. Since all sounds are created by vibrations, even the slightest whisper will send sound waves through the bottle. However, the sound waves created by a whisper will feel different when they strike the balloon surface than the sound waves created by a shout.

Save the balloon-covered bottle from this activity to use with Activity 6 on page 200.

## Activity 4:
## Vibrations And Pitch

**Each student will need:**
one medium-size rubber band
two pencils
one hardcover textbook

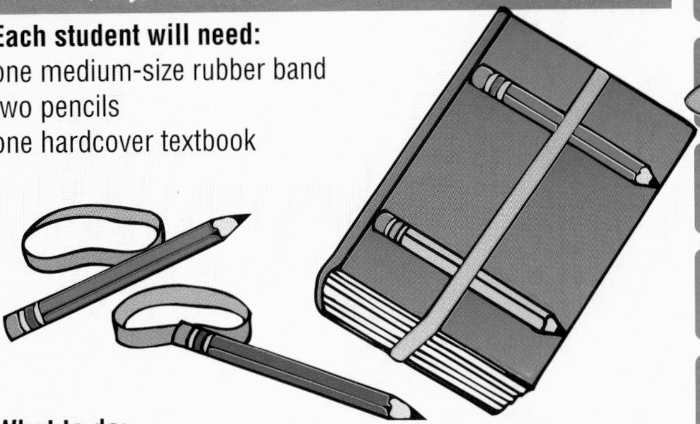

**What to do:**

To begin distribute the rubber bands and establish appropriate safety guidelines. Then challenge each youngster to use his rubber band to make a variety of noises. Next make sure that each youngster has two pencils and a hardcover textbook; then show the students how to use their supplies to create a sound maker. (See the illustration. Make sure there are no twists in the rubber band.) Once the sound makers are made, allow ample time for the youngsters to investigate the different sounds they can make using these unique contraptions. Use the questions below to encourage experimentation.

**Questions to ask:**
1. What happens when you pluck and strum the rubber band?
2. How can you make a loud sound? a soft sound?
3. What happens when you move the pencils closer together? farther apart?

### This is why:

This activity provides another chance for students to see the relationship between vibrations and sounds. In addition you can help youngsters discover that pitch (the highness or lowness of a sound) is relative to vibration speed, and that vibration speed is determined by the size of the vibrating object. In the case of the sound maker—when the pencils are at opposite ends of the textbook, the elevated portion of the rubber band is at its greatest length. Plucking the band in this position produces slow vibrations that in turn create a low sound. To create a higher sound, faster vibrations are needed. This can be achieved by moving the pencils closer together, thus shortening the length of the elevated portion of rubber band. A person's vocal chords are similar to rubber bands. One reason female singers often have higher singing voices is because their vocal chords are normally shorter than men's.

## Activity 5: Check Out These Vibrations!

**You will need:**
a small, colored paper plate
a tablespoon of white rice
a radio or tape player with a large speaker

**What to do:**
Gather the youngsters around your audio equipment. Position the equipment so that the paper plate can be placed directly on top of the speaker. Then carefully sprinkle the rice on the paper plate. Turn on the music. As students observe, vary the volume of the music and (if possible) play several different musical selections.

**Questions to ask:**
1. What is happening to the rice? Why?
2. What happens when the speaker volume is increased? decreased?
3. Does the music affect the movement of the rice? Why or why not?

### This is why:

A sound recording is really a series of vibrations. As the vibrations (or sound waves) leave the speaker, they cause the speaker to vibrate. This makes the rice appear to be dancing. When the volume of the speaker is increased, more energy is released. This creates stronger vibrations, which in turn increase the movement of the rice. Since each musical selection is a collection of unique vibrations, the rice reacts differently each time a new musical selection is introduced.

## Activity 6: The Human Ear

**You will need:**
the bottle-and-balloon project used in Activity 3
a simple diagram of the inside of the human ear

**What to do:**
Repeat or review Activity 3 with the students. It is important that the youngsters remember the vibrations they felt on the surface of the stretched balloon. Next display a diagram of the inside of the human ear.

**Questions to ask:**
1. What part of the ear do you think captures sound waves that are in the air?
2. What part of the ear might vibrate like the balloon covering on the bottle?

### This is why:

Sound waves travel through the air at all times. Any noise heard is the result of sound waves. The outer ear is designed to collect sound waves and funnel them inside the ear. Once inside the ear, the sound waves travel down the ear canal. At the end of the canal lies the eardrum. When the sound waves strike the eardrum, it vibrates like the surface of the stretched balloon (Activity 3). The vibrations from the eardrum are then sent to the brain in the form of a nerve message. This entire process happens very quickly and continues all day long.

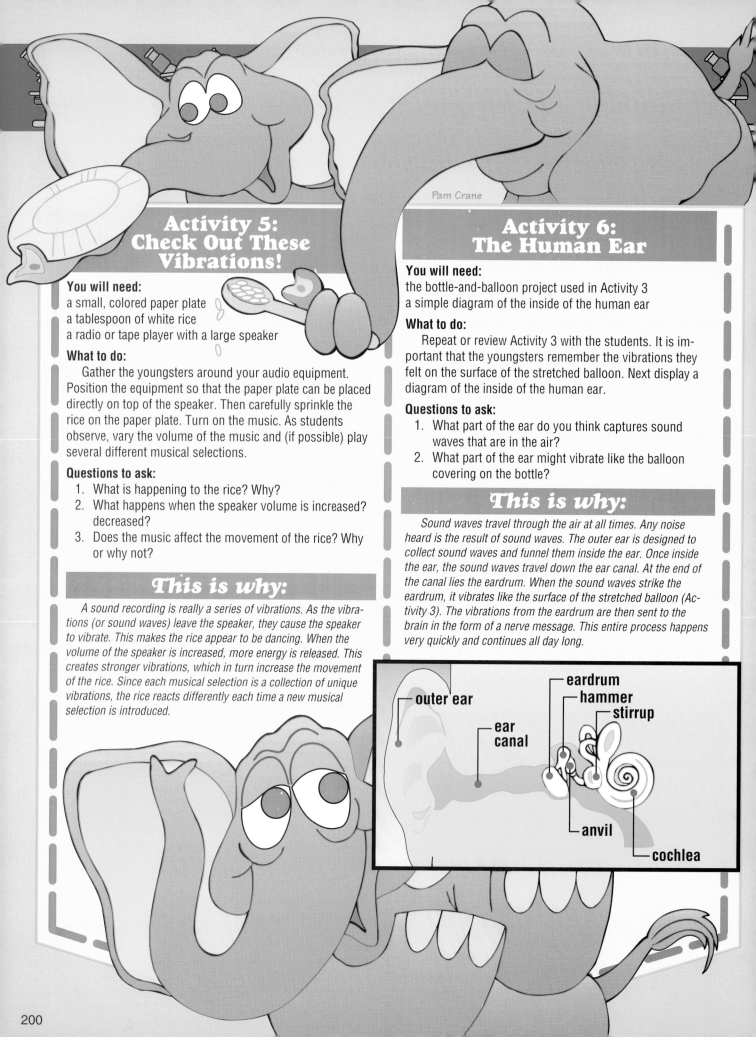

- outer ear
- ear canal
- eardrum
- hammer
- stirrup
- anvil
- cochlea

Pam Crane

# SOCIAL STUDIES UNITS

# A CONTINENTAL APPROACH
## TO INTERNATIONAL GAMES

Playing games is an important part of childhood—and it's fun besides! With this game plan, your students are introduced to games that are played in other parts of the world. As an added bonus, they learn about the seven continents, too.

## DESTINATION: ASIA

Asia is the largest continent in both population and size. The continent covers almost a third of the world's land area!

### Vietnam

*You can expect squeals of laughter—and twisting and turning—as students play this game from Vietnam.*

#### Catch A Carp's Tail
**Number Of Players:** six per line
**Equipment Needed:** none
**To Play:** Each group of six players stands single file to form a carp. With the exception of the first player in line (the head), each player places his hands on the hips of the player in front of him. To play the game, the head tries to tag the tail (the last player in line). The children in the middle of the carp must hang on tight to prevent the fish from pulling apart. When the head tags the tail, the tail moves to the head position and the game starts again.

### Burma

*This country in Southeast Asia is not quite the size of Texas, but it has almost three times as many people!*

#### Hiding The Stone
**Number Of Players:** an even number, eight or more
**Equipment Needed:** a small stone
**To Play:** Divide students into two equal teams—A and B. Each team sits single file on the floor so that the resulting lines are parallel. All players extend their legs straight ahead of them. Except for the first player in each line, each player's feet should barely touch the back of the teammate who is seated in front of him. To begin play, hand the stone to the first player of team A. The objective is for the player to hide the stone under the knees of one of his teammates. To do this, the player goes up and down his line of teammates, putting his hand under the knees of each child in line. When he returns to his position, the first player of team B guesses where the stone was placed. If the player is correct, the player from team A who hid the stone must join team B. Then the player from team B who guessed correctly hides the stone under the knees of one of his teammates. However, if the player from team B guesses incorrectly, he must join team A, and the next player in line for team A gets to hide the stone. Play continues in this manner. The team having the most players when time runs out is the winner.

## Denmark

*Almost completely surrounded by water, Denmark is well-known for its fishing industry. This game from Denmark is quite fishy and fun!*

### The Fish Game

**Number Of Players:** an even number, eight or more
**Equipment Needed:** two chairs less than the total number of players
**To Play:** Pair students and declare one couple to be IT. This couple is called the whales. Each of the remaining couples secretly selects the name of a fish; then it positions a pair of chairs somewhere in the playing area and sits in them. To begin play, the whales march about the playing area, weaving in and out between the chairs, calling out the names of fish. If a couple's secret fish name is called, the pair must march in line behind the whales. After the whales have called out as many fish names as they know or want, they declare, "The ocean is calm!" This signals all seated players to march in line behind the whales. The whales lead the students for as long as desired, but when they suddenly call out, "The ocean is stormy!" all couples run to find chairs. The couples may not separate. The couple left standing becomes the whales for the next game. Be sure to have each seated couple secretly choose a new fish name before the next round of play begins.

## DESTINATION: EUROPE

Unfortunately we can't provide a game from the more than 40 countries of Europe! However, your youngsters are sure to enjoy the following games from Denmark and Spain. Assist your students in finding these locations on a world map; then let the playing begin!

## Spain

*Spain is famous for its bullfights, castles, and sunny climate. This game can introduce students to several Spanish cities.*

### Come On Over!

**Number Of Players:** an even number, eight or more
**Equipment Needed:** none
**To Play:** Divide students into two teams; then line up the teams so that they face each other. There should be about ten feet between the two teams. Name each team for a different city in Spain, such as "Valencia" and "Madrid." The object of the game is for the citizens of one city to capture all the citizens of the other. To begin play, choose a player from Valencia to travel to Madrid. Each player from Madrid extends one hand, palm up. The visitor from Valencia walks down the line and rubs his hand over the extended palms. Eventually the visitor claps the palm of one Valencia player. This player chases the Madrid player as he runs for home. If the Valencia player tags the Madrid player before he reaches his team line, the Madrid player is taken captive and returned to Valencia with his captor. If the player is not tagged, the Valencia player returns home alone. Play continues with a Valencia player traveling to Madrid and repeating the same actions. The game is over when one city is captured, or time runs out, in which case the city with the most people is declared the winner.

## DESTINATION: AFRICA

The continent of Africa is about four times the size of the United States. Within this vast continent there are more than 50 countries and territories! Help students locate the continent of Africa on a world map; then help them find the African countries where the next two games are played.

## Egypt

*This Egyptian tug-of-war game has been played in Egypt for centuries—and it is still played in Egyptian schools today.*

### Tug-Of-War

**Number Of Players:** an even number of three-player teams
**Equipment Needed:** a large grassy playing area, a long length of string or yarn, a whistle
**To Play:** Lay the length of string down the center of the playing area. Have half of the teams line up single file behind the string. On the other side of the string and directly opposite these teams, have the remaining teams line up single file. Have each team leader (the player closest to the string) clasp hands with the team leader opposite him, while the rest of the players hold onto the waists of the teammates in front of them. At the sound of the whistle, each team tries to bring its opponents across the string to its side by pulling and leaning backwards. When a team is tugged over the line, both teams involved sit down. When all the teams are sitting, the round is over. Then rotate the teams so that each team has a new opponent and play another round.

## Ghana

*Because of its warm climate, Ghana is home to many types of snakes. Here's a fun game that puts this cold-blooded reptile in the spotlight!*

### Big Snake

**Number Of Players:** ten or more
**Equipment Needed:** a large, defined indoor or outdoor playing area, several cones, a whistle
**To Play:** Choose one child to play the snake. Using the cones, the snake marks off a corner of the playing area as its home. The snake stays in its home as the rest of the players roam the playing area. At the sound of the whistle, the snake runs out of its home and tries to tag free players. A player who is tagged must join hands with the snake and become a part of its body. The snake's head (the original snake) and tail (the last player to join the snake) are the only students who may tag free players. If the snake's body pulls apart, blow the whistle and send the snake home. When the snake has regrouped, blow the whistle again to signal that the snake is rejoined and ready to play. Free players may try to break apart the snake's body. The game ends when everyone is caught or out of breath!

# DESTINATION:
# ANTARCTICA

Your visit to the bottom of the globe will be brief. Find Antarctica on a world map. Find out what your youngsters know about this icy wonder. Remind students that because of the extreme weather of Antarctica, few people live there—in fact, only a small number of scientists call Antarctica their home.

# DESTINATION:
# AUSTRALIA

*Australia is unique because it is the only country that is a continent. As students locate Australia on a world map, inform them that Australia produces a large amount of our world's wool.*

### Sheepdog Trials
**Number Of Players:** eight or more, divided into teams of equal numbers of players
**Equipment Needed:** a large playing area, a defined starting line, two inflated balloons per team (provide a different color for each team), one jump rope per team, one 3" x 12" strip of cardboard per team
**To Play:** Create a starting line in the center of the playing area. Divide students into equivalent teams, and line up each team single file behind the starting line. Opposite each team, at the far end of the playing field, use a jump rope to form a pen. At the back of each pen, leave an entrance. Place two sheep (balloons) in front of each team and hand the first player in line a sheepdog (cardboard strip). On your signal, the first player of each team uses the sheepdog to guide his sheep down the course and into his team's pen through the rear entrance. The first player to have both of his sheep in the pen scores a point for his team. Continue play until all players have herded the sheep. The team with the most points wins.

# DESTINATION:
# SOUTH AMERICA

South America is the fourth-largest continent in the world and is home to almost a fourth of all the known animals in the world! Help students find South America on a world map; then give them map-related clues so that they can guess the country in which each of the following games is played.

## Peru
*This educational jump-rope game called "El Reloj" (EL ray-loh) is a popular children's game in Peru. The faster the game is played, the more exciting it becomes!*

### The Clock
**Number Of Players:** eight or more
**Equipment Needed:** a long jump rope (15–20 feet)
**To Play:** Select two rope turners. As they practice turning the rope, have the remaining players line up single file about ten feet away from the turning rope. When the rope turners are turning the rope so that it swings in a complete circle and lightly touches the ground at the bottom of each turn, begin play. The first player in line runs through the rope without a jump. The second player runs in, jumps one time, and runs out as the players say, "One o'clock." The third player follows, jumps two times, and runs out as the players say, "Two o'clock." The game continues with this jump pattern until one player makes 12 consecutive jumps (12 o'clock). If a player touches the rope or misses the correct number of jumps, he exchanges places with a rope turner and the game begins again.

## Bolivia
*Players must keep their eyes on a handkerchief when they play this Bolivian game!*

### The Handkerchief Game
**Number Of Players:** nine or more
**Equipment Needed:** a handkerchief
**To Play:** Place a flattened handkerchief in the middle of the playing area. Divide students into four teams and one IT. Have each team sit in single file facing a different edge of the handkerchief. When the teams are in position, IT circles around the group and drops the handkerchief behind a player seated at the end of one team. The players on the team jump up and run around the group. IT takes a vacated spot. The last player to return is without a seat and becomes the new IT.

# DESTINATION:
# NORTH AMERICA

The third-largest of the seven continents, North America spans from the icy Arctic to the warm tropics. After students have located the continent on a world map, help them find Canada and Mexico—since a game from each of these countries is provided. If desired, have students locate the United States, too; then take a bit of time to play some of your students' favorite games.

## Canada

*Many of the games that are played in Canada and the United States were played in the colonial days. These games have been played and taught and adapted so many times that today it's next to impossible to know where the games originated. This game from Canada may feel familiar to your students.*

### Pass The Broom

**Number Of Players:** eight or more
**Equipment Needed:** a long-handled broom, music that can be quickly stopped and started
**To Play:** Students stand in a large circle formation, facing inwards. Each student holds one hand behind his back. Pass a broom to one player. While the music is playing, the players pass the broom around the circle in a designated direction. The child who is holding the broom when the music stops must drop out of the circle. Continue play in this manner until only one student remains!

## Mexico

*The title of this next game brings to mind the beautiful parrots and other colorful birds that flourish in Mexico's lush rain forests.*

### The Little Parrot

**Number Of Players:** eight or more
**Equipment Needed:** a small object such as a pebble or bean bag
**To Play:** Students sit on the floor in a large circle, facing inwards. Give one player the small object. This student becomes player 1. She turns to the player on her right (player 2) and asks, "Won't you buy this little parrot?" Player 2 asks, "Does it bite?" Player 1 answers, "No, it does not bite," and hands the object to player 2. Player 2 turns to the player on her right (player 3) and asks, "Won't you buy this little parrot?" Player 3 asks, "Does it bite?" Player 2 does not answer the question, but instead turns to player 1 and asks, "Does it bite?" Player 1 answers, "No, it does not bite." Player 2 repeats the answer to player 3 and then hands over the object. Play continues in this manner, with the question "Does it bite?" always being referred back to the first player for the answer. The answer is likewise passed from player to player until it reaches the player who asked the question. The game is over when the last player in the circle turns to player 1 and asks her to buy the parrot—and she responds, "Yes! I will buy the parrot for it does not bite!"

# Hear Ye! Hear Ye!
## Read All About Colonial Times

Betwixt and between the starched-collared Pilgrims and the stalwart, plodding pioneers, there lived a gritty, industrious collection of Americans known as the colonists. They were a reasonable lot, willing to farm the land and salute the Union Jack. When it became apparent that Mother England and good King George were demanding more than that, this independent-minded assembly of adventurers mustered the courage to take a stand against the most powerful nation in the world. They resolved to inaugurate a great experiment in freedom called democracy—and that made all the difference!

*books reviewed by Deborah Zink Roffino*

### A Williamsburg Household
*Written by Joan Anderson*
*Photographed by George Ancona*
*Clarion Books, 1988*

Breathtaking color photographs and stimulating text provide a fascinating look at what life was like for blacks and whites in Williamsburg, Virginia, just prior to the Revolutionary War. The story focuses on events of a fictional family in a typical colonial household.

### Phoebe The Spy
*Written by Judith Berry Griffin*
*Illustrated by Margot Tomes*
*Scholastic Inc., 1977*

Bravery can be ordinary citizens doing what they are certain must be done to guarantee the spread of a cause—in this case, freedom. This short chapter book offers the true story of a young black girl who risked her life to be a spy for the colonists. It's an engaging read-aloud for primary-aged listeners.

### The Joke's On George
*Written by Michael O. Tunnell*
*Illustrated by Kathy Osborn*
*Tambourine Books, 1993*

This fact-based story of Washington's unique friendship with Charles Willson Peale—portrait painter, cutting-edge museum curator, father of 17—affords an opportunity for students to see aristocrats at rest. Even George Washington—the man behind the stoic face on the dollar bill—could get flustered and chuckle at his own shortcomings. These small lessons serve to remind students that the men and women of history were multi-dimensional characters—real people with whom they may have a great deal in common.

### Betsy Ross
*Written & Illustrated by Alexandra Wallner*
*Holiday House, 1994*

Folk art in bright country colors decorates this glimpse into the life of a rather self-reliant rebel. Elizabeth Griscom Ross Ashburn Claypoole—a daughter of Pennsylvania Quakers—was a bit of a spitfire for the mid-1700s. She married outside her faith, outlived two husbands, and found a third by the age of 32. Betsy, very unlike most Quaker women, ran her own upholstery business for most of her life. The legend of her sewing the first American flag is the reason history notes this industrious American.

### Dear Benjamin Banneker
*Written by Andrea Davis Pinkney*
*Illustrated by Brian Pinkney*
*Gulliver Books, 1994*

Benjamin Banneker—a free black man with a burning desire to be a mathematician and a scientist—was born in Maryland in 1731. He fulfilled his dreams against enormous odds. Like George Washington, he became a surveyor. Like Ben Franklin, he published yearly almanacs. Like men who would fight and die years after his own death, he spoke out against slavery. This is the story of Banneker's correspondence with Secretary Of State Thomas Jefferson—a politician who spoke out against slavery, yet owned slaves. Refreshing and impressive oil-painted scenes enhance this story of a remarkable man.

## Thomas Jefferson:
## A Picture Book Biography
*Written by James Cross Giblin*
*Illustrated by Michael Dooling*
*Scholastic Inc., 1994*

This red-haired boy wonder wasn't just a colonist, he was the catalyst who authored the very document that provoked the British. This man—who would become a president and would single-handedly expand the new nation to double its size—was painfully shy, according to this well-written chronicle of Thomas Jefferson's life. Oil paintings capture the majesty of Monticello and the intense, sensitive, and enigmatic man who lived there. Thomas Jefferson was a man who would do much to shape the course of a nation.

## In 1776
*Written by Jean Marzollo*
*Illustrated by Steve Björkman*
*Scholastic Inc., 1994*

Playful illustrations sizzle with the energy of a fireworks display, activating this celebration of the American Revolution. Rollicking verse describes touchstones of history—the colonists' outrage at the King of England, how the Declaration of Independence came to be, and George Washington's important role in the fight for liberty. The joy of independence is the focus of this elementary explanation.

## Paul Revere's Ride
*Written by Henry Wadsworth Longfellow*
*Illustrated by Ted Rand*
*Dutton Children's Books, 1990*

Invite your youngsters to come along, on the eighteenth of April, that cool spring night in 1775 when a nation is born. Shadowed watercolors add mystery and realism to the rolling hills and thick forests of New England. Whether mostly fact or fiction, this Longfellow poem—in tribute to the silversmith's role in the war against Mother Britain—remains an integral part of our national heritage.

## The Baker's Dozen:
## A Colonial American Tale
*Retold by Heather Forest & Illustrated by Susan Gaber*
*Harcourt Brace Jovanovich, Publishers; 1988*

Before the birth of the nation, near Albany, New York, there lived a baker who became celebrated around the colonies for his unparalleled cookies. As his breads, cakes, and reputation rose, so did his ego and alas, his greed. This delicious explanation for how the term "a baker's dozen" became part of the nation's jargon and a customary token of good measure is bathed in soft watercolors.

## A Picture Book Of Benjamin Franklin
*Written by David A. Adler*
*Illustrated by John and Alexandra Wallner*
*Holiday House, 1990*

Benjamin Franklin began his life as the youngest son in a family of 17 children, and when he died he was considered one of America's greatest men. This account of Franklin's life is packed with the type of information that appeals to young learners. The sketches, in full color, offer details of the man and the era. As a writer, scientist, inventor, and statesman, Franklin was the father of American culture.

# Picturing The Past
## Learning About Colonial Times

*They came to the New World for different reasons, and with them they brought traditions native to their homelands. Little did they know that the strange environment they encountered would alter those traditions and lead to a uniquely American lifestyle that was a blend of the familiar and the original. Enhance your study of colonial America with the following activities.*

ideas contributed by Theresa Ives Audet and Karen Gibson

## Helpful Background Information

The colonial period began in 1607 with the settlement of Jamestown and ended with the start of the Revolutionary War in 1775. It began with a few hardy colonists. By the time it was over, more than 2,000,000 European settlers called the New World home. Instead of the rough, primitive conditions of the earliest settlers, there was a land of thriving farms and plantations, prosperous towns and small cities, and well-established schools, churches, and institutions of government. No longer solely dependent on foreign shipments of basic goods, these later colonists grew and produced enough to maintain a brisk trade with England and other countries. What began as scattered settlements along the Atlantic coast grew to 13 flourishing colonies and a frontier that stretched westward for hundreds of miles.

## Pomander Balls

Fragrant pomander balls were often hidden in baskets or placed in cupboards of colonial homes to hide unpleasant cooking odors. Colonial women often placed small pomander balls in their handkerchiefs when they traveled so they could sniff their sweet smell instead of foul street odors. Plan to make pomander balls at the beginning of your colonial study. The completed projects need to be stored in a cool, dark place for about two to three weeks. So by the time your colonial study is completed, the projects will be ready to take home!

**Materials:**

a firm apple, orange, lemon, or lime
whole cloves
ribbon
cinnamon
cheesecloth

string or yarn
a fork or toothpick
a dish
a wire hairpin

**Steps:**

1. Use a fork or toothpick to prick a hole in the skin of the fruit; then insert a clove in the hole. Repeat—studding the entire fruit with cloves. Keep the cloves close, but be careful not to break the skin between the cloves.

2. Stick the tips of a wire hairpin into the fruit at the stem; then roll the fruit in a dish of cinnamon.

3. Place the fruit in the center of a piece of cheesecloth. Bring the corners of the cheesecloth together and twist them around the hairpin. Tie the corners around the hairpin using a length of yarn or string; then tie a ribbon bow around the yarn.

4. Allow the fruit to dry in a cool, dark place for about two to three weeks or until the fruit hardens. Prick small holes in the cheesecloth; then place the pomander ball in a drawer or hang it in a closet.

## The Thirteen Colonies

You can count on students learning the names, locations, and sizes of the 13 colonies after a few rounds of this high-interest math game. Enlarge the map on page 212 onto a length of bulletin-board paper or cardboard. Using the chart, assign each colony a point value. (If a more difficult game is desired, increase the point values.) Place the resulting gameboard for two to four players on the floor, along with a container of five pennies. Before play begins the players decide what game score will indicate the final round of play. Then, standing in a predetermined location, each player takes a turn tossing the five pennies—one at a time—onto the gameboard. The object is to earn points by having each of the five pennies land in a different colony. When all five pennies have been tossed, the player adds up the total points he scored and verifies the amount with the other players. (A penny that lands on a boundary line does not earn any points and may not be tossed again.) The game continues until one player reaches the score determined at the start of the game. The player with the highest score at the end of that round of play is declared the winner.

| Colony | Points |
| --- | --- |
| Massachusetts | 5 |
| New Hampshire | 5 |
| New York | 2 |
| Rhode Island | 10 |
| Connecticut | 5 |
| Pennsylvania | 2 |
| New Jersey | 10 |
| Delaware | 10 |
| Maryland | 5 |
| Virginia | 2 |
| North Carolina | 2 |
| South Carolina | 2 |
| Georgia | 2 |

# School Days

*What was school like 250 years ago? Children of wealthy colonists had tutors or were sent to private schools. Colonists established some public schools, but most children from poor families were taught by their parents at home. Because some parents could not read or write, they primarily taught their children obedience, religious teachings, and skills they needed in daily life. The colonists, however, firmly believed that education was the way to rise in the world. So by 1647 laws were passed to provide schools for children in towns of 50 families or more.*

## Hornbooks

The first school that boys and girls went to in colonial days was called a *Dame School.* The teacher was a woman, and most often the children came to her home to learn to read and write. Instead of schoolbooks the students used *hornbooks.* Each hornbook was a thin piece of board with a handle. A printed page (which usually included letters of the alphabet, numerals, and a prayer or verse from the Bible) was mounted on one side of the board. This page was covered with a clear piece of horn. The handle of many hornbooks had a hole so that the hornbook could be worn around a child's neck or fastened to his belt with a length of rope or twine. A child left Dame School once he could read and write everything on his hornbook!

Students will enjoy using these present-day hornbooks. To make a hornbook, mount a brown construction-paper copy of the pattern on page 211 onto tagboard; then cut it out and punch a hole where indicated. Use a marker to personalize the hornbook and add desired details before laminating the cutout for durability. At each dotted line, make a slit and insert a paper clip. Staple a 6 1/2-inch square of clear acetate atop the hornbook; then thread a length of yarn though the hole and tie the yarn's ends. The resulting hornbooks can be used at school or used for homework. To incorporate the hornbooks into your daily activities, each morning distribute a colonial-related assignment on a 5 1/2-inch square of paper. Ask students to clip the papers to their hornbooks and complete the assignment during the day. Or distribute a similar-sized homework assignment. Students clip the homework assignment to their hornbooks, then carry their hornbooks home. The hornbooks and the completed assignments should be returned on the next school day.

## The New England Primer

Older students used a book called *The New England Primer.* It taught the alphabet using two-line rhymes, some of which taught moral values such as "A *dog* will bite a thief at night." Create your own updated version of *The New England Primer* by assigning each pair of students one or two letters of the alphabet. Have each pair write and illustrate a two-lined rhyme for each letter. Then have students copy their rhymes and mount their illustrations on large pieces of paper to make a class big book.

## Learning A Trade

A boy (and sometimes a girl) often left home at the age of 14 to become an *apprentice* to a *craftsman.* For the next three to seven years, he would become part of the master's household and learn the master's trade. The apprenticeship benefited everyone. The boy's parents had one less to feed, clothe, and house. The master had a helper. And the boy not only learned a trade but was also taught to read and write by his master.

Here's a fun way to find out what trades your youngsters might have pursued during colonial times. Distribute student copies of page 214. Discuss the jobs listed below. Explain that some craftsmen were shopkeepers who sold their goods to the public. The shops were often identified by wooden signs hanging outside the shops' doors. Have each student choose a trade he would have liked to apprentice in had he lived in colonial days, then design a sign for his shop!

### Some Colonial Occupations

**Blacksmith:** melted iron to make nails, hinges, and tools.
**Cooper:** made barrels.
**Cordwainer:** cut and sewed shoes and boots.
**Glassblower:** made glassware such as bottles and drinking glasses.
**Hatter:** made a variety of hats.
**Housewright:** designed and built homes.
**Joiner:** made fine wooden furniture.
**Printer:** published, edited, and printed newspapers and books.
**Shipwright:** built ships.
**Silversmith:** melted silver coins to make teapots and bowls.
**Storekeeper:** sold supplies in a store.
**Tanner:** processed animal hides into leather goods.
**Wigmaker:** created wigs out of cow, horse, or human hair.

# Colonial Games

*Every morning colonial children got up early and helped with family chores. They even helped after school and into the night. Colonial children did not have as much time to play as youngsters do today, but when they did play, they had loads of fun. In fact several of the games that colonial kids played are still played today! Here are a few games your students are sure to enjoy:*

**Hopscotch:** Today's version of hopscotch is very similar to the colonial version. Colonial youngsters, however, drew their hopscotch squares in the dirt with sticks and used rocks for their markers.

**Leapfrog:** Students may also recognize this partner game. To play, one partner squats down. The other partner places his hands on the squatter's back, leaps over the squatter, and then squats down. His partner stands up and likewise leaps over him. Play continues in this manner for as long as desired.

**London Bridge Is Falling Down:** Colonial kids sang and acted out this tune in much the same manner as youngsters do today.

**Squat Tag:** To play this game of tag, one player is chosen as It. The rest of the students are runners. A runner cannot be tagged when he is in a squatting position. When a predetermined number of runners have been tagged, a new It is chosen.

**Stone Poison:** You need one less stone than there are players to play this game of tag. Arrange the stones (rather large in size) on the playing field. Choose one player to be It. When It tags a player, this player becomes the new It. A player cannot be tagged if she has one foot resting on a stone.

**Blindman's Bluff:** This colonial favorite was played in the same manner as it is today.

**Hop, Skip, Jump:** Turn this colonial game into a high-interest math activity for partners. Beginning at a designated starting point, each player takes a turn completing the three motions—hop, skip, and jump—without pausing. The object is to cover as much distance as possible. A player's partner marks his final landing point and together they measure the distance traveled. Each player tries to improve his personal best during the allotted time.

## Colonial Quilts

No colonial home was without quilts because no home was without drafts! Many colonial women shared friendship quilts with friends and relatives. Each person wrote his or her name in a quilt block and embroidered it with colored thread. The woman then sewed all of the quilt squares together to make a friendship quilt.

To make a giant friendship quilt, divide the class into groups of four students. Give each child a copy of page 213. Have each student complete a quilt square by following the directions on the reproducible. Then provide each student with an eight-inch construction-paper square. Use two colors of construction paper so that you can mount the finished quilt in an alternating pattern on a bulletin board. If desired attach gathered crepe paper to the outer edges of the display for a quilt border; then add the title "Our Friendship Quilt."

## A Colonial Celebration

Conclude your study of colonial America with a patriotic party! For refreshments decorate a white sheet cake to resemble Old Glory—the colonial American flag. To do this use blue food coloring to tint a portion of white frosting. Brush the blue frosting into a rectangle as the background for the stars; then cover the remainder of the cake with the white frosting. Arrange 13 yogurt-covered raisins in a circle atop the field of blue. Then use red hots, strawberry slices, or red licorice pieces to create seven red stripes on the cake. Fruit punch (red, of course!) makes a refreshing beverage.

To make some noisemakers for the affair, have each student bring to school one empty bathroom tissue roll. To make a noisemaker, center an empty tissue roll on the long side of a 10" x 12" rectangle of red, white, or blue tissue paper. Wrap the paper around the roll and secure it with glue. Gather the paper at one end of the roll and tie it with a length of white or blue yarn. Drop ten dried beans or kernels of unpopped corn into the open end of the tissue roll; then gather the paper at the end of the roll and tie it with a second length of yarn or string. When the glue is dry, shake the resulting rattle and make a whole bunch of noise!

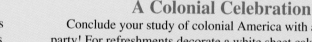

This hornbook belongs to _____.

# The Colonies In 1775

Use with "The Thirteen Colonies" on page 208.

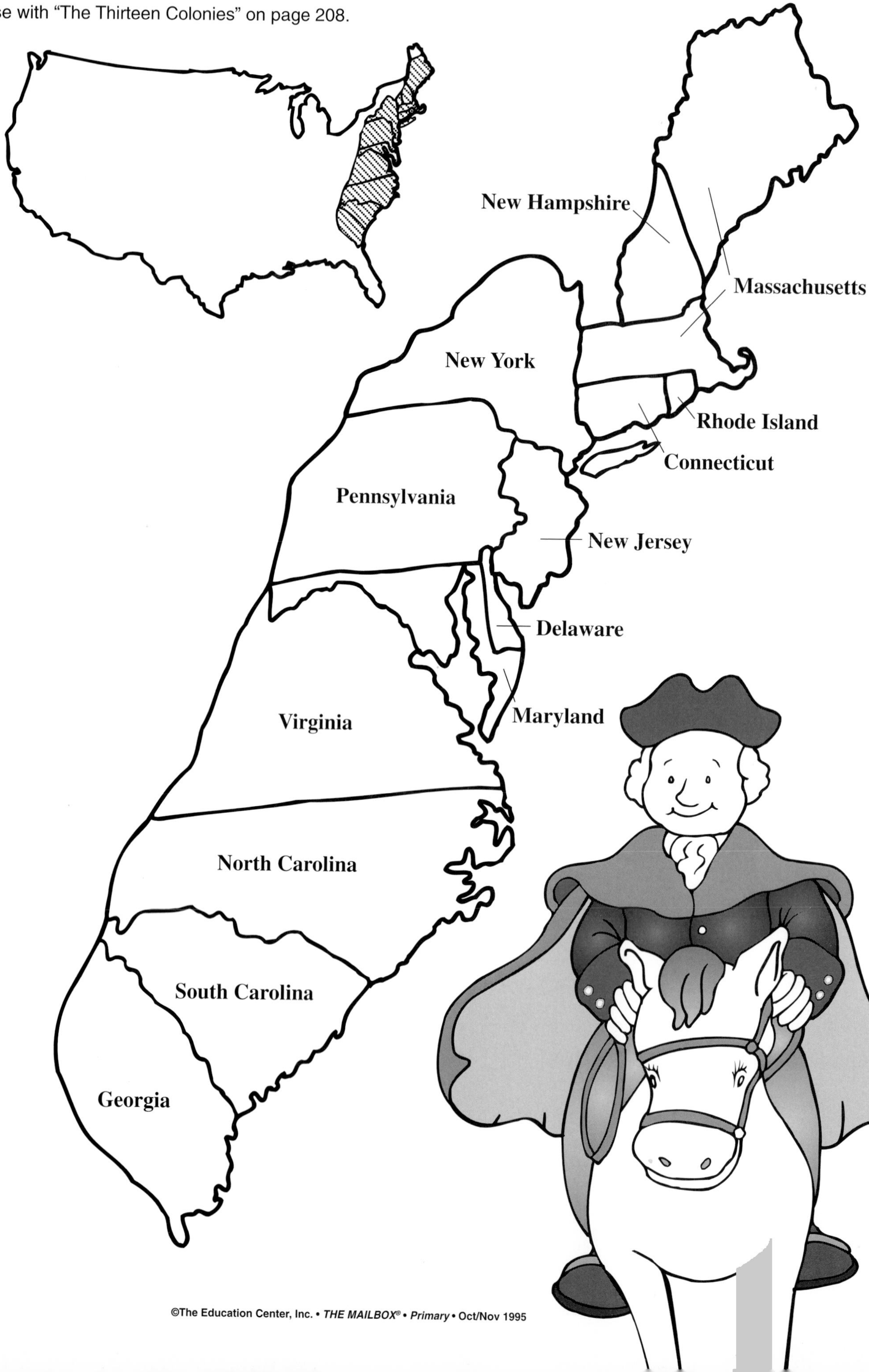

New Hampshire

Massachusetts

New York

Rhode Island

Connecticut

Pennsylvania

New Jersey

Delaware

Virginia

Maryland

North Carolina

South Carolina

Georgia

# Making A Friendship Quilt

Work together with your classmates to make a quilt square for a friendship quilt.

| 5 | 1 | 6 |
|---|---|---|
| 2 | 7 | 3 |
| 8 | 4 | 9 |

**To make a quilt patch:**
1. Write your name in box 1. Then use crayons or markers to decorate the box.
2. Ask a friend to write his or her name in box 2 and then decorate the box.
3. Complete box 3 and box 4 like you did box 2. Ask two different friends.
4. In boxes 5–9, draw and color one of the patterns below. Or make your own pattern.
5. Cut out the quilt square and glue it to a piece of construction paper.

**Patterns:**

**Pattern**
Use with "Learning A Trade" on page 209.

## Welcome To Mexico

Mexico is often described as a land of contrasts. To the north are dusty deserts; to the south are lush rain forests. There are hot, tropical coastlines. Flat plateaus are surrounded by high, mountainous areas. You'll also find huge cities and tiny villages—the populated areas and the pristine wilderness. Enlist your youngsters' help in finding Mexico on a physical map; then help the students locate the mountainous, flat, and coastal regions of Mexico along with its capital—Mexico City.

Next find your state on the map. Decide as a group if it would be better to drive or fly to this fascinating country. Propose a route of travel to and through Mexico and discuss the things that might be seen along the way. Conclude the lesson by reading aloud a book like *Mexico* by Karen Jacobsen (Childrens Press®, 1982) to give students more background information about our southern neighbors.

Travel to the land of sunshine and *sombreros*—Mexico. Use these across-the-curriculum ideas to teach your *muchachos* and *muchachas* about our neighbors south of the border. *Olé!*

*ideas by Michele Converse Baerns*
*and Stacie Stone*

## Grocery-Bag Garments

Typical dress in many parts of Mexico includes T-shirts, blouses, jeans, pants, skirts, and jackets. But in rural areas, many natives of Mexico still wear traditional clothing such as *guayaberas*—loose cotton shirts, *huaraches*—thick-soled sandals, or *huipiles*—cotton dresses trimmed with embroidered flowers. A wool scarf called a *serape* may be worn by a man on chilly nights. A *rebozo*, or shawl, is worn by a woman when she has visitors or goes into a village.

Dress up your study of Mexico by having students make their own serapes or rebozos. To begin have each student cut out the side panels of a large grocery bag so that it will lay flat. Then have the students use tempera paint and paintbrushes, markers, or crayons to decorate their serapes and rebozos. When the projects have dried, have students hole-punch a series of equally spaced holes along each end of their projects. Then, using three-inch lengths of colorful yarn, show students how to loop a yarn length through each hole as shown. When the serapes and rebozos have been completed, have students model their Mexican garb for their classmates. Plan for students to wear the garments again during a culminating activity like "It's A Celebration!" on page 219.

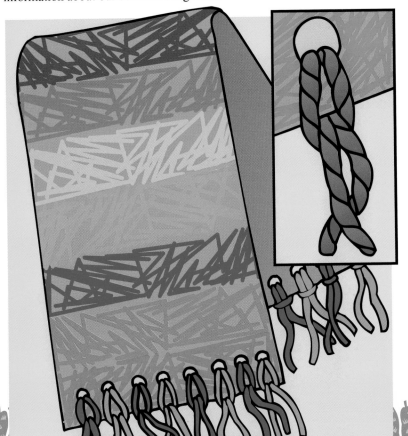

# Mexican Munchies

*Taquitos, tacos, tamales*—mmm, tantalizing! Many of the foods from Mexico are made from corn. This is because corn, or *maize*, has been an important crop in Mexico for thousands of years. Corn is used—dried or fresh—in main courses, soups, desserts, and drinks. Most importantly, the corn is ground into flour and used to make tortillas—flat, pancakelike bread. Tortillas are eaten at almost every meal. They are the basis for other Mexican foods such as *burritos* and *quesadillas*. Use these recipes to give your students a taste of Mexico.

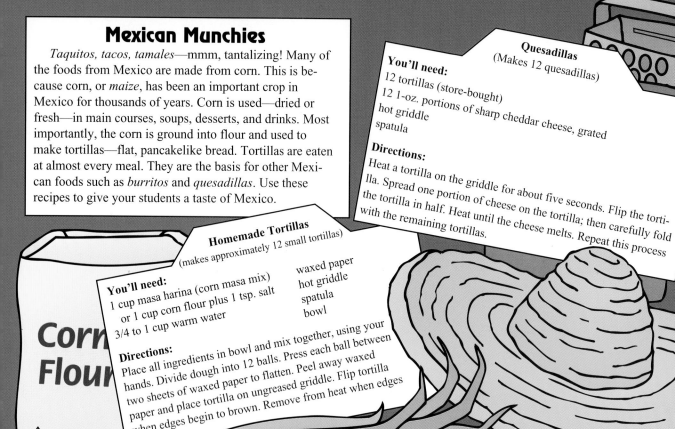

### Quesadillas
(Makes 12 quesadillas)

**You'll need:**
12 tortillas (store-bought)
12 1-oz. portions of sharp cheddar cheese, grated
hot griddle
spatula

**Directions:**
Heat a tortilla on the griddle for about five seconds. Flip the tortilla. Spread one portion of cheese on the tortilla; then carefully fold the tortilla in half. Heat until the cheese melts. Repeat this process with the remaining tortillas.

### Homemade Tortillas
(makes approximately 12 small tortillas)

**You'll need:**
1 cup masa harina (corn masa mix)
or 1 cup corn flour plus 1 tsp. salt
3/4 to 1 cup warm water
waxed paper
hot griddle
spatula
bowl

**Directions:**
Place all ingredients in bowl and mix together, using your hands. Divide dough into 12 balls. Press each ball between two sheets of waxed paper to flatten. Peel away waxed paper and place tortilla on ungreased griddle. Flip tortilla when edges begin to brown. Remove from heat when edges are brown.

## A Spectrum Of Spanish

Familiarize your youngsters with a bit of Spanish—the most commonly spoken language in Mexico. *My World Of Spanish Words* by Debbie MacKinnon (Barron's Educational Series, Inc.; 1995) is a wonderful classroom resource. The book's simple design and colorful photographs make it a terrific teaching tool.

When students are familiar with Spanish color words, they'll enjoy creating a Spanish color version of *Brown Bear, Brown Bear, What Do You See?* by Bill Martin Jr. (Henry Holt & Company, Inc.; 1992). Create the story as a class; then copy the text onto 12" x 18" sheets of white construction paper—patterning the format after the original story. Have the students illustrate the resulting pages; then bind the pages into a class booklet titled "Bear Moreno, Bear Moreno, What Do You See?"

### Color Word Translations

| | | | |
|---|---|---|---|
| **brown** | morena, moreno | **purple** | morada, morado |
| **red** | roja, rojo | **white** | blanca, blanco |
| **yellow** | amarilla, amarillo | **black** | negra, negro |
| **blue** | azul | **gold** | ora, oro |
| **green** | verde | | |

## Codex Books

Long ago the Maya were the most powerful group in Mexico. They were expert mathematicians, astronomers, and architects. One of the first writing systems in North America was developed by Mayans. It used pictures or symbols—called *heiroglyphs* or *glyphs*—to represent words and ideas. These glyphs were written on walls and in Mayan books called *codices*. Codices were different from modern-day books in that they were pleated and had to be unfolded in order to be read. Each codex told stories about Mayan gods and other significant people.

Students will enjoy creating a classroom codex that features people who are important to them. On a 9" x 12" sheet of white construction paper, have each student use crayons or markers to illustrate a significant person in her life. Then have each student write a sentence on her paper that explains *why* that person is, or has been, significant. To assemble the codex, position the student pages side by side. Place a 9" x 12" sheet of construction paper at the beginning and one at the end of the series of papers; then tape the long edges of the papers together. Fold the resulting booklet accordion-style. Decorate and write the title "Our Class Codex" on the front cover; then display the classy codex in your classroom library.

## Casa, Sweet Casa

Homes throughout Mexico vary widely. City dwellers might live in modern homes and apartments. Others may live outside the city in colonial-style homes that share a courtyard with several other families. Many of these homes are built of *adobe*—sun-baked bricks of earth and straw. Mexicans who live in rural areas of Central Mexico also use adobe to build their homes.

This adobe brick-making opportunity is sure to thrill your future architects and builders! Each student needs a clean and empty eight-ounce milk carton, a plastic spoon, one-half cup of dry dirt, one-half cup of powdered plaster of paris, one-quarter cup of water, and a small amount of dry grass or straw clippings.

To make his brick, a student combines the dirt and plaster of paris in his milk carton; then he stirs in the water. He adds grass clippings to the mixture until it thickens. Then he uses his spoon to smooth the top of his project. Place the projects on a sunny shelf to harden and dry. (This will take several hours or overnight.) Then have each student tear the milk carton away from his project to reveal an adobelike brick.

If desired, students can decorate their projects to resemble adobe homes. Provide markers, paintbrushes and tempera paints, and other desired craft supplies for decorating purposes. Then have the students create a village by arranging their adobe homes on a sheet of poster board. To complete the class project, invite students to add construction-paper trees and roads, and a variety of other decorations.

## Handwoven Baskets

Handwoven baskets are a popular craft item in Mexico. Your students are sure to be impressed with the results of this basket-weaving project! For each student you will need a clean and empty plastic margarine tub (or something similar—about 12 ounces in size) and three yards of raffia (available at your local craft store)—one yard of red, one yard of green, and one yard of natural. Prepare the containers for distribution by making an odd number of vertical cuts in the container. (The cuts should be about one inch apart and should stop at the base of the container. This will result in a series of plastic strips.) To begin his project, a student ties and knots one end of a length of raffia around one plastic strip—making sure his knot is on the inside of his container and the raffia is pushed to the bottom of the plastic strip. (Provide assistance as needed.) Then he weaves the length of raffia in and out of the strips of plastic until he uses the entire length—making sure the exposed end of the raffia is inside the container. He then repeats the process (starting where the last length of raffia ended) with the remaining lengths of raffia until the container is covered. After taping down any exposed ends of raffia inside his container, the student uses a permanent marker to label the bottom of his project with his name or initials. His handiwork is now ready to be displayed at your classroom market.

## To Market, To Market

In villages all over Mexico, market day is a weekly highlight. People come to buy or sell food and items like baskets, rebozos, flowers, and clay figurines. Share the story *Saturday Market* by Patricia Grossman (Lothrop, Lee & Shepard Books, 1994) to give students a better understanding of the happenings at a local market. Then select students to move several unused desks to an area of the classroom to create a marketplace. While several students cover the individual desks with brightly colored paper, have a small group of youngsters design a sign that reads *"La Plaza—The Market."*

See "Handwoven Baskets," "Corn-Husk Crafts," and "Mexican Pottery" for craft ideas that can be displayed at *La Plaza.*

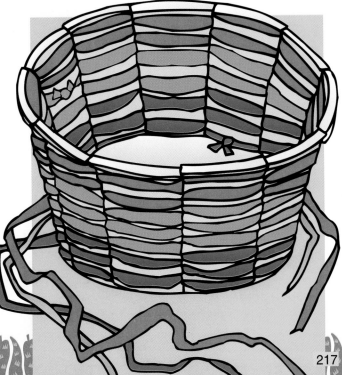

## Corn-Husk Crafts

These "a-maize-ing" dolls will delight your little amigos. To make a corn-husk doll, each student needs one 6-inch and one 18-inch length of tan twisted paper, a one-foot length of yarn, a black felt-tip marker, and a scrap (about 3" x 6") of brightly colored fabric. Assist each student in untwisting his lengths of twisted paper. To make a doll, a student bends the 18" strip in half lengthwise without creasing the paper. Then he places the six-inch strip between the bent strip, creating the arms for his doll. To secure the arms in place, he holds one end of his yarn length at the back of his project; then he wraps the yarn length diagonally around the project, crisscrossing it as shown. When he approaches the end of the yarn, he ties a knot at the back of the project. Using the black felt-tip marker, the student adds facial features to his doll. To complete the project he drapes his fabric scrap around the doll's shoulders to resemble a rebozo or a serape. Display the corn-husk dolls in your classroom marketplace.

## Mexican Pottery

Mexico is known for its brightly decorated pottery. Each student can create her own Mexican-style pottery using a three-inch ball of Crayola® Model Magic™, and permanent markers or acrylic paints and a paintbrush. After each student has molded her compound into the shape of a small animal, have her set it aside overnight so it will harden slightly. The next day, the student can decorate her figurine as desired. Add the colorful pottery to your marketplace display!

*Michelle McAuliffe and Marsha Black, Greensburg, IN*

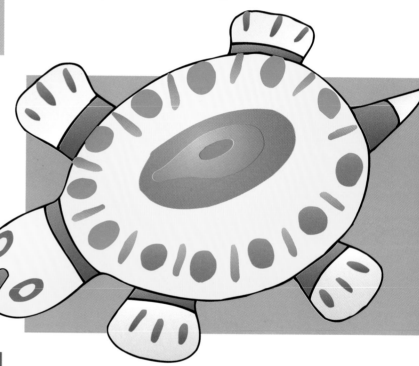

## Fiesta, Fiesta!

People all over Mexico enjoy fiestas! Fiesta parties and festivals are held for a variety of reasons. A fiesta can be a birthday celebration, a tribute to a local hero, or an acknowledgement of an important day in Mexico's history. Many religious fiestas, like Christmas and Easter, are celebrated nationwide. While each fiesta is different, many begin at dawn with the ringing of church bells or an explosion of fireworks. Colorful parades, dancing, music, food and drink, rodeos, and/or bullfights may follow.

To learn more about some of the holidays for which people in Mexico hold fiestas, divide students into four groups. Have a different group research each of the following: Christmas traditions in Mexico, Easter traditions in Mexico, Mexico's Independence Day, and Cinco De Mayo. Then have each group present information about the holiday it researched. Conclude the activity by discussing how celebrations in the United States are similar to or different than celebrations in Mexico.

## Comparing Cultures

Once students have been introduced to the culture of Mexico, have them compare life in Mexico to life in the United States. Display a chart like the one shown to initiate a discussion about a variety of topics. Ask student volunteers to record the observations of their classmates on the chart; then display the chart on a bulletin board. Invite students to add to the chart as they acquire more information.

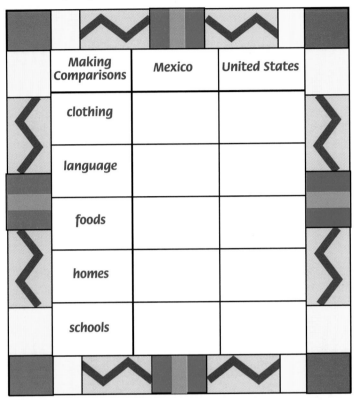

| Making Comparisons | Mexico | United States |
|---|---|---|
| clothing | | |
| language | | |
| foods | | |
| homes | | |
| schools | | |

## It's A Celebration!

Conclude your Mexico-related activities with a celebration of learning! Encourage students to invite their families to your classroom fiesta. The guests of honor can stroll through the classroom marketplace and view the student-made wares, then check out the student-created adobe village. As the visitors snack on a sampling of Mexican foods, the students can model the serapes and rebozos they made earlier in the unit. A presentation of the codex book and an oral reading of "Bear Moreno, Bear Moreno" will definitely be in order. If you are musically inclined, lead the students and your guests in a medley of songs (see "Song Collections") or add to the festive mood by playing selections from *Papa's Dream,* a recording that features traditional Mexican folk songs with a bit of classic rock 'n roll. (Available from Music For Little People at 1-800-727-2233: cassette #2089 @ $9.95; CD #D2089 @ $15.95.) A fun time is sure to be had by all!

## Song Collections

**De Colores And Other Latin-American Folk Songs For Children**
*Selected, Arranged, and Translated by José-Luis Orozco*
*Illustrated by Elisa Kleven*
*Dutton Children's Books, 1994*

This collection reflects all of Latin America across the pages, but author Orozco grew up in Mexico City. Combining his childhood recollections and adult research, this musician/author includes music notes. The verses are written in Spanish and English. Whimsical pictures dance over the brightly edged pages. Look for examples of architectural style, native instruments, and festival attire.

**Los Pollitos Dicen: The Baby Chicks Sing**
*Collected And Adapted by Nancy Abraham Hall &*
*Jill Syverson-Stork*
*Illustrated by Kay Chorao*
*Little, Brown And Company; 1994*

Music and bilingual text lie over lighthearted watercolors in this collection of traditional games, nursery rhymes, and songs from Spanish-speaking countries. An excellent resource that offers universal themes in appealing, singsong verse.

## Outstanding Teacher Resources

**Fiesta! Mexico's Great Celebrations**
*Written by Elizabeth Silverthorne*
*Illustrated by Jan Davey Ellis*
*The Millbrook Press, 1992*

This book is an explosion of information on the various Mexican fiestas.

**Mexico: The People**
*Created by Bobbie Kalman; with photographs*
*Crabtree Publishing Company, 1993*

From The Lands, Peoples, And Cultures Series, this book looks at the way of life of Mexican people, including family life, education, religion, city and village life, and work. Two other books from the series—*Mexico The Culture* and *Mexico The Land*—are also packed with information for a study of Mexico.

**A Taste Of Mexico**
*Written by Linda Illsley; with photographs*
*Thomson Learning, 1995*

Through a study of the foods of Mexico, the country's culture and geography are explored.

# Read Your Way Through Mexico

Find your travel ticket within the pages of this festive literature collection.

*books reviewed by Deborah Zink Roffino*

## Saturday Market

*Written by Patricia Grossman*
*Illustrated by Enrique O. Sánchez*
*Lothrop, Lee & Shepard Books; 1994*

Across the globe they are called flea markets, bazaars, and emporiums. In Mexico, they are the venue for the farmers and craftsmen who sell the fruits of their weekly labors. In the detailed descriptions of the folks who cross the market square, readers find a liberal sampling of Spanish vocabulary, explained in context. Bubbling with noise and excitement, the Saturday market shows off the wares, the clothing, and the culture of Mexico.

## Lorenzo, The Naughty Parrot

*Written by Tony Johnston & Illustrated by Leo Politi*
*Harcourt Brace Jovanovich, Publishers; 1992*

In this longer story, Johnston offers a clear picture of a rural Mexican family. The loudest member of this close-knit group is Lorenzo—a parrot who thinks he is a watch-dog. This possessive and overbearing pet has a squawk-ing opinion on every action in and around the residence. But nobody minds—in fact, they love it.

Spirited illustrations offer insight into life in the house and in the village.

## Diego

*Written by Jonah Winter & Illustrated by Jeanette Winter*
*Alfred A. Knopf, Inc.; 1991*

Diego painted everywhere. From the time he was a small boy, he re-created everything he saw. This beginning biography detailing the early years of Mexican artist Diego Rivera—with text in both Spanish and English—is a Reading Rainbow™ Review Book and the recipient of The New York Times Best Illustrated Children's Book Award. Diego's story is that of a gifted artist with the singular obsession to celebrate the beauty of Mexico.

## The Iguana Brothers: A Tale Of Two Lizards

*Written by Tony Johnston & Illustrated by Mark Teague*
*The Blue Sky Press, 1995*

This duo of laid-back lizards from Mexico are brothers and best friends. Given to random bouts of thinking, followed by long hours of lazing in the sun, Dom and Tom crawl through three low-key adventures. Communicating in an endearing "Span-glish" language, this pair will be a hit for enthusiastic and reluctant readers.

## The Old Lady And The Birds

*Written by Tony Johnston & Illustrated by Stephanie Garcia*
*Harcourt Brace & Company, 1994*

Shadow boxes, filled with collages of natural materials, depict a weathered Mexican woman passing the hours in harmony with her garden. She is alone—but never forlorn. She feeds the birds, chides them with love, and protects them. It is a touching story of friendship written in simple text.

## The Piñata Maker: El Piñatero

*Written & Photographed by George Ancona*
*Harcourt Brace & Company, 1994*

Piñatas, long a Mexican tradition, are becoming an ever-growing part of holiday celebrations across the United States. Curiosity about the origin and construction of this fun-filled art form is satisfied in this bilingual, photographic look at Tio Rico, a piñata maker in southern Mexico. Behind the faces in Ancona's candid shots, readers glimpse the architecture and inhabitants of Tio Rico's village.

## The Sad Night: The Story Of An Aztec Victory And A Spanish Loss

*Written & Illustrated by Sally Schofer Mathews*
*Clarion Books, 1994*

Youngsters learn in school that Cortés conquered the Aztecs in Mexico in 1519. This story—with blazing illustrations rendered in the style of Aztec codex art—displays the magnitude of that cultural clash. Moctezuma, as the Aztecs called their leader, laid down his awesome power before the Spaniards, believing that Cortés was the god Quetzalcoatl. Only once were the Aztecs victorious over the invaders. A riveting narration of Mexico's history.

## Postcards From Mexico

*Written by Helen Arnold; with photographs*
*Raintree Steck-Vaughn Publishers, 1996*

This collection of colorful postcards takes the reader on an exciting journey through Mexico. Each pictorial representation is accompanied by a brief, written message that describes the highlights of that particular stop. A kid-pleasing travel journal.

# A Folklore Sampling

## The Little Ant

*Written by Michael Rose Ramirez*
*Illustrated by Linda Dalal Sawaya*
*Rizzoli International Publications, Inc.; 1995*

This Mexican folktale teaches resolving conflict and taking responsibility for one's actions. There's a profusion of tropical colors and animated, bilingual text. Like the house that Jack built, the story cumulates, shifting the blame for a little ant's broken leg down a line of larger-than-life characters.

## The Moon Was At A Fiesta

*Written by Matthew Gollub*
*Illustrated by Leovigildo Martinez*
*Tambourine Books, 1994*

Jealous of the merriment that occurs in the daytime, the moon decides to plan a fiesta of her own. She enlists the *padrinos,* who gather the prerequisite food, music, and lanterns. The moon's gala is festive, but the price is high when the villagers go to bed at dawn and cannot fulfill their responsibilities the following day. The author and illustrator have combined their talents to create a sumptuous original tale set amid the rich folk culture of the illustrator's homeland of Oaxaca.

# Italy

*Buon giorno!* That's Italian for "Good day!" Use the suggestions in this interdisciplinary unit and you'll not only have a good day—you'll have several good days of captivating learning experiences. It's the perfect way to inform and enlighten your students about the fascinating country and culture of Italy.

## A "Boot-iful" Country

To kick off your study of Italy, have students locate the country on a globe or a world map. Ask students to name the countries that border Italy to the north; then have them look along Italy's western coastline to find the islands of Sicily and Sardinia. Explain that both of these islands, along with approximately 70 smaller islands, are part of Italy, too. Then ask students to study the shape of Italy. Some students may correctly identify Italy as a peninsula. Urge them to keep looking until they spot a tall, high-heeled boot. Wow! Italy really is a "boot-iful" country!

## Uno, Due, Tre

Long ago in Rome, people played this popular number game. No doubt youngsters will also enjoy the game. To play, two students sit facing each other, hiding their right hands behind their backs. On a count of *tre* (3), both players declare a sum from *due* (2) to *dieci* (10), and at the same time bring forward their right hands with one to five fingers extended. Both players quickly add up the total number of fingers extended. If the finger sum equals the sum declared by a player, that player wins the round. To keep score, give each twosome ten tokens to place in a pile between them. When a player wins a round, he earns a token. The token may be taken from the game pile or it may be taken from his partner's earnings. The winner of the game is the player who wins all the tokens or who has the most tokens when playing time is over.

## A Book You Can Count On!

In his book *Count Your Way Through Italy* (Carolrhoda Books, Inc.; 1990), author Jim Haskins serves up some delicious lessons about the history and culture of Italy as he teaches his readers to count from one to ten in Italian. A sprinkling of Italian words, customs, mythology, geography, and culinary delights provide students with a colorful overview of the country. It's a great *antipasto* to your Italy unit! After sharing the book with your students, create a classroom counting chart like the one shown. Plan to incorporate Italian number words into your classroom conversations and encourage students to do the same.

SARDINIA

ITALY

Adriatic Sea

SICILY

**Counting In Italian**

| | | |
|---|---|---|
| 1 | uno | (OO-no) |
| 2 | due | (DOO-ay) |
| 3 | tre | (tray) |
| 4 | quattro | (KWAHT-troh) |
| 5 | cinque | (CHEEN-kway) |
| 6 | sei | (say) |
| 7 | sette | (SEHT-tay) |
| 8 | otto | (OHT-to) |
| 9 | nove | (NO-vay) |
| 10 | dieci | (DYAY-chee) |

## Spiffy Spelling

Salute spelling practice the Italian way—it's as easy as ABC! Each student needs a 9" x 12" sheet of white construction paper, two strips of 4" x 9" construction paper (one red and one green), glue, and a bowl of alphabet pasta. To make a flag of Italy, a child aligns and glues her green and red paper strips atop her white paper as shown. Next the student uses her pasta letters to spell several weekly spelling words or words related to Italy; then she glues the words she spelled atop her flag. The completed projects are a delightful reminder of Italy's colorful flag.

*Michele Converse Baerns—Gr. 2, Sevierville Primary School, Sevierville, TN*

## Hot Stuff!

Believe it or not, Italy is home to four active volcanoes! Help students locate the volcanoes on a map. Mount Etna—the largest and most active of the four—is located on the island of Sicily, Mount Vesuvius is near Naples, and Stromboli and Vulcano form two of the Lipari Islands. In ancient Rome, people believed that Vulcan, the Roman god of fire, lived in a blacksmith shop beneath a mountain. When he pounded his anvil, sparks and smoke shot up his chimney. In fact, it is from the Roman god Vulcan that we get the word *volcano*. Today scientists know that volcanoes are caused by other activities inside the earth. Ask students how they think volcanoes are formed. Then use the hands-on activities on pages 156–159 to further investigate these mountains that sometimes blow their tops!

## Plenty Of "Pasta-bilities"

Italians love pasta! While every region of Italy has its own food specialty, pasta is considered the basic food of the country. In Pontedassio, Italy, there is even a Spaghetti Historical Museum! Imagine a museum dedicated to the history of pasta. To acquaint students with several types of pasta, ask each youngster to bring to school a small amount of uncooked pasta shapes. As a class, sort the resulting pasta collection and determine how many different pasta shapes you've collected. Then list the name of each pasta on a poster-board cutout and use hot glue to attach a piece of the corresponding pasta near each name. In no time at all, your students will be pasta pros!

No doubt you'll have plenty of leftover pasta pieces. Here are some more "pasta-bilities" for putting your classroom collection to good use.

**Use Your Noodles:** Have students measure classroom items using pasta as units of measurement. Check it out! This art table is ten lasagna noodles long!

**Paper Pasta:** Give each student pair a length of yellow paper and a piece of pasta. Have each twosome trim its paper to resemble its pasta piece. Then, using crayons or markers, the pair labels the cutout with words that describe its pasta.

**Pigmented Pasta:** Create a colorful collection of manipulatives for patterning activities. Combine the uncooked pasta; then divide it into several large, resealable plastic bags. Pour a generous amount of rubbing alcohol and food coloring into each bag; then securely seal the bags. Shake the contents of each bag until all the pasta pieces are a desired color; then step outdoors, open each bag, and spread the pasta pieces on newspaper to dry. (The odor of the alcohol disappears as the pasta dries.) Combine the dried pasta and store it in an airtight container for later use.

*Michele Converse Baerns—Gr. 2*

## Italian Folklore

Introduce your students to a sampling of Italian folklore. The following titles are a great place to start. Before you begin, emphasize that these stories have been shared throughout the history of Italy and do not represent life in Italy today.

*books reviewed by Deborah Zink Roffino*

### Grandfather's Rock: An Italian Folktale
*Written by Joel Strangis & Illustrated by Ruth Gamper*
*Houghton Mifflin Company, 1993*
The setting is Southern Italy, with the spring-green earth bathed in yellow sun. Here the roots of love grow deep and affect the tough decisions of a family. This picture book tells the tale of a family barely surviving. Thus when Grandfather can no longer live alone, when he needs a place to live and people to care for him, the family feels the strain. When it seems as if there is no other option than to take Grandfather to the old folk's home, the children devise a loving plan for keeping Grandfather in their home.

### The Mysterious Giant Of Barletta: An Italian Folktale
*Adapted & Illustrated by Tomie dePaola*
*Harcourt Brace & Company, 1984*
Long ago in the warm south of Italy, legend holds, an imposing stone sculpture once stirred to life to save the little town of Barletta. This joyful piece of folklore suggests clever planning, wishful thinking, and warm affection that can arise from friendship.

### Petrosinella: A Neapolitan Rapunzel
*Retold & Illustrated by Diane Stanley*
*Dial Books For Young Readers, 1995*
Predating the Grimm brothers' version of Rapunzel by 200 years, this is a lovely, less violent, and more satisfying version of a classic tale. The luxuriant hair still tumbles out of a dark, menacing tower, but this time from the clear-thinking head of a strong female protagonist. Leading her man, Petrosinella achieves happily-ever-after with some creative outwitting of the ogress and just a tad of magic.

### Amzat And His Brothers: Three Italian Tales
*Remembered by Floriano Vecchi & Retold by Paula Fox*
*Illustrated by Emily Arnold McCully*
*Orchard Books, 1993*
With origins stretching back at least six generations, these fanciful Italian folktales are overflowing with comedy and creative resolutions. The characters are instantly memorable, making these three tales treasures for reading aloud. Lively pen-and-ink drawings appear on random pages.

**Pam Crane**

Baernserati

*designed by Scott Baerns*

## Grand Prix Of Shapes

Vroom! Fire up an interest in sports cars and geometric shapes with this one-of-a-kind activity! Display several pictures featuring Italian-made sports cars. *Fiat, Ferrari, Lamborghini, Maserati,* and *Alfa Romeo* are Italian exports that are sure to impress your students. Explain that Italy is not only one of the world's leading producers of automobiles—it is also famous for manufacturing sleek, fast cars of exquisite design. Allow time for students to study and discuss the cars on display. Then challenge each child to design a flashy car for a famous Italian carmaker. Explain that this particular carmaker is looking for cars created with geometric shapes. Provide a colorful supply of paper and an assortment of geometric-shaped templates. Then let the fun begin! Each student cuts out desired geometric shapes, arranges the shapes on a 9" x 12" sheet of white construction paper, and glues the shapes in place. Additional details—along with the name of the car and its designer—can be added with crayons or markers. Prepare to wave the checkered flag! With this activity, everyone's a winner!

*Michele Converse Baerns—Gr. 2, Sevierville Primary School, Sevierville, TN*

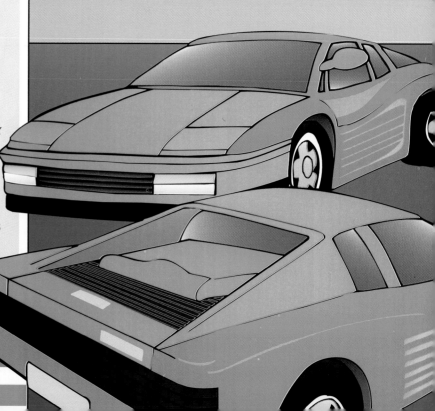

## The Italian Marketplace

Food is important to the Italian way of life. And the marketplace is where Italians can buy the freshest of cooking ingredients. Italian markets are usually held outdoors in city squares, and they are always lively and colorful. It is here where people gather to buy and sell food, to swap stories and recipes, and to visit neighbors. After a morning of shopping, an ice-cream vendor is always a welcome sight. Italy has a most delicious ice cream called *gelato*.

Your youngsters will be only too happy to taste a bit of Italian culture. Using the recipes below, students can make individual servings of bruschetta and *gelato!*

## The Nose Knows!

Well, in Pinocchio's case, anyway! The magical story of this wayward puppet was written over 100 years ago by the Italian author Carlo Collodi. No one really knows why Collodi chose to write about a puppet, but it might have been because puppetry has delighted the young and the old of Italy for centuries.

There are three types of puppets: hand puppets, marionettes, and rod puppets, although many puppets have features of more than one type. Students will enjoy making and operating these rod-type puppets. To make the head of the puppet, use crumpled newspaper to stuff a paper lunch sack. Poke a cardboard tube into the opening of the bag to form the neck; then use masking tape to secure the bag to the tube. Decorate the face of the puppet. Be creative! To make the puppet body, fold a two-foot square of cloth in half. Cut a small slit in the center of the folded cloth. Then poke the end of the cardboard tube through the hole as shown. To make hands (paws, wings, etc.) for the puppet, cut out the desired shapes and staple them inside the folded cloth. Then tape a drinking straw or similar device to one of the puppet's hands. To operate the puppet, hold the tube in one hand and the drinking straw in the other. Then let the fun begin. Can you make your puppet wave, scratch its nose, and salute?

### Bruschetta

**Ingredients:**
one slice of fresh Italian white bread
1/2 tablespoon olive oil
2 fresh basil leaves
2 tablespoons chopped fresh tomatoes
salt and pepper

**Directions:**
Brush the olive oil on the slice of bread. Put the two basil leaves on top of the oil; then spread the tomatoes over the bread. Sprinkle with a desired amount of salt and pepper. Enjoy!

### Gelato

**Seal inside a small, resealable plastic bag:**
1/2 cup milk
1/4 teaspoon vanilla
1 tablespoon sugar

**Then:**
Fill a gallon-size, resealable plastic bag half-full of crushed ice; then add 1/2 cup of salt. Place the small, sealed plastic bag inside the larger bag. Seal the large bag; then shake the mixture for about five minutes or until the contents of the small bag solidify. Spoon the gelato into a serving cup and enjoy!

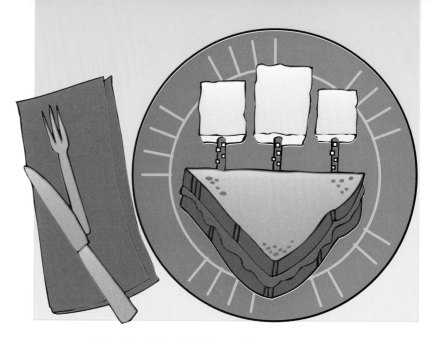

## Famous Italian Artists

Italy has a rich tradition of painting and sculpture. But when you rattle off the names of these four famous Italian artists from long ago, there's little doubt that your youngsters will stare at you in disbelief! The artists' names are Leonardo, Michelangelo, Raphael, and Donatello! Explain that these historical men (no, not the turtles!) created many sculptures and paintings that have been preserved to this day. Show students pictures of these men's work, taking care to share only those pictures from encyclopedias and other resources that are appropriate for student viewing. Explain that most of the artwork created by these men was modeled after someone or something that was very important to the artist or to the people of Italy. Set up several painting and sculpting centers in your classroom. Encourage youngsters to create paintings and sculptures of people or things that are important to them, their families, their school, their town, or their country.

## He Sailed The Ocean Blue

Another famous Italian your students will surely recognize is Christopher Columbus. Born in 1451 in Genoa, Italy, Columbus is most remembered for his first voyage from Spain to the New World in 1492. In all, this great explorer made four journeys. *The First Voyage Of Christopher Columbus 1492* by Barry Smith (Viking Penguin, 1992) traces Columbus's first voyage step-by-step. A removable foldout map at the back of the book makes charting his course a classroom event. In *All Pigs On Deck* (Delacorte Press, 1991), author Laura Fischetto offers information that focuses on the purpose of Christopher Columbus's second voyage. This warm and rollickingly funny picture book suggests that of all the people and products Columbus carried across the Atlantic, only the pigs—the most rowdy and difficult passengers—were suitable inhabitants for the New World.

After reading about Christopher Columbus—a man who followed his dreams—invite students to talk about their personal dreams for the future. Be sure to share a personal dream of your own, too! For a fun finale, plan to have students make a yummy, ship-shaped snack. To make an edible ship, prepare a peanut-butter sandwich on brown bread. Cut the sandwich diagonally and place one half on a paper plate, reserving the other half for another ship. Insert pretzel sticks in the cut edge of the sandwich; then position rectangular pieces of white bread on the pretzel sticks to represent sails. Smooth sailing!

## Pizza With Pizzazz

Hot, cheesy, and topped with just about anything—pizza has become one of America's favorite foods. And Americans owe their thanks to an Italian baker from Naples who invented the stuff in the early 1700s! Put some pizzazz into your students' creative writing with this hot-and-spicy activity. Arrange several pizza-slice cutouts that you have programmed with creative-writing prompter on an aluminum pizza pan; then place the pan, a red-and-white checkered tablecloth, paper plates, and a supply of paper at a center. A student serves himself a slice of pizza on a paper plate and completes the corresponding writing activity. For added fun, give each child a writing journal in the shape of a pizza slice. Students can decorate and personalize their journal covers as desired, then complete each writing activity on a different journal page. Any way you slice it, this writing center is just too good to pass up!

# Then And Now

Today Italy is a very prosperous country. But there was a time when it was very poor. Many Italians bravely left their country in search of better opportunities. Many of these Italians emmigrated to America. Their lives were difficult, but the dream of a better life helped them persevere. Ask students how they think America would be different today if Italians had not emmigrated to America. Guide them to realize that these brave people of long ago not only enriched their lives, but they enriched our lives as well.

The following picture books tell stories of our country's immigrant past. They show readers that the values that helped create our country—hard work, hope, and love—came from near and far.

*books reviewed by Deborah Zink Roffino*

### Silver At Night
*Written by Susan Campbell Bartoletti & Illustrated by David Ray*
*Crown Publishers, Inc.; 1994*

The dawn of the twentieth century saw an unprecedented wave of young, strong Italians heading for America and a more promising future. This simple story, illustrated in shadows that add depth and texture, reveals the intensity of the struggle to make a new life. Massimino leaves his beloved Perina and his beautiful homeland, heads across the sea, and finds himself deep in the coal mines of Pennsylvania. He dreams and he learns on this journey—and he discovers what it means to be rich.

### Peppe The Lamplighter
*Written by Elisa Bartone & Illustrated by Ted Lewin*
*Lothrop, Lee & Shepard Books; 1993*

The shadows lay thickly across the cobbled streets of Little Italy in this poignant Caldecott Honor book. Turn-of-the-century faces, some with bowler hats and others with swept-up hair, reveal the cares of the Italian immigrants in America. Here the self-esteem and dreams of a father cross and conflict with those of his son. This is a book about love and respect. It is a book about setting goals and assessing values. It is also a book about European ways and American attitudes. Children may only see the strong love of a family in pain, but that will be more than enough to make this book a favorite.

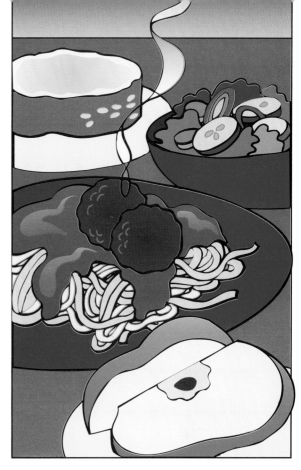

## *Arrivederci!*

That's good-bye in Italian! (Pronounced "ar-ree-ve-DARE chee.") For a fun conclusion to your study of Italy, prepare an Italian feast. To whet your students' appetites for pasta, read aloud *Strega Nona* by Tomie dePaola. In this kid-pleasing tale, a magic pot bubbles out of control, spewing pasta every which way. At the conclusion of the story, reveal the pot in which you plan to cook pasta for the feast! Your menu could include spaghetti, tossed salad, and fresh Italian bread. For dessert serve fresh fruit—a popular dessert choice in Italy. Enlist the help of your students and their parents in preparing the feast. To add ambiance, have each child make a red-and-white checkered placemat by coloring a 12" x 18" sheet of white construction paper. When the feast is over and the mess is cleared away, delight your full-bellied youngsters with more tales of Strega Nona. She's quite the lady! (Strega Nona returns in *Strega Nona's Magic Lessons* and *Strega Nona Meets Her Match*, both written and illustrated by Tomie dePaola.)

*Michele Converse Baerns—Gr. 2*
*Sevierville Primary School, Sevierville, TN*

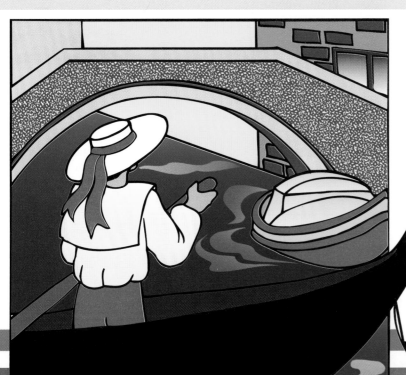

# Book It To
# The Caribbean!

Come to the Caribbean islands—breathtaking isles that rise above the shimmering surface of blue-green waters. See the vibrant colors and feel the soft, balmy breezes. Hear the bustling marketplaces as the excited chatter of young children rises above the screech of the taxis, the frenzied squawks of wild parrots, and the pong of the sweet steel drums. It takes just a touch of imagination to picture yourself in the shade of rustling palm fronds as you and your students savor these delightful island books.

*books reviewed by Deborah Zink Roffino*

## Fiction And Folklore

### Coconut Mon
*Written by Linda Milstein & Illustrated by Cheryl Munro Taylor*
*Tambourine Books, 1995*
Savor the rhythm and flavor of the Caribbean in this very simple counting book that follows the exuberant Coconut Mon around his island. Splashed with outrageous, nearly iridescent hues, the colors of the Caribbean shine through on every page.

### Jasmine's Parlour Day
*Written by Lynn Joseph & Illustrated by Ann Grifalconi*
*Lothrop, Lee & Shepard Books; 1994*
Shark 'n bake, sugar cakes, poulari balls, and much more line the seaside parlours and make the feast for young Jasmine's day at the market. Golden-washed pages add warmth to the sun, sand, and sweet smiles of the children of Trinidad.

### Island Baby
*Written & Illustrated by Holly Keller*
*Mulberry Books, 1992*
Young Simon nurses a baby flamingo back to health under the watchful eyes of a wise old friend. Simple stylized pictures, spicy colors, and an easy story of loving and letting go make this book a precious choice.

### Flamboyan
*Written by Arnold Adoff & Illustrated by Karen Barbour*
*Harcourt Brace & Company, 1988*
Written as prose, this magical story reads like poetry. It tells of a young island girl—born with flaming red hair—who is drawn to all the colors and excitement of island life. Radiant pages are matched with lyrical language to form a surreal vision of the sensory experiences in the tropics.

### Josephine's 'Magination: A Tale Of Haiti
*Written & Illustrated by Arnold Dobrin*
*Scholastic Inc., 1973*
Welcome to a bustling marketplace in Haiti. Readers befriend sweet, imaginative Josephine and get a peek at the climate, the geography, and the culture of these island people.

# The Tangerine Tree
*Written by Regina Hanson & Illustrated by Harvey Stevenson*
*Clarion Books, 1995*

Papa is going to New York for a very long time. While he is gone from Jamaica, Ida promises to tend to her studies and to Papa's precious tangerine tree. A strong family theme is present in this soft and warm view of Jamaica. Sweet, hot colors glow from the pages.

# Tap–Tap
*Written by Karen Lynn Williams & Illustrated by Catherine Stock*
*Clarion Books, 1994*

Now that Sasifi is eight years old, she can help Mama at market. But when the youngster quickly grows weary from the weight of her fruit-filled basket and repeatedly requests to ride the tap-tap, Mama wonders if the child is up to the task. Riotous watercolors washed in tropical sun illustrate this rite of passage for a young Haitian child.

# Paco And The Witch
*Retold by Felix Pitre & Illustrated by Christy Hale*
*Lodestar Books, 1995*

This Puerto Rican folktale is brimming with Spanish vocabulary offered in context. Resplendent colors create joyous artwork and a mischievous mood as Paco must outwit an old witch. The resolution shows youngsters a whole new way to look at a crab!

# An Island Christmas
*Written by Lynn Joseph & Illustrated by Catherine Stock*
*Clarion Books, 1992*

How different is an island holiday celebration? Merriment bubbles on the pages in this joyful account in dialect from the Caribbean. Rosie enthusiastically gathers the *sorrel* fruit for the traditional holiday drink and assists Tantie as she makes the black currant cakes. Watercolors—washed pale by tropical sun—lure the reader through rows of pastel cottages, where people trail the *parang band,* singing holiday tunes.

# Tukama Tootles The Flute: A Tale From The Antilles
*Retold by Phillis Gershator & Illustrated by Synthia Saint James*
*Orchard Books, 1994*

From the Antilles comes this vibrant folktale with powerful giants and a young boy who doesn't always listen to his grandmother. Magical nonsense verse paints the pitch of the boy's flute, producing a musical lilt to the reading. The young boy discovers that Grandma knows best.

# My Two Worlds
*Written by Ginger Gordon & Photographed by Martha Cooper*
*Clarion Books, 1993*

Christmas at her grandparents' house in the Dominican Republic is an exhilarating experience for young Kirsy Rodriguez of New York City. This photographic chronicle of Kirsy's holiday trip highlights several of the contrasts between her two worlds: the weather, the customs, the foods, and the housing.

# Poetry And Song

## Caribbean Alphabet
### Written & Illustrated by Frané Lessac
### Tambourine Books, 1989

Weaving the exotic into the familiar, this alphabet book is packed with particulars. Stylized gouache paintings with the enthusiasm of island festivals illustrate a phrase or a set of words for each letter of the alphabet. Ingenious, informative, and enormously appealing, this is an engaging introduction to island living.

## Coconut Kind Of Day: Island Poems
### Written by Lynn Joseph & Illustrated by Sandra Speidel
### Lothrop, Lee & Shepard Books; 1990

The bold color and lively spirit of island life come alive with these delicious verses. The *palet man,* the cricket-playing boys, Mama, the teacher, and even the *jumbi man* are included. Several corners of island life merge in this coconut kind of a day.

## I Have A News: Rhymes From The Caribbean
### Collected by Walter Jekyll & Illustrated by Jacqueline Mair
### Lothrop, Lee & Shepard Books; 1994

More than a dozen effervescent Jamaican folk rhymes provide resounding patterns of color and sound for your readers. The first reading is challenging—but the rhythm is infectious, and the information packed within the different selections offers clues to life in the islands.

## Caribbean Carnival: Songs Of The West Indies
### Written by Irving Burgie & Illustrated by Frané Lessac
### Tambourine Books, 1992

No Caribbean festival is complete without music. Here are the lyrics and scores from the most famous calypso tunes. "Michael, Row The Boat Ashore"; "Day-O"; "Yellow Bird"; and "Jamaica Farewell" are featured with nine other joyous Caribbean songs. Lively folk art decorates the resonant pages.

## Caribbean Canvas
### Written & Illustrated by Frané Lessac
### Wordsong, 1987

The stunning Caribbean artwork of Frané Lessac that accompanies a collection of island poems and proverbs results in an enchanting anthology. From the exhilaration of the dances to the serenity of a churchyard, the view is authentic and lovely.

## A Caribbean Dozen: Poems From Caribbean Poets
### Edited by John Agard and Grace Nichols & Illustrated by Cathie Felstead
### Candlewick Press, 1994

Illustrated with robust patterns, collages, and colors, this spicy collection of poetry is the work of 13 Caribbean natives who spread their memories across the festive pages. Listen for the ping-pong song of steel drums as the words trip along to a reggae beat.

Pam Crane

## Not A Copper Penny In Me House: Poems From The Caribbean
### Written by Monica Gunning & Illustrated by Frané Lessac
### Wordsong, 1993

Vivid verses detail architecture, education, language, marketplaces, lazy Sundays, and wild weather as readers tag along with a Jamaican youngster as she runs through a variety of island-life experiences. It's a child's-eye view of the tropics.

# The Caribbean: A Tropical Paradise

Feel like a tropical getaway? Drop anchor in the Caribbean and explore the warm seas and sandy beaches, luscious tropical fruits, rhythmical calypso music, and so much more. It's time for a little fun in the sun!

*ideas contributed by Jennifer Gibson & Doug L. Poage*

## Islands In The Sun

The Caribbean, as the West Indies is commonly called, is perhaps best known as the ideal vacation spot. This beautiful chain of islands borders the Caribbean Sea and forms a 2,500-mile arc from Florida to Venezuela. Within the arc there are more than 30 large islands and several smaller ones. The islands are divided into three groups: the Bahamas, the Greater Antilles (Cuba, Jamaica, Puerto Rico, and Haiti), and the Lesser Antilles (the Windward and Leeward Islands). Use a map to show students where the Caribbean islands and the Caribbean Sea are located. Explain that the Caribbean islands are actually the tips of undersea mountains, and are the result of volcanic activity deep in the earth. Invite students to share their impressions of the Caribbean, from climate to natural resources. Find out why they think the Caribbean is one of the world's most fascinating places to visit.

To whet your youngsters' appetites for this tropical paradise, cut up a fresh coconut and distribute small chunks for the students to sample. Then read aloud one or more of the delightful island books featured on pages 228–230.

## Sounds Of The Caribbean

During your study of this island paradise, fill your classroom with sounds of the Caribbean. Each of the following recordings can be purchased from Music For Little People (1-800-727-2233):

- *Smilin' Island Of Song* by Cedella Marley-Booker. This collection of reggae and calypso music for children features favorites such as "Tingalayo," "Banana Boat Song," and "Sweet Guava Jelly."
- *Reggae For Kids: A Collection Of Music For Kids Of All Ages*
- *Positively Reggae: An All Family Musical Celebration*

## Tropical Travel Logs

What better way for a youngster to keep track of his tropical adventures than in a personalized travel log? On white construction paper, duplicate a class supply of the journal cover on page 234. Have each youngster fold his copy in half, then decorate and personalize the resulting journal cover as desired. Assist each child in stapling a supply of blank paper between his completed cover. Encourage students to record interesting facts, information, illustrations, and personal anecdotes related to their Caribbean adventures in their tropical travel logs.

## A Melting Pot

The Caribbean is a true melting pot of cultures, which makes it one of the most fascinating places to visit. The Arawak Indians were among the first inhabitants of the islands. The Caribs followed; then came the Spanish, English, French, and other Europeans who brought with them slaves from West Africa. Later, workers from China and India moved to the islands. More recently Lebanese, Syrians, and others have made the Caribbean their home. The result is a unique blending of cultures. Explain that the Caribbean is known for the warmth of its climate as well as its people. Invite students to talk about the benefits of living in a melting pot such as the Caribbean. *The Caribbean And Its People* by T. W. Mayer (Thomson Learning, 1995) is an excellent reference for further investigation.

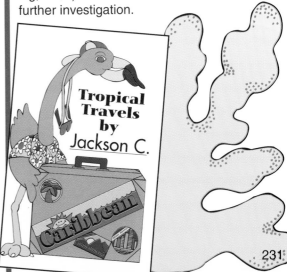

Tropical Travels by Jackson C.

# Pirates Of The Past

Years ago pirates were plentiful in the Caribbean Sea. The numerous islands provided ideal hiding spots for pirates and their precious loot. Blackbeard was a fierce pirate who attacked ships in the Caribbean from 1716 to 1718. Students will enjoy singing about a legendary scoundrel who once terrorized Caribbean waters.

## Blackbeard

*(sung to the tune of "The Ants Go Marching One By One")*

Blackbeard raided ships at sea,
Ho, ho! Ho, ho!
Blackbeard raided ships at sea,
Ho, ho! Ho, ho!
He was a fierce leader of pirate
    men.
They terrorized the Caribbean.
And the Jolly Roger flew,
When Blackbeard set sail with his
    crew!
Ho, ho, ho, ho! Ho, ho, ho...

Blackbeard raided ships at sea,
Ho, ho! Ho, ho!
Blackbeard raided ships at sea,
Ho, ho! Ho, ho!
He looted their treasures and
    buried them in
The islands of the Caribbean.
And the Jolly Roger flew,
When Blackbeard set sail with his
    crew!
Ho, ho, ho, ho! Ho, ho, ho, ho!

# An Undersea Kaleidoscope

Tropical fish pack the warm, clear waters and the coral reefs of the Caribbean Sea, creating a paradise for scuba divers. The bright colors of tropical fish make them relatively easy to spot and their unusual names—like balloon fish, angelfish, triggerfish, hogfish, and parrot fish—give clues to their unique shapes. Show students several colorful illustrations and photographs of coral reefs and tropical fish; then display the pictures near a bulletin board that you have covered with blue or aqua background paper. During the next day or two, arrange for each student to illustrate a coral reef in crayon on the bulletin board. Then have each student create a colorful foil fish (see "Dazzling Tropical Fish") to showcase at the display.

# Dazzling Tropical Fish

These tropical fish have plenty of razzle-dazzle! To make a foil tropical fish, crumple a large piece of aluminum foil; then flatten the foil, leaving it somewhat crinkled. Stir a few drops of food coloring into each of several small containers of white glue. Brush a thin, even coat of several colors of tinted glue onto the foil, allowing some of the colors to mix. Let the glue dry. The next day cut the foil into small pieces and separate them by color. Using a crayon, draw the outline of a tropical fish on a sheet of black construction paper and cut it out. Glue the foil pieces on the cutout, trimming and overlapping them as desired. Display these dazzling tropical fish as described in "An Undersea Kaleidoscope."

# Market Day

Market days bubble with noise and excitement. Women—many with children in tow—bring fruits, vegetables, baked goods, and crafts (such as handmade baskets, pottery, and jewelry made from coral) to sell on market day. If they are lucky, they'll find wealthy tourists to buy their wares. Read aloud *Tap-Tap* by Karen Lynn Williams (Clarion Books, 1994) or *Jasmine's Parlour Day* by Lynn Joseph (Lothrop, Lee & Shepard Books; 1994) to give students a better understanding of the happenings at a local market.

**Pam Crane**

## A Taste Of The Tropics

The tropical climate of the islands creates perfect growing conditions for a variety of tropical fruits. Some fruits, like bananas, are produced for export to other countries. The following recipes are a fun way for students to sample the fruits of the Caribbean. For other tropical fruit recipes and foods with a traditional Caribbean flavor, have students assist you in making a dish from *Cooking The Caribbean Way* by Cheryl Davidson Kaufman (Lerner Group, 1988) or *A Taste Of The Caribbean* by Yvonne McKenley (Thomson Learning, 1995). Both books feature specialty recipes from various Caribbean islands and include interesting information about Caribbean cuisine.

### Fruity Island Punch
(makes about 12 small servings)
1 small can of crushed pineapple
2 cups of chilled orange juice
1 cup of maraschino cherries
1 banana, peeled and sliced
1/2 cup of fresh strawberries, tops removed

Combine ingredients in a blender. Mix for about two minutes, until thick and foamy. Serve immediately.

## Smooth Sailing

Many snapshots taken in the Caribbean show colorful sailboats, yachts, and cruise ships. A lot of activity takes place on, in, and around the waters of the Caribbean. Windsurfing is popular in some locations, as is surfing. Create a wave of exciting writing with this unique booklet project. To make the front cover of her booklet, a student cuts a wave design along the top edge of a 6" x 9" sheet of dark blue construction paper; then she stacks and staples a supply of 5" x 8 1/2" writing paper between the front cover and a 9" x 12" sheet of light blue construction-paper back cover. Next she uses construction-paper scraps and markers or crayons to create a tropical scene above the wave line. On her first booklet page, she writes "Fun In The Sun: A Caribbean Adventure by [student's name]". Then she writes a sun-filled story on her remaining booklet pages.

### Tropical Baked Bananas
unpeeled bananas (1/2 per child)
sugar
grated coconut
lemon juice
cinnamon

Preheat oven to 375°F. Without removing the peel, cut each banana in half lengthwise. Arrange the bananas on a cookie sheet and bake them in their peels for 15 minutes. Peel the skins from the bananas. Have each child sprinkle his serving of banana with his choice of coconut, lemon juice, sugar, or cinnamon.

## It's As Caribbean As A, B, C

For a fun culminating activity, have each child create a page for a Caribbean *ABC* big book. Ask students to brainstorm words related to the Caribbean as you write their ideas on the chalkboard, grouping together words that have the same beginning letters. After each child has chosen a different letter of the alphabet, have him copy and complete the following alphabet sentence near the top of a 12" x 18" sheet of white construction paper: [alphabet letter] is for [a corresponding word from the class list].Then have each student illustrate his entire page using crayons or markers. While students are working, ask each one in turn to sign a booklet page labeled "Authors and Illustrators."

To assemble the big book, enlist your youngsters' help in sequencing the pages; then place the autographed page on top. Hole-punch the project and use metal rings to bind the project between two slightly larger pieces of poster board. Entitle the class big book "The *ABCs* Of The Caribbean."

S is for steel drum.

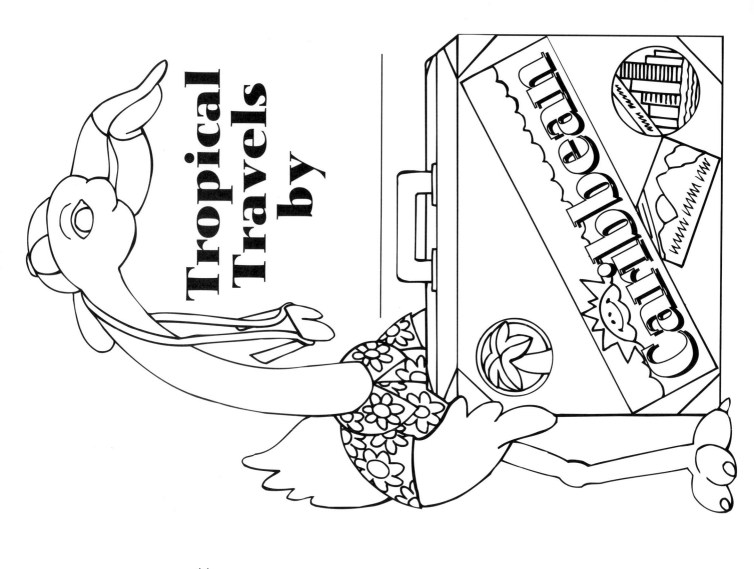

# Tropical Travels by Caribbean

# Fascinating Facts About Flamingos

 Most flamingos are from three to five feet tall.

 A flamingo can have more than 25,000 feathers on its body.

 All flamingos have black wing feathers.

Flamingos get their pretty pink coloring from the food they eat. That's why not all flamingos are the same color of pink!

 All flamingos live near water.

 Flamingos live in *colonies*, or groups. Some colonies have more than 1,000 members!

 The world's largest colony of flamingos lives in the Caribbean.

# LANGUAGE ARTS UNITS

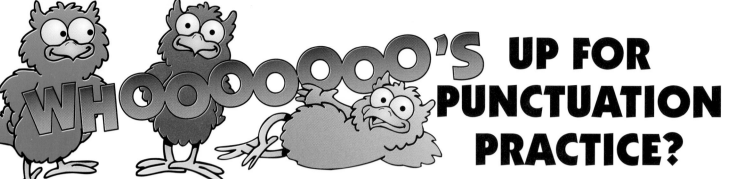

# WHOOOOOOO'S UP FOR PUNCTUATION PRACTICE?

Some days, does it seem as though your youngsters just don't give a hoot about punctuation? No need to stay up nights thinking of ideas when this topflight collection is right at your fingertips!

## All Aboard!

Get students' punctuation skills on the right track by making this nifty punctuation train. To begin, draw and cut out a train engine, three boxcars, and a caboose from tagboard. Use a permanent marker to write the words "Today is" on the train's engine; then display the cutouts near the calendar. Program blank cards with the seven days of the week, the 12 months of the year, the numerals 1 through 31, and the two years within this school year. Using a red marker, insert commas after the days of the week and the dates; then place periods after the years. Attach the appropriate cards to the train. Each day have a student look at the current cards on the train and tell which ones need to be replaced. After the sentence is brought up-to-date, have the class read the information aloud. As they read, have students use hand signs to represent the punctuation marks. This daily review will keep your youngsters' punctuation skills on track!

Pamela S. Lasher—Gr. 2, Grand Rapids Baptist Academy, Grand Rapids, MI

## It's A Holdup!

With this idea your students will be holding all the cards—period, question mark, and exclamation-point cards, that is! Have each student use three blank index cards and a dark marker or crayon to make punctuation cards. Once the cards are ready, students listen as you say a sentence. Each student decides which punctuation mark belongs at the end of the sentence and holds up the corresponding card. You can evaluate at a glance your students' punctuation skills.

Doreen Carlo—Gr. 2
Broadview Elementary
Pompano Beach, FL

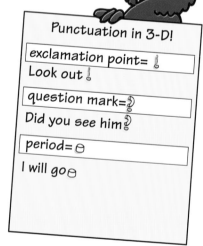

| Today is | Monday, | November | 6, | 1995. |

### Punctuation in 3-D!

exclamation point= ⫚
Look out ⫚

question mark=⫰
Did you see him⫰

period=⊖
I will go⊖

## Munchable Marks

Try using 3-D punctuation marks in your classroom to reinforce students' punctuation skills. In advance, program a chart with sentences that end with periods, question marks, and exclamation points; but instead of writing the punctuation, glue the following items after each sentence: period = a miniature marshmallow, question mark = a piece of elbow macaroni and a small dried bean, exclamation point = a pretzel stick and a small dried bean. Discuss the chart with your students; then distribute glue and the food items to each student. Students refer to the chart and use the appropriate items to punctuate sentences in a writing assignment. After checking students' work, invite them to munch on leftover pretzels and marshmallows!

Leigh Anne Newsom—Gr. 3, Greenbrier Intermediate, Chesapeake, VA

## Lotto Fun

Reinforce punctuation skills by adding a new twist to the ever popular game of lotto. Distribute blank lotto cards and markers to your students. Have each child program the spaces with periods, question marks, and exclamation point. When the cards are complete, read aloud a sentence from a deck of unpunctuated sentence cards. Each student then decides which punctuation mark ends the sentence and places a marker on a space containing that mark. Continue reading additional sentences from the card deck. The first student to fill a row and say, "Lotto!" wins the game, if she can locate one used sentence card to match each of the punctuation marks in the winning row. Each child will be a winner when she discovers how much fun practicing punctuation can be!

Doreen Carlo—Gr. 2

## Colorful Cards

Here's a bright idea for helping students polish their punctuation skills. Write several sentences on a transparency, omitting ending marks. Supply each student with one green, one blue, and one yellow index card. Have each student program his blue card with a period, his green card with an exclamation point, and his yellow card with a question mark. Using an overhead projector, display the first sentence on the transparency and ask each student to select the punctuation card that correctly fits the sentence. Ask each child to wait for your signal, then hold up the selected card. Reveal the remaining sentences one at a time for students to punctuate.

*Tonya Byrd, William H. Owen Elementary, Fayetteville, NC*

## Annie Apostrophe

Your students will find that learning to use apostrophes is a breeze when they get a little help from a friend named Annie Apostrophe. Make Annie by cutting an apostrophe shape from tagboard. Add appealing facial features and laminate her for durability. On the chalkboard write a word or sentence in which an apostrophe is needed; then invite a student to insert Annie Apostrophe into the space where the apostrophe belongs. A little masking tape (or magnetic tape for a magnetic chalkboard) will keep Annie in place. Repeat this procedure until each student has had at least one turn to position Annie. After students become familiar with Annie Apostrophe, you might want to introduce them to her cousin, Connie Comma!

*Julie Mazzarino—Gr. 1, American Heritage School, Plantation, FL*

The ducks saw the child□holding a bag of peanuts□"Let's go□" said the mother duck□The three ducklings□swam behind their mother□

## Transforming Textbooks

Get new uses from outdated reading books by using them for punctuation practice. Affix correction tape (or small pieces cut from white, self-adhesive labels) to cover the punctuation marks on a story page copied from an old basal reader. Once the punctuation marks are hidden from view, attach a few extra pieces of correction tape to act as distractors. Laminate the page. Place the page in a center along with a wipe-off marker and an unaltered duplicate of the page. Challenge students to take turns writing appropriate punctuation marks and referring to the unaltered page to check the accuracy of their work.

*Cindy Lonergan—Special Education, Disney Elementary, Tulsa, OK*

A machine makes your work easier □. There are lots of different kinds of machines □. The lever □, inclined plane □, screw □, and pulley are names of some machines □. Do you know the names of any other machines □?

## What A Combination!

When your purpose is punctuation practice, ensure meaningfulness by connecting punctuation, literature, and student writings. Ahead of time, determine which punctuation mark to emphasize; then write it on a chart similar to the one shown below. After introducing (or reviewing) the featured punctuation mark, challenge each student to browse through one of the books that he is currently reading to find an example of a sentence in which the punctuation mark is used. Write these examples on the chart. Discuss each sentence and its punctuation mark; then leave the chart on display for future reference. To extend the learning, ask each student to examine a sample of his previous writings and correct any punctuation mistakes that he now notices.

*Mary E. Fagan—Gr. 1, Public School #9, Brooklyn, NY*

## Take Note!

Stick with this idea and your students will be punctuating pros before you know it! Write a class-dictated paragraph on chart paper, omitting punctuation but leaving spaces large enough to accommodate small sticky notes. As students read aloud the class paragraph, have them identify each place where punctuation is missing and attach a sticky note to that spot. On each note, have a student record the missing punctuation mark. After the entire paragraph has been correctly punctuated, have students reread it; then remove the sticky notes. Put the chart and a pad of sticky notes where students can again supply the punctuation.

*April Johnson—Gr. 3, Morningside Elementary School, Perry, GA*

| PUNCTUATION | EXAMPLES |
|---|---|
| Question Mark  ? | 1. Well, what do you think?<br>2. Why not?<br>3. How about Dr. Grizzly?<br>4. Where have you been?<br>5. Who is that speaking? |

# Write About It

Feast on this bountiful collection of exciting writing ideas!

### Creative Writing With Confetti

This spellbinding writing activity is sure to enchant your youngsters! Purchase a supply of holiday-shaped confetti. Introduce each confetti shape and write its name on the chalkboard. Encourage students to refer to the resulting word bank as they write seasonal stories. Then have each student copy her completed story on a blank sheet of paper, substituting confetti shapes for the corresponding words. Invite students to share their tales aloud; then bind these remarkable rebus stories into an eye-catching book.

*Carol Ann Liske—Gr. 3, Betty Adams Elementary School, Westminster, CO*

### Making Tracks Toward Descriptive Writing

In *The Island Of The Skog* by Steven Kellogg, a group of brave mice set sail and eventually land on an island. There they discover the sole inhabitant's enormous footprint. A surprise is in store for everyone when the footprint maker is revealed. After reading the story aloud, have each child cut a footprint shape from a portion of a sponge and sponge-paint a series of footprints across a 9" x 12" sheet of construction paper. On a second sheet of construction paper, have each student use crayons or markers to illustrate a creature that could have made the footprints. Next have each youngster describe his creature on a sheet of writing paper. As you gather and exhibit the creature illustrations for all to see, have each student glue or tape his written description to the back of his footprint project. For a finale, have each child take a turn reading aloud his description while his classmates listen carefully, study the student's footprint project, and then try to identify the corresponding creature illustration.

*Michelle Thomas—Gr. 2, A. J. Martin Elementary, Sugar Land, TX*

### Butterflies In My Belly

If you're looking for a way to set your students' writing skills aflutter, try this! As a class discuss the meaning of the saying "I have butterflies in my stomach." Then ask students to talk about times they have felt butterflies in their stomachs and to describe the events that provoked these feelings. Next distribute story paper and two butterfly stickers to each student. Ask each youngster to illustrate herself and attach the butterfly stickers to the stomach of her artistic likeness. Then have each student write about an event that caused her to get butterflies. Encourage students to share their completed projects. Knowing that butterflies find their way into lots of bellies can be comforting to your students.

*Anne Cutberth, Nixa Espy Elementary, Nixa, MO*

### Award-Winning Books

Each year the American Library Association awards the Caldecott Medal to the illustrator(s) of the book it considers to be the most outstanding picture book of the preceding year. Past winners of this award have been the illustrators of *The Polar Express* (1986), *Owl Moon* (1988), and *Grandfather's Journey* (1994). Share several Caldecott Medal–winning books with your students and discuss their outstanding features. As a follow-up writing activity, have each student select a picture book that he feels is worthy of a similar award and write a paragraph about the book. Each paragraph should include the book's title, its author and illustrator, a description of the artwork, and reasons the student feels this book should earn an award. If desired have students design construction-paper awards that can be paper-clipped to the chosen books. Compile the written projects into a book entitled "The Best Picture Books: A Classroom Guide." Display the award-winning books and the student-published guide in your classroom library.

*Nancy Wojcik—Gr. 2, Hayes Elementary School, Kennesaw, GA*

# Write About It

Slide into winter with this cool collection of writing activities.

"What would you like to talk about, Rudolph?" asked Santa. Rudolph hung his head. Then he replied, "It's about the sleigh, Santa. I can't lead the team." "Well, my goodness, Rudolph!" exclaimed Santa. "Why not?"

## Clever Conversations

Writing conversations is a fun and effective way to reinforce the use of quotation marks. Provide a creative conversation starter, such as a dirty sock talking with a clean shoe, or a snowman begging the sun not to melt it. Ask each student to write a conversation between the characters. Have students use quotation marks to denote direct quotes. If desired, divide students into pairs, and have the partners read and role-play the conversations that they wrote.

*Barbara Langford—Gr. 3, Brandon Elementary, Columbus, MS*

What if it snowed every day of the year?

What if a bear came to your house looking for food?

## Bright Ideas

Create interest in journal writing by inviting students to pen the writing topics. In advance mount a large Christmas tree cutout on a bulletin board and reproduce a class supply of colorful holiday light patterns. Pose a "What if…" question to your students, such as "What if you could jump inside your favorite storybook?"; then have each student respond to the question in her writing journal. Next distribute the holiday light patterns. Ask each child to cut out and program her pattern with a "What if…" question. Display the programmed lights on the Christmas tree cutout. Each day select a different writing topic from the tree. After students have responded to the topic in their journals, encourage them to share their entries with their classmates. The child who created the writing topic for the day will glow with pride when she hears what her classmates have written.

*Traci Indlecoffer—Gr. 1, Edgewood Elementary, Minneapolis, MN*

## Calendar Story Collection

Don't toss out last year's calendar! You can use the calendar pictures as unique story starters. Display a calendar picture and ask students to share their thoughts about it. On chart paper record all of the ideas offered by the students. Then have each student write a story about the picture, referring to the idea chart if desired. Invite students to share their stories aloud. For a unique display, stack the stories and staple them together along the top margin. Then attach the stories to the calendar picture as shown. Display the calendar story collection in a prominent location.

*Diane Fortunato—Gr. 2, Carteret School, Bloomfield, NJ*

The Birds That Forgot To Fly South
Pete and Chipper are bluebirds. Every winter they fly to Florida so they will not be cold. But one winter, they overslept and when they woke up, it had already snowed! They had forgotten to fly south!

### Recipe For Peace

**Ingredients:**
7 cups friendship
3 cups freedom
1 1/2 cups sharing
5 tablespoons caring
love
harmony

**Directions:**
In a large bowl, combine friendship and freedom. Stir in sharing and mix well. Pour the mixture into a heart-shaped pan and sprinkle it with caring. Bake at 350° for one hour. Serve warm with lots of love and harmony.

## Recipe For Peace

Follow up a series of lessons on Martin Luther King, Jr., by having students cook up a recipe for peace. On the chalkboard write a student-generated list of some of the principles that Martin Luther King, Jr., promoted. Then encourage students to refer to the list as you cooperatively write a "Recipe For Peace." For an extra measure of fun, invite students to illustrate what *peace* means to them. Copy the class recipe on poster board; then use the students' illustrations to create an eye-catching border.

*Carol Majewski—Gr. 3, St. Mary School, Jewett City, CT*

# Write About It

Put your students' writing skills back in business.
These creative-writing activities really work!

### Sticker Story Starters

Looking for a way to get your students stuck on creative writing? Gather a collection of incentive stickers in various designs and sizes. Cut sticker sheets apart and place individual stickers in a bag. Each student selects a sticker to place on his paper, then writes a story inspired by the sticker design. Using the sticker as part of the illustration, the student draws a picture to match his story. Now that's a creative writing idea with real "a-peel"!

*Patty Young—Grs. 1-4, Haymarket, VA*

### Fantasy Islands

Whisk your youngsters off to the islands for this creative-writing adventure! Engage students in creating travel brochures for imaginary islands that they would like to visit. First have each student accordion-fold a 12" x 18" sheet of white paper into a four-panel brochure. On the front cover, a student illustrates and writes the name of his island. Then he fills the rest of his brochure with such information as the official island bird, tree, song, and symbol. Your enthusiastic youngsters will think writing is pure paradise!

*Kim Walding—Gr. 2, Newton Rayzor Elementary, Denton, TX*

### Author Of The Week

Put your young authors in the spotlight with this idea! Write each of your students' names on a Popsicle® stick; then place the sticks in a can. At the beginning of each week, draw a stick from the can and declare the student whose name is on the stick the "Author Of The Week." Send home with the student a briefcase or bookbag filled with motivational writing and book-making supplies. Items might include pencils, paper, story starters, shape book patterns, and a variety of art materials. Plan for the student to return the briefcase and share her writing at the end of the week. Be sure to provide a special chair for the author to sit in while she reads her original work to the class.

*Patsy Blakley—Gr. 2, Haskell Elementary School, Haskell, TX*

### Creative Creature Writing

Zebras with giraffe necks and mice that roar may be just what your youngsters are looking for! Enhance creative writing by reading aloud the book *You Look Ridiculous Said The Rhinoceros To The Hippopotamus* by Bernard Waber (Houghton Mifflin Company, 1979). In this story a hippopotamus decides he wants to change his appearance. The results are literally laughable. At the conclusion of the book, challenge youngsters to blend the body parts of various animals to make new creatures. Have each student draw, name, and write about his creature. Suggest that each child include information about his creature's habitat, food preference, personality, and interests. Display the creations on a bulletin board entitled "Really Ridiculous Creatures," or bind them into a class book. These creatures may not be real, but the skills your students gain from this exercise will be!

*Gina Parisi—Gr. 2, Demarest Elementary School, Bloomfield, NJ*

# Write About It

Shower your budding authors with this assortment of writing activities.

## Out-Of-Sight Stories

These student-made, astronaut-shape booklets are out of this world! To make a booklet, a student colors a white construction-paper copy of the pattern on page 242, adding his own facial features. He cuts out the pattern. Then, using the resulting cutout as a template, he traces and cuts out a supply of shaped writing paper and a construction-paper back cover. He then staples his writing paper between his two covers. Ask each youngster to write his name and date on the first page of his booklet. Explain that the remainder of the booklet is for writing about adventures he thinks he could have as an astronaut. Blast off!

*Sandra Maxwell—Gr. 1, W. H. Owen Elementary, Fayetteville, NC*

## Look Who's Talking

Here's an idea that's a real conversation starter! From discarded magazines, cut a supply of pictures featuring two or more people or animals. Each student chooses a picture and glues it in the center of a 12" x 18" sheet of colorful construction paper. The student studies the picture and decides what he thinks each person or animal might be saying or thinking. Then, on writing paper, he writes each character's dialogue inside a different conversation bubble. After outlining each conversation bubble with a black marker or crayon, he cuts out the bubbles and mounts them near the appropriate characters. Display this clever conversation project on a hallway bulletin board titled "Look Who's Talking!"

*Phoebe C. Sharp—Gr. 1, Gillette School, Gillette, NJ*

## Earth Day Poems

Put your young poets to work writing Earth-friendly poems for Earth Day—and at the same time, reinforce nouns and verbs! On the chalkboard write a student-generated list of nouns that relate to the environment. Then ask the class to brainstorm verbs that relate to the nouns listed. Explain that the verbs must end in *-ing*. Write several of the students' suggestions next to the corresponding nouns. To write an eight-line Earth Day poem, a student writes a title followed by a list of seven noun-verb pairs. His final line is a phrase or sentence that summarizes his topic. Invite students to illustrate and share their prose with their classmates. Repeat the writing activity with any variety of themes or topics.

*Zelphia Hutchinson—Gr. 3, Fort Washington Forest Elementary, Fort Washington, MD*

## Bunches Of Bubbles!

Youngsters will have a blast blowing—and writing about—bubbles! For a prewriting activity, head outdoors with your youngsters, a container of bubbles, and a student supply of bubble-blowing wands. As students blow bubbles, emphasize the colors, shapes, sizes, and movements of the different bubbles. Back in the classroom, begin a lively discussion about what it might be like to float in a bubble. Ask questions like "What would it feel like?", "Where would you go?", and "How long would your bubble ride last?" Then, on writing paper, have each child write about an adventure he might have inside a floating bubble.

To showcase the students' bubble stories, have each child draw a giant bubble shape on a 12" x 18" sheet of drawing paper, then use watercolors to paint his bubble. When the projects are dry, have each student cut out his giant-size bubble and attach his bubble story in the center of his cutout. For a three-dimensional effect, loosely cover each project with a layer of thin, clear plastic (dry-cleaner plastic works well). Then mount the projects for all to see!

*Phoebe C. Sharp—Gr. 1*

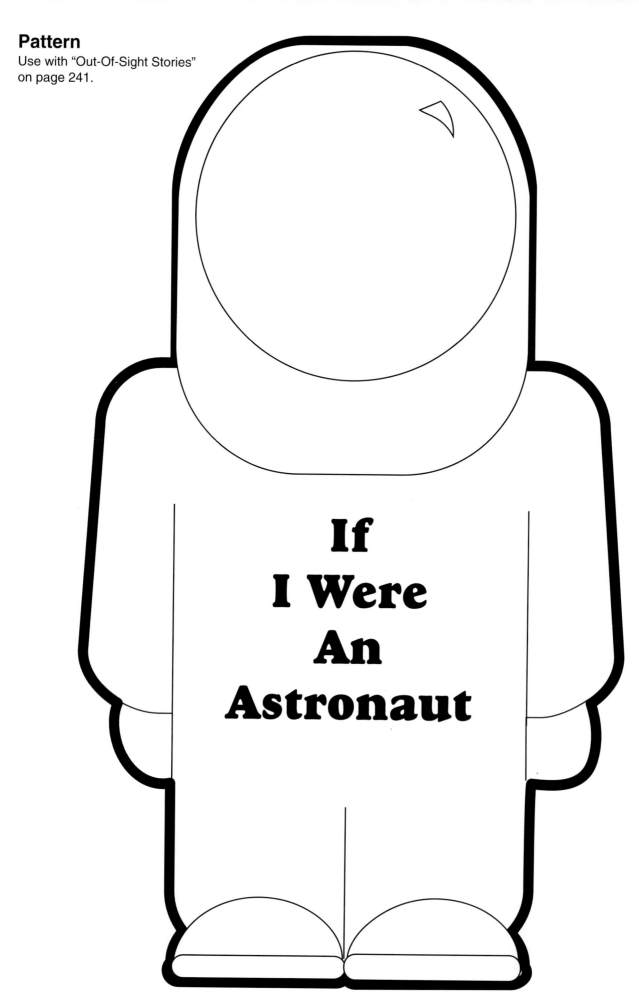

If
I Were
An
Astronaut

# Hot Off The Press!

## Utilizing The Newspaper In The Classroom

Extra! Extra! Read all about it! Here's the inside scoop on using the newspaper in the classroom. We've gathered newsworthy tips and activities from a most reliable and respected source—our trusty subscribers—and we've published the best of the batch in this news-breaking collection. You can count on us to deliver!

## Easy Does It

The format of newspapers makes them difficult for students to handle. To keep the oversized pages from slipping and sliding, place several staples down the left-hand edge of each newspaper.

Dee Ann Bates
Hawthorne Elementary
Oklahoma City, OK

## Not Just For Grown–Ups!

Beginning readers often think that the newspaper is just for adults. Use this activity to convince your youngsters that they can read the newspaper, too! Have each student choose a different newspaper article and circle each word in the article that he can read. Then ask each student to count the number of circled words and write that number near the top of the article. By gum, students can read the newspaper!

Sally Bivins—Gr. 1, Apache Elementary School, Peoria, AZ

## Front–Page News

Get the scoop on front-page news! Enlist your youngsters' help in comparing and contrasting a similar news story from two different newspapers. Read aloud the two articles; then as a class create a large Venn diagram that shows the similarities and differences between the two stories. This activity also works well with sports coverage and movie reviews.

Kelly Pflederer—Gr. 2, Academy Of The Sacred Heart, St. Louis, MO

Pam Crane

## Comic Capers

This large-group sequencing activity leaves youngsters smiling from ear to ear! To prepare for the fun, each student cuts out her favorite comic strip from a discarded newspaper. She cuts apart the individual frames and mounts each one on a construction-paper rectangle; then she sequences the mounted frames and programs the backs for self-checking. Next she writes her name and the name of her comic strip on a library pocket before she randomly slips the pieces of her project inside. To begin the large-group activity, each student places her project on her desktop. The students then move from desk to desk along a prearranged route and work the projects their classmates have prepared. There'll be plenty of reading, sequencing, and chuckling taking place!

Marcia Dosser—Gr. 1
Eastern Tennessee State University School, Johnson City, TN

## Attention–Grabbing Advertisements

Students may be surprised to discover the number of advertisements found in a newspaper. Display a few newspaper pages; then use a colored marker to circle the ads featured. As a class, critique the advertisements. Discuss what makes an effective ad and why the newspaper is a good medium for advertisers. Then challenge each child to create an attention-grabbing newspaper advertisement for a brand-new product or service. Set aside time for students to share their creative work; then showcase the ads around the school!

Lilly Schultz—Resource Teacher, Washington Elementary School, Auburn, WA

## Movie Madness

Interpreting a movie schedule is a picture-perfect way for students to practice reading and interpreting information. Give each group or individual a similar movie listing from the newspaper. Pose a series of questions that require the students to interpret the information at hand. Be sure to include some problem-solving challenges as well!

Lilly Schultz—Resource Teacher

## News And Views

Reinforce comprehension, critical thinking, and writing skills with this newsworthy idea. Each week bring to school a different newspaper article that you feel will be of special interest to your youngsters. Read the article aloud; then discuss it as a class. Pose several questions that require students to think critically about the information presented. In conclusion have each child write a paragraph that describes and defends his opinion about the news topic. Mount the completed paragraphs along with the featured news article on a bulletin board entitled "News And Views."

Laura Horowitz—Gr. 2
Plantation, FL

**Room 301 Classifieds**

## Classy Classifieds

Put your youngsters' writing skills to the test when you ask them to pen classified ads! Distribute several pages of classified ads for students to study. Discuss the kinds of information included in the ads and why some ads are more appealing than others. Also read aloud your local paper's guidelines for writing a classified ad. Then have each student write a brief ad in which he is selling or seeking an item or a service. After a student's ad has been proofread by a classmate, he copies it on a two-inch-wide paper strip. Collect the paper strips and mount them on blank paper as shown. Draw lines as needed; then photocopy a class supply of the project for your youngsters' reading enjoyment.

*Pam Doerr—Substitute Teacher, Elizabethtown District, Elizabethtown, PA*

## Scavenger Hunt

Youngsters love scavenger hunts—so you can count on an enthusiastic response when you suggest this activity! Each student needs a newspaper, a copy of page 250, scissors, and glue. A student finds each requested item in his newspaper, cuts it out, and glues it in the corresponding box. To reprogram the scavenger hunt, photocopy the page and white-out the boxed text. Make this your master copy. Then program a copy of the master and duplicate student copies. Using this technique, you can create a different newspaper scavenger hunt each week!

*Dee Ann Bates, Hawthorne Elementary, Oklahoma City, OK*

**Boy Finds Alien In Backyard!**

## Picture This!

High-interest newspaper photos make excellent springboards for creative writing. Cut out and code a supply of newspaper photos and their accompanying text. Store the text for later use. Each child chooses a photo and writes a brief news article about the pictured event. Remind reporters to address the elements of *who, what, when, where,* and *how* in their stories. Have each reporter mount the final draft of his article and its corresponding photo on construction paper. Then display each completed project along with the original newspaper text. You can bet this bulletin board will be read through and through!

*Valerie Suttmiller—Gr. 2, Incirlik Elementary School, Incirlik, Turkey*

## Dear Editor

The local paper in Danville, Illinois, publishes a children's editorial section. Each week a topic or a question is provided and children are encouraged to submit written responses of 50 words or less. The students enjoy the writing challenge and they are always eager to read the replies that are published. If your local paper is unable to offer this educational opportunity, consider publishing a weekly classroom (or school) newspaper that offers a similar writing opportunity. Hot off the press! The first edition of the *The Students' Tribune!*

*Mary Park—Learning Disabled Grs. K–8*
*Daniel School, Danville, IL*

**The Students' Tribune**

# Comic Booklets

Use the Sunday comics to turn a parts-of-speech review into a barrel of laughs! To make a comic booklet, label a 6" x 9" rectangle of construction paper for each part of speech to be reviewed. Staple the resulting pages between construction-paper covers. For each booklet page, locate one comic-strip frame that has a written example of the featured part of speech. Use a crayon to underline the example; then cut out the frame and mount it on the appropriate booklet page. To complete each page, write a brief definition of the spotlighted part of speech. Add a title and byline to the booklet cover, and this newspaper project is complete!

Susan M. Stires—Gr. 3, Alamo Elementary School, Wichita Falls, TX

# Tracking Down Numbers

Energize a math review with a number search! Each youngster needs crayons and a few newspaper pages. Challenge students to find numerals based on certain criteria. Directions could include, "Use a red crayon to circle a three-digit numeral that has a six in the tens place," and "Draw a green box around a numeral that is greater than 75." Provide a greater challenge with directions like "Find two numbers whose sum equals ten. Draw a yellow star on each number." The possibilities are endless! Be sure students understand that this activity includes an element of chance like the game of bingo. This will prevent students from feeling frustrated if they cannot find all the numbers.

Kelly Malandra—Gr. 3, Lorane Elementary School, Exeter Township, PA

# Making Comparisons

Comparing newspapers from different communities provides a wealth of learning opportunities. As a class choose several communities from which you'd like to obtain newspapers. Divide the class into small groups; then ask each group to compose a letter that requests a sample newspaper and offers to pay for the requested newspaper and mailing costs. Mail the letters to the communities on your class list. (Most libraries have a reference, such as *Editor & Publisher International Year Book* or *Gale Directory Of Publications And Broadcast Media,* that lists the names and mailing addresses of newspapers.) When each paper arrives, compare and contrast its news coverage to that of your local paper for the same day. Students will enjoy comparing the comics, the weather, and the movie selections, too. Be sure to send a thank-you note to each newspaper that participates in your project.

Pam Doerr—Substitute Teacher, Elizabethtown District, Elizabethtown, PA

# A Continental Study

Learning the continents of the world is in the bag with this individual booklet project. To make a booklet, stack eight flat paper bags; then staple the bags together along the left-hand edge. Personalize, attach a cutout of the world, and write the title "Our World Around Us" on the top bag. On each of the following bags, attach and label a cutout of a different continent. To complete his booklet, a student cuts out newspaper articles and determines where each news event took place. Then he slips each article into the appropriate continent bag. Encourage youngsters to find five or more articles per continent.

Patti A. Devall—Gr. 3, St. Anthony Grade School, Effingham, IL

## As Easy As ABC!

Searching for a quick-and-easy review of alphabetical order? Look no further than the daily news. Ask each student to cut out ten or more words from a newspaper, then glue the words on his paper in ABC order. For a more challenging activity, ask students to cut out words that represent an assigned theme (like weather, sports, or music) or a category (like verbs, adjectives, or nouns).

Pam Negovetich—Gr. 3, Ready Elementary, Griffith, IN

## What A Great Photo!

Get a little help from the newspaper for a great sentence-writing activity. Ask each youngster to find a newspaper photo that she really likes, then cut it out and mount it on construction paper. For a writing assignment, challenge each student to write a question, a statement, a command, and an exclamatory sentence about her picture. The students are writing about topics they enjoy—and when the activity is completed, you'll have a clear indication of each student's sentence-writing capabilities. Later showcase the mounted pictures at a creative-writing center. You'll have a gallery of writing inspiration!

Pam Negovetich—Gr. 3

## Graph It!

This class graphing activity is full of laughs! Cut out the comic strips featured in your local newspaper. Count the strips you have; then divide the class into an equal number of groups. Give each group one comic strip and ask the group to count the words shown on its strip. Enlist your students' help in graphing the results on a class graph and in interpreting the information presented. If desired repeat the activity for several days using current comic strips each time. Students will enjoy comparing and contrasting the data, and making predictions about the comic strips for the following day, such as "I predict that Garfield will have the least number of words."

Susan Barnett—Gr. 3, Northwest Elementary School
Fort Wayne, IN

## Shop 'Til You Drop!

For this activity choose a local grocery store's advertising supplement from your newspaper and use it to create a shopping list. If you're designing a center activity, you'll only need one supplement. If you're planning to have your youngsters complete the activity simultaneously, you'll need one supplement for every one or two students. (Enlist your youngsters' help in gathering the supplements, or ask a local grocer for additional copies.) Display the shopping list and challenge each student to use his advertising supplement to determine the total cost of the items. Include a list of discount coupons that the students may apply to their purchases, if desired. Depending on the nature of the shopping list, a variety of math skills can be reinforced. Students are also learning important consumer concepts. Shop on!

Shannon Tovey—Gr. 3, George Peabody Elementary School, Dallas, TX

## Understanding Headlines

So what's in a headline? Challenge students to find out! Read aloud a newspaper headline and ask students to predict what the corresponding article will be about. When all of the predictions are in, read the article aloud or give a brief summary of it. Then reexamine the headline and determine what the key words are. Repeat the activity several times. For a fun twist, read aloud a newspaper article and challenge students to write an appropriate headline!

Tammy Brinkman & Kimberly Martin—Gr. 3
Dellview Elementary
San Antonio, TX

Zorkian Caught In Sticky Situation?!?!

## Making Use Of Maps

The newspaper is an excellent resource for maps—from local city maps to maps of the world. To take advantage of this offering, create a special file for newspaper maps. Each time a unique map is featured, clip it out and file it for later use. Most of the maps are easy to enlarge or duplicate. Or you can laminate the maps for individual student use. You'll soon wonder how you ever got along without this excellent resource.

Tammy Brinkman & Kimberly Martin—Gr. 3

## Mugging It Up

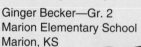

This activity is a sight to see! Ask each student to bring to school a coffee mug. Personalize the bottom of the mugs; then display the mug collection on cup hooks or store it in a classroom cupboard. One morning a week, use the mugs to serve a desired beverage; then distribute a newspaper page to each child. On the chalkboard list several items for the students to find in their newspapers, such as two nouns, a contraction, a compound word, three plurals, and an action verb. As students sip their beverages, they read their papers and use crayons to circle the requested items. The students feel quite grown-up as they enjoy the daily news!

Ginger Becker—Gr. 2
Marion Elementary School
Marion, KS

## Happily Ever After

For one-of-a-kind writing inspiration, check the Lost & Found listing in the classified ads. Cut apart and store the individual listings in a container. When you have a student supply, have each child draw a listing from the container and glue it to the top of his story paper. Then have each child write and illustrate a story that describes how a family pet is reunited with its family or how a family becomes the proud owner of a stranded pet.

Terry Kelly—Gr. 3, Prospect Elementary, East Cleveland, OH

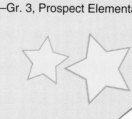

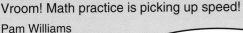

## Pulverized

## Action Packed!

If you're looking for verbs, try the sports page—it's packed with action! Challenge students to locate a predetermined number of past, present, and/or future-tense verbs on their newspaper pages. Or have students find ten past-tense verbs in the newspaper, then write the present and future tenses of the verbs on their papers. You'll have plenty of verbs and plenty of possibilities for skill reinforcement!

Pam Williams, Lakeland, FL

## Autos For Sale

Shopping for cars is a unique way to provide students with practice in reading large numbers. Each student needs a newspaper page that lists automobiles for sale. Youngsters can choose the cars they'd like to buy and read aloud the corresponding prices. Or ask each student to read aloud the highest (lowest) priced car on his page. Sequencing car prices is also an excellent way to reinforce place-value skills. Vroom! Math practice is picking up speed!

Pam Williams

**TURBO SPACE CRUISER** for sale. Like new condition. **CHEAP.** $12,090.00

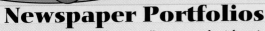

**WHAT'S THE WEATHER?**

## Graphing The Weather

Tracking the weather offers lots of learning opportunities. For a weeklong graphing activity, have students graph the daily high and low temperatures of cities across the country. To do this a student chooses a city that appears daily in the local paper's weather column and records the information on a duplicated graph. At the end of the week, students can report their cities' high and low temperatures for that week. The class can then determine which city had the highest (lowest) temperature of the week and locate the corresponding cities on an appropriate map. Students can also graph and tally precipitation readings. Who knows? Youngsters may even like to test their talents at making weather predictions!

Theodora Gallagher—Gr. 1, Carteret School, Bloomfield, NJ

## Newspaper Portfolios

These nifty (and newsy!) carryalls are perfect for storing or transporting newspaper projects. To make a portfolio that holds 9" x 12" projects, stack and align two full-size sheets of newspaper. Position the papers so that the center crease runs horizontally across the papers. Create a three-inch fold along the right and left edges of the project and along the bottom of the project as shown. Keep these folds in place as you bring the bottom of the project upward and make a fold along the crease line. Staple along each side. Fold down the top of the project to create a flap. Crease this fold; then unfold the flap and punch two holes near the center of the resulting crease— about four inches apart. For added durability, attach lengths of tape to both sides of each hole and repunch the holes. To make a sturdy handle, repeatedly thread a length of yarn through the holes; then securely tie the yarn ends. Refold the flap and your portfolio is ready to use!

Theodora Gallagher—Gr. 1

Name ______________________________________________ Newspaper Scavenger hunt

# A Nose For The News

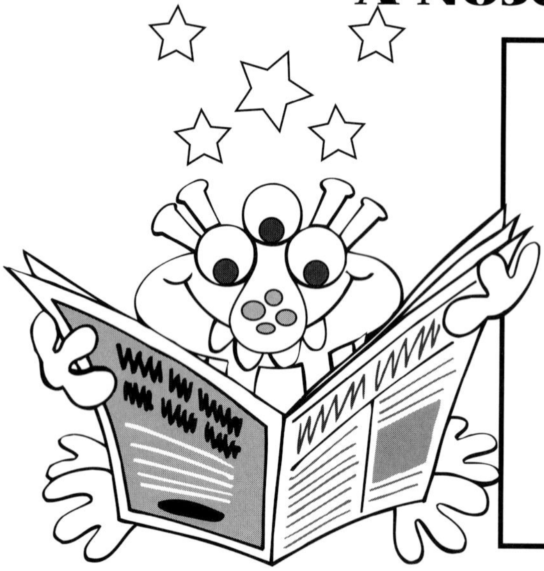

**Five Compound Words**

**Your Age**

**Three Color Words**

**Three Numbers Larger Than 50**

**An Animal**

**Five Contractions**

**Two Rhyming Words**

**Four Odd Numbers**

**Two Different Countries**

**A Day Of The Week**



**Note To Teacher:** Use with "Scavenger Hunt" on page 245.

# Seasonal Units

# A Bushel Of Back-To-School Ideas

Get to the core of your back-to-school planning with this bushel of our subscribers' best ideas! These are the pick of the crop—just what you need to put the polish on a new school year.

## Getting To Know You

Here's a picture-perfect way to help your students get to know one another better. During the first week, ask students to bring to school a few snapshots of their families and themselves engaged in various activities. Also ask each child to fill out an auto-biographical page listing such favorites as hobbies, foods, television shows, and games. Provide for each child a blank page from a loose-leaf photo album. On the front side of the page, a student can arrange his family photos, adding captions if desired. Insert these pages into the album; then attach each child's autobiographical information to the album page that is facing his photographs. Once the album is complete, establish a checkout system so that each child can share the album with his family.

Loretta Brabant—Gr. 1, Peshtigo Elementary Learning Center, Peshtigo, WI

## That's My Bag

Excite your students about the prospect of a new school year. A week before school begins, send a letter and a paper lunch sack to each of your future students. In the letter, ask students to place items in the bag that are clues to their hobbies, personalities, or summer experiences. Your students' first-day jitters will be replaced with the excited anticipation of sharing the contents of their bags.

Sharon Bayus—Gr. 3, Cortland Elementary, Cortland, OH

## I'm Special

As students begin to focus on making friends in their new class, give them the opportunity to think about what makes each of them so special. Read the book *I Like Me!* by Nancy Carlson (published by Viking Kestrel). Discuss with your class the characteristics that the pig in the story liked about itself. Have students list traits that they think make them unique. Lead youngsters to understand that their interests, feelings, hobbies, likes, and dislikes help make them whom they are. Give each student a copy of the student inventory on page 257. Collect the completed sheets and bind them into a class book. Students can leaf through the book to learn a few things about their new friends. Best of all, each child may realize that one of his very best friends is himself!

Maureen Burke Iannacone—Reading Specialist, Enfield Elementary, Oreland, PA

## Name Cards

Children can learn a lot from each other, as this child-centered activity proves. Cut several sentence strips in half; then write each child's first and last names on one of the resulting cards. Now that your preparation is complete, use these name cards to teach a variety of skills. To focus on alphabetizing, have students work together to arrange their name cards in alphabetical order by first or last names. Help students learn to recognize their classmates' names by asking a different student each day to pass the name cards out to their rightful owners. Highlight phonics by placing the name cards in a center; then challenge students to find names that contain specific consonant or vowel sounds. For math, graph the number of letters in each name to find out which name length is most commonly found. Students can also use their name cards as models of correct penmanship. Learning occurs much more readily when it is made personally relevant. What can be more personal to a child than his own name?

Judy Lively—Gr. 1, East LaFollette Elementary, LaFollette, TN

## Officer D.E.A.L.

Take the law into your own hands when establishing your classroom management system. Make or purchase a puppet resembling a police officer for use in laying the groundwork for classroom discipline policies. When Officer D.E.A.L. (the puppet) arrives on the scene, students must Drop Everything And Listen. Officer D.E.A.L. can explain classroom rules, consequences for misbehavior, and rewards for good behavior. Explain to students that he will remain in the local precinct (your classroom) so that he can discuss rule infractions, lend an ear when a student has a personal problem, or pat a youngster on the back for a job well done. All in all, your youngsters may find that having this special friend in class is a pretty good deal.

Ernestine K. Goldstein—Gr. 2, Little Creek Elementary School, Norfolk, VA

## Personal Pledge

In many classrooms, saying the Pledge Of Allegiance is a routine start of each day. Adding a little twist to this routine will help your students make the most of each learning-filled day. Ask your students what they think they would like to accomplish each day. Encourage them to list ways they can achieve these goals. Then charge them with the duty of writing a class pledge that includes these ways. Display the final version of the class pledge for all to see. After students have said the Pledge Of Allegiance, lead them in saying their own pledge to their class. This pledge will inspire unity among your students as they aim for a common goal. Thus, you'll be engendering patriotism to both country and class.

Don Bertke—Grs. 1–2, E. J. Brown School, Dayton, OH

### Our Class Pledge

I pledge allegiance to my class
And to the principles for which it stands.
I can learn anything I set my mind to.
I must listen to learn.
My teacher and classmates will support me.
If I do my very best, I will succeed in life.
I must try at all times to do those things that
Will make me proud of myself.

## Orderly Outlines

This year, put a trace on all those center materials that can be so difficult to locate. Before you begin sending students to centers, place the center materials in the areas where you will keep them for the year. Trace outlines of the materials on construction paper. Tape the construction-paper outlines to the shelves or tables on which the materials will lie. Tell students to place center materials on top of the outlines that match them. If outlines are not covered, you will immediately know what materials are missing. Your materials management problems will vanish without a trace.

Melinda Reynolds—Gr. 2, Gardnerville Elementary School, Gardnerville, NV

## Down To Earth

Get your students talking on the first day of school with this nature-related icebreaker. Design a questionnaire that features questions having a nature theme. You might ask, "Who has seen a bald eagle?", "Who has picked up trash?", or "Who has gone camping?" Be sure to include at least enough questions or signature spaces to represent the number of students in your class. Circulate the questionnaire among your students. Explain that each student should sign his name beside one question that describes an event in which he has participated. When everyone has signed the questionnaire, gather the students in a comfortable area and encourage them to talk about their experiences. Not only will your youngsters learn a lot about each other, but they will also find they already have a common bond: a love of nature.

Julie Decker—Gr. 3, St. Anthony School, Loyal, WI

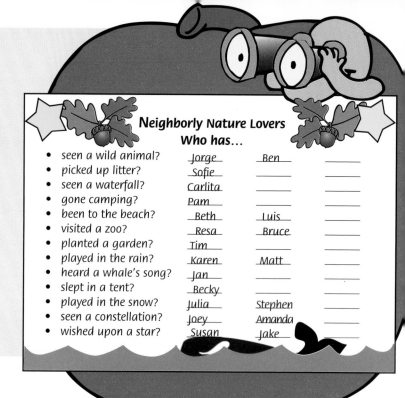

**Neighborly Nature Lovers Who has...**

| | | | |
|---|---|---|---|
| • seen a wild animal? | Jorge | Ben | |
| • picked up litter? | Sofie | | |
| • seen a waterfall? | Carlita | | |
| • gone camping? | Pam | | |
| • been to the beach? | Beth | Luis | |
| • visited a zoo? | Resa | Bruce | |
| • planted a garden? | Tim | | |
| • played in the rain? | Karen | Matt | |
| • heard a whale's song? | Jan | | |
| • slept in a tent? | Becky | | |
| • played in the snow? | Julia | Stephen | |
| • seen a constellation? | Joey | Amanda | |
| • wished upon a star? | Susan | Jake | |

## Hands-On Teacher

Your students will really have fun lending a hand with this project. You will need a plain, white T-shirt in your size, fabric paints in various colors, and several small paintbrushes. Lay the shirt on a newspaper-covered table and slip a cardboard T-shirt form inside. Using a paintbrush, cover a student's hand with fabric paint. Have her press her handprint on the T-shirt. Then, using a fine-tip bottle of black fabric paint, write the student's name on top of the handprint she made. Repeat the process until each child has taken a turn. Now you have a colorful keepsake to remind you of this class. Wear it proudly to Open House, PTA meetings, and anywhere else you want to show off your "hand-some" group.

Wanda Cimermancic—Gr. 1, Jefferson Elementary, Hibbing, MN

## The Parent Post

Establish open lines of communication with parents right from the start. Hang a bulletin board just outside your classroom door. On this bulletin board, post newsletters, parenting articles, your class schedule, special assignments, and the dates of upcoming events. As parents arrive to pick up their children or meet with you for a conference, they can glance at the board to catch up on what's going on in your classroom. Attach a pencil, a pad of notepaper, and some thumbtacks to the bulletin board so that parents can leave notes for you if you are not available when they drop by. Your thoughtfulness will be greatly appreciated. And that's good news!

Ruth Howell, Spartanburg, SC

Parent Post

News:

Book Sale    Research Projects

Bob will be out on Friday.
Mrs. Jones

TAKE ONE!

Field Trip Forms

Notepaper

# Nifty Nametags

These no-fuss nametags can save you plenty of time and money. Rather than purchasing expensive nametags that seldom last long, gather some cute Post-It™ Brand notes in designs that correspond to your class themes. For extra durability, mount the notes on construction paper; then laminate and cut around the shapes. Write your students' names on the shapes with a permanent marker. If desired, make extras and label them to use for counting, sorting, patterning, and flannelboard activities. Once you see how easy to make and versatile these nametags are, you'll really want to stick with them.

Jeri Moskowitz, El Cajon, CA

# Personalized Yearbooks

As the year begins, plan for a spectacular way to celebrate its end. Starting on day one and continuing throughout the year, take lots of photographs of your students engaged in various school-related activities. When you have the film developed, order double prints. Keep one set of pictures in a classroom photo album. File the other set in a box under the names of the students who are in the photos. Keep a running tally of the number of snapshots that are filed for each child. You will need an equal number of snapshots (ten or more) per student. Near the end of the year, begin making an individual yearbook for each class member. Mount each student's photos on heavy paper and add appropriate captions if desired. Staple each student's pages between an eye-catching cover. Present the students with their personalized yearbooks during the last week of school, at a time when all the youngsters are present. These special gifts will enable students to literally look back and remember what a terrific year and teacher they had!

Kara K. Koenig—Gr. 3, Hooven Elementary, Cincinnati, OH

Ian at recess.

Ian and Kendra reading together

The Halloween costume parade.

Ian's dad at the class picnic.

# Learning Log

The fact that school days are packed with high-interest activities does not seem to prevent many children from claiming that they did nothing all day long. This calendar-based activity helps students keep track of their learning day by day. At the beginning of each month, give students a blank calendar page to keep at their desks. Have students label the dates of the month in the calendar's boxes. Starting with the first school day of the month, ask students to draw pictures illustrating one of the activities that took place that day. Encourage them to write brief sentences describing the activities they chose. At the end of each successive day, allot time for students to complete the appropriate box on their calendars. At the month's end, your students will have a concrete reminder of what went on in class for that month. Send the calendars home with the students. When asked what they have done in school, your students can show that they've been as busy as bees!

Doris Hautala—Gr. 3, Washington Elementary, Ely, MN

September

| Monday | Tuesday | Wednesday | Thursday | Friday |
| --- | --- | --- | --- | --- |
| | 5 Bingo | 6 | 7 | 8 |
| | 12 | 13 | 14 | 15 |
| | 19 | 20 | 21 | 22 |
| 25 | 26 | 27 | 28 | 29 |

# Gumballs Aren't Just For Chewing

Sink your teeth into this suggestion for counting to 100. Design a poster-board bubble-gum machine. Laminate, cut out, and display the gumball machine within easy reach of your students. Place a colorful collection of gumballs (removable, self-sticking dots) nearby. On the first day of school, have a student choose a dot of any color to place on the machine. Explain that one gumball represents one day of school. Each day ask a different student to add one more gumball to the machine. On the 100th day of school, have students peel off the dots and graph them by color. Students can use the resulting graph to answer questions like "Which color was chosen most often?" and "How many more blue dots are there than green?" The array of questions is endless, as is the fun your class will have participating in this activity.

Sue Elliott, Ruskin, FL

## Stuffed Signature Critter

Here's a unique way to remember guest speakers and other noteworthy classroom visitors. Purchase a stuffed autograph animal (which can be found in gift shops), or make one using a stuffed animal pattern and plain muslin. As a guest speaker concludes her presentation, have a student thank her for coming and request that she sign the autograph animal. Your kids will give this unusual method of keeping mementos their roars of approval.

Susan Robinson—Resource Room, Lloyd Harbor Elementary, Huntington, NY

## Positive Postcards

This idea is positively perfect for encouraging students to look for the best in their classmates. As the school year begins, assign each student a Secret Pal. Keep a supply of postcards, or index cards cut to postcard size, on hand. Throughout the year, when a student witnesses a positive trait of her Secret Pal, she notes it on a postcard—along with any complimentary comments she would like to include. Then she sends the postcard to her Secret Pal via classroom or regular mail. As the recipient of the postcard rushes to share the news with her classmates, a domino effect of positive feelings ensues. The writer is pleased to have her words shared with others, the Good Samaritan is tickled to have been noticed, and the rest of the class is anxious to do what it takes to repeat the process for themselves. As your youngsters' observation and writing skills increase, so will their self-esteem.

Dear Derrick,
Hi! Today I saw you do some nice things for others. It was sure lucky that you had an extra pencil for Josh. Sharing your baseball and glove with everyone at recess was awfully swell, too! See ya!
Your Secret Pal

Derrick Shelton
Ms. Newsom's
3rd Grade
Room 213

Leigh Anne Newsom—Gr. 3, Greenbrier Intermediate School, Chesapeake, VA

## From Finish To Start

You have them every year—students who finish their assignments ahead of their classmates, then turn to you for additional work. This year make the Challenge Chart part of your classroom routine. To create a Challenge Chart, compile on a piece of poster board a list of interesting learning activities that can be completed independently. Number the choices so students can record the numbers of the activities that they choose to do. Individual record sheets will help you to keep track of which choices students are making, how often the chart is being utilized, and which activities seem to be most and least popular. When a child completes an assignment in less than the allotted time, he can use his free time constructively by choosing an activity from the chart. Be forewarned! You may never again hear the words, "What do I do now?" Instead, you'll be greeted with, "I'm finished, but I'm just getting started!"

Virginia A. Shaw, Los Angeles, CA

### Challenge Chart

1. Write a new ending for an old fairy tale.
2. Create your own comic strip.
3. Measure 20 items in the classroom using a metric ruler.
4. Illustrate a book that you just

## Hill Of Beans

This math activity is worth a million! To teach your youngsters the concept of one million, request that parents donate bags of dried beans. Establish free-time counting centers that each contain beans, ten small paper cups for grouping beans into tens, a larger container in which to place counted beans, and a sheet for recording the name of the counter and the number of beans counted. When one million beans have been counted, you'll be ready to celebrate! Spread a large tablecloth on the playground. Ask students to estimate how tall a hill of one million beans will be. Then have students pour individual containers of counted beans onto the tablecloth. Keep on adding beans until the entire million beans are in a pile. Measure to see which student's estimate is closest to the actual height of the hill. When the learning is complete, donate the dried beans to food kitchens. There is no end to the usefulness of these bounteous beans!

Diann Messman—Gr. 3, Joshua Intermediate School, Cleburne, TX

# I Am Special!

Me

Hi! My name is _____
_____ .

I like me because _____
_____
_____
_____
_____ .

How I would make the world a better place:

*My Family*

*One Wish*

**My Hobbies**

# My favorite...

book _____

movie _____

TV show _____

food _____

color _____

season _____

**Note To Teacher:** Use with "I'm Special" on page 252.

# Pokin' Around The Pumpkin Patch

Harvest a crop of fun-filled learning with real pumpkins! Enlist the help of your students, a local grocer, or your school's parent group in gathering a class supply of small pumpkins. Then use the following tips and hands-on activities to cultivate math, observation, and writing skills.

*ideas by Felice McCreary, Buda Intermediate, Buda, TX*

### The Perfect Patch

A pumpkin patch is the perfect spot for storing pumpkins when they are not in use. Choose a location that's large enough to house a class supply of pumpkins. To prepare the patch, have students cut out and attach construction-paper pumpkin leaves to lengths of yarn; then display the resulting greenery in the patch. If desired, enlist your students' help in creating an eye-catching scarecrow to guard the classroom crop.

Before students place their pumpkins in the patch, have each child dangle a numbered tag from his pumpkin's stem. To make the tags, hole-punch a class set of construction-paper leaf cutouts and label each one with a different number. Each student chooses a cutout, threads a length of yarn through the hole, and ties the yarn ends. The pumpkin owners should remain anonymous until the first activity has been completed. Be sure that you have a pumpkin in the patch, too!

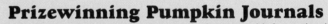

### Prizewinning Pumpkin Journals

In the activities that follow, students are asked to record information in journals. With your students' help, you can make the needed journals in a jiffy. You will need a class supply of pages 260 and 261, four sheets of blank white paper per child, two 9" x 12" sheets of orange construction paper per child, and several tagboard templates in the shape of the large pumpkin shown on page 260. Each student will also need scissors, crayons or markers, and access to a stapler.

To make a journal, a student uses a template to trace a pumpkin shape on each sheet of unprogrammed paper. He cuts out the pumpkin shapes—including the duplicated ones—and stacks the resulting cutouts in the following order: orange cutout, two white cutouts, cutout A, cutout B, two white cutouts, orange cutout. After aligning the cutouts and stapling the stems together, he personalizes his journal cover.

My Journal

Charlie Crow

### Activity One: Whose Pumpkin Is It?

Sharpen your students' observation and writing skills by having each child write a detailed description of her pumpkin. At the pumpkin patch—without revealing which pumpkin is hers—a student carefully studies her pumpkin. Back at her desk, on a blank journal page, she describes her pumpkin in detail. When the students have finished writing, each child takes a turn reading aloud her description and challenging her classmates to identify her pumpkin by number. When a child's pumpkin has been identified, she takes it to her desk. To keep the interest level high, have a student claim his pumpkin if it hasn't been identified after five guesses.

When the last student pumpkin is claimed, leaving only yours in the patch, ask students to name their pumpkins. Ask each student to write her pumpkin's name on its leaf-shaped tag.

### Activity Two: Problem Solving With Pumpkins

Your pumpkin patch is packed with problem-solving opportunities! Pose several pumpkin-related word problems for your students to solve. Have students use their pumpkins to demonstrate how to solve the problems. Then have each student write and solve two pumpkin-related word problems on a blank journal page. Have each child take a turn reading aloud one problem he created. When a classmate supplies the correct answer, the student's turn is over.

## Activity Three: Sizing Up Pumpkins

Divide students into small groups to complete the following measurement activities:

### Circumference

Each group needs one measuring tape, pencils, and its pumpkins and journals. To begin, ask students to estimate the circumference of your pumpkin. Record several estimates on the chalkboard; then measure the actual circumference of the pumpkin and write this measurement on the board. Discuss the results as a class.

Next have each child turn to cutout A in his pumpkin journal and locate the circumference chart. On the chart, have each student list the pumpkin names in his group and log a circumference estimate for each one. Encourage students to apply the outcome of the previous demonstration to their estimates and to discuss their estimates within their group. Then, in turn and using the provided measuring tape, each group member measures his pumpkin's circumference. All group members record the resulting measurement on their circumference charts. Urge students to evaluate their estimates after each measurement is recorded, reminding them that unconfirmed estimates can be adjusted.

### Height And Weight

Using the same teaching technique described in "Circumference," have students complete the height and weight charts in their pumpkin journals. Each group needs a ruler for the height activity and scales for the weight activity.

## Activity Four: Sink Or Float

Divide students into small groups. Each group needs its pumpkins and journals, pencils, crayons or markers, a supply of paper towels, and a water-filled container large enough to hold the entire group's pumpkins. Ask students to turn to a blank page in their journals and answer the following questions: Do you think a pumpkin will sink or float in water? Why? Next have the students rest their pumpkins on top of the water without letting go of the pumpkin stems. On a count of three, have the students release their pumpkins. Discuss the results of the experiment as a class. Then ask each student to remove his pumpkin from the water and dry it off. Lastly have each child summarize and illustrate the activity in the remaining space on his journal page.

## Activity Five: Counting Seeds

Before introducing this activity, prepare the students' pumpkins by creating a removable lid in the top of each one. Do the same to your pumpkin; then remove its lid, pulp, and seeds. Discard the pulp and count the seeds. Note the seed count; then store the seeds inside the pumpkin in a plastic bag. Replace the pumpkin lid.

Divide students into small groups. In addition to its pumpkins, journals, and pencils, each group needs a supply of paper towels and one resealable plastic bag per child. Using the teaching technique explained in "Circumference" (Activity Three), have students estimate and determine the number of seeds in their pumpkins. The chart for this activity is found on journal cutout A. However, unlike the previous exercises, allow group members to simultaneously scoop out their pumpkins and count the resulting seeds into their plastic bags. When the entire group has completed the exercise, each member can share his final count so that the rest of his group can record it on their charts. Send the seeds home with the students. Provide toasting instructions if desired.

## Activity Six: Graphing The Results

Students may work individually or in groups to complete this activity. To begin, have students turn to cutout B in their pumpkin journals. Explain that each student will create a graph that compares the circumference, the height, the weight, or the seed count of six pumpkins. First have each student label his graph to reflect his graphing choice. For example, a student who is graphing pumpkin heights labels his graph "Comparing Pumpkin Heights" and "Number Of Inches." Then he programs the graph in one- or two-inch increments. To complete his graph, he records the names of six pumpkins along the lower edge and colors the graph to show the heights of the pumpkins listed. A student can use information from his height chart and/or gather new information from his classmates to complete his graph.

## Pumpkins With Personality

For a fun finale to your pumpkin activities, let students decorate their pumpkins before they carry them home. Provide assorted arts-and-crafts supplies for the decorating endeavor. If desired, students can illustrate their decorated pumpkins on their remaining journal page. Students will be pleased as pumpkins to carry home these pumpkin projects!

## Just Ripe For Reading

These picture books are perfect for a pumpkin-related unit!

*The Pumpkin Blanket*
Written & Illustrated by Deborah Turney Zagwÿn
Fitzhenry & Whiteside, 1990

*Pumpkin Pumpkin*
Written & Illustrated by Jeanne Titherington
Greenwillow Books, 1986

*The Pumpkin Patch*
Written & Photographed by Elizabeth King
Dutton Children's Books, 1990

*Pumpkins: A Story For A Field*
Written by Mary Lyn Ray & Illustrated by Barry Root
Harcourt Brace Jovanovich, Publishers; 1992

*The Great Pumpkin Switch*
Written by Megan McDonald & Illustrated by Ted Lewin
Orchard Books, 1992

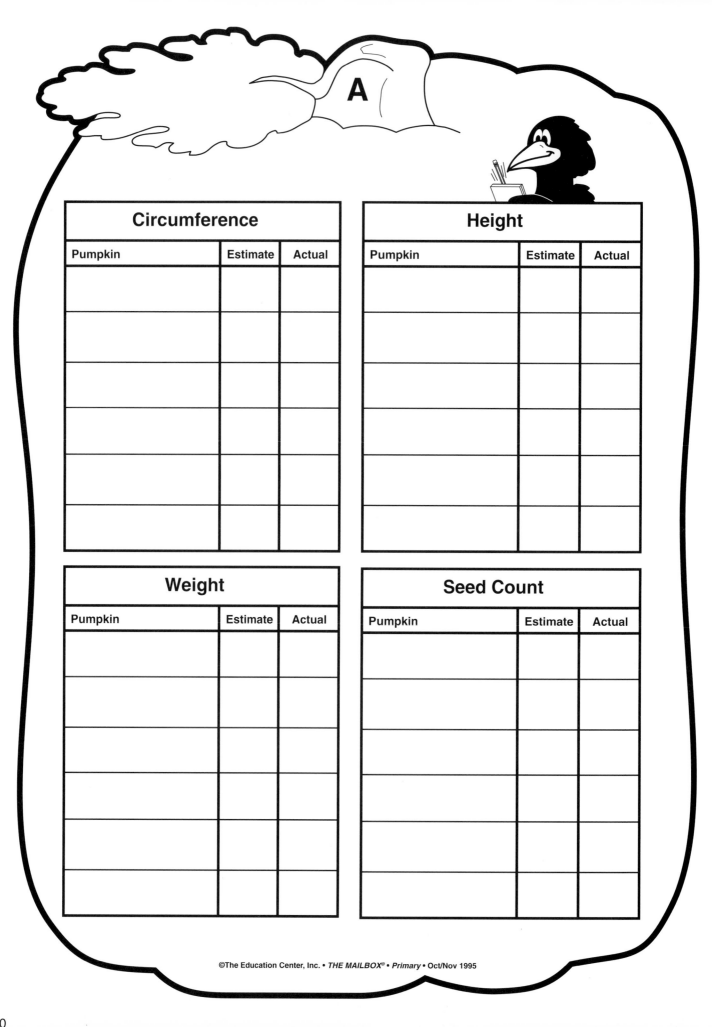

## Circumference

| Pumpkin | Estimate | Actual |
|---|---|---|
|  |  |  |
|  |  |  |
|  |  |  |
|  |  |  |
|  |  |  |
|  |  |  |

## Height

| Pumpkin | Estimate | Actual |
|---|---|---|
|  |  |  |
|  |  |  |
|  |  |  |
|  |  |  |
|  |  |  |
|  |  |  |

## Weight

| Pumpkin | Estimate | Actual |
|---|---|---|
|  |  |  |
|  |  |  |
|  |  |  |
|  |  |  |
|  |  |  |

## Seed Count

| Pumpkin | Estimate | Actual |
|---|---|---|
|  |  |  |
|  |  |  |
|  |  |  |
|  |  |  |
|  |  |  |

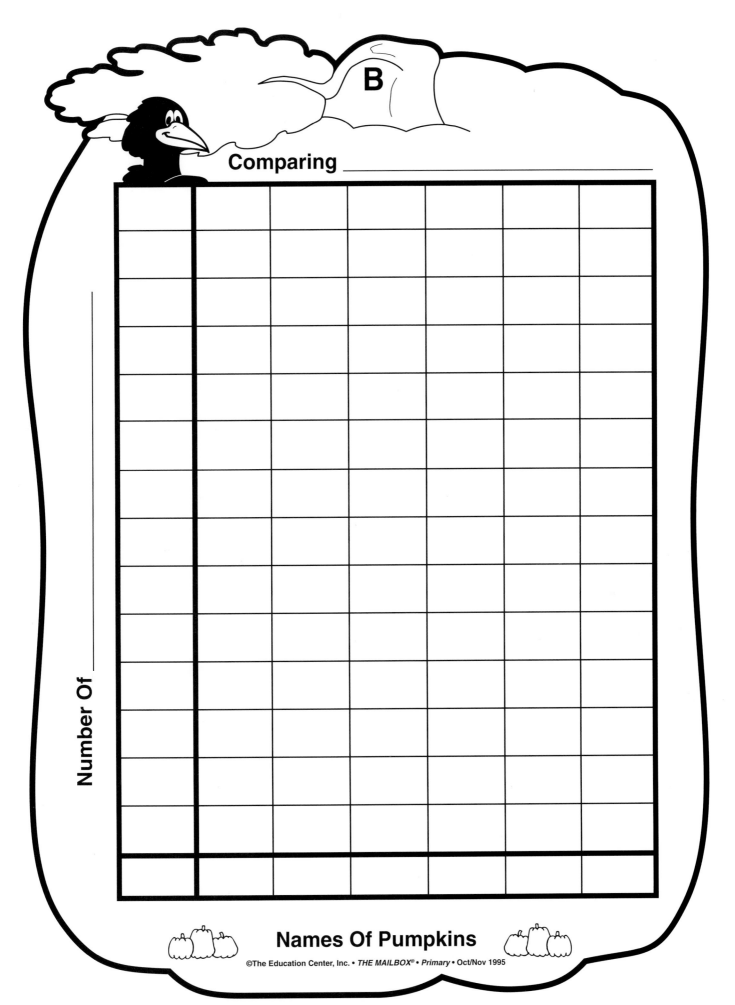

**B**

Comparing _____

**Number Of** _____

**Names Of Pumpkins**

# Hip! Hip! Hooray! It's The 100th Day!

How about that! It's the 100th day of school. Time *does* fly when you—and your students—are having fun. Celebrate your 100th day together with these fun-filled activities. Hip! Hip! Hooray!

*ideas contributed by Ann Higgins, St. Davids, Ontario, Canada*

### Collecting 100 Items

In preparation for your 100th-day celebration, challenge each youngster to collect 100 items in the category of his choice. Specify that all 100 items must fit inside a small box or clear, nonbreakable container. On the 100th day, display the collections in a hallway or in your school library.

### 100 Feet

Just how long is 100 feet—student feet, that is? Provide your students with construction paper and scissors, and have them find out! Based on the number of students present, help the class decide how many shoe tracings each child will need to provide so that the total number of shoe cutouts will equal 100. Then have the students trace their shoes and cut out the shapes. Number the cutouts; then tape them end to end on a wall. Finally have your students measure the trail of cutouts. Compare its length to the actual length of 100 feet.

### Spend It!

With this activity youngsters will discover some of the items they can buy with $100.00. Using play money, have the class count aloud 100 one-dollar bills. Then provide students with catalogs or sections of catalogs. Ask each student to find and cut out pictures of items that cost $100.00 or close to that amount. Have each student glue his pictures onto art paper and label them. Bind the pages together to create a class catalog of items that cost $100.00. Let's do some shopping!

### In 100 Years...

Help each student determine the year he will turn 100 years old. Then have him draw a picture of how he thinks he might look when he is that age. Encourage youngsters to write about their lifetime experiences or to describe what they think being 100 years old might be like.

## Read On!

Youngsters will be surprised when they discover how many words they can read and spell. Ask the class to brainstorm a list of 100 words that they can read and spell. Challenge older students to list 100 science, math, or social studies words. One, two, three,....

## The Pieces Fit

This hands-on activity is more than just fun! While participating, students will have hands-on experience with the number 100, and they will also strengthen their abilities to work cooperatively in a group. Divide the class into small groups; then give each group a 100-piece jigsaw puzzle to complete. Hey! Teamwork really counts!

## Ten Groups Of Ten

Students are sure to give this idea a big thumbs-up! Provide each child with a piece of paper, a marker, and an ink pad. Have each child print his thumbprint onto his paper 100 times in groups of ten. As he prints each group, encourage him to circle the set and label it with the appropriate increment of ten. There you have it—ten groups of ten!

## Measure It

Can't get enough of the number 100? Stretch out the fun of the 100th day with this measurement activity. Have students estimate which classroom items might be 100 centimeters long. Then provide students with measuring tapes to measure and verify their guesses. Record the actual lengths of the items on a chart for all to see.

In 100 years, there will be robot salad bars.

## Future Forecast

Help students calculate the year that it will be 100 years from now. Discuss ways the community might have changed. Also have students draw and describe items that might be invented during the next 100 years.

## 100 Good Deeds

Wrap up your 100th-day activities on a positive note! As a class, brainstorm a list of 100 good deeds. Challenge each youngster to commit to doing one or more of the good deeds listed. Your list of 100 will be only the beginning of many good deeds to come.

# Patterns

Use with "Introducing The Theme" on page 265. Duplicate on construction paper. Tape a Hershey's Kiss® with almonds in the space above the poem.

Here's a little drop of gold
From a merry secret elf
Who thinks that you should be told,
"Thanks for giving of yourself!"

**Have a very merry day!**

Here's a little drop of gold
From a merry secret elf
Who thinks that you should be told,
"Thanks for giving of yourself!"

**Have a very merry day!**

# Elf Clip Art

Use with the activities on page 265.

# A Little Elfin Magic

## Fun Thematic Activities For Your Little Elves

Who does Santa count on to help him get ready for the busiest night of the year? His hardworking elves, that's who! Bring that spirit of helpfulness and fun into your classroom with the following thematic activities—all designed to turn your students into happy, ho-ho-holiday elves!

*ideas by Bev Wirt—Gr. 1, Marshall Ranch School, Glendale, AZ*

Pam Crane

### Introducing The Theme

After Thanksgiving, ask your media specialist to help you collect several picture-book versions of the old German tale, "The Elves And The Shoemaker." Don't forget to check in fairy-tale or folklore anthologies for different variations as well. After sharing the versions with your students, discuss differences and similarities in the tales. Emphasize that the elves helped the shoemaker and his wife with no expectation of reward.

Next talk about people in your school who serve your students and deserve a pat on the back. List these people on the chalkboard; then distribute copies of the cards on page 264 to small groups of students. Direct students to color the cards, making sure not to color over the poem. Then have them place small rolls of tape on the bottoms of Hershey's Kisses® with almonds (the "little drop of gold") and attach them to the cards as shown. Let pairs of students secretly deliver these notes to office workers, cafeteria staff, specialty teachers, and other support personnel. After they've returned from their secret mission, treat your elves to a snack of E.L. Fudge® Sandwich Cookies, which are cut in the shape of the popular Keebler® elves.

Here's a little drop of gold
From a merry secret elf
Who thinks that you should be told,
"Thanks for giving of yourself!"
**Have a very merry day!**

## Extend the elf theme with the following fun activities:

- **Art:** Decorate your walls, bulletin boards, or hallways with colorful elves that will cheer anyone in need of a holiday lift! Provide each student or student pair with scissors, glue, construction paper, pom-poms, glitter or glitter pens, and other art materials to make the magical elf shown. (Depending on the age of your students, you may wish to precut the head, feet, hands, and hat for each child's elf.

- **Math:** Direct students to take off their shoes and place them in a pile at the front of the classroom. As a class, sort the shoes into different categories (laced/no laces, white/colored, sneakers/non-sneakers, etc.). Then display the results of your sorting on a large graph.

- **Reading:** Read additional stories about elves and other types of little magical people such as leprechauns, fairies, etc. Have students compare the different types of little folks. Then have them make simple stick puppets to use in retelling their favorite stories.

- **Motivation:** Keep excitement about your elfin theme high by decorating student reproducibles, awards, and notes with the elf clip art on page 264. To use the clip art, copy page 264 Cut out the graphic you wish to use; then glue or tape it onto your master before duplicating student copies. Or enlarge the graphics to use on bulletin boards, signs, or other classroom displays.

- **Writing:** After students have read about elves, let them write their own stories about the little creatures on paper that has been decorated with the clip art on page 264.

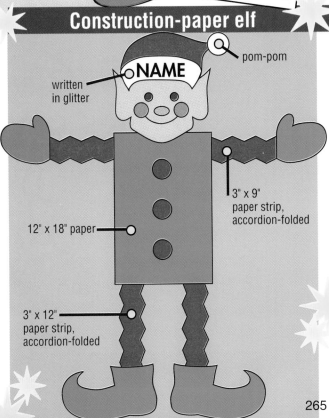

### Construction-paper elf

pom-pom

NAME
written in glitter

3" x 9" paper strip, accordion-folded

12" x 18" paper

3" x 12" paper strip, accordion-folded

# Happy, Happy New Year

All around the world, people welcome the new year! Most New Year celebrations focus on family and friends—putting the old year to rest and looking forward to the new year with great anticipation. However, not all New Year celebrations take place on the same day or in the same way! Introduce your youngsters to a variety of New Year's customs, using the ideas in this fun and festive unit!

*ideas contributed by Susan Morphew and Lisa Reep*

## Japan

In the Land Of The Rising Sun, the new year is welcomed with great seriousness. It is a time for new beginnings—a fresh start. Homes are cleaned, personal debts are paid, and efforts are made to wrap up all unfinished business from the previous year before the January 1 celebration.

### Rice Is Nice

Traditional foods are a prominent part of the Japanese New Year celebration. Rice cakes are a popular New Year's food. They are believed to bring good fortune if eaten for at least the first three days of the New Year. In *Bamboo Hats And A Rice Cake,* written by Ann Tompert and illustrated by Demi (Crown Publishers, Inc.; 1993), a penniless couple decides to trade a most precious possession in order to have rice cakes for the New Year. This elegant adaptation of a traditional Japanese tale also teaches a lesson in human kindness. After an oral reading of the story, serve your youngsters a snack of mini rice cakes. Invite students to talk about times when acts of kindness have brought them good fortune.

### Good-Luck Tree

If you went to Japan on New Year's Day, you could see a tree covered with white blossoms—or so you might think! The white blossoms are really strips of white paper bearing fortunes. The people in Japan buy the fortunes and tie them onto bare-branched trees for good luck. To sprout a good-luck tree in your classroom, secure a bare tree branch in a container filled with sand or plaster of paris. Invite students to write fortunes for the new year on 1" x 12" strips of white paper, then loosely tie the fortunes on the "good-luck tree"!

# Iran

The first day of the Iranian New Year coincides with the first day of spring. The celebration begins on March 21 and ends 13 days later. The holiday is called *No Ruz,* which means "new day." It is a time of gift giving and visiting friends and family. Families often travel long distances to be together with as many members of the family as possible.

## Growing Grains

A few weeks before March 21, it is customary for people to plant tiny bowl gardens. Tiny grains of wheat, barley, or other grains are placed in shallow bowls of water or laid upon damp cotton. By the New Year, the grains have sprouted. The new sprouts, called *sabzeh,* symbolize spring and a new year of life and growth. What better time to put your youngsters' green thumbs to the test? Distribute a variety of seeds for students to sprout. Have each youngster place his seeds in a shallow bowl of water. Before long, greenery will be cropping up all over!

## Head Outdoors

*Sizdah Bi Dar,* the 13th day after No Ruz, is the end of the New Year celebration. On this day it is considered unlucky to stay indoors, so everyone plans to picnic outdoors. The idea is for families to get out of their homes, taking any bad luck with them. This year chase away any bad luck that might be lurking in your classroom by eating lunch outdoors with your youngsters on a designated date. The event will be a fun change of pace—and you can never have too much good luck!

# Greece

In Greece, New Year's Day (January 1) is also the Festival Of St. Basil. St. Basil was a kind and generous man. For many Greek children, he is their equivalent of Santa Claus. Before youngsters go to bed on New Year's Eve, they place their shoes by the fireplace, hoping that St. Basil will fill them with gifts.

## St. Basil's Cake

On New Year's Day, a cake called St. Basil's cake, or *Vassilopitta,* is served. Baked inside the cake is some type of a small treasure—usually a small ring or a coin. It is believed that the person who finds the treasure in her slice of cake will have a lucky year! Serve your youngsters slices of a cake you've baked after hiding a small treasure within. Remind students to eat their cake carefully so as not to swallow any good luck that might be headed their way!

*Tet* is the most important holiday in Vietnam. The celebration—which ushers in a new year and the start of spring—usually occurs in late January or early February, and lasts for at least three days. Tet is a time for families to be together in happiness and goodwill. The preparation for Tet is much like that for the Chinese New Year: houses are cleaned, lavish meals are planned, and new clothing is purchased. On the eve of the New Year, people stay up late so that they can each be doing a good deed when the clock strikes midnight. These deeds are believed to bring good fortune in the new year.

## Chuc Mung Nam Moi!

(CHOOK MUNG NAHM MOY)

That means "Happy New Year!" in Vietnamese. To learn more about the celebration and the symbols associated with Tet, read aloud *Têt: The New Year* written by Kim-Lan Tran and illustrated by Mai Vo-Dinh (Simon & Schuster Books For Young Readers, 1992). This lively story is told through the eyes of immigrant children who—while adjusting to new customs in America—still honor the traditions of their people.

## Wee Wee Oink

If you hear a pig cry, there will be a shortage of food.

## Woof, Baaaa, Meow!

Some people believe that the first animal sound of the Vietnamese New Year can predict the events of the coming year. Hearing a dog bark is considered good luck because a dog's bark can scare away burglars. If a buffalo cry is heard—indicating a weary buffalo—a year of hard work is predicted. For this follow-up activity, give each youngster a six-inch square of white construction paper. Ask each child to draw and color an animal on his paper, then invent a New Year's prediction based on the animal and its cry. In turn, have each child present the animal he drew and share his prediction. For an eye-catching display, mount the illustrations on a paper-covered bulletin board entitled "Animal Sounds Of The New Year." Above his posted picture, have each child use a colorful marker to write the sound his animal makes. Older students can write their animal-related predictions on paper slips that can be mounted below the pictures.

# Belgium

In Belgium, December 31 is filled with New Year's Eve festivities and the new year begins on January 1.

## Colorful Promises

It's a custom in Belgium that the children prepare New Year's greetings for their parents. Each child's greeting normally includes wishes of good health and happiness in the coming year, along with promises that describe how the child plans to improve his behavior during the next 12 months! These notes are written in advance on colorful paper that the children have purchased with their own money, then tucked away until the children read them aloud to their parents on New Year's morning. For a fun writing activity, have your students write similar New Year's greetings for their parents. Provide an assortment of colorful paper for the students to use.

> Dear Mom,
> Happy New Year! I hope this year is a good one for you! I hope you stay well and happy all year long. I promise to help you have a good year by being a kid you can be proud of. I will try my best in school and I will help you around the house. I promise to listen to you, too. I love you, Mom!
>
> Love,
> Chase

# Ethiopia

*Enkutatash,* the Ethiopian New Year, is celebrated in Africa on the first day of the Ethiopian month of *Maskarem,* which usually falls around September 11. In Ethiopia the holiday comes at the end of the rainy season when the wildflowers are in full bloom. Children gather the wildflowers and arrange them in small bunches. Then, on New Year's Eve, the youngsters go from house to house singing, dancing, and delivering flowers along with New Year's greetings.

## New Year's Nosegays

In the spirit of the Ethiopian New Year, suggest that students give these colorful flowers to special friends or neighbors on New Year's Day. To make a New Year's nosegay, fold a 9" x 12" sheet of green construction paper in half. Starting at the fold, make a series of cuts equal distances apart, stopping approximately one inch from the opposite edges of the paper. Invert the fold (without creasing it) and glue the straight edges together. Beginning at one end, loosely roll up the greenery and staple to hold it in place. Cut out and glue an assortment of colorful construction-paper flowers on top of the greenery. If desired, have each student write a brief New Year's message and attach it to his nosegay. Happy New Year!

# Scotland

In Scotland the last day of the year (December 31) is known as *Hogmanay*. There are a number of theories about how this name originated. One theory suggests that the name came from an old French expression that had to do with lucky mistletoe! Many of the customs of Hogmanay date back hundreds of years, and some are still in practice today.

## First-Footer

Many old superstitions connected with Hogmanay are still observed today. One of these is called *first-footing*. There are people in Scotland who believe that the first person to enter their homes on New Year's Day can influence the outcome of the year ahead. A tall, dark-haired visitor (or *first-footer*) is believed to bring good luck. A flat-footed first-footer is considered to be unlucky! Tap into your youngsters' creativity by having them write far-fetched first-footer tales. A tale might describe how a family makes sure that its first visitor of the new year will bring good luck or how a family tries to prevent an unlucky first-footer from entering its home. The more far-fetched the tales, the better! Be sure to set aside time for these tall tales to be told.

## "Auld Lang Syne"

One Hogmanay custom that is now worldwide is the singing of "Auld Lang Syne" at the stroke of midnight on New Year's Eve. Have students stand in a circle and join hands as they sing a rousing chorus of this popular New Year's Eve song!

# Ecuador

In Ecuador, South America, December 31 marks the celebration of *Año Viejo* (AHN-yo vee-AY-ho) or "Old Year." For this day, a family creates a figure of the old year by sewing together an old shirt and pants, then stuffing the shape with straw. The resulting scarecrow-type figure, called Old Year, is displayed in a window or in the front of the family's home. The family members also write a will for Old Year that lists their personal shortcomings. At midnight on December 31, the will is read with much amusement. Then a match is lit, and Old Year and his will go up in flames—and so do all the family's faults, or so they say. Now the family has a fresh start for the new year!

## Good-Bye, Old Year!

Say good-bye to the old year and welcome in the new one with a clean slate! Ask each child to draw and color a picture of a scarecrow-type figure (Old Year) on a sheet of drawing paper. Next instruct each youngster to turn his paper over and list any faults he thinks he has. On the count of three, have the youngsters wad up their completed work, bid the old year good-bye, and toss away their faults by depositing their crumpled papers in a designated trash can. Then, as a class, carry the trash can to a school custodian and ask him to safely dispose of its contents. Happy New Year!

# China

The Chinese New Year is the most exciting and colorful time of the year! All Chinese festivals are celebrated according to a Chinese lunar calendar. The Chinese New Year marks the first new moon of the first month of the new year. On our calendar, this falls between January 20 and February 20.

## Sweeping Out The Old

In preparation for Chinese New Year, everyone joins in housecleaning. This is symbolic for "sweeping out the old, and welcoming in the new." Engage your youngsters in a similar activity by assigning jobs for a classroom cleanup. Once the room is sparkling clean, gather the students together for a treat of apple and orange slices. Explain that the Chinese believe that red and orange are colors of joy. Apples also symbolize good luck for the new year!

## New Year's Eve

On the eve of the new year, Chinese families celebrate at a reunion feast. If any family member is unable to attend, a place is set for him along with an empty chair to symbolize his presence. Traditional holiday foods such as fish, poultry, pork, beef, vegetables, and noodles are served. After the feast, children receive red envelopes from family members. These envelopes contain good-luck money for the new year.

In *Sam And The Lucky Money*, written by Karen Chinn and illustrated by Cornelius Van Wright & Ying-Hwa Hu (Lee & Low, 1995), a young Chinese American boy named Sam receives a red envelope of good-luck money from his grandparents. Excited by the notion that this year he is old enough to spend his good-luck money as he chooses, Sam sets his hopes so high that his New Year's Day shopping trip ends in disappointment. A surprise encounter with a stranger helps Sam discover that no gift is too small when it comes from the heart. At the conclusion of the story, invite students to talk about the valuable lesson that Sam learned and how they could learn from Sam's experience as well.

## New Beginnings

On New Year's Day, everyone is on his best behavior. Many Chinese families believe that whatever happens on this day determines the family's luck for the entire year. In some families it is also customary to get new haircuts and buy new clothes for New Year's Day. This is believed to prevent the evil spirits from recognizing family members, and it enables the family to have a fresh start in the new year.

In celebration of the Chinese New Year, invite your students to make a fresh start in the classroom. On the top half of a 12" x 18" sheet of drawing paper, ask each student to illustrate a portrait of himself sporting new clothes and a new haircut. On the lower half of his paper, the student can list three to five desirable behaviors he plans to display from this day forward. Display the completed projects on a bulletin board or compile them into a class booklet. How's that for a fresh start?

Ted

1. I will not hit my brother unless he starts it.
2. I will close my mouth when I eat.
3. I will make my bed most of the time.
4. I will put my bike in the garage.
5. I will finish my homework.

# Making A Difference

## African-American Trailblazers

African-Americans who have dared to fight racism and fulfill their dreams are at the heart of black history. Use these teaching suggestions to enrich your celebration of Black History Month.

### Calendar Companions

Introduce your students to a variety of famous African-Americans with this pictorial plan. After your daily calendar activity, present a picture of a famous African-American. (Clip pictures from resources like newspapers and discarded magazines.) As a class discuss the featured African-American and how he or she has influenced the growth and development of our nation. Then showcase the picture near your calendar display. On each day that follows, challenge students to recall the contributions of the famous person(s) on display before introducing that day's featured African-American. By the end of the month, your students will know a wealth of information about famous African-Americans—and you'll also have a striking display!

Amy Hall—After-School Program, Tree House Day Care, Robinson, IL

### Something To Talk About

Here's a teaching format that youngsters are sure to love. Pair students and have each twosome research a different African-American. Then ask each pair to present its information in the format of an interview. To do this, one student role-plays an interviewer and the other role-plays the African-American who has been researched. Encourage the students to dress for their parts. These high-interest presentations are sure to bring rave reviews. If possible, videotape the event. Move over Oprah! You've got plenty of competition headed your way!

Pamela Whitted, University School, Johnson City, TN

### Charting African-American Contributions

Compile your youngsters' research efforts on an easy-to-read chart like the one shown. As each youngster makes a discovery, write it on the chart. Before long you'll have an abundance of information that can be used in a variety of ways. For example, each student can create a booklet of African-American contributions. To do this a student describes and illustrates a different contribution on each page of a blank booklet. Or challenge students to illustrate things that all people today can do that result from the efforts of African-Americans. Showcase these illustrations and a border of colorful hand cutouts on a bulletin board entitled "Applauding The Contributions Of African-Americans."

Agnes Tirrito—Gr. 2
Kennedy Elementary School
Texarkana, TX

| African-American Trailblazers | |
| --- | --- |
| Name | Contribution |
| Rosa Parks | • Civil Rights Activist |
| Neal Loving | • Aviator |
| Harriet Tubman | • A Leader of the Underground Railway |
| Colin Powell | • Chairman of Joint Chiefs of Staff |

# A Celebration Of Differences

Celebrate the differences among people with this baking project. With your students' help, prepare a batch of your favorite rolled cookie dough. Then, using a cookie cutter, have each child cut out a body shape from the rolled dough. As the cookies bake, talk about how the cookies were made. Guide students to conclude that while the shapes of the cookies may vary, the cookies are all the same on the inside. When the cookies have cooled, ask each student to decorate a cookie to his liking. To encourage creativity, provide several colors of frosting and a wide variety of edible cookie decorations. Have each student display his work of art on a napkin at his desk. Provide time for students to admire their classmates' cookies. Lead the students to conclude that the differences among the cookies make them unique and special. Then, as the youngsters consume their creations, help them apply this important concept to the world around them.

Patsy Blakley—Gr. 2, Haskell Elementary School, Haskell, TX

# A Literature Link

Plan to read aloud several inspirational picture books that feature contemporary African-American characters. Here are a few titles that your youngsters are sure to enjoy.

**Our People** • *Written by Angela Shelf Medearis & Illustrated by Michael Bryant • Atheneum, 1994*
As a young girl and her father playfully explore great moments of African-American history, she learns that her people have had a glorious past and that she can have a glorious future.

**Boundless Grace** • *Written by Mary Hoffman & Illustrated by Caroline Binch • Dial Books For Young Readers, 1995*
The spunky heroine of *Amazing Grace* is back! Grace is reunited with her father—a man who left home when Grace was very small and who now lives in Africa. Grace discovers that even though she and her father live on different continents, the two are connected at the heart.

**Joshua's Masai Mask** • *Written by Dakari Hru & Illustrated by Anna Rich • Lee & Low Books Inc., 1993*
In this modern African-American fable, a young boy realizes that he's proud of his talents and happy to be himself.

**Tanya's Reunion** • *Written by Valerie Flournoy & Illustrated by Jerry Pinkney • Dial Books For Young Readers, 1995*
This is a heartwarming new tale about the beloved characters from *The Patchwork Quilt*. When Tanya and her grandma go to help with preparations for a big family reunion, Tanya learns about the history of the farm where Grandma grew up.

**Uncle Jed's Barbershop** • *Written by Margaree King Mitchell & Illustrated by James Ransome • Simon & Schuster Books For Young Readers, 1993*
Uncle Jed was a man with a dream. Sarah Jean—his niece and now a grown lady—tells the poignant story of her Uncle Jed, his dream, and what he taught her.

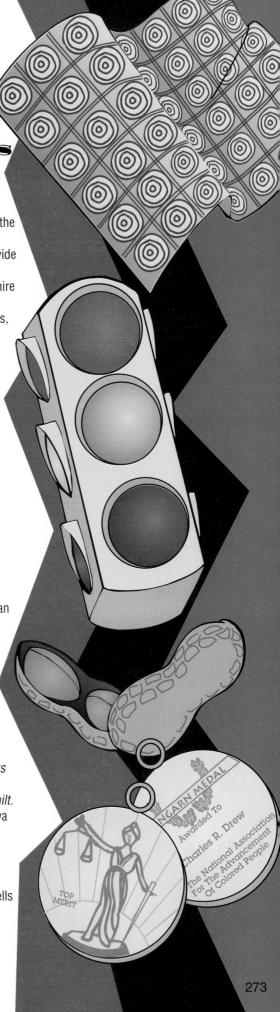

# The Olympic CHALLENGE

## Record-Breaking Activities For The 1996 Olympic Games

Teach your students about the 1996 Olympic Games by planning a classroom, grade-level, or schoolwide celebration. The following activities are guaranteed to score a perfect ten with your youngsters!

*ideas by Stacie Stone*

### From Greece To Atlanta

Prior to the opening of the 1996 Olympic Games, a lighted torch will be carried from the site of the first Olympic Games in Greece to the Olympic stadium in Atlanta, Georgia. To help students visualize the torch's route, find Greece on a large world map and use a sticky dot to mark its location. Display a torch cutout near the sticky dot and explain to students that the torch will be carried by plane from Greece to its entry point into the United States—Los Angeles, California. With your youngsters' help, find Los Angeles on the map and mark its location. Also find and mark Atlanta. Inform students that a relay of runners will carry the lighted torch along a predetermined route from Los Angeles to Atlanta, with the last relay runner lighting the Olympic flame in Atlanta during the Opening Ceremonies of the 1996 Olympic Games. The Olympic flame will burn throughout the games.

### Read Your Way To Atlanta!

Build enthusiasm for the 1996 Olympic Games and your classroom celebration with this reading challenge. Refer students to the torch cutout that is displayed on your world map (see "From Greece To Atlanta"). Under the watchful eyes of your students, remove the cutout and "fly" the torch to Los Angeles. As you reattach the cutout to the map, remind students that from this point a relay of runners carries the torch to Atlanta. Then reveal that you'd like the students to transport the classroom torch to Atlanta by reading! Give each student several copies of a reading record slip (see the pattern on page 277). Explain that each time a child completes a book, he fills out a record slip and deposits the slip in a designated container. Every few days tally the record slips received and award one mile for each page read. Then, using the scale on your map, move the torch toward Atlanta the appropriate distance. When the torch arrives in Atlanta, begin your classroom Olympic celebration!

*(The actual route of the torch relay is approximately 15,000 miles and passes through 42 states. A direct route from Los Angeles to Atlanta equals 2,145 miles. If a direct route is taken for the reading relay, a classroom of 20 students, each of whom reads an average of eight pages per day, seven days a week, will reach Atlanta in about two weeks.)*

**Headed To Atlanta!**
ATLANTA OR BUST!
**Olympic Reading Record**

Name: _____

Title Of Book: _____

_____

Number Of Pages: _____

_____

*Granted with special permission from the U.S. Olympic Committee.*

## World-Class Geography

Athletes from all over the world will travel to Atlanta to participate in the 1996 Olympic Games. Ask students to name countries that they would like to represent during your classroom Olympic celebration and write their suggestions on the chalkboard. After each country has been located on your world map, narrow the field to five or six countries. On individual sheets of tagboard, write the names of the chosen countries. Then, below each country's name, list the students who will represent that country. For easiest management, attempt to form teams of equal numbers.

## Team T-Shirts

These student-decorated team T-shirts are sure to add to your students' Olympic spirit! Ask each child to bring to school a plain, white T-shirt; then have each team meet to determine how to decorate its team shirts. Ask each team to sketch its shirt design on scrap paper, making sure that the name of the team's country is included in its design. Then let each team take a turn decorating its shirts with fabric markers or paints. Have each child insert a cardboard cutout or several thicknesses of newspaper inside his shirt to prevent the markers or paint from bleeding though to the back of the shirt. Set the shirts aside to dry.

## The Opening Ceremony

Plan your opening ceremony to coincide with the arrival of the classroom torch in Atlanta (see "Read Your Way To Atlanta!" on page 274). Arrange for the school principal to greet the students in the school gym. Invite parents and neighboring classrooms to the ceremony if desired. Wearing the decorated T-shirts, each team carries its flag into the "stadium." Enlist your students' help in determining the correct order of the teams' arrivals. After the principal has greeted the students, have the youngsters recite a class oath that they wrote for this Olympic occasion. Then let the games begin!

## National Flags

An opening ceremony would not be complete without a display of national flags! Have each team locate a picture of its country's flag, then create a likeness of the flag on a 12" x 18" sheet of construction paper. Construction-paper scraps, crayons, markers, or paints may be used. Display the flags around the classroom until it's time for the teams to carry them for your opening ceremonies.

*Granted with special permission from the U.S. Olympic Committee.*

275

# Let The Games Begin!

Let your students experience the thrill of victory as they complete these winning activities!

### Spelling Relay

Pass it on—this spelling relay is loads of fun! Each team forms a line so that its members are standing shoulder to shoulder. Designate a captain for each team and supply her with a stack of index cards that are programmed with review spelling words and a team baton (a paper-towel tube). On your signal, each captain passes her baton to the first member on her team. Then she reads aloud a spelling word. The team member holding the baton spells the word aloud. If she spells the word correctly, she passes the baton to the next team member. If she does not spell the word correctly, she may either try to spell the word again or request a different word. The baton may only be passed when a correct spelling is given. The team captain then reads aloud a spelling word to the next player holding the baton. Play continues in this manner until the last player in the team correctly spells a word. This player passes the baton back to the captain and the team immediately sits down. The first team seated wins the relay. Repeat the game as many times as desired, choosing different team captains each time.

### The Word-Problem Weight Lift

Can your students hold their weight in this word-problem game? You will need a supply of word problems that vary in difficulty. Use the following categories to sort or label the problems: lightweight (least difficult), middleweight, and heavyweight (most difficult). Write the following code on the chalkboard along with the names of the teams: lightweight = 1 point, middleweight = 3 points, heavyweight = 5 points. To begin play, ask one member from each team to stand. In turn each player chooses a category and attempts to solve the problem that is read aloud to him. If he answers correctly, he writes the appropriate number of points on the chalkboard next to his team name before he sits down. If he answers incorrectly, he sits down. When all players are seated, ask another member from each team to stand. Repeat the procedure. Continue play in this manner until all team members have attempted to answer one or more questions. Then tally each team's points to determine the winning team!

### Javelin Throw

Before you head outdoors for this Olympic competition, have each student personalize a milk cap or other similar object to use as a marker. Then give each team a tape measure and an empty, cardboard wrapping-paper tube. Each team lines up single file behind a designated throwing line. Then, in turn, each team member throws the cardboard-tube javelin. His milk cap is used to indicate where his throw lands. After each team member has taken his turn, the team uses its tape measure to determine the length of the longest throw. The team with the longest throw wins the event. For more fun, at the conclusion of the javelin throw, collect the cardboard tubes and give each team a small, sponge-type ball. It's time for the shot put competition!

### A Balancing Act

To create a mock balance beam, use chalk to draw a 4" x 16' rectangle on an outdoor blacktop surface. Then give each team time to create a routine or a series of movements that its members will perform on the beam. Award teams points for creativity, balance, and participation. If possible, capture this event on video!

*Granted with special permission from the U.S. Olympic Committee.*

## The Awards Ceremony

Once your Olympic events have been completed, gather students together for a closing ceremony. If desired, return to your established stadium. Present each student with a participation award (below) and a gold medal for exceptional sportsmanship. To make a gold-medal award, attach a large, gold-foil sticker to a tagboard circle. Hole-punch the circle and thread a length of red, white, and/or blue ribbon through the hole; then tie the ribbon ends.

## Olympic Treats

No doubt all of the Olympic activity will leave your Olympians hungry and thirsty, so be prepared with a supply of napkins, drink cups, munchies (see the recipe below) and juice.

### Field Games Mix

**Ingredients:**
1 bag of javelins (pretzel sticks)
1 box of shot puts (round corn cereal)
1 package of discuses (seasoned bread flats)
a dash of your favorite Olympic seasoning

Mix all the ingredients in a large bowl.

*Granted with special permission from the U.S. Olympic Committee.*

---

# Headed To Atlanta!

## Olympic Reading Record

Name: _____

Title Of Book:_____

_____

### Number Of Pages:

_____

_____
Parent Signature

---

_____'s

participation in

# The Olympic Challenge

earns *gold medal* recognition!

## Congratulations!

_____
Signature

_____
Date

# Buzzing Into Summer

Your happy hive will be humming with excitement when you try these teacher-tested ideas to end the school year.

## Summer Fun List

This nifty list of summertime activities can keep youngsters as busy as bees when school lets out! Ask students to brainstorm things to do and titles of good books to read during summer vacation. Write the students' suggestions on chart paper, labeling each child's suggestion with his name. Then type the completed list and make student copies. Encourage students to refer to their list of peer suggestions when they're looking for something to do this summer. That all-too-common summertime phrase, "I'm bored!", will become a thing of the past!

Kelly A. Wong—Grs.1 & 2
Berlyn School, Ontario, CA

## Autograph Celebration

Your youngsters will be buzzing about these student-made autograph booklets long after the school year is over. To make the front cover of the booklet, glue colorful tissue-paper squares on a 9" x 12" sheet of construction paper so that the squares slightly overlap. Then, using a paintbrush, brush a thin layer of diluted glue over the tissue paper. This will result in the colors bleeding together for a pretty effect. When the cover is dry, hole-punch two holes in the left margin. Then use the cover as a guide to punch holes in a supply of blank paper and a 9" x 12" construction-paper back cover. Stack and align the project. Thread a length of yarn through each hole; then securely tie each length's ends. Have each child write his name and grade on the front cover of his completed autograph book; then provide time for each student to gather written messages and autographs from his classmates.

Kristin McLaughlin—Substitute Teacher
Boyertown Area Schools, Boyertown, PA

## Making A Beeline

Creating a resumé is a fun and effective way for students to reflect on their growth during the past school year. Duplicate student copies of a resumé like the one shown. Before students begin the activity, talk about their next year's goals. Ask students to brainstorm the skills they've learned during the past year as you write their ideas on the chalkboard. You may also want to provide a sample character description to help students generate their own ideas. And lastly remind students that their character references should be three adults whom the students feel know them well. After students have completed their resumés, set aside time for students to share their impressive work. If desired, photocopy each student's resumé so that he may present a copy of it to his next year's teacher!

Anne Marie Fluck—Gr. 2
Loring Flemming Elementary, Blackwood, NJ

## Tokens Of Thanks

How can you show appreciation for your "un-bee-lievably" helpful volunteers? Present each volunteer with one of the following inexpensive and easy-to-make gifts:
- an addition flash card with the message "Thanks for adding so much to our school."
- a crayon with the message "Thanks for bringing color to our students' lives."
- a glue stick with the message "Our volunteers help us stick together."
- a pair of scissors with the message "I just couldn't cut it without you!"

Your volunteers will "bee-m" with delight after receiving one of these gifts!

Barbara McCreary—Gr. 5
Ridge Elementary School, Henrico County, VA

## Travel Brochures

Once your youngsters have created these travel brochures, they'll be eager to share them with students who plan to enter your classroom or grade level next fall! Explain that the purpose of a travel brochure is to enlighten its reader about the area or place featured on the brochure. Show students several travel brochures that you've obtained from a travel agency. Then challenge each youngster to create a brochure in which your classroom (or grade level) is the travel destination. As a class, brainstorm ideas for the travel brochure. Include the topics that are listed on the brochure on page 283. Write the students' ideas on the chalkboard; then give each youngster a copy of page 283 to complete. When the pages are finished and cut out, demonstrate how to fold the brochure along the thin lines so that the programming remains on the inside. Then have each student unfold his brochure, flip it over, and print "Take A Trip To _____" on the far right panel. To finish his brochure, a student decorates the two remaining panels with illustrations of favorite activities, projects, or events; then he refolds the brochure.

Mary Ann Reed—Grs. 2–6 Math Resource
West Wyomissing Elementary
West Lawn, PA

## Memory Day

Invite the families and friends of your busy bees to an end-of-the-year Memory Day! For this special occasion, display photographs around the classroom that feature your students engaged in a variety of school-related activities. Also enlist your youngsters' help to create a colorful chalkboard display. To do this, write the title " 'Sea' What We Have Learned" on the board. Then ask each child to draw two sea animals on the chalkboard and write one sentence that describes something he learned this year. Provide colored chalk for the activity. During the Memory Day event, invite students to share memory booklets that they have designed. For a fun finale, show a video that contains a compilation of events from the past school year. Student-made refreshments could also be served!

Linda Valentino—Gr. 2
Minisink Valley Elementary School
Slate Hill, NY

## Sweet Awards

Supplement your academic end-of-the-year awards with sweet treats that highlight positive personality traits. Awards could include the following:
- a package of LifeSavers® for the student who is always willing to help
- a Snickers® candy bar for the student who has a great sense of humor
- a Bit O' Honey® candy bar for the student who exhibits kindness toward others
- a 3 Musketeers® Bar for those students who stick together through thick and thin
- Hershey's® Hugs™ and Kisses® for all students!

Diane L. Bishop—Gr. 2
Assumption Catholic School
Denver, CO

## End-Of-The-Year Memoirs

Here's a honey of an end-of-the-year writing activity! On the chalkboard write a student-generated list of favorite events, activities, and projects from the past school year. Then give each student a blank writing booklet in which to pen her memoirs of the past school year. Instruct each student to write the title of her book on the first booklet page. Next ask each child to think of someone who encouraged her this year or helped make her year extra-special; then have her write a dedication to that person on page two of her booklet. On page three, have each student list the events, activities, and/or projects from the class-generated list that she plans to write about. This page will become her table of contents. When the student has finished writing her memoirs, have her number her booklet pages and complete her table of contents, then illustrate her booklet cover to her liking.

Mrs. S. Mates—Gr. 2
Public School 206
Brooklyn, NY

## Student Surveys

On a scale of one to five, this activity rates a five! Enlist your students' help in naming subject areas learned, and activities and projects completed during the past school year. List the students' responses on the board. Type the list and duplicate a copy for each student. Then, using a scale of one to five, ask the students to score each activity on their lists—with five being the best score. Collect the surveys and use them to determine which activities and topics were most popular among your youngsters. Utilize this information as you make teaching plans for the following year.

Mary Jo Kampschnieder—Gr. 2
Howells Community Catholic, Howells, NE

## Showcase Tea

Looking for a "bee-autiful" way for students to share their writing talents? Try having a tea party. To inform parents of the special event, have each student create an invitation to be sent home. On the day of the tea party, enlist students' help in covering tables with floral fabric or colorful paper and placing a potted flower atop each table. As guests arrive, have a recording of classical music playing. During the party have each child share a favorite piece of original writing from the past school year. If time allows, invite parents to write stories under their youngsters' guidance. These writing efforts can also be shared. Conclude the event by serving cookies and tea or apple juice.

Terry Gross—Gr. 2
Asher Holmes Elementary School
Morganville, NJ

## End-Of-The-Year Notes

The recipients of these warmhearted thank-you notes are sure to be "bee-dazzled" by your youngsters' kind words. Ask students to name school personnel whom they would like to thank for helping to make their school year run smoothly. Write the students' ideas on the chalkboard. Be sure to include your school principal, secretary, nurse, custodians, and cafeteria workers. Next ask students to describe how each of these people has helped to make their school a better place. List the students' ideas near the appropriate name(s) on the chalkboard. Then, on provided writing paper, ask each student to write a thank-you note to one of the people listed on the board. Take measures to be sure that a fairly equal number of notes are being written to each spotlighted person. After the thank-you notes have been edited and illustrated, bind the thank-you notes for each deserving person between student-decorated construction-paper covers. Plan to present these booklets of heartfelt thank-you notes during the final days of the school year.

Christina MacTaggart—Gr. 2
Hemby Bridge School
Indian Trail, NC

## Buzzing Down Memory Lane

Here's a picture-perfect way to end the school year. Give each student a copy of a multiple-picture frame like the one shown. Ask each student to print his name and the school year in the rectangular shape at the bottom of the sheet. In each of the remaining spaces, instruct the student to draw pictures of various events or activities that have taken place during the school year. Then have each student cut out his project and glue it on a 9" x 12" sheet of colorful construction paper. Laminate the projects for durability; then have each student take his impressive picture frame home as a reminder of his fun-filled year.

adapted from an idea by Kate Cassorla—Grs. K–1
Yavneh Hebrew Academy
Los Angeles, CA

## End-Of-The-Year Party

No need to buy paper supplies for your end-of-the-year party. Use the leftover paper products from your Valentine's Day, Easter, Halloween, or Christmas parties. This economical idea will give students a chance to recall the fun times that they had during the parties at which the paper products were originally used. Remember when we searched for the missing pumpkin during the Halloween party?

Diane Fortunato—Gr. 2
Carteret School, Bloomfield, NJ

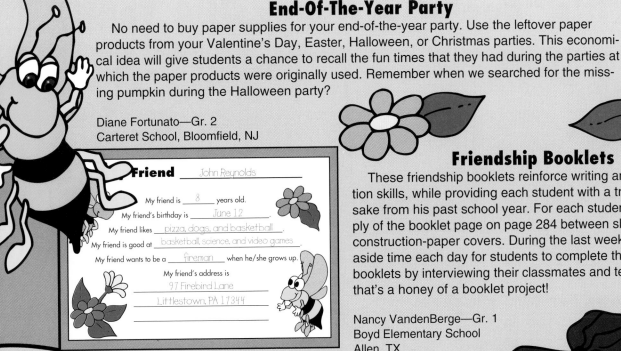

**My Friend** John Reynolds

My friend is ___8___ years old.
My friend's birthday is ___June 12___.
My friend likes ___pizza, dogs, and basketball___
My friend is good at ___basketball, science, and video games___
My friend wants to be a ___fireman___ when he/she grows up.
My friend's address is
___97 Firebird Lane___
___Littlestown, PA 17344___

## Book Storage

This quick-and-easy tip speeds up end-of-the-year textbook collection, and it will also save you time next fall. Give each student a plastic grocery bag and a duplicated textbook form like the one shown. After each student has completed his form, he secures his textbooks inside his plastic bag and tapes his completed form to the outside of his bag. Collect the labeled bags and store them for the summer. In the fall distribute a bag of books to each student in your class. Instruct each student to carefully remove the textbook form from the bag and write his name on the bottom line. Collect the forms and presto—you have a record of which textbooks each student has in his possession!

Sandra Morris—Gr. 3
Champion Elementary School
Warren, OH

## Friendship Booklets

These friendship booklets reinforce writing and communication skills, while providing each student with a treasured keepsake from his past school year. For each student staple a supply of the booklet page on page 284 between slightly larger construction-paper covers. During the last week of school, set aside time each day for students to complete their friendship booklets by interviewing their classmates and teacher. Now that's a honey of a booklet project!

Nancy VandenBerge—Gr. 1
Boyd Elementary School
Allen, TX

Michelle Stone
Name

**1995–96 School Year**

Math | # _28_
Science | # _14_
Social Studies | # _8_
Health | # _2_
English | # _5_
| 1996–97

Name

## It's "Bee-n" A Honey Of A Year!

If you're looking for a unique way to review skills and concepts taught during the past school year, then look no further. Here's a honey of a game that's intended to do just that. Duplicate two copies of the open gameboard on page 282. Program the open spaces on each gameboard with a different set of review challenges. Then duplicate each version of the gameboard for one-half of your students. Pair students and give each twosome one copy of each gameboard version, a coin, and two game markers. Instruct each student to color one gameboard. If desired have each student glue the gameboard he colored onto a 9" x 12" sheet of colorful construction paper. Then each pair chooses one of its gameboards and begins play. When the winner of this game has been determined, the twosome plays a second game using its other gameboard. Each pair may continue alternating play between its two gameboards until game time is over.

Michele Anszelowicz—Gr. 1
Mandalay Elementary
Wantagh, NY

It's "Bee-n" A Honey Of A Year!

**Start**

Name 3 compound words.

Tell a number sentence that equals 17.

Buzz ahead one space.

Name the days of the week in order.

Say the sounds of 5 long vowels.

Name these words in ABC order.
egg bed foot

Name the months of the year.

**Oops!** Lost your stinger. Go back one space.

Name two authors we studied.

What country is north of the United States?

Buzz ahead one space.

Name one animal that lives at the South Pole.

Count by 5's to 100.

**Finish**

**Directions for two players:**
1. Place your markers on Start.
2. In turn, flip the coin and move:
   Heads = 1 space
   Tails = 2 spaces
3. Read and answer or do what is written on the space.
   If your answer is approved by your partner, you may stay.
   If your answer is not approved, return to your original space.
4. The first player to reach Finish wins.

# It's "Bee-n" A Honey Of A Year!

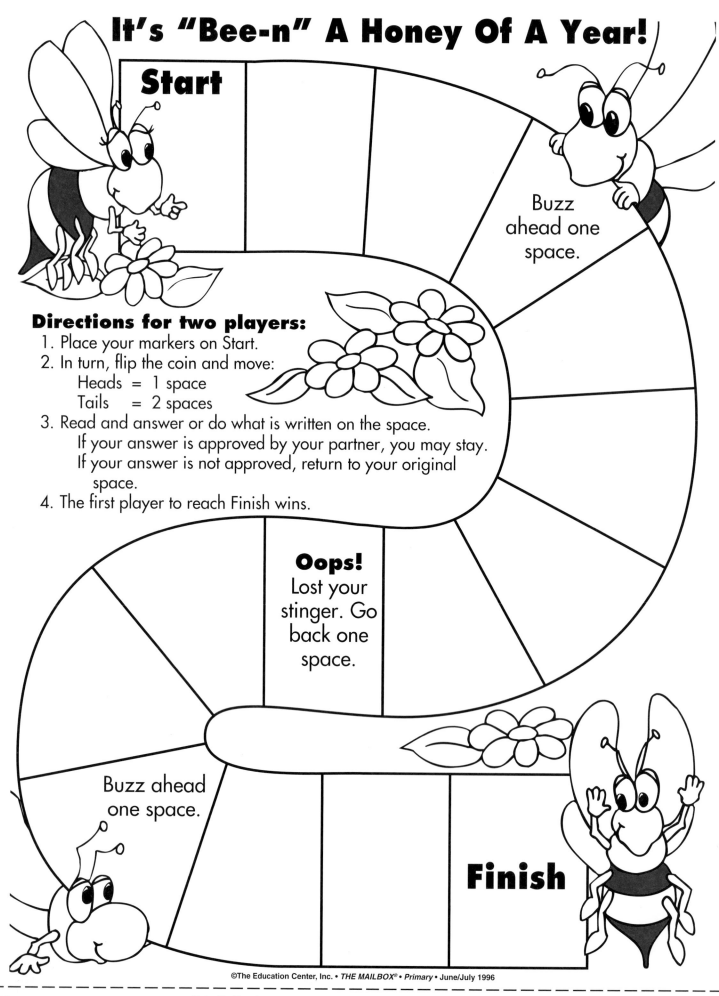

**Start**

Buzz ahead one space.

**Directions for two players:**
1. Place your markers on Start.
2. In turn, flip the coin and move:
   Heads = 1 space
   Tails = 2 spaces
3. Read and answer or do what is written on the space.
   If your answer is approved by your partner, you may stay.
   If your answer is not approved, return to your original space.
4. The first player to reach Finish wins.

**Oops!** Lost your stinger. Go back one space.

Buzz ahead one space.

**Finish**

**Note To Teacher:** Use with "It's 'Bee-n' A Honey Of A Year!" on page 281.

Draw a picture of something you needed to know this year.

# Things you will need to know...

# Things you get to do while you're there...

# What you will learn...

Draw a picture of something you learned this year.

©The Education Center, Inc. • *THE MAILBOX*® • *Primary* • June/July 1996

Use with "Friendship Booklets" on page 281.

# My Friend _____

My friend is _____ years old.

My friend's birthday is _____.

My friend likes _____.

My friend is good at _____.

My friend wants to be a _____ when he/she grows up.

My friend's address is

_____

_____

_____

©The Education Center, Inc. • *THE MAILBOX*® • *Primary* • June/July 1996

# My Friend _____

My friend is _____ years old.

My friend's birthday is _____.

My friend likes _____.

My friend is good at _____.

My friend wants to be a _____ when he/she grows up.

My friend's address is

_____

_____

_____

©The Education Center, Inc. • *THE MAILBOX*® • *Primary* • June/July 1996

# Teacher Management Tips

# LIFESAVERS...management tips for teachers

### Favorite Reproducibles

If you're always scrambling to locate your tried-and-true reproducibles, try organizing them with this great tip. You will need a three-ring binder with dividers. Label one divider for each month of the school year. Three-hole-punch your favorite reproducibles (student activities, parent letters, party notices) and place them into the binder according to the month in which they will be used. Your reproducibles will be right at your fingertips when you need them.

Cheryl Sneed—Gr. 1, Winters Elementary, Winters, TX

### Reward-Winning Restaurant

When you're ready to reward hardworking or well-behaved students, invite them out to lunch! Don't worry; you won't have to go far to find a suitable restaurant. Your own classroom will do nicely. On the day of the special lunch, decorate a table with a fancy tablecloth and a centerpiece. Play soft background music and provide dessert if desired. Students will enjoy eating their lunches in style. Who knows? You might even earn a four-star rating for your charming classroom cafe.

Marilyn Cameron—Gr. 3
Gray Elementary
Houston, TX

### Organization Is A Shoe-In

It can be difficult to keep track of the items your students bring to you each morning. With this idea, the solution to this problem is in the bag! Hang a plastic shoe organizer with see-through pockets within reach of your youngsters. Write each student's name on a different pocket. When a student has something that needs to be given to you, he can simply place it in his plastic pocket. The item will be there until you find time to retrieve it.

Cindy Wood—Gr. 1
Cedar Lake Christian Academy
Biloxi, MS

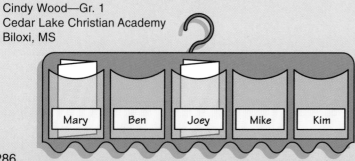

Mary  Ben  Joey  Mike  Kim

### Marshmallow Shoes

Before venturing out into the school hallways, have your youngsters put on imaginary marshmallow shoes. Explain to students that noisy feet can disturb other students who are hard at work. Because marshmallows are soft and noiseless, shoes having marshmallow soles are perfect for wearing when quiet walking is needed. Don't be surprised to find your students slipping off their humdrum footwear and opting for their imaginary shoes, even without your asking!

Judith Casey—Substitute Teacher, Chatham School District
Chatham, NJ

### Colorful Crate

Lining students up from recess can be hectic, especially at the beginning of the year when students are not yet familiar with their classmates. Keep your students in the right spot with this great idea. Take a colorful, weatherproof crate with you when your class goes outside for recess. Encourage youngsters to place play equipment, toys or clothing items that are not being used in the crate. Explain that students should line up behind the crate when recess ends. Not only will your youngsters get back to the right room, but so will all of their belongings.

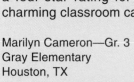

Ellen Bieleski, Elk Lake School, Dimock, PA

### Calling All Parents

Children are notorious for placing in their pockets important papers which are never again seen in recognizable form. To make sure vital information is being received by parents, laminate a class set of manila envelopes like the one shown. Inform parents that papers requiring immediate attention will be carried home in these envelopes. Also include in each envelope a checklist that indicates what action(s) needs to be taken and, if desired, a receipt form to be signed and returned in the envelope the following day. This system keeps parents and teachers informed!

Susanna Zumbro & Maggie Griffin
Britt Elementary
Snellville, GA

IMPORTANT INFORMATION
Please read and...
○ sign and return.
✓ review with your child.
✓ keep at home.
○ contact me.

IMPORTANT INFORMATION
Please read carefully.
Return the envelope on the next day of school.
☆ Thank you! ☆
Mrs. Griffin
Mrs. Zumbro

### Teaching On Tape

Providing make-up work for the student who is absent can be time-consuming. Let technology lend you a hand. On a day when a student is absent, tape-record lessons, discussions, and any oral tests given. When the student returns, send the tape home with him so that he can catch up on missed concepts and work assignments.

Sherry Thrush—Substitute Teacher, Highland Heights, OH

# LIFESAVERS...management tips for teachers

## Table Management Tool

Here's a great management idea to use when your students are working at tables. Number each table and color-code each student's table space. Refer to table numbers when praising groups of students who are exhibiting positive behaviors. When it is time to tidy up, call out a color. All students who are represented by the color chosen are responsible for cleanup duty. Your room will be spiffy in a jiffy!

Mae Purrenhage—Grs. 3–5
Jackson Elementary
Fort Campbell, KY

## Good Manners Detective

Enlist your students' help in recognizing and encouraging good manners. Each morning remind students to be on the lookout for good manners. At the end of the day, ask students to recall instances in which their classmates exhibited good manners; then invite one student to tell the class about the good manners that she saw being practiced. Afterwards have her announce the names of the students she thought were particularly well-mannered. Thanks to this great idea, your students will soon come to expect from themselves the same good manners they are looking for in each other.

Kathleen Ann Weisenborn—Gr. 2
Fricano Elementary School, Lockport, NY

## Nameless Papers

Enlist your students' help in putting an end to nameless papers. Give each group (or row) of students a paper cup that is to be displayed on a different group member's desk each day. Before an assignment is turned in, the student with the cup on his desk verifies that all papers in his group have names. Each time a group successfully submits only papers with names, place a wooden craft stick in its cup. When a group has earned a designated number of craft sticks, present its members with a special reward or privilege.

Kay A. Fuller—Gr. 2
Clearview Elementary School
Brogue, PA

## Roll Out The Red Carpet

Students feel like royalty when they receive the red-carpet treatment for personal successes. Place a square of red carpet underneath the desk of each student who demonstrated outstanding behavior or academic progress the previous school day. Present each student with a red certificate that entitles him to a specified number of rewards and/or privileges throughout the day of his reign. Though each student steps down from his throne when the day is done, his positive feelings about himself will have just begun.

Margie Siegel—Gr. 2
Wren Hollow Elementary
Ballwin, MO

Today Samuel Crump received the Red Carpet treatment!

## Desk Pockets

Help students stay organized with colorful desk pockets. To create a class set of pockets, personalize a file folder for each student. Keeping the folders folded, laminate each one. Trim away the laminating film, leaving a 1/4-inch margin. To convert each folder into a pocket, use an X-acto® knife to slit the laminating film. Then attach each student's folder to his desk with a strip of clear Con-Tact® paper or packing tape. Ask students to keep unfinished work in their pockets. At the end of the day, any papers remaining in the pockets are taken home as homework. The colorful folders are also a nifty place for students to display their sticker collections.

Robin Polson-Avra—Gr. 2
New Caney Elementary
New Caney, TX

Name

Lisha

## Now Hear This!

With this idea you can quietly capture the attention of students actively engaged in conversational activities. Simply whisper a direction for students to follow, such as "If you can hear me, touch your ear," or "If you can hear me, raise your hand." As youngsters begin to notice their classmates following your directions, they will tune in to find out what you are saying. Before you know it, your entire class will be all ears.

Beth Bill
Prospect Elementary
Lake Mills, WI

# LIFESAVERS...management tips for teachers

## Paper Of The Day

Encourage students to carefully complete their work with this paper-of-the-day plan. Conclude each day by presenting one outstanding assignment that was completed that day. Enlist your students' help in identifying the positive qualities of the paper such as neatness, accuracy, originality, and completeness. Then showcase the paper in a special frame designed for this purpose. A round of applause for the proud owner of the paper of the day is definitely in order!

Debbie Byrne—Gr. 1, Candor Elementary, Candor, NY

## Reusing Desktags

If changes in your student enrollment make it necessary for you to purchase several sets of desktags each year, try this idea. Laminate a class supply (plus a few extras) of unprogrammed desktags. Then, from clear Con-Tact® covering, cut a class supply of strips. Each strip should be approximately one inch longer and wider than a desktag. Use the strips to cover and adhere the desktags to your students' desks. Then, writing atop the clear covering, use a permanent marker to personalize each desktag. When a student moves away, peel away the strip of programmed covering. You'll be left with a good-as-new desktag that can be used again and again!

Marie Lain—Gr. 1
Marjory Stoneman Douglas Elementary, Miami, FL

## Party On Pluto

This out-of-sight motivational plan encourages stellar student behavior! On a bulletin board covered with black paper, mount cutouts of the sun and each of the nine planets. Use a pushpin to attach a spaceship cutout to the sun. Then mount a trail of star cutouts that begins at the sun, ends on Pluto, and connects all the planets in between. Each time the class demonstrates terrific behavior, move the spaceship forward one star. If the spaceship lands on a planet, reward the class with a special privilege such as five minutes of extra recess. When the spaceship lands on Pluto, treat your youngsters to a well-deserved stellar celebration! Far-out!

Jennifer Ellis—Gr. 3, Tom Green Elementary, Buda, TX

## Wristband Reminders

Remind students and parents of upcoming events with wristband reminders. Keep a supply of 8 1/2" x 1" paper strips on hand. When you wish to send a reminder home, write the desired message on the chalkboard and have each student copy the message onto a paper strip. Ask each child to wrap his resulting reminder around his wrist so that you can tape or staple the ends of the strip together. These nifty reminders are the perfect fit for any occasion!

Tara Murphy—Gr. 1
Oconee County Primary School
Watkinsville, GA

## Storing Letter Cutouts

Here's a tip for organizing your bulletin-board letters. Sort letters by style, size, and/or color; then place each group of letters in a gallon-size, resealable plastic storage bag. Three-hole-punch the plastic bags as shown and place them in a three-ring notebook. Store the binder in a handy location. The next time you need letter cutouts, you'll have them neatly organized and ready to use!

Angela Virostick
West Hill Elementary
Sharon, PA

## Filing Correspondence

Minimize the risk of misplaced parent correspondence with this easy filing system. Label a file folder for each student; then alphabetically file the folders in a handy location. Whenever you receive parent correspondence (whether it be a note explaining an absence or a note of praise or concern), file the correspondence in the appropriate child's folder. If any questions arise about past parent communications, you'll have everything you need at your fingertips. The folders are also the perfect place to record your contacts with parents. To do this attach a form to the inside of each folder that provides space for recording the date, the time, and the reason for each contact, as well as a place for jotting down the outcome of the conversation.

Alicia Stenard—Grs. K–1, Nebo Elementary, Nebo, NC

# LIFESAVERS...management tips for teachers

## Storing Supplies

Put an end to students fishing through their desks looking for hidden supplies. Personalize a resealable plastic bag for each student; then punch a hole in each bag directly below its seal. Have each youngster seal the supplies he does not use on a daily basis inside his bag. Use metal rings to suspend the bags from plastic clothes hangers—one hanger per row or group of student desks. Store the hangers in an easily accessible location. When the supplies are needed, select students to retrieve and distribute the supply bags for their groups.

Margaret Ann Rhem—Gr. 3
Western Branch Intermediate
Chesapeake, VA

## Directions Director

Use this idea to encourage students to listen carefully to oral directions. Each week appoint a student helper to be the Directions Director. Explain that it is the responsibility of this student to carefully listen to and remember your oral instructions. Any students who did not listen carefully must ask the Directions Director for assistance. Not only will you be free to help students in other ways, but your youngsters' listening skills are bound to improve!

Sherry Kay—Gr. 2, Fox Prairie Elementary, Stoughton, WI

## Clever Cleanup

If you need help keeping your classroom tidy, enlist the help of litter-eating Egabrag (*garbage* spelled backwards). Cut the shape of a dust ball from gray construction paper; then add facial features and the message "Please feed Egabrag!" Use clear Con-Tact® covering to attach the cutout to your classroom trash can. When you start to see signs of classroom litter, a gentle reminder such as, "Did I just hear Egabrag's tummy growl?" will have students cleaning up in no time!

Jo Fryer—Gr. 1
Kildeer Countryside School
Long Grove, IL

## Sample Book

To help you remember which shapes can be created on your school's die-cut machine, make a sample book. To do this, gather one sample of each shape. Categorize the shapes as desired; then glue the shapes onto the pages of a blank booklet or spiral notebook. Use divider tabs to label the different sections of the sample book. There you have it—a shipshape sample book!

Karen Bryant—Gr. 3
Rosa Taylor Elementary
Macon, GA

## Praising With Popcorn

Promote class cooperation by sponsoring a popcorn party. You will need a bag of unpopped popcorn, a small scoop, and a large transparent container. Each time you notice students working well together, place a scoop of popcorn in the container. When the container is full of popcorn, plan a popcorn party. What a tasteful way to encourage positive interactions between students!

Stella Levy—Gr. 3, Hackley School, Tarrytown, NY

## Daily Schedule

Keep your youngsters abreast of each day's events by posting your daily schedule on a pocket chart. Write the numerals 1 through 12 on index cards; then position the cards in sequential order on the chart. Next cut a supply of sentence strips in half and label each strip with the name of a different subject, class, or event that takes place on a recurring basis. To program the chart, position the labeled strips on the pocket chart in the order that they will occur. Store any unused strips nearby. At the end of each day, reprogram the chart to show the next day's schedule of events.

Tricia Peña—Gr. 3
Acacia Elementary
Vail, AZ

| Daily Schedule | | | |
|---|---|---|---|
| 1 | Opening | 9 | Lunch |
| 2 | Spelling | 10 | Math |
| 3 | Reading | 11 | Presentations |
| 4 | Group | 12 | Science |
| 5 | Art | | |
| 6 | Recess | | |
| 7 | Story | | |
| 8 | P.E. | | |

Centers

Reports

Games

# LIFESAVERS...management tips for teachers

## Color-Coded Flowerpots

These one-of-a-kind flowerpots are a fun way to color-code groups (or tables) of students' desks. Use a different color of paint to decorate an inexpensive plastic flowerpot for each group. Also make several like-colored tissue-paper flowers per pot. Tape each flower to one end of a wooden skewer or a green pipe cleaner, and attach construction-paper leaves to the resulting stems. When the painted pots are dry, put a layer of rocks in the bottom of each one (for added weight). Trim a piece of florist's foam or Styrofoam® to fit inside each pot; then press the foam in place and poke the flower stems into the foam. Present each group of students with a pot-o'-blooms. "Just look at that yellow group! Each of its members are ready to begin."

Marie Lain—Gr. 1
Marjory Stoneman Douglas Elementary
Miami, FL

## Organizing Centers

Organize materials for your daily center activities in a jiffy! Establish a color for each of your learning centers; then color-code a resealable plastic storage bag to match each center. In each center bag, place the materials that are needed to complete the center. When center time is over, ask one child at each center to seal the remaining center materials in the center bag.

Cindy Wood—Gr. 1, Cedar Lake Christian Academy, Biloxi, MS

## Absent Folders

Use these colorful file folders to organize work for students who are absent. Label each of several folders "Absent Folder"; then write a cheery message on each one. Laminate the folders for durability; then store them in a convenient location. When a student is absent, place an "Absent Folder" on his desk. Ask a student helper to place the absent student's assignments in the folder throughout the day. When a parent or sibling comes to retrieve the student's work, or when the student returns to school, the missed assignments are in one handy location.

Tricia Peña—Gr. 3
Acacia Elementary
Vail, AZ

You Were Missed!

## Quiet Transition

Stuffed animals can help make classroom transition times quiet times. Keep a collection of stuffed animals handy. When you call students to the rug for storytime, ask your Student Of The Week to observe his classmates and identify five or more youngsters who move to the story area quickly and quietly. Then have him present each of these students with a stuffed animal that he may hold while the story is being read.

Kerry Ojeda—Gr. 1, Paul Ecke Central School, Encinitas, CA

## Calendar Time-Saver

Tired of removing staples or masking tape each time you reposition the dates on your monthly calendar? Check your local office supply store for a "restickable" adhesive glue stick. Apply a generous coating of the adhesive to the back of calendar date cards; then press the dates on the calendar. Since the adhesive is "restickable," the dates are easy to reposition. Use the same technique to attach special messages and notes. This is a time-saver you're sure to stick with!

Barbara Turner—Gr. 3, Pelham Road Elementary, Greenville, SC

## Sharing Sessions

Just in time—a great idea for managing student sharing sessions! Each day set aside time for a predetermined number of students to share their "egg-citing" news. Display an hourglass egg timer; then, as each student starts to share his news with the class, invert the timer. If the sand in the timer runs out before the youngster is finished, inform him that his sharing time is over and ask him to wrap up his story. Before you know it, students will be summarizing their stories so that they can make the most of their sharing sessions.

Judith Casey—Substitute Teacher: Grs. K–4
Chatham School District
Chatham, NJ

# LIFESAVERS...management tips for teachers

## Conference Waiting Area

When children are involved in the editing and publishing stages of a writing project, it is crucial for them to meet with the teacher several times. To reduce interruptions during individual conferences, set up a "Conference Waiting Area." Place four chairs near where student-teacher conferences are held. Students wishing to see the teacher take a seat. If all the seats are full, a student remains at her desk until one of the chairs becomes available. The circle of children waiting for a conference with the teacher will be a thing of the past.

Sandra Lankford—Gr. 2
Lancaster Elementary
Orlando, FL

## Snazzy Slipcovers

These colorful slipcovers are sure to be a hit with your next year's class. And if you purchase your fabric on sale, the cost of each slipcover is nominal. To make a slipcover that will easily fit over the back of a student's chair, cut a length of fabric that is twice the height of the chair back plus two additional inches for the hemline. The width of the fabric should equal the width of the chair back plus four additional inches. Fold the fabric in half with right sides together. Sew two half-inch side seams; then hem the bottom edge. Turn the fabric right side out and you have a ready-to-use slipcover. Sew slipcovers to recognize student birthdays, the student of the week, and your weekly table captains.

Janice Greenenwald—Gr. 2
Komarek School
North Riverside, IL

## Magazine Binders

If your summer "To do" list includes organizing your back issues of *The Mailbox®* magazine, try this great tip. Label each of six three-ring binders for a different magazine edition. Three-hole-punch each *Mailbox®* magazine and place it in the appropriate binder in sequential order. Continue this practice each time you receive a new magazine issue. To make your binders even more usable, keep a photocopy of each end-of-the-year index at the front of your August/September binder.

The Mailbox Magazine
August/September Issues

Joan Hodges—Gr. 2
Lantern Lane Elementary
Missouri City, TX

## Useful Boxes

Fishing for a way to get organized? A tackle box may be just what you need! Tackle boxes come in a variety of sizes and some models even have adjustable compartments. Sort and store your overhead supplies inside the compartments of a small tackle box. Or stock a large tackle box with paper-grading supplies like rubber stamps and stamp pads, stickers, and colorful pens. You may also want to keep a tackle box near your desk for sorting paper clips, safety pins, and other odds and ends. If you're scrambling to get organized, this "reel-y" good idea is a great catch!

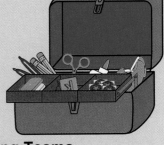

Peggy McAllister—Gr. 2
Kluckhohn Elementary
Oyens, IA

## Creating Teams

Here's a simple way to divide students into teams or groups. To create four teams, you need four different colors of construction paper. From each color, cut the number of three-inch cards that equals one-fourth of your student enrollment. When it's time to play, randomly distribute the cards to your youngsters and ask students to group themselves by color. Four teams will result in a quick, easy, and colorful manner.

Mary Dinneen—Gr. 2
Mountain View School
Bristol, CT

## Good Behavior Bulletin Board

Ahoy, mateys! Here's the key to great student behavior! Program a paper strip with the title "The Key To The Treasure Is Good Behavior!"; then staple the paper near the top of a bulletin board. Use a pushpin to suspend a key cutout below the first letter in the title. Staple a decorated treasure chest cutout to the right of the paper strip. Tuck a small card labeled with a class reward or privilege behind the treasure chest. Each time that the class exhibits exemplary behavior throughout the day, move the key to the right one letter. Continue in this manner until the key reaches the treasure chest. Then remove the card and reveal what treasure the students have earned. No doubt your youngsters will do their best to be as good as gold!

Fran Rizzo—Gr. 3
Brookdale School
Bloomfield, NJ

The Key To

# Teacher Report Card

Teacher's name: _____

Rate your teacher.
Use the rating scale.

| Rating Scale | | | |
|---|---|---|---|
| **+** = yes | **✓+** = sometimes | **✓** = no | **?** = I'm not sure |

**I think my teacher…**                                                              **Rating**

| | |
|---|---|
| is kind to everyone. | |
| treats students fairly. | |
| is good at answering questions. | |
| expects me to do my best. | |
| gives good directions. | |
| prepares interesting lessons. | |
| is well prepared. | |
| cares about her students. | |
| is a good listener. | |
| has a good sense of humor. | |
| is understanding. | |
| makes learning fun. | |

Additional comments: _____

_____

©The Education Center, Inc. • THE MAILBOX® • Primary • Oct/Nov 1995 • Debbie Nierath—Gr. 3, St. Joan of Arc, St. Clair Shores, MI

**Note To Teacher:** Duplicate and distribute student copies of the report card. Talk about why students receive report cards during the school year. Then explain that you would like to know how well you are doing as a teacher, too. Discuss the importance of being fair and honest during an evaluation. Then guide students through the evaluation. Older students may complete the activity independently.

292

# OUR READERS WRITE

# Our Readers Write

## Hot-Air Balloon

Bedazzle your budding readers with this student-made balloon project! To make a hot-air balloon, use a template to trace two balloon shapes on construction paper. Color the shapes as desired; then cut them out. With one cutout atop the other, use a hole puncher to punch evenly spaced holes around the edges. Lace a length of yarn through the holes, leaving the bottom edge of the project open. Insert a desired amount of newspaper stuffing in the opening; then lace the remaining holes and tie and trim the loose yarn ends. Below the project, suspend a clean and empty margarine tub (or similar container) from yarn lengths. In the resulting basket, a child can collect items or pictures of items that begin with the letter *b*. Learning the sound of *b* will be a breeze!

Cathy Collier—Learning Disabled
Teacher: Grs. K–3
Southeastern Elementary
Chesapeake, VA

## Let's Get Acquainted

Hosting a student teacher can be exciting. Add to the excitement by getting students involved in planning for her arrival. To do this, have each student write a letter of introduction to the new teacher that includes a self-portrait or a snapshot of the child. Package the letters, along with copies of your lesson plans, a class schedule, a student-teacher handbook, and other pertinent information. Mail the welcome package a few weeks before the student teacher is to begin her teaching experience. If arrangements can be made for the student teacher to visit your class prior to her starting date, enlist students' help in planning a get-acquainted party in her honor.

Phil Forsythe—Gr. 3
Northeastern Elementary
Bellefontaine, OH

## Magnificent Manners Magnets

Replenish your classroom treasure chest with these inexpensive, easy-to-make magnets. Cut out child-friendly pictures from magazines, newspapers, or wrapping paper. Mount the pictures onto tagboard; then laminate and cut out the pictures. Attach a strip of magnetic tape to the back of each cutout. When a student displays great classroom manners, reward him with a magnet. Encourage the child to display the magnet on his family's refrigerator as a reminder of how terrific he is!

Jeanne Bennett—Substitute Teacher
Upshur County Schools
Buckhannon, WV

## The Number's Up

Here's a handy way for students to answer multiple-choice questions in unison. Read the question and each numbered answer to the class. Count to three and have students hold up the number of fingers that represents the answer they are choosing. A quick glance can show you how well your students comprehend the concepts you are evaluating.

Phyllis Handler—Gr. 2, Arnold Elementary, Dover, DE

## Gift-Wrapped Books

Increase interest in the newest arrivals to your bookshelves by adding an element of surprise. When you receive books that you have ordered for the class library, wrap them with colorful paper. Gather students in a cozy area. In turn, have students select, unwrap, and present the books for all to see. Wow! Reading really is a gift!

Beth Bill, Prospect Elementary, Lake Mills, WI

The Little Mouse And The Kitten

## Instructional Postcards

You might be surprised to find that much of the information you need to teach your class about the 50 states can be found on postcards. Check gift shops, variety and grocery stores, and even museums for postcards of each state. Many postcards provide pictures of the state as well as information regarding state symbols, points of interest, state capitals, and the history, geography, and resources of the state. The cards are portable, easily filed, and inexpensive.

Robin Andrews—Gr. 2
Eakin Elementary
Nashville, TN

FLORIDA Tallahassee

Nashville
TENNESSEE

## Teaching On Tape

Parents are vital teachers for their children. These tape-recorded teaching sessions can make it easier for parents to help their youngsters at home with skills they are learning at school. Each time you introduce a new concept, videotape yourself teaching the concept. Make the resulting tapes available for checkout. Parents will appreciate this opportunity to see just exactly how you teach the skills at hand.

Tammi Romenesko
Central Elementary
Winchester, KY

## Communicating Clearly

Let these transparent sentence strips spread the news to parents about what goes on in your classroom each day. Using transparency film, cut a class supply of 3" x 9" strips. Using a permanent marker, program each strip with the phrase "Ask me about" and a handwriting line. (See the illustration.) Staple a strip on the front of each student's homework folder. At the end of the day, have each student use a dark crayon to write a subject or activity that he would like for his parent(s) to ask him about. The programmed strips should be taken home, shared with parents, wiped clean, and returned to school. The rewards of this method are clear—communication is fostered be-tween parents and their children as well as between parents and the teacher.

Victoria Schirduan—Gr. 1, Plantsville School, Plantsville, CT

## Picture-Perfect Memories

Here's a fun way to strengthen your students' memories. Display a picture in the morning for about five minutes; then remove it. Later in the day, find out what your students can recall about the picture. If the students have trouble remembering details about the picture, shorten the amount of time between when you remove the picture and when you ask them about it. Gradually lengthen the time for students until their memory skills improve.

Sr. M. Henrietta, Villa Sacred Heart, Danville, PA

## Letter Of The Week

With this activity, learning alphabet sounds is in the bag. A few days before you begin studying a particular letter of the alphabet, send home with each student a paper lunch sack with the upcoming letter printed on one side. Ask each youngster to place in her bag objects that begin with the designated letter. On the day that you introduce the alphabet letter, ask each student to share and name the contents of her bag. If desired record the name of each object on the chalkboard.

Carrie Damron
Lynchburg, VA

## Daily Warm-Up

Start getting your youngsters' math and grammar gears tuned up as soon as they enter the classroom each morning. Provide a student activity sheet divided into five sections—one for each day of the week. Then each morning display a math review problem and an incorrectly written sentence on the board. Challenge youngsters to solve the problem and rewrite the sentence correctly in the appropriate spaces on their papers. As you grade their papers, place a foil star beside each correct answer. As a reward for diligent work, students skip the warm-up on Friday for any subject in which they have already earned four stars for the week.

Kimberly Jones-Gravel—Gr. 3
Public School 27
Albany, NY

## Visions Of Cupcakes

Encourage each of your students to do his best when completing assignments by comparing his finished product with a cupcake. Explain that when a child does his work correctly, he has made the cupcake itself. When he colors his work or does the extra-credit portion, he adds the icing to the cupcake. When he writes neatly and carefully, he adds the candy sprinkles. From now on your students will experience sweet success!

Ann Scheiblin
Bloomfield, NJ

## Sustained Silent Writing

Promote writing by using a variation of the familiar "sustained silent reading" technique designed to encourage reading. Set aside a 15- to 20-minute period of time each day for writing. Students may write about the events of the day, an assigned writing topic, or topics of their own choosing. Model the importance of writing during this activity by engaging in writing yourself. Because all energies are focused on writing, creativity is sure to flourish!

Nancy Murray—Gr. 2
Forest Hills Primary
Walterboro, SC

## Scent Words

Making scratch-and-sniff cards is a "scent-sational" way to teach sight words! To make a card, a student copies a sight word on an index card and places the card inside a box lid. Using a squeeze bottle, he traces over each letter with a thin trail of glue. Next he sprinkles each letter of the word with an aromatic spice such as cinnamon, nutmeg, or ginger; then he sets the project aside. When the project is dry, shake off the excess spice and, in a well-ventilated area, spray the card with acrylic sealer. When appropriate, return the card to the student. The student can release the aroma by lightly scratching the letters.

Shari Miller, Pittsburg, KS

## Welcome To Our Room

Moving to a new school can be a stressful experience for a child. Your class can help newcomers feel right at home by giving them welcome sacks. At the beginning of the year, have students decorate white paper lunch sacks. Fill the sacks with items similar to those provided for the class on the first day of school—pencils, erasers, crayons, stickers, a list of needed supplies, a copy of the class rules, and a class schedule. You may even wish to include a welcome letter dictated by your class and signed by each student. When a new student arrives, select one youngster to present him with a welcome sack and serve as his buddy for the day. New youngsters will surely feel lucky to have made a move to such a warm, thoughtful classroom.

Kathy Blocker, Forest North Elementary, Austin, TX

## Are You Learning?

Children seem to have an uncanny talent for memorizing song lyrics. So why not capitalize on this talent when teaching the purpose of adjectives? Students will enjoy learning the following lyrics, sung to the tune of "Are You Sleeping?"

Adjectives, Adjectives
Describe a noun!
Describe a noun!
Tell us shape and color.
Tell us size and number.
Spice up a sentence!
Spice up a sentence!

Ann Margaret Neal—Gr. 2
Encino Park Elementary
San Antonio, TX

## Absentee Assignment Sacks

Why wait until the end of the day to gather assignments for absent students? Instead label three or four small tote bags "While You Were Away...." When a student is absent, place a bag at his desk. As each work page is distributed, place a copy in the bag. Jot down book assignments; then place the assignments and necessary books into the bag, too. If appropriate, tuck in a get-well card. At the day's end, the bag is ready to send home with a parent, sibling, or neighbor of the absent child.

Michael C. Zeidler—Gr. 2
Thomas Jefferson Elementary
Wausau, WI

## Pen-Pal Cards

Helping students keep track of vital information regarding pen pals can be challenging. With a package of index cards, your students' pen-pal problems may be permanently solved. When the first letters from your children's pen pals arrive, have each student write her pen pal's name on an index card along with her pen pal's address, classroom teacher's name, and any other pertinent information. If a picture accompanies the letter, it can be attached to the index card. Encourage each student to turn the card over and record any personal facts that her pen pal shares. When it is time to write back, the notes on the index cards can help students create more personal letters.

VaReane Heese
Omaha, NE

## Feelings Chart

Here's a nifty way to get a feeling for the emotional tone of your classroom each day. Create a poster-board chart like the one shown, listing a variety of emotions. Laminate the board and attach a wipe-off marker. Each morning have students write their names under the emotions that best describe their current feelings. The chart makes a great springboard for group discussions about the causes and effects of different feelings. Erase the chart at the end of each day to get youngsters off to a fresh start the following morning.

Sharon Tobin—Gr. 2
Stewarts Creek Elementary
Carrollton, TX

## Star Of The Week

Give your student star of the week the chance to shine extra brightly! In addition to the personal memorabilia that she brings to school for her week in the spotlight, ask her to complete several construction-paper stars that you have partially programmed. Display the completed stars, along with the student's personal effects, at your star-of-the-week exhibit. Your students will enjoy learning about their special classmate and she will relish her time in the limelight. What better way to foster a glowing self-esteem!

Kristin McLaughlin—Substitute Teacher
Boyertown Schools
Boyertown, PA

## Sentence-Strip Books

Add new life to your instructional sentence strips by compiling them into books. The next time you display sentence strips focusing on specific events in a story, don't put them away when the lesson is finished. Instead, sequence the strips; then staple them into a miniature booklet. Youngsters will enjoy seeing familiar words appear in another context. When you see how inexpensively you can increase the size of your class library, you'll use this idea again and again.

Rhonda Pearce—Gr. 1
Anne Watson Elementary
Bigelow, AR

## Students As Teachers

When your weekly newsmagazines arrive, let each youngster step out of his everyday role and into a new one—yours! Divide students into small groups and distribute the magazines. Then assign each group a different news story. Explain that each small group must teach its story to the rest of the class. To do this a group introduces five vocabulary words from its assigned story, then uses the words to teach a phonics or study-skills lesson (clapping out syllables, underlining vowels, etc.). Next the group either reads the story aloud—taking turns—or it selects student volunteers to read. Then the group asks the class five questions about the story. When the questions have been answered correctly, the group's teaching time is over. Your youngsters may find that teaching is a fun way to learn! Of course, you already knew that!

Jo Bressan—Gr. 2
Jefferson Park Elementary
El Paso, IL

## Fond Farewell

Saying good-bye to a student who is moving is never easy. Using a tape recorder and a blank cassette tape, your youngsters can say good-bye in a memorable way. Begin by taping your own personal message to the departing student. Then arrange for each student to tape-record a message telling the student why he was a good friend and why he will be missed. Slip the completed tape and a snapshot of your class inside a cassette case; then give your class gift to the student on his last day. What a thoughtful way to say, "Farewell."

Mary Lynn Vinal—Gr. 2
Dodge Elementary School
East Amherst, NY

## Expect Good News!

The next time you plan to call a parent with good news about his child's performance or behavior, send home a note explaining your intentions. Both the parent and child can eagerly await your phone call—making the call even more special. And the advance notice gives the parent time to think of any questions or concerns that he's been wanting to share with you. It's a perfect plan for positive parent communication.

Michele Lasky Anszelowicz—Gr. 1
Mandalay School
Wantagh, NY

## Edible Words

Whet your youngsters' appetites for spelling with this daily activity. Each morning, have students select one word from the lunch menu. Challenge students to use the letters within the chosen word to make additional words. At the day's end, compile your students' efforts on a laminated chart. Then, as a class, count to find the grand total of words spelled. Your students will really develop a taste for this motivational method of practicing spelling.

Carolyn Kanoy—Gr. 2
Old Town Elementary
Winston-Salem, NC

## Picture Perfect!

Many magazines are terrific sources for the kinds of pictures you can use in your classroom. Enlist the help of parents in collecting a variety of magazine pictures for instructional use. Ask parents to search for, cut out, and sort pictures from magazines they no longer want. You may wish to provide the names of categories for which you are most interested in obtaining pictures, such as animals, people, foods, and plants. Once you have received the pictures, students can use them in numerous ways—for example: matching pictures that rhyme, illustrating self-written books, or making rebus stories.

Paulette Hammond—Gr. 1
Chalkville Elementary
Birmingham, AL

## Drawing In Circles

Cling onto this idea for recycling empty tape rolls! When a roll of tape is used up, place the remaining ring at your art center. If a student needs to draw a circle, he can choose a ring and use the inside or outside of the ring as a template.

Diane Fortunato—Gr. 2
Carteret School
Bloomfield, NJ

## Parent-Child Response Journals

Periodically use parent-child response journals to extend the self-discovery writing process and enhance parent-child communication. On the chalkboard write one journal topic designed for the student and one for the parent. Each child responds to the student topic, records the parent topic in his journal, and takes the journal home so that his parent can respond to the appropriate topic. Encourage each parent to discuss his journal response with his child before sending the journal back to school. Some parent/child topics that you might use include the following: "The most important lesson my parent (child) taught me…", "If I could do anything differently…", and "The way I would describe my family (child)…." Your students will learn as much about themselves as they do about writing.

Pamela M. Szegedy
Erieview Elementary School
Avon Lake, OH

The most important lesson my parents taught me was to share. Now my friends share with me.

The most important lesson my child taught me…

## Handling Supplies

Don't toss out those empty detergent boxes with handles! They are perfect for storing students' art supplies. Decorate the empty boxes with colorful, self-adhesive paper; then number one box for each small group of students. Place each group's glue bottles, crayons, scissors, markers, and rulers in its box. Store the boxes where they can easily be found. When a group needs art supplies, one student retrieves her group's box. This reduces the number of students gathering supplies, and keeps materials in a central location. Organization and recycling—a welcome combination!

Ann Margaret Neal—Gr. 2
Encino Park Elementary
San Antonio, TX

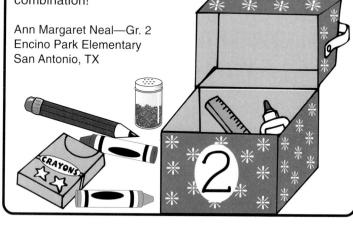

## Plastic Bags And Paper Pieces

When a student must put away an unfinished cut-and-paste project to begin working on something else, keeping track of the small pieces can be a challenge. Resealable plastic bags are the perfect storage solution! Attach a magnetic or self-adhesive cup hook to each child's desk. From each hook, suspend a resealable plastic bag labeled with the student's name. A student places the pieces of his unfinished project inside his plastic bag and returns the bag to the hook. Now keeping pieces together is in the bag!

Ann Margaret Neal—Gr. 2

## Beautiful Borders

Make eye-catching bulletin-board borders using seasonal and/or decorator fabrics. To make a border, laminate a desired amount of fabric. Cut the fabric into strips or trace the outline of a desired border pattern onto the fabric and cut it out. Attach the cloth border to your bulletin board. When it's time to remove the border, simply roll it up and store it for later use. These colorful and durable borders are a cut above the rest!

Kendria Sanders—Gr. 1
Goldonna Elementary School
Goldonna, LA

## Recess Puzzler

When recess is cancelled due to inclement weather, pull out the puzzles! You will need one jigsaw puzzle (no more than 100 pieces) for every two or three students. Number the box lids for easy identification; then distribute the puzzles. Signal the students to begin working. To increase the level of difficulty, ask students to refrain from talking. When three puzzles have been assembled, ask all students to stop. Record, in the order of completion, the puzzle numbers and the names of the students who completed them. Then have each group disassemble and return its puzzle to the box. Rotate the groups to different puzzles and repeat the activity. Continue in this manner until recess time is over. Once the puzzles have been put away, have students study the information you recorded. Students may notice that particular puzzles or groups of students are listed with some frequency. If this is the case, challenge students to interpret these findings.

Cassie Black—Gr. 3
Little River Elementary
Woodstock, GA

## Colorful Ceiling

Here's a bright idea for livening up the appearance of your classroom. Cut and curl lengths of colorful ribbon; then hang the ribbons from the ceiling of your room to create a cheery, festive atmosphere at party time or anytime.

Christine Wirtanen—Gr. 1
Northeast Elementary
Evergreen Park, IL

## No-Slip Flannelboard Tip

If you're looking for a way to keep your cutouts from sliding off the flannelboard, don't let this great tip slip by! Glue small pieces of sandpaper to the back of your flannelboard shapes. Make sure the rough side of the sandpaper is facing out. The sandpaper will adhere securely to the flannelboard. Now that's a solution you can stick with!

Sr. M. Henrietta
Villa Sacred Heart
Danville, PA

## Morning Math

Keep math skills sharp with this great pointer. For each day of the week, design a math word problem that correlates to your current literature selection. Write the word problems on literature-related shapes; then laminate and cut them out. Present the first word problem on the morning that the story is introduced. One student reads aloud the word problem. After giving his classmates time to solve the problem on their own, he calls on one student to record the equation on the chalkboard, and another to solve the problem for the class. Repeat this procedure each morning until all of the cards are used, or until you have completed the story; then begin again with a new story and a new set of math cards. Combining literature and math is truly "no problem"!

Lana Stewart—Gr. 2
Haskell Elementary
Haskell, TX

The Legend of the Indian Paintbrush
retold and illustrated by Tomie dePaola

If Little Gopher used four handfuls of berries to make one pot of paint, how many handfuls of berries would he use to make three pots of paint?

## Paper Pen Pal

Your youngsters will be involved in this activity in a few minutes flat. Read aloud *Flat Stanley* by Jeff Brown (HarperCollins Children's Books, 1989). In the story Stanley—after being flattened—takes advantage of his slender physique by traveling to California in an envelope. To set the stage for a related activity, have each student create a construction-paper likeness of Flat Stanley. Then ask each child to bring to school the address of a friend or relative who lives out of state. Next have each student write a letter to his friend or relative. In his letter he introduces Stanley and requests that Stanley be returned, after a brief visit, with a letter explaining what Stanley did during his visit. Each student then addresses an envelope and places Stanley and his letter inside. When the envelopes are in the mail, entitle a bulletin board "Flat Stanley's Travels" and display a map of the United States there. As each child's Flat Stanley returns, have him find and mark on the map where Stanley has been; then read aloud the accompanying letter.

Nancy Conner—Gr. 2
Turnpike Christian School
Grand Prairie, TX

Nov. 10, 1995

Dear Lashay,
I was happy to hear from you. Stanley came to school with me. He sat with me at lunch. Mrs. Ives showed us the state of Texas.

## Estimating Erasers

Erase the guesswork over how to fill your estimating jar. Purchase inexpensive erasers in a variety of shapes and sizes. If desired, fill your jar with seasonally appropriate erasers, or erasers that match your current thematic study. Not only do the erasers look attractive in the jar, they make great student prizes when the estimating activity is complete.

Kathleen Darby—Gr. 1
Community School
Cumberland, RI

## Handmade Treasures

Focus on the true spirit of giving by hosting a handmade gift exchange. Send home with each student a list of ideas for making a gift. For example, a student could make an original comic book, jewelry from thread and beads, or bookmarks from poster board and stickers. As the gifts are opened, each child will be eager to see how excitedly his own homemade gift is received. Through this experience your youngsters can learn firsthand that the greatest gifts are those from the heart!

Pa Negovetich
Gr. 3
Ready School
Griffith, IN

## Photo Graphs

Here's a great tip for graphing with your youngsters' photographs. Laminate a photograph of each child; then attach a magnet to the back of each laminated snapshot. On a magnetic board, prepare a bar graph outline. With students' input, select a subject for the graph and label the columns accordingly. Have each student attach his magnet in the appropriate column. Ask the students to evaluate the resulting graph. Your students' graphing skills will soon be picture-perfect!

Sherryl Robertson—Gr. 1
Social Circle Elementary
Social Circle, GA

Favorite School Lunch

hot dog | pizza | spaghetti | burrito | hamburger

## Colorful Candies

Stretch your candy-buying dollars by purchasing packages of green and red M&M's® during after-Christmas sales. Separate the green candy pieces from the red ones; then place them in two different resealable plastic bags. Store the candy in a freezer. When Valentine's Day rolls around, thaw out and use the red candy to win your young valentines' hearts. On St. Patrick's Day, you'll be in luck again when the leftover green candy will come in handy! Now that's a sweet bargain!

Karen Harper—Gr. 1, Cany Reynolds School, Dunaville, GA

## Storing Borders

Put a cap on your bulletin-board border storage woes with this idea! Save the empty cardboard tubes from jumbo rolls of wrapping paper. To prepare each tube, glue one end-cap securely in place. Insert borders into the cylinder; then attach the remaining cap to protect the borders. Label each tube so that you will know at a glance where to find the border you need.

Audrienne Teach, H. V. Helbing Elementary, Euless, TX

## Book-Order Wish Lists

Don't toss out those extra book-club order forms! Here's a way to use them to teach money skills. Each student will need a book-order form, paper and pencil, and perhaps a calculator. Ask each child to browse through the order form and make a list of books that she would like to "purchase," being sure not to exceed an established price limit. To increase the challenge, designate a price range and ask students to make several different lists of book purchases that would fall within the specified price range.

Emily Goren—Gr. 3
Cary Elementary
Cary, NC

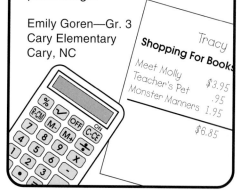

Tracy
Shopping For Books

Meet Molly        $3.95
Teacher's Pet       .95
Monster Manners    1.95

$6.85

## Reading Round

Add some adventure to your oral reading practice with a set of Uno® cards. Prepare the card deck by removing all cards that read "Draw 2" and "Draw 4"; then gather a group of students into a reading circle. Explain to students that the luck of the draw will determine the order in which they will read. For example, when a numeral card is drawn, the next reader is determined by counting around the circle. If a student draws a "zero" card, he continues reading another section. If a student draws a "Reverse" card, the direction of the reading changes from clockwise to counterclockwise (or vice versa). If a student draws a "Skip" card, the person sitting next to the reader will be skipped over for one turn. A "Wild" card gives the current reader the chance to choose the next reader. Once the rules have been discussed, begin by reading the first selection yourself. Draw a card and, unless you have drawn a "Reverse" card, proceed in a clockwise direction. How do you make reading fun? It's in the cards!

Nikole Winter—Substitute Teacher, Antioch, TN

## Padded Dice Plates

Get on a recycling roll by making padded dice holders from plastic frozen-food containers. Simply cut a piece of felt to cover the bottom of a clean plastic container. When your students are playing a dice game, ask them to roll their dice in a padded container. The felt padding will make for a much quieter game.

Ann Margaret Neal—Gr. 2
San Antonio, TX

**Good Morning!**
We're going to have a great day! I even have a surprise for you! Please be seated quickly and quietly.

## Good-Morning Messages

Greet your children at the start of each day with a "Good Morning" message. Place a brief message and/or instructions on the classroom door frame for each student to read as he enters the room. Each student will feel as if he has been personally greeted by you, even if you are unable to speak to him individually at that moment. What a cheerful way to begin each day!

Carolyn Kanoy
Winston-Salem, NC

## Managing Money

Since collecting project money from students can be a challenge, here's a way to simplify the process. On the outside of an envelope, have each student write a personalized note explaining what the requested money will be used for and how much is needed. Send the unsealed envelopes home. When a parent receives the envelope, she will have both the information she needs and a container in which to place the money. The personalized envelopes make it easy to identify which students have returned their money to school and reduce the possibility that money will be lost along the way.

Carolyn Matheson—Gr. 1
Florence Elementary
Southlake, TX

Dear Mom,
My class is going to the zoo on January 26.
I need $2.10 for admission.
Love,
Sofie

## The "Magic Bag"

Add a little pizzazz to upcoming lessons with a "magic bag"! To make the bag, use fabric paints and other craft materials to decorate a large pillowcase. Make a casing and thread a drawstring through it. Then fill the bag with materials needed to complete an upcoming lesson. Display the closed bag in a prominent classroom location. When it's time to begin the "magic bag" lesson, there's no doubt that you'll have your students' undivided attention!

Kristin McLaughlin
Substitute Teacher

## Talents Day

Host a Share-Your-Talents Day, and watch each child's self-esteem grow! Begin by writing a note to inform parents about the upcoming talents day. In the note encourage each parent to help his child identify and practice one talent or skill. Provide a list of possible skills that might be considered, such as braiding hair, tying special knots, flying a kite, or turning a cartwheel. On Share-Your-Talents Day, ask each youngster to demonstrate his skill for his classmates and parents or other relatives who can attend. Invite the audience to share positive comments about the students' performances. Your youngsters will be amazed at what a talented bunch they are!

Kathy Britton—Gr. 1, Holmes Elementary, Spring Lake, MI

## Comic-Relief Reading

To reach those reluctant readers, tickle their funny bones! Create high-interest reading materials by placing age-appropriate comic strips in a photo album. If desired, encourage students to contribute some favorite comic strips of their own. Shelve this comic-strip collection alongside other class library books. Your youngsters will be eager to check it out!

Kristin McLaughlin—Substitute Teacher
Boyertown Area Schools, Boyertown, PA

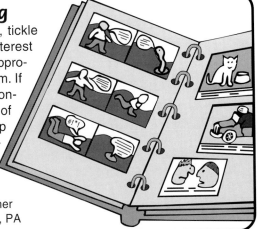

## Edible Penguins

These "egg-ceptional," edible penguins make a one-of-a-kind snack! To make a tasty penguin, start with a boiled-egg body. Using a toothpick, attach a jumbo black olive head to the most narrow end of the egg. Cut a second jumbo black olive in half to make wings, and attach them with toothpick halves. Cut wedges from two carrot rounds to make penguin feet. Use dabs of cream cheese or peanut butter to attach the feet and a tiny carrot nose. Now that's a cool bird!

Linda L. Sherman
Gr. 1
Robert Morris
School
Batavia, NY

## Far-Out!

Set the stage for your next space unit with this out-of-sight display! Using colorful paper and various craft materials, create a fictional planet and several of its inhabitants. Attach the resulting cutouts to a bulletin board. From white paper, cut out several large speech bubbles; then label each one with a different fact about the fictional planet along with an Earth-related question. As students learn facts about the Earth and its solar system, they can add their own make-believe creatures and planetary facts to the display.

Angie Carpenter—Gr. 2
Hamlow Elementary
Waverly, NE

The planet Jowesi has five moons. How many moons does Earth have?

## Beat The Blues

Try this unique method for beating those wintertime blues! On a selected day, encourage each student to wear blue clothing. Play some blues music; then ask students to brainstorm ideas for beating the wintertime blues. Record students' suggestions on a chart. This activity will go a long way toward perking up your youngsters, and the resulting chart is a permanent resource for students who may need help in beating the blues!

Kathleen C. Weisenborn—Gr. 2
Fricano Elementary, Lockport, NY

## Organizing Word Cards

If keeping track of loose vocabulary word cards is a challenge, you're likely to find this tip useful! Purchase a set of spiral-bound index cards. Write each vocabulary (or spelling) word on a different card. Use an index tab to label each word list or category. Because it's unlikely that cards will get lost, these vocabulary booklets are perfect for individual student study or group games.

Laurie Mick—Grs. K–2
Special Education
Patterson Elementary
Holly, MI

frost
blizzard

## A Large Letter

Help your youngsters keep their letter-writing skills in top form with a giant class-written letter. Ask students to dictate a class letter. Then copy the letter—in correct form—on a brightly colored length of bulletin-board paper. Mount the letter so that it can be seen from each child's desk. Write the different parts of a letter on individual sentence strips; then attach the strips to the appropriate locations on the class-dictated letter. Encourage students to refer to the giant letter as they pen letters to their pals.

Beth Martin Sine—Gr. 3
Dr. Brown Elementary, Waldorf, MD

## Wintertime Puzzles

Establishing a jigsaw-puzzle exchange is a fun and easy method for fostering parent/child involvement. Begin by suggesting that each family purchase a puzzle that they can complete over the course of several evenings. Keep a small supply of your own puzzles to loan to parents, as well. When a child and her parent have successfully completed their puzzle, ask them to disassemble it and send it to school. Then send the child home with one of your puzzles or a puzzle that another child has returned. This winter will be full of interactive fun for students and parents alike!

Angela Simmons—Grs. 2–3
Okolona Elementary School
Louisville, KY

## Appetizing Vocabulary

This large or small group game creates an appetite for new vocabulary words! Provide a list of ten or more words. Ask each youngster to draw a large tic-tac-toe grid on his paper and write a different vocabulary word from the list in each space. Give each player a small container of dry cereal pieces. To play, randomly call out the vocabulary words. If the called word is on a student's grid, he covers the space with a piece of cereal. When a student has covered three words in a row (in any direction), he declares, "Tic-tac-toe!" To win the game, he must correctly read aloud each word in his row. When the game is over, each player eats the cereal pieces on his gameboard; then a new game begins. Now that's appetizing vocabulary!

Karen Saner—Grs. K & 1
Burns Elementary
Burns, KS

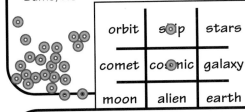

| orbit | s(o)ip | stars |
|-------|--------|-------|
| comet | co(s)mic | galaxy |
| moon | alien | earth |

## Picture This!

Turn special classroom events into lasting memories with pictorial folders! Each time you develop a roll of classroom snapshots, sort the photographs by events. Mount each set of photos inside a colorful file folder and write a narrative caption near each snapshot. On the front of each folder, note the corresponding event and the date that it occurred. Laminate the projects and display them in your classroom for your youngsters' viewing enjoyment. If desired, establish a checkout system that allows interested students to take the folders home overnight. By the end of the school year, you'll have an impressive collection of lasting memories.

Jill Zukerman—Gr. 2
Hudson Elementary School, Solon, OH

## Spelling Journals

These individualized journals foster spelling skills. Whenever a child learns that she has misspelled a word, she lists the correct spelling of the word in her journal. A student may discover misspelled words when she evaluates corrected papers or when she's working with adults and classmates. As students make additions in their spelling journals, offer words of encouragement and recognize those youngsters who are expanding their spelling vocabularies by using words in their daily writing that are less familiar and more challenging. Periodically ask each student to create her weekly spelling list using words listed in her journal.

Joyce L. Abele, Berne, NY

## Write On!

Here's a one-of-a-kind writing pad that puts beginning writers in touch with letter formation. To make a writing pad, seal approximately eight ounces of tinted hair-setting gel inside a medium-size resealable plastic storage bag. Use durable tape to secure the bag to a piece of white poster board as shown. Place the project at a writing center. A student uses one finger to press the shape of a letter into the pad of gel. To erase his work, he gently rubs the pad with the palm of his hand until the gel is evenly distributed inside the bag. There's no doubt that this writing pad will make a big impression on your little ones.

Mary Ann Garza, La Pryor, TX

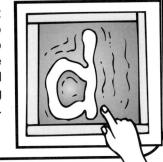

## Private Work Space

These nifty and easy-to-make desktop screens create privacy for working students. To make a screen, tape together two same-size cardboard pieces (at least 15 inches tall), leaving a small gap to ensure that the pieces can be folded together. Cover the entire screen with decorative self-adhesive paper. Store the ready-to-use screens in an easily accessible location. When a youngster desires a private work space, she retrieves a screen and sets it up on her desktop. These screens are especially useful during testing sessions.

Alyce Pearl Smith—Gr. 1
Butzback Elementary, Germany

## Now Listening To...

If you've discovered that softly playing classical music helps maintain a relaxed and quiet atmosphere in your classroom, here's a tip for you. Post a laminated sign that reads "Now Listening To..." near your audio equipment. Store a dry-erase marker and an eraser nearby. Whenever there's background music playing, be sure that the name and composer of the musical piece are noted on the sign. Before long your youngsters will be making musical requests by name—and that will be music to your ears!

Sheila R. Chapman—Gr. 3, Elm Street School, Newnan, GA

## Creating Sunny Days

Brighten a cloudy day with this self-esteem booster. Ask each student to write his name on a sheet of blank paper, then display the paper on his desktop. Be sure to do the same yourself! Then have each student take his pencil and move from desk to desk, stopping at each one to write a positive comment on each person's paper. For easy management, have students move along a pre-determined route. Students will beam with delight when they return to their desks and read the sunny messages that are awaiting them.

*Laura Mihalenko—Gr. 2, Truman Elementary School, Parlin, NJ*

Kevin

You are nice to everyone.

I like your smile.

You are good at math.

You tell funny jokes.

## Edible Phonics

Students can sink their teeth into these phonic lessons! To maximize student interest, plan to serve a food item that reinforces the phonic sound you are teaching. For example, when you teach the *gr* blend, serve *gr*its. Invite students to mun*ch* on *ch*ips as they learn about the digraph *ch.* Youngsters are sure to remember each tasty lesson and its corresponding phonic rule.

*Theresa Pierce—Gr. 1*
*North Hills Christian School*
*Salisbury, NC*

## Organizing Manipulatives

Picture yourself saving time distributing math manipulatives! It's a snap when you store individual sets of manipulatives inside empty 35mm film containers. Label the outside of each container with its contents; then store the containers in a handy location. Now your manipulatives can be distributed and collected in a jiffy.

*Tammy Sivley—Gr. 3*
*Dr. W. J. Creel Elementary*
*Melbourne, FL*

20 washers

Let's mun**ch** on some **ch**ips.

## An Author's Chair

Here's a fun way to spotlight the authors your youngsters study. Purchase an inexpensive plastic chair and use a permanent marker to label it "Authors' Chair." At the conclusion of each author study, ask a student to write the author's name on the chair and draw an object or character that represents the author's work. Provide colorful permanent markers for this purpose. At the end of the year, make plans to raffle off the chair. Students can earn tickets for the drawing by reading books!

Donna Henry
Portsmouth Catholic School
Portsmouth, VA

## Moving Desks

Enlist your students' help in changing the classroom seating arrangement with a game of Memory Move. In advance explain (or draw on the board) the new seating arrangement; then designate where each student will sit. On your signal, each student quietly and cooperatively moves his desk and chair to their new locations.

*Rachelle Dawson—Gr. 3*
*Nashua Elementary, Kansas City, MO*

## See-Through Reading Guides

It's clear—these reading guides can help students who are having difficulty following a line of print. To make four reading guides, laminate two 1/2" x 12" construction-paper strips, leaving a predetermined amount of blank space between them. (The blank space must accommodate a line of print.) Cut the laminated strip into three-inch sections. Store your supply of reading guides in a location that's easy for students to access.

*Pam Tobias—Resource Assistant*
*Serna Elementary*
*San Antonio, TX*

then the dog bar**k**ed.

## Make Each Day Special

Planning one special activity per day is sure to please your youngsters. But if you're looking for rave reviews, enlist your students' help in planning the activities! Post a laminated chart like the one shown that lists each day of the week. Every Friday afternoon set aside time for students to choose the following week's special activities; then use a wipe-off marker to write the activities on the chart. Or write a student-generated list of special activity ideas; then enlist your youngsters' help in copying each idea on a paper slip. Place the written suggestions in a container and ask a different student to draw an activity for each day of the next week. The following Friday ask five more students to draw activities from the container. Continue in this manner until all the ideas have been implemented; then repeat the brainstorming part of the activity.

Pamela Cobler Packard—Gr. 3, Campbell Court Elementary, Bassett, VA

### Make Every Day Special

Monday-ten minutes extra P.E.

Tuesday-sing a song

Wednesday-art project

Thursday-free reading time

Friday-filmstrip

## Plastic Book Protectors

Whether you're protecting books from inclement weather or gooey surprises inside student bookbags—resealable plastic bags will do the trick. Make available a supply of gallon-size bags; then ask students who are taking books home to seal their books inside plastic bags before transporting them. When the books are returned, the plastic bags can be recycled.

Michael C. Zeidler—Gr. 2, Thomas Jefferson Elementary, Wausau, WI

## Picturesque Mapping Skills

Reinforce map skills with discarded calendar pictures! Collect calendar pictures that feature sights from around the United States. Mount each picture on construction paper; then label the back of each one with the state it represents and a brief description of the sight shown. Laminate the mounted pictures for durability. For a fun mapping activity, distribute the pictures. In turn ask each student to display his calendar picture and read aloud the information from the back. Then, on a map of the United States, the student or a classmate locates the corresponding state.

Victoria Cavanagh—Gr. 2, St. Catherine Of Siena School, Nutley, NJ

## Magic Number Game

Presto! This fast-paced game reinforces basic subtraction facts or basic addition facts with sums of nine or less. Give each child a set of ten cards that have been labeled with the numerals zero through nine. To play, call out a series of nine fact problems—each having a different answer from zero through nine. After each problem is called, a student removes the corresponding answer from his stack of cards. At this point each student should be down to one card. On your signal, the students call out, "Magic number!" and display the last card in their stacks. A quick glance shows you which students are mastering their facts.

Susan Nye—Gr. 2
Holland Elementary
Virginia Beach, VA

## Hooray For Homework!

This stellar idea encourages students to complete and return their homework assignments on time. Cut five large stars from tagboard and label each one for a different day of the school week. Attach a strip of magnetic tape to the back of each cutout. Mount a banner that reads "Hooray For Homework! We Did It!" on a magnetic surface. Every day that all present students turn in their homework assignments, post the corresponding homework star near the banner and congratulate your youngsters on their stellar performance. If desired, declare a "No Homework Day" after a predetermined number of consecutive stars have been earned.

Katherine Gartner—
    Special Education Grs. 1 & 2
Oxhead Road Elementary School
Centereach, NY

Monday

Tuesday

Hooray For Homework! We Did It!

## Keeping In Touch

Maintain outstanding parent-teacher communication by establishing weekly goals. Each week determine which parents you will contact by phone or in writing regarding their youngsters' positive performance in school. Make plans to call each student's family at least once a month. This positive interaction demonstrates your desire to keep the lines of communication open.

Christy Meyer, Honolulu, HI

Magic Number!

## Borrower's Bag

What do flash cards, puppets, books, and games have in common? Each of these items can help youngsters practice responsible borrowing habits. Label each of two canvas bags "Borrower's Bag" and store a small notepad in each one. Every Friday invite two different students to each fill a bag with a predetermined number of classroom items that he would like to borrow for the weekend. Each child lists the items he will be taking home on the provided notepad. Then he leaves the notepad with you. When the borrower returns his bag, he checks off each returned item on the notepad and gives you his list. He then returns the classroom items to their proper places, stores the blank notepad in the Borrower's Bag, and returns the bag.

Karen Dufault—Gr. 2, Killdeer Public School, Killdeer, ND

## Neighborhood Lotto

This simple twist on the game of lotto leaves more students feeling like winners. To play Neighborhood Lotto, distribute a lotto card and a supply of markers to each student. You will also need a supply of stickers to give away as prizes. Before play begins, announce that three games will be called before players must clear their cards. In addition, each time a winner is identified, the students who sit to the left and right of him win, too! Students love the results of this game variation. After three games are played and the game winners have been rewarded, have students clear their cards for another rousing trio of games.

Sue McDowell—Grs. 3–4, Kennedy Elementary School, Willmar, MN

## Naming Nouns

Here's a group activity that's a shoe-in for learning nouns. Each week divide students into small groups. Challenge each group to brainstorm a list of nouns that fit a certain criteria, like nouns that would fit in a shoebox or nouns that make noise. After a predetermined amount of time, ask one member from each group to read aloud the nouns on his group's list. Record the nouns on a poster-board chart that can be displayed in the classroom. Later in the week, ask students to incorporate the posted nouns into a writing activity.

Diane Fortunato—Gr. 2
Carteret School, Bloomfield, NJ

### Shoebox Nouns

| | | |
|---|---|---|
| pen | scissors | nail |
| yo-yo | pencil | hamburger |
| dice | ball | shoe |
| ring | jacks | calculator |
| tape | eraser | wallet |

## Take-A-Break Cards

**TAKE A BREAK**

☆ ☆ ☆ ☆

Name Mickey

Take-A-Break cards can motivate students to be on their best behavior—even when spring fever hits. Whenever you see a student behaving responsibly, reward her with a gold star she can affix to her card. When a student earns a predetermined number of stars, she redeems her card and takes a break from a lesson or work assignment. During her break she may read a book, spend time on the classroom computer, complete an art activity, etc. Each time a student redeems a card, present her with a new one!

Nancy Rispalje—Gr. 1
American Heritage School
Plantation, FL

## Animal Math

Here's a fast and easy way to practice math facts and word problems. Use your Unifix® cubes to represent animals. For example, while figuring rain-forest word problems, use the green cubes to represent frogs and the brown cubes to represent sloths. While solving word problems about polar animals, have the white cubes represent polar bears and have the black cubes represent penguins. For added appeal, have students use pages from theme-related notepads as counting mats.

Angie Kelley—Gr. 3
Weaver Elementary School
Weaver, AL

## Story In A Bag

Strengthen your youngsters' comprehension and oral-communication skills with this follow-up activity. After students have either read a book or had a book read to them, ask each student to choose his favorite part of the story. To complete the project, a child decorates the outside of a white paper lunch bag to show where his favorite part of the story took place. Then, on white construction paper, he illustrates each character who had a role in this part of the story. Next the student cuts out his story characters and stores them in his decorated bag. When the projects are complete, pair the students. In turn, have each partner use his character cutouts and lunch-bag scenery to retell his favorite story part. Then encourage each youngster to take his story-in-a-bag presentation on the road so that he can share it with his friends and family.

Diona Durham
Special Education Grs. K–5
Ontiveros School
Santa Maria, CA

## Name Ball

A game of Name Ball will help familiarize a new student with his classmates' names. Have students stand in a large circle formation; then hand a sponge-type ball to one player. To begin play, the player holding the ball calls out the name of a classmate and tosses the ball to that student. The student who receives the ball names a different classmate and tosses the ball to that student. If the intended receiver misses the ball, she sits down. If the ball thrower makes a bad throw, she sits down. Seated students may rejoin the game after three successful tosses have been made. Your youngsters will have a ball helping their newest classmate learn their names.

Nancy Lujan—Gr. 3
C. I. Waggoner Elementary
Tempe, AZ

## Subtraction Derby

Get your youngsters on a math roll with this large-group subtraction game. Gather two dice. Visually divide your chalkboard in half and label one half "Class" and the other half with your name. Write the numeral 99 below each title. Ask each student to personalize a sheet of blank paper and write the numeral 99 at the top. Pass one die to a student and keep the second die for yourself. To begin play, the student rolls the die and calls out the displayed number. On their papers, the students subtract the called number from 99. Simultaneously solve the problem on the chalkboard under "Class"—making sure to conceal your answer until students have completed their work. To take your turn, roll your die on a student's desk; then complete the corresponding subtraction problem on the chalkboard under your name. Continue alternating turns with your class, making sure that the class die is passed from student to student along a predetermined path. The first "team" to reach zero wins!

| Ms. Newsom | Class |
|---|---|
| 99 | 99 |
| -4 | -6 |
| 95 | 93 |
| -6 | -2 |
| 89 | 91 |

Leigh Anne Newsom—Gr. 3
Greenbrier Intermediate, Chesapeake, VA

## Challenge Box

A challenge box provides your early finishers with fun, challenging reproducible activities—without using a lot of paper! Make a copy of each of several enticing reproducibles that you do not plan to incorporate into your daily activities. Mount each activity on construction paper and attach a corresponding answer key to the back. Laminate the pages and place them in a decorated box labeled "Challenge Box." Near the box store a container of wipe-off markers. When a student has free time, she helps herself to a challenge-box activity. After completing the activity, she checks her work, then wipes away the programming before returning the activity and the wipe-off marker to their respective locations. Each month provide new activities in the challenge box.

Jennifer Lynn Fabry—Gr. 3
Woodview Elementary, Grayslake, IL

Challenge Box

## A Handsome Gift

This student-made gift will be a hands-down favorite! Add a squirt of liquid soap to liquid tempera paint; then use a paintbrush to brush a thin layer of the paint on the palms of each student. Each student presses his hands onto the bottom of a heavy, white paper plate. When the paint has dried, use a hot glue gun to attach a border of rickrack around each student's project. On writing paper each student copies the poem shown in his best handwriting, then signs and dates his work. To make a card, a student mounts his writing on construction paper. When the glue has dried, he folds the construction paper in half so that the poem is inside the resulting card. He then decorates the outside of the card to his liking. Moms and dads will be thrilled with these gifts of love!

Jo Franco—Grs. K–5 Basic Skills
Lincoln School, Harrison, NJ

Here are my prints—
You've seen them before.
On the walls, the woodwork,
And the bathroom door.

Those special prints—
You've scrubbed patiently.
But these you may keep
For a nice memory.

Love,
Tom

## Backup Leader

This backup plan will be a hit with your students. Each week when you select a line leader, also select a backup leader. The backup leader stands at the end of the line and is responsible for making sure all his classmates are in line, turning off the classroom lights, and shutting the classroom door. If the line leader is absent, the backup leader fills in until he returns. Now it's an honor to be last in line!

Peter Tabor—Gr. 1
Weston Elementary
Schofield, WI

## Tally Marks

This idea for practicing skip-counting is bound to become a class favorite. Each day ask a different student to choose a topic like "My Favorite Movie" and provide three or four answer choices. Write the information on the chalkboard and have students cast their votes by a show of hands. Use tally marks to record the student votes. As a group count the tally marks by fives and ones to determine each total; then challenge students to determine the most- and least-favorite choices.

Carolyn Jones—Gr. 1
Lake Lucina Elementary
Jacksonville, FL

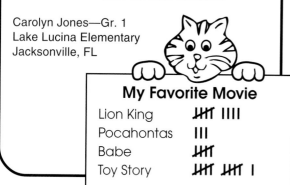

**My Favorite Movie**

| | |
|---|---|
| Lion King | ЖЖ IIII |
| Pocahontas | III |
| Babe | ЖЖ |
| Toy Story | ЖЖ ЖЖ I |

## Spell-A-Page

Sharpen students' listening and spelling skills with this terrific tip. When you need to direct students to a certain page in their books, spell out the page number. Before you know it, students will be able to turn to page "t-w-e-n-t-y" as quickly as they used to turn to page 20!

Mary Dinneen—Gr. 2
Mountain View School
Bristol, CT

## How Far Is It?

Learning how to accurately use a map scale to determine distance is tricky! Here's a tip that can keep your youngsters right on track. Have each student position a sticky note directly below the map scale, then transfer the scale onto the sticky note. Now the student has a movable map scale that makes measuring and calculating map distances a breeze!

Rita Peat—Gr. 3
Cleveland Elementary, North Elkhart, IN

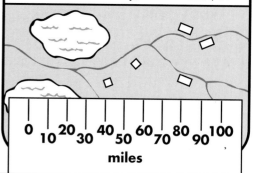

## Quotes For Mom

If you've kept a file of endearing quotes spoken or written by your youngsters, you are well on your way to making the perfect Mother's Day gift. If you haven't, plan to use this idea next year. Write a Mother's Day newsletter that includes at least one quote spoken or written by each student. Have each child decorate a business-size envelope. Then, inside each envelope, slip a copy of the newsletter, a tea bag, and instructions that encourage Mom to relax with a cup of brewed tea as she reads her unique Mother's Day surprise.

Theresa Pierce—Gr. 1
North Hills Christian School
Salisbury, NC

## Word Clubs

Reinforce word-recognition skills with word-club memberships! To join a word club, a student must read a list of words that relate to a specific topic. For example, to join the Springtime Word Club, a student must read 20 spring-related words. When the student is successful, he is presented with a Springtime Word Club membership certificate, and his name is written on an official Springtime Word Club poster like the one shown. To introduce a new club, announce a topic and enlist your youngsters' help in creating a list of words related to the topic. Send each child home with a copy of the finalized word list, and post a related word-club poster in the classroom. By the year's end, you'll have an impressive display of your youngsters' reading accomplishments!

Carole Curcio—Gr. 1
Hampton Elementary
Hampton, NJ

## Where In The World?

Improve geography skills by imitating Carmen San Diego. Mount a United States map on a bulletin board along with the title "Where In The World Is Your Teacher Today?" Each morning post several clues that reveal which state you are hiding in that day. Clues might include a river, mountain range, or lake located in the state; or the name of the state flower or capital. For additional reference, provide map-related books near the display. Students will look forward to revealing your location at the end of the day. After your location has been confirmed, students can color in the corresponding state on their own duplicated maps.

Kim Hermes—Gr. 1, Furry Elementary, Sandusky, OH

## Nutritious Quilt

Culminate your nutrition unit with this class quilt project. Assign each student a different alphabet letter, excluding the letter *X*. Using a letter stencil, each student draws his assigned letter on a 9" x 12" sheet of drawing paper. Then he colors his letter and illustrates a healthful food that begins with the same letter. For the letter *X*, program a sheet of drawing paper with the words "X-tra Helping." Also illustrate two additional quilt blocks as desired. Alphabetically assemble the quilt blocks in seven rows of four squares each, placing one additional quilt block at the beginning and one at the end of the quilt. Use strips of colorful cloth tape to join the quilt blocks as shown. Suspend the completed project in the school cafeteria for all to see!

Sr. Bernadette Cole—Gr. 1, Presentation Of Mary Academy, Hudson, NH

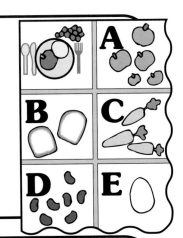

## Bird Mask

Here's an art project that's for the birds! Have each student create a bird mask like the one shown using colorful tagboard, feathers, markers, craft glue, and a wooden craft stick. If desired, precut the tagboard pieces. For a fun finale to a bird unit, ask each youngster to recite a poem, share an interesting fact, or give a report related to birds while wearing her bird mask. These presentations will definitely be something to chirp about!

Candy Whelan—Gr. 3
Garlough Elementary
West St. Paul, MN

## End-Of-The-Year Gift Stationery

Personalized stationery makes a nice end-of-the-year gift and it encourages letter writing, too. Attach a photo of each child to a separate sheet of lined paper; then make multiple copies of each sheet. Use a length of colorful ribbon to bundle each student's personalized stationery and a supply of envelopes. If desired, tuck a stamped envelope that you have addressed to yourself inside each child's bundle. Set aside time for students to exchange addresses so that they can keep in touch with one another over the summer, too!

Dana Hughes—Gr. 1, Pritchett School
Buffalo Grove, IL

## Colorful Window Decorations

Keep these student-painted window decorations on display until the last day of school! Have each child use permanent markers to sketch a desired scene on a length of plastic wrap. Then have each student paint his scene, using colorful tempera paint that contains a bit of liquid soap for easy cleanup. When the paint has dried, the student may use permanent markers to add more details. To display the projects, press the unpainted side of each piece of plastic against a window and secure the corners of the project with clear tape. The windows will look like they're painted. On the last day of school, quickly peel away the tape and plastic wrap.

Michelle Beagle—Grs. K–2, A. D. Owens School, Newport, KY

## Easy-To-Make Stencils

If you've been using an X-acto® knife and coffee-can lids to make stencils, here's an easier way! Purchase inexpensive, clear report covers. Cut each cover on the fold to create two lengths of plastic. Using a fine-tipped permanent marker, trace desired patterns on the plastic; then use scissors to carefully cut out each stencil. The resulting stencils are very durable. And since report covers come in a variety of colors, you can create color-coded stencil sets!

Deanne Wilhelm—Gr. 1
Taft Elementary, Middletown, OH

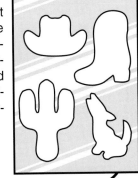

## Classy T-Shirts

Students will love wearing matching, sponge-painted T-shirts on field day, on field trips, and during end-of-the-year festivities. Ask each child to bring to school a white T-shirt. Demonstrate the painting process by painting a white T-shirt that you have brought to school. To paint it, place a cardboard cutout inside the T-shirt to prevent paint from bleeding through to the back of the shirt. Then use fabric paints and precut sponge shapes (or a stencil and sponge pieces) to paint desired artwork on the front of the T-shirt. When the shirt is dry, use fine-tip fabric markers to add desired details. Display your T-shirt at the painting station and encourage students to paint their T-shirts in the same manner. These matching T-shirts are sure to promote camaraderie among your students.

Debra Kain—Gr. 2, Sewell School, Sewell, NJ

## Menu Mania

Hook your youngsters on this end-of-the-year math review! Divide students into small groups and ask each group to design a food menu complete with prices. If desired ask the groups to create thematic menus, such as a seafood menu for an end-of-the-year pirate theme. Encourage each group to first brainstorm a list of foods and beverages, then assign a price to each item. Next have each group create its menu on a sheet of white poster board. Display the resulting menus around the classroom. Each day ask a different group to open its restaurant. Have the group assemble near its menu and give each member a blank pad of restaurant order forms (or something similar) and a supply of play money. The other students become customers and take turns placing orders at the restaurant. Each order is recorded and tabulated by a group member and then verified by the customer. Using play money, the customer pays his bill and waits to receive any change he is due. A multitude of math skills are reviewed each day!

Lisa Lemmings—Gr. 3
Westside Elementary
LaGrange, GA

## Planetary Order

To help students remember the order of the planets from the sun, teach them the following silly sentence: **M**y **V**ery **E**ducated **M**other **J**ust **S**erved **U**s **N**ine **P**izzas. The bold letters stand for the planets Mercury, Venus, Earth, Mars, Jupiter, Saturn, Uranus, Neptune, and Pluto. Invite students to write more silly sentences to remind them of planetary order. Ask each student to write her silly sentence on a construction-paper strip; then mount the reminders where students can easily refer to them.

Laura Horowitz, Plantation, FL

## Space-Saving Listening Station

Build a state-of-the-art listening station with just a few supplies and a minimal amount of space. Place your tape player and headset(s) on a desired table or desktop. On the wall about two feet above the equipment, secure two closet brackets about three feet apart. Rest a round rod of adequate length on the brackets as shown. Store each book-and-tape set in a resealable plastic bag; then use clothespins to attach each bagged set to a hanger. Suspend the hangers from the rod. For additional storage space, secure a board (approximately 1' x 3 1/2') to the top of the brackets.

Linda Guillot & June Jone
Chapter 1 Reading, Grs. K–5
Rosenthal Elementary
Alexandria, LA

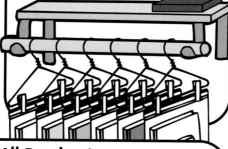

## Silly Sentences

There'll be giggles galore when this subject-and-predicate activity is completed! For each student cut one tagboard sentence strip and six construction-paper sentence strips of equal size; then cut the construction-paper strips in half to create 12 cards. On scrap paper have each student write six sentences and circle the subject of each one. To make a flip book like the one shown, a student copies each subject and each predicate on a different construction-paper card. Next he stacks his subject cards, aligns the stack atop the left half of his tagboard strip, and staples the stack to the tagboard near the left end. In a similar manner he stacks, aligns, and staples his predicate cards near the right end of the tagboard strip. Students will have a ball flipping the cards and reading the resulting sentences.

Carolyn Stickney—Chapter I, Grs. 1–3
Roseborough School, Mt. Dora, FL

## Nifty Bookmarks

These colorful bookmarks are easy to make and inexpensive! Cut book-related artwork from book order forms and publisher's catalogs; then glue the resulting artwork onto construction-paper strips. Use markers to add desired details; then laminate the bookmarks for durability. These bookmarks promote interest in a variety of books, and they also make excellent student incentives and gifts.

Karen Bryant—Gr. 3
Rosa Taylor Elementary School
Macon, GA

## Calling All Readers!

Do your students beg to be chosen for oral reading? To promote fairness, use Xs to create a simple seating chart like the one shown. When a child is chosen to read aloud, color a circle over the corresponding X. When all the Xs on the chart become colored dots, you will know that every child has had a chance to read. Then it's time to make a new chart and begin the procedure again.

Kelly Placek—Gr. 3
Lemasters Elementary, St. Louis, MO

### Reading Chart

## A Sunny Message

If you're looking for a unique way for your youngsters to express their gratitude to a parent volunteer, school secretary, or other deserving person, this bright idea is for you! From yellow paper cut a large circle; then cut out a yellow, triangle-shaped ray for each student. Add facial details and a desired message to the circle cutout. Then have each student decorate his ray with a brief message or an illustration. Attach the rays to the circle as shown. There'll be plenty of bright, sunny smiles when your youngsters present their special thank-you.

Lara O'Brien—Gr. 2
Lexington Park Elementary
Lexington Park, MD

Dear Ms. Owens
You are "sun-sational"!

## Shared Learning

Everyone benefits from this daily review! Near the end of the day, ask a student to describe one thing he learned during school that day. On the chalkboard write "[student's name] said," followed by the student's exact words. As you write the statement on the board, enlist your youngsters' help with correct spelling and punctuation. Then have each child copy the statement of the day on provided paper, using his best handwriting. Parents will look forward to seeing these papers each day!

Hayley MacDonald—Gr. 1, Town And Country Elementary, Tampa, FL

## Zipper Them!

Keeping track of game pieces becomes much easier when the loose pieces are safely zipped inside a pencil case or plastic storage bag. Use a hole puncher and two metal rings to attach the zippered container to the gameboard. Lost game pieces will become a thing of the past!

Donna Tobey—Gr. 1
Gulliver Academy
Coral Gables, FL

## Author On Tour

### Official Book Tour

Each time an author in your classroom becomes published, arrange for the student to take her latest book on tour. Determine a tour date; then schedule brief appointments with the school principal, the school nurse, a former teacher, and other school staff for that day. On the day of the tour, clip an official-looking badge like the one shown to the young author's clothing and give her a list of her scheduled tour stops. Each staff member who hears the youngster's story writes a brief comment and signs the back cover of her book. You can bet your students will keep publishing their stories right up to the very last day of school!

Susan Bunte—Grs. K–3
Crest Hills Year-Round School, Cincinnati, OH

## Reader Of The Week

Encourage reading success and recognition by spotlighting one student reader each week. Stock a reading center with easy-to-read books. Encourage student pairs to practice reading aloud at the center. Then, once a week, select a different student volunteer to choose a book from the center and read it aloud to his classmates. Photograph the student reading. When he completes the book, ask the audience to share positive comments about the student's reading. Record the comments on chart paper; then mount the comments and the student's photo on a bulletin board like the one shown. Read on!

Heather C. Hedman-Devaughn—Gr. 1
Pasadena Lakes Elementary School
Pembrook Pines, FL

### This Week's Reader

What we liked about Todd's reading:
• He read with expression! (Zita)
• He showed pictures. (Ed)
• He read smoothly. (Kim)
• He read loud. (Jan)

### Notes Of Praise

Dear Dakari,
I really enjoyed your book report. You spoke in a clear voice and told many interesting details about your book. Keep up the good work!
Mrs. Wong

Here's an easy way to make sure that every student receives at least one teacher-written note of praise per month. At the beginning of the month, personalize one page of a seasonal notepad for every student; then use the pad for writing messages of praise. Tuck the written messages into students' desks, cubbies, or lunchboxes. Be sure to use all of the personalized notepad pages before the end of the month.

Kim Wong—Gr. 2, Olney Elementary, Olney, MD

## Fact Cards
Use with "For The Birds" on page 191.

| | | |
|---|---|---|
| **Resplendent Quetzal**<br>I am the national bird of Guatemala. My green tail feathers can be two feet long! | **Northern Jacana**<br>My extralong toes allow me to walk on floating plants without sinking! Some people call me a *lily-trotter.* | **Cuvier's Toucan**<br>I am very playful. Sometimes I use my colorful beak to toss fruit to other toucans. |
| **Red-Fan Parrot**<br>When I get excited, I spread my red crest into a broad fan. Sometimes I use my feet to put food in my beak. | **Harpy Eagle**<br>Beware! I am fearsome and I can fly 50 miles per hour. | **Three-Wattled Bellbird**<br>I have a big mouth! I can swallow large fruits and I have a very loud call! |

**Page 105**

| | |
|---|---|
| 1. red | 6. purple |
| 2. purple | 7. red |
| 3. purple | 8. purple |
| 4. purple | 9. purple |
| 5. blue | 10. blue |

**Page 106**

| | | |
|---|---|---|
| 1/2 | 2/4 | 4/8 |
| 1/4 | 2/8 | 4/16 |
| 1/3 | 2/6 | 4/12 |

**Page 107**

| | |
|---|---|
| 1. opinion | 7. opinion |
| 2. fact | 8. fact |
| 3. fact | 9. fact |
| 4. fact | 10. opinion |
| 5. opinion | 11. fact |
| 6. fact | 12. opinion |

FRIENDS FOREVER

**Page 159**

1. false
2. false
3. false
4. true
5. false
6. false
7. true
8. true

# Answer Keys and Pattern

Use pattern and writing suggestions with "Poetic Planter" on page 63.

**Page 179: Where Are The Deserts?**
**Page 185: Desert Wildlife Locations**

| | |
|---|---|
| Gila monster | = North American deserts |
| saguaro cactus | = only in the Sonoran Desert |
| oryx | = Arabian Desert and deserts in Africa |
| jerboa | = deserts in Asia and Africa |
| camel | = The one-hump camel shown is a *dromedary camel.* It is native to the hot deserts of Arabia and North Africa, but it has also been introduced to parts of America and Australia. The two-hump camel (not shown on the map) is called a *Bactrian camel.* It is native to the cooler central Asian deserts. |
| emu | = deserts in Australia |

**Page 123**
*(Items listed should be illustrated.)*

| | | | |
|---|---|---|---|
| TV | dime | Golden Ticket | bowl of soup |
| tube of toothpaste | wad of chewed gum | peanuts | newspaper |
| several candy bars | Wonka Bar | bread | dollar bill |

**Writing Suggestions:**
Line 1: name of this person
Line 2: three present-tense verbs that tell actions of this person
Line 3: phrase telling where this person can be found
Line 4: another phrase telling where this person can be found
Line 5: another phrase telling where this person can be found
Line 6: a summarizing thought about this person

# Index

316

7  21202 04502  5